Learning, Culture and Community in Online Education

Steve Jones
General Editor

Vol. 21

PETER LANG
New York • Washington, D.C./Baltimore • Bern
Frankfurt am Main • Berlin • Brussels • Vienna • Oxford

Learning, Culture
AND Community
IN Online Education

RESEARCH AND PRACTICE

Caroline Haythornthwaite & Michelle M. Kazmer
EDITORS

PETER LANG
New York • Washington, D.C./Baltimore • Bern
Frankfurt am Main • Berlin • Brussels • Vienna • Oxford

Library of Congress Cataloging-in-Publication Data

Learning, culture and community in online education: research and practice /
edited by Caroline Haythornthwaite, Michelle M. Kazmer.
p. cm. — (Digital formations; vol. 21)
Includes bibliographical references.
1. Distance education. 2. Education—Effect of technological innovations on.
3. Educational technology—Social aspects. 4. Library Education Experimental
Program. I. Haythornthwaite, Caroline A. II. Kazmer, Michelle M.
III. Series: Digital formations; v. 21.
LC5800.L45   371.35'8—dc22   2004009962
ISBN 978-0-8204-6847-1
ISSN 1526-3169

Bibliographic information published by **Die Deutsche Nationalbibliothek**.
Die Deutsche Nationalbibliothek lists this publication in the "Deutsche
Nationalbibliografie"; detailed bibliographic data are available
on the Internet at http://dnb.d-nb.de/.

Cover image: *Into the Light* © Larry Kanfer, www.kanfer.com
Cover design by Lisa Barfield

The paper in this book meets the guidelines for permanence and durability
of the Committee on Production Guidelines for Book Longevity
of the Council of Library Resources.

© 2004, 2017 Peter Lang Publishing, Inc., New York
29 Broadway, 18th floor, New York, NY 10006
www.peterlang.com

All rights reserved.
Reprint or reproduction, even partially, in all forms such as microfilm,
xerography, microfiche, microcard, and offset strictly prohibited.

Printed in the United States of America

Contents

Foreword: Reflecting on Best Practices ix
Amy Bruckman

Introduction: Multiple Perspectives and Practices
in Online Education xiii
Caroline Haythornthwaite & Michelle M. Kazmer

EDUCATION ONLINE

1 Navigating the Advantages and Disadvantages
of Online Pedagogy 3
Nicholas C. Burbules

2 Maintaining the Affordances of Traditional Education
Long Distance 19
Bertram C. Bruce

EXPLORING COMMUNITY

3 Community Development among Distance Learners:
Temporal and Technological Dimensions 35
*Caroline Haythornthwaite, Michelle M. Kazmer,
Jennifer Robins, & Susan Shoemaker*

4 Catch a Cyber by the Tale: Online Orality and the Lore

vi • Learning, Culture, and Community in Online Education

  of a Distributed Learning Community 59
  Betsy Hearne & Anna L. Nielsen

5 Juggling Multiple Social Worlds: Distance Students
  Online and Offline 89
  Michelle M. Kazmer & Caroline Haythornthwaite

6 Disengaging from Online Community 111
  Michelle M. Kazmer

NEW CHALLENGES AND NEW FEATURES IN ONLINE SETTINGS

7 Affordances of Persistent Conversation:
  Promoting Communities That Work 129
  Caroline Haythornthwaite & Alvan Bregman

8 Affording a Place: The Persistent Structures of LEEP 145
  Jennifer Robins

9 Changing Patterns of Participation: Interactions in a Synchronous
  Audio+Chat Classroom 163
  Karen Ruhleder

10 Over-the-Shoulder Learning in a Distance
  Education Environment 177
  Michael B. Twidale & Karen Ruhleder

TEACHING AND LEARNING ONLINE

11 Teaching and Learning Online: LEEP's Tribal Gleanings 197
  Pat Lawton & Rae-Anne Montague

12 Faculty Perspectives 215
  Rae-Anne Montague & Linda C. Smith

13 The Virtual Classroom as Ludic Space 229
  Christine A. Jenkins

MANAGEMENT AND ADMINISTRATION

14 The Distance Education Program from the
Management Perspective 245
Leigh S. Estabrook

15 User-Centered Support and Technology in LEEP 255
Jill Gengler

16 Reshaping Traditional Services for Nontraditional Learning:
The LEEP Student in the Library 267
Susan E. Searing

17 The View from Campus Administration 283
Lanny Arvan

LEEP Bibliography
compiled by *Rae-Anne Montague* 291

Contributors 297

Amy Bruckman

Foreword: Reflecting on Best Practices

We've all heard the predictions from pundits:

> The economics of education are changing. Distance learning can provide higher quality education at a lower price. A broad trend toward learning at distance is inevitable, and any institution that does not embrace it will lose market share.

> The modern information economy demands a more highly educated work force. To meet that need, we need to provide flexible, quality educational options for lifelong learning. Education is no longer primarily for the young. Distance approaches can best meet the needs of adult learners needing to integrate education, career, and family.

Counterpundits of course reply:

> In reality, distance education delivers lower quality education at higher cost. The hype behind distance learning is motivated primarily by an unexamined technological positivism.

> When you hear "distance learning," think "correspondence course." Correspondence courses fill an important societal function—providing lower quality education at a lower cost. This makes new opportunities available to segments of the population. However, do not confuse distance ed/correspondence courses with the kind of education that takes place in our elite institutions—they are entirely different phenomena.

There are probably some elements of truth in all of these perspectives. What is most striking, however, is how little real evidence is behind any of these statements. The reality is more complex and more interesting, subtler than popular punditry even hints.

Quality of distance learning varies widely. On the one hand, university faculty members with no training in education often jump on the bandwagon, for example, by simply pointing a video camera at their existing lectures (to the distress of both students and professional educators alike). At the other end of the spectrum, institutions like Britain's Open University have carefully and thoughtfully refined the practice of distance learning on a large scale for generations. The very best practitioners, however, are often too busy practicing to be able to distill that experience for the benefit of others.

As a result, it's a pleasure to introduce this volume. LEEP (Library Education Experimental Program), the distance education program offered by the Graduate School of Library and Information Sciences at University of Illinois at Urbana-Champaign, is a strong example of best practices in the field. In this volume, Haythornthwaite, Kazmer, and colleagues have pulled together a breadth and depth of thoughtful reflection on those practices.

As we see in all the essays included, understanding distance learning is not primarily about technology. Technology is one piece of the puzzle, but by no means the focus. Technology is just one component of a socio-technical system—a combination of people, social practices, new and old technologies designed to support learning. In a learner-centered design process, technology is added only where appropriate. Designers begin with learner needs and choose technologies to meet those needs, rather than starting with technological tools and searching for uses. Yet this is not to say that technology is neutral. LEEP teachers and students in these essays document how the special affordances of technology help shape the evolution of social structures (both deliberate and emergent) to create a new kind of community.

Furthermore, a distance learning community is not created full-blown—it evolves over time. These papers about LEEP document the gradual evolution of a culture. Like members of any culture, LEEPers have rituals of initiation and disengagement. Community members have multiple distinct roles that interact in complex fashions. They even, as we shall see, have their own forms of folklore. How does one design a culture? LEEP as a case study provides a wealth of insights.

In the end, the whole adds up to more than just a volume about distance learning. In the process of reflecting on LEEP, many insights emerge that are applicable to broader issues of pedagogy, learning communities, and learning technologies. Anthropologists travel to study geographically isolated cultures not so much out of an inherent interest in the exotic as an interest in the mundane. If we know a bit more about kinship or cockfights in Bali, we also know a bit more about transcendent human issues in our families and communities. Defamiliarization helps reveal issues of broader relevance. Similarly, carefully reflecting on our practices in distance learning environments sheds light on practices in traditional classrooms. These essays about learning in LEEP are valuable not just for their contribution to the growing literature on distances approaches, but also for the insight they provide into fundamental issues of community and pedagogy in learning environments of all kinds.

Caroline Haythornthwaite
Michelle M. Kazmer

Introduction: Multiple Perspectives and Practices in Online Education

The New Face of Distance Education

In 2001, The Pew Internet and American Life Project (http://www.pewinternet.org) found that 5 percent of adult U.S. Internet users—more than 5 million people—had taken a class online for college credit, and 1 percent (one million) were online taking a course on any given day. For the 2000–2001 academic year, the National Center for Education Statistics (2003) estimated that approximately three million people were enrolled in distance education courses offered by accredited two- or four-year degree-granting institutions. Of those institutions, 56 percent (2,320) offered distance education, and 12 percent intended to start offering distance education within three years. These institutions use a mix of technologies: 90 percent of those already offering programs use asynchronous Internet as the primary mode of instructional delivery (and 88 percent of those intending to offer courses expect to use this means); 51 percent use primarily synchronous Internet means, 41 percent prerecorded video, 29 percent CD-ROM, and 19 percent multiple modes.

These numbers convey the amount of interest and activity already vested in creating and providing online, Internet-based, education, and how much more there will be in the near future. These statistics show a significant number of people and programs, even though they do not include the instructors, faculty, and support staff involved in course delivery; administrators making the programs run; and families and coworkers who support the degree takers. As more people become involved, either centrally or peripherally, in online distance education, the more we need to know and understand the impact of such programs.

This book presents papers on social, technical, administrative, and pedagogical aspects of online distance education. The papers include work directed toward the practice of online education, as well as research on online environments. As a whole they show how the questions we already have about such programs (e.g., how to establish a program, how to teach online) must be supplemented by questions addressing the environment as a whole (e.g., how to create and sustain a community of learners, how to provide technical assistance at a distance). The collection goes beyond best practices to include, in the words of one of the authors, better practices (Burbules, this volume). And these better practices include taking a wider view of what is involved in setting up not just distance course delivery, but rich, online learning environments.

While the topic examined is different in each chapter, the book is brought together around its primary example, which is the LEEP (Library Education Experimental Program) master's degree program, begun in 1996 by the Graduate School of Library and Information Science (GSLIS) at the University of Illinois at Urbana-Champaign (UIUC). This program has been an outstanding success, with over 95 percent retention rate of students, faculty commitment to the endeavor, and general recognition for delivering high-quality education. In 2001 the program was awarded the Sloan Consortium (Sloan-C) Award for Most Outstanding Asynchronous Learning Network (ALN) Program (http://www.aln.org/aboutus/awards2001.asp).

The program has been more than just an educational project. LEEP is also an early innovation in Internet use. The efforts put into making this program a success represent early lessons on how to engage in the activities needed to do so: how to exchange information, build a distributed learning community, manage new technology and new ways of teaching, operate in an online environment, and change the face of educational practice. Since its inception, LEEP has been evaluated and assessed for its pedagogical and online practices. The research on this program represents a wealth of information about new online practices, including teaching, learning, managing projects, maintaining relationships, building community, and developing a culture.

While reports of the ongoing work of LEEP and research presentations have been made and published, their diversity means they can only be found in many different locations, addressed to many different audiences both academic and professional. This book brings that work together in one place to show the diversity of questions raised when creating this kind of environment, as well as the diversity of perspectives that have been brought to the study of it. While this is not a book about educational outcomes (i.e., whether on-campus students score better on tests than off-campus students), it is a book about *program outcomes*. What satisfies students and faculty? What makes it possible to learn and teach at a distance? How do you maintain relationships with instructors and among students without regular face-to-face contact? How does being online change relationships, conversations, and learning?

This book presents a unique combination of papers about research and practice around an online distance degree program. While many books collect local wisdom on how to create, run, teach, and learn in an online environment, we are unaware of books that combine noneducational research with educational practice. Why include research? Because asking research questions, using the backgrounds from computer science, information science, education, communications, and so forth, opens up what we see. Here we explore distance education from the perspectives of community, conversation, computer-mediated communication, technical support, as well as pedagogy. As a result, we gain a more rounded view of the complexity that constitutes the whole of an online program, and that is what we want to convey with this book.

Who You Gonna Call?

To demonstrate the kind of complexity involved in an online distance program, and what kind of a problem we think it is, let's consider the following questions: When you set out to build and operate an online program—aiming to provide quality education for students who cannot, or choose not to, move to an on-campus facility—what kind of a problem is it? Who are you gonna call to fix it?

Is it a technical problem?—in which case you call on computer software designers, implementers, vendors, and operators. Is it an institutional problem?—in which case you negotiate with educational administrators, education boards, etc. Is it an administrative problem? If so, you plan, negotiate, and gain the cooperation of faculty, instructors, student organizations, and staff. It's always an educational problem, so how do you learn to teach online? Indeed, how do you learn that you have to learn how to teach online (i.e., to become aware that it is not a seamless transition)? But is it an information problem? Should the focus be on how to deliver information across space and time, including library materials, lectures, course notes?

But wait—maybe it's a workplace problem, so perhaps the negotiations are with future employers (or even current employers) of your students. Or maybe it's a recruitment and retention problem, so the effort is in bringing in, retaining, and graduating students who are exemplary models of your program. Oh, but heck, how do you retain students in the lean environment of text-based communication? Maybe it's a student experience problem and efforts should be focused on providing a positive student experience. But how do you do that? What makes for a positive online experience when pursuing a degree?

What kind of a problem is an online degree program? It is, indeed, all of those listed above, and undoubtedly a number more not listed. It is also not just one of the above—it is not just a technical problem or an educational problem—it is a problem at the meeting place of social, technical, administrative, and pedagogical considerations.

xvi • Learning, Culture, and Community in Online Education

Addressing the Nexus

This book addresses this nexus. It provides multiple perspectives on the online experience that is LEEP, and as such shows the many perspectives that can, and often need to be addressed when creating and maintaining distance programs. Through chapters from administrators, philosophers, faculty, librarians, and technical staff, and researchers in education, computer science, folklore, information science, and sociology, we gain a rounded view of the complexity that constitutes the whole of an online program. Although the LEEP program and its students, faculty, and staff, have been the focus of most of the research studies in this volume, the net result is not a book about LEEP. Rather, it is an examination of a variety of social and educational phenomena that occur within the socio-technical environment that is LEEP.

The emphasis on LEEP comes naturally from our involvement in it. Most contributors are faculty, students, former students, or staff in GSLIS, many of whom have been involved since LEEP's first year of operation in 1996. In particular, Leigh Estabrook, dean of the school from 1986 to 2001 and now professor in GSLIS, spearheaded the establishment and ongoing administration of LEEP, and Linda Smith, professor and associate dean of GSLIS (and interim dean, 2001 through 2003) has had major responsibility for all aspects of LEEP's operations since its inception, including managing faculty assignments for LEEP, course offerings, student needs, and as administrative liaison. Both have been also been active in research, publications, and presentations on LEEP practices (see the LEEP bibliography in this volume, and online at http://www.lis.uiuc.edu/gslis/degrees/leep_bib.html for papers by these and other contributors to this volume).

Those not affiliated with GSLIS each have their own significant track records in online education (Arvan, Bruckman, Burbules). In these contributors we have a group of people who have been actively addressing issues and creating solutions for delivery of high-quality online education. Whether pursued through organized research efforts, administrative, educational, or technological evaluation and improvement, each contributor has spent a number of years engaged in helping in our understanding of what makes a successful online environment.

The LEEP Program

We provide here details of the LEEP program and environment, both to ground the book in its primary example, and to give background that does not need to be repeated in later chapters.

LEEP Program Option

LEEP is a program option for the master's degree at GSLIS that started with its first cohort coming to campus (see below) in summer 1996, and starting online classes in fall 1996. As an option rather than a separate program, the course requirements are the same for students at a distance as for those on campus (ten courses, including two required courses).[1] Currently, approximately half of the LEEP students are in-state Illinois students, and half reside out of state (see Estabrook, this volume, for budgetary details about LEEP, as well as a history of its inception; see also Estabrook, 2003). So far, students have come from 46 of the 50 U.S. states, and 14 countries (see Estabrook, this volume); 320 have graduated with master's degrees in Library and Information Science from 1997 to spring 2003.

Boot Camp and On-Campus Sessions
There are two on-campus, face-to-face requirements for LEEP students. First, students accepted into this option must begin their program by attending an intensive two-week on-campus session named *boot camp* by the students. In this session they complete one of the required courses and also receive training in technology use. When the program began, the fifty to sixty incoming students started together in one cohort. As incoming classes have increased in size, it has become necessary to run two of these sessions back-to-back each summer (starting in 1998).[2]

The second face-to-face requirement is that students attend a mid-semester, on-campus session for each course they are taking. Every semester GSLIS runs a week of sessions, with one day set aside for each course offered. Attendance is mandatory at these sessions. Instructors use this time to give experiences and teach materials not easily conveyed online. Students use this time to catch up with boot camp companions, use the physical resources of the library (for details on distance provision of library services, see Searing, this volume), meet with faculty and faculty advisors, and put faces to the names of people in their classes. Each midterm on-campus session includes an optional social evening where faculty and students come together for dinner and conversation.

At a Distance, Online
After boot camp the remaining courses needed for the degree are taken at the student's home location, via the Internet. The work of coming to class, getting to know others, discussing class work with students and faculty, working on group projects, accessing course readings, and submitting homework happens via the Internet and almost entirely through the LEEP online environment.

The LEEP site is accessible by password to registered students, and GSLIS faculty and staff. The home page organizes information on courses (current and past), technical help, and access to lists of current students; the page also offers quick links to

Web-based e-mail, bulletin boards, and file transfer, and a help site on managing passwords. Also available as a quick link is a site for submitting and maintaining personal biographies. Students create and post their own biographies, which are then available to any LEEP member with a click of the mouse from the list of current students, and the lists of students in each class. This gives both LEEP students and faculty a quick look at the people in their classes and how they describe themselves. Also prominent on this page is an area marked Help! which links to a "who to contact for what" site. General bulletin boards with titles such as The Essentials, GSLIS Community, Professional Associations, and Scholarships, Fellowships, Assistantships & Jobs provide current general information for students.

The LEEP technology provides a coordinated site and common environment for the delivery of LEEP classes. Thus, routines for each class look much the same. Class home sites have standard links to the syllabus, course archive, Web-based class bulletin boards, and for logging in to the synchronous "live" lecture sessions. Other standard links include access to the list of class members, current class slides, electronic reserves, and an electronic chalkboard facility. As explained further below, classes meet here for live lectures, and asynchronous discussion via class bulletin boards. The LEEP format of class management has proved so popular with faculty that now all courses have a LEEP presence, providing facilities for on-campus course participants to post and/or review materials, manage class memberships, and have class-based, bulletin-board discussions.

Distance Course Delivery and Communication Technologies
Instructors make use of both synchronous and asynchronous online interaction with students. Lectures are delivered live using *streaming audio*[3] along with online slides or Web pages. A demonstration is available online that gives a flavor of the LEEP lecture experience (see *The LEEP Experience: An Instructor's Perspective,* by Christine Jenkins at http://leep.lis.uiuc.edu/demos/jenkins/). While some instructors offer live sessions as frequently as once a week, others offer them only several times a semester (relying instead on asynchronous technologies). Local faculty use the Instructional Technology Office's (ITO) facilities to deliver lectures, with ITO staff literally at hand in the office (for more on ITO and its work, see Gengler, this volume). Lecturers who are located at a distance from campus also have ITO staff at hand, but virtually, as they lecture from their own offices or homes. Travel plans are not an obstacle, and not an excuse for missing class. Although instructors can pretape a lecture, many choose to connect from hotel rooms or other remote sites in order to give their classes (incoming phone calls can be redirected to broadcast the audio portion to students). Lecturers also may have live office hours, where they use Internet Relay Chat (IRC) for *synchronous text chat* with students.

During live sessions, all students gather virtually in the main class chat room. The names of all those signed in for the day's class are visible to class participants. Students use IRC to submit questions during the lecture; text submitted to the class chat room is visible to all members of the class, and recorded. Separate chat rooms can be used for nonrecorded break-out sessions, and facilities such as chalkboards can be used to write notes in a common online place, visible to those in the chat room. Such work can be shown to the class as a whole by having all members move into the particular chat room.

An important part of the LEEP system is that lectures and chat from the main class chat room are recorded and available for later viewing through the LEEP Web facilities. Being unavailable for the live audio lecture is not an obstacle, and there is again no excuse for missed lectures. All lectures are archived in this way. As LEEP enters its eighth year, all archives are still available (as more years accumulate, the issue of what to do with those archives and how long to keep them needs to be addressed; see Lynch, 2002).

An important aspect of the live online classes is that students are there together in the class. Ever since a student first propagated the information about how to use it, students have been making regular use of the IRC *whisper* facility to direct comments to specific others in the class, without the text being recorded or visible to anyone else. This backchannel provides a way for friends to talk to each other during class, both for socializing and for clarifying class content.

Web-based bulletin boards are used in most classes for discussion and exercises that stretch over the time between synchronous sessions. There are also Web boards that contain programwide announcements, course announcements and discussions, and other threads of interest to LEEP students.

Each student has an e-mail address with the domain name of the university. E-mail acts as a primary form of communication for dyadic or small group interactions in LEEP. Students use e-mail to reach other students, instructors, GSLIS administrators, and the LEEP assistants who provide technical support. They have access to their own telephones and to a toll-free 800 number to call GSLIS instructors or staff. Phone conversations are less common than e-mail communication, but are used to reach the same people. In general, the more students need to communicate, whether for working together or for social interaction, the more means of communication they use (see the studies by Haythornthwaite, 2001, 2002a).

Other Web resources for members include Web site space for coursework and Web page editing software. Homework and assignments are generally handed in via the Internet as Web pages, Web board postings, or attachments to e-mail. Students also send in assignments by fax and sometimes by regular mail. Many courses include group projects; students coordinate their own interactions to complete these projects, calling on instructors as necessary. In-class presentations can be done by having students call in to GSLIS and having their phone conversation broadcast via LEEP. Such presentations are usually accompanied by a Web page or slide display that can be seen by all students. Assignments, grading, and comments are returned to students via regular mail or e-mail.

Support

LEEP technical staff members provide caring and expert technical support (see Kazmer, 2000; Gengler, this volume). LEEP students also gain support from the university librarians, and in particular the Library and Information Science (LIS) librarian and staff (see Searing, this volume). The library system provides access to many online journals and resources, as well as to a variety of print-based resources. Students also find access to additional technologies and technical help from Internet Service Providers (ISP), employers and coworkers, and family and extended family. As described in many chapters in this book, other students are a prime source of support, particularly social support (e.g., see Haythornthwaite et al., 2000, reprinted in this volume).

Questions about Online Education

In making the effort to put a whole degree or program online, there is always the worry that it will not be accepted. While many have embraced online education, there are still concerns that haunt such programs. In particular there are concerns about not meeting on-campus standards for learning outcomes, providing an impoverished social environment, having poor interaction between instructors and students, failing to provide a community of learners as on-campus sites do, and not satisfying employers that the degree is as good as one earned on campus. Perhaps the first concern of any program builder is: Will it work? As our "Field of Dreams" (Robinson, 1989), if we build it, will they come? Will students come to our courses and employers hire our graduates? While we can't predict outcomes for any particular program, the papers in this book give some ideas of what concerns and needs must be met to make it work.

Is online education a better mousetrap (with apologies to the mice)—in other words, will it be economically viable or even profitable? For a time, efforts in online education were seen as ways to save money, and the "greater throughput with lower cost" model might, justifiably, have concerned many. If we have one resounding lesson from online education, it is that it does not save money or time or faculty or staff, but is still worth doing, and worth doing well. Neither should any student imagine that a program worth doing will save them time. Both students and faculty become deeply embedded in online interaction that stretches and expands the lecture hours into the course week. More so than in offline courses, discussion happens and continues throughout the week as an integral part of the course design. Success depends on achieving participation and knowledge sharing not only among faculty and students, but also among students themselves.

Is it as good as a face-to-face environment? Are learning outcomes equivalent? We do not address this directly in this book. As mentioned above, our focus is more on program outcomes than course learning outcomes. But we rely on the many studies that show "no significant difference" to support the idea that it is, at the very least, *as good as* a face-to-face learning environment (see Hiltz, 1994; Russell, 1999; and the TeleEducation NB site associated with the book: http://teleeducation.nb.ca/nosignificantdifference/index.cfm). However, we also want to make an argument that when many students are embedded in local contexts relevant to what they are learning, and have the opportunity to share those ideas, online distance education may prove *better than* face-to-face, on-campus instruction (Kazmer, 2003).

Like any other educational enterprise, there are better and worse practices in online teaching. There should always be an active pursuit of improvement in how we provide education, and we should be actively sharing our experiences with other teachers. As faculty and instructors venture online, a key concern is: How do we teach online? What works and what does not? Learning and accumulating this knowledge takes time and some trial and error, but a body of literature is now emerging giving guidance in this direction (e.g., Barab, Kling, & Gray, 2004; Bourne & Moore, 2003; Eisenstadt & Vincent, 2000; Koschmann, 1996; Koschmann, Hall & Miyake, 2002; Simonson, 2003; Small & Paling, 2002; Twigg, 2001). Of particular note in the LIS field is a recent compilation of contributions from twenty-eight schools that offer courses at a distance (Barron, 2003). This volume collects knowledge from decades of distance education, providing guidance for future successful practice. In LEEP, mechanisms for evaluation have been in place since the first year of the LEEP program (see Estabrook; Lawton & Montague, this volume). The most recent collection of "tribal knowledge" was gathered in August 2002, and is shared here in this volume in the paper by Lawton and Montague.

An intriguing outcome of asking all these questions about the online environment is how it often opens up the "black box" of offline teaching, giving a "heightened awareness" of one's teaching: "This heightened awareness can be both illuminating and humbling. We find that the instructional design process becomes less implicit and more of a deliberate enterprise. Sometimes this leads us to make changes in the way we do things or to try out new approaches, not only in our online courses but in our on-campus classrooms as well" (Ko & Rossen, 2001, p. 277).

This awareness leads us to reexamine all sides of what we are doing. Bruce (this volume), for example, reexamines the affordances of traditional classrooms and asks what we may want to preserve online; and Burbules (this volume) discusses how immersion, an attribute most often associated with computer-based virtual reality experiences, really tells us about essential attributes of education in any environment.

We may also want to ask how what we are learning about online practices can enhance our offline teaching and learning. In particular, we may want to see how to incorporate the new kinds of interaction and participation possible online into our offline classes (e.g., the student–student help giving described by Ruhleder, this volume), and pay attention to the important role of community in helping students deal with frustrations (e.g., Haythornthwaite et al., 2000). Indeed, as asynchronous learning networks (ALN) become companions to on-campus classes, such studies become input for hybrid practices combining on- and offline teaching and learning. In GSLIS, online classes now often include on-campus students, challenging what it means to receive an on-campus degree. Also as noted above, faculty have become so attached to the LEEP environment that all classes have a LEEP presence, challenging the idea that a clear separation can continue to be made between on- and offline teaching practices.

Faculty are often concerned about dealing with the added work involved in distance education, and administrators with getting and keeping faculty interested in this form of course delivery. LEEP addresses the added work by giving course relief while preparing and teaching a course online for the first time. In general, responses have been very positive to teaching online. GSLIS Associate Dean Linda C. Smith (personal communication, November 12, 2003) reports that findings from a faculty survey (presented in an unpublished evaluation report completed by the Committee on Extended Education and External Degrees of the Graduate College at UIUC), offer insights into the kinds of positive outcomes LEEP faculty report from teaching online. She reports that observations in response to the question "What impact, if any, has the program had on your career?" include: "sparked overall interest in educational technologies and incorporating educational technology into on-campus courses," "provided a new view towards teaching," and "increased new research, publishing, and presentation opportunities." Observations in response to the question "What impact, if any, has the program had on you?" include: "developed new views on pedagogy; and made me a better teacher."

Smith notes that these kinds of responses, and the experiences of LEEP faculty, show that online teaching, in creating heightened awareness about teaching, fosters what Kathleen McKinney has defined as "scholarly teaching." As defined by McKinney, "*scholarly teaching* involves taking a scholarly approach to teaching just as we would take a scholarly approach to other areas of knowledge and practice. . . . Thus, scholarly teachers do things such as reflect on their teaching, use classroom assessment techniques, engage in systematic course design, update their courses, discuss teaching issues with colleagues, try new teaching techniques, and read and apply the literature on teaching and learning in their discipline" (McKinney, in press). Similarly, Smith sees that online teaching has stimulated engagement for some in the *scholarship of teaching and learning*,[4] in other words, the "systematic reflection on teaching and learning made public" (Illinois State University, http://www.cat.ilstu.edu/sotl/index.shtml), which "goes beyond scholarly teaching and involves systematic study of teaching and/or learning and the public sharing and review of such work through presentations or publications" (McKinney, in press). For example, Betsy Hearne and doctoral students Kathleen McDowell and Anna Nielsen are engaged in studies comparing instruction of children's literature and storytelling in the face-to-face classroom and in the virtual LEEP classroom. Studies cited in the LEEP bibliography include a number of papers and presentations reflecting the scholarship of teaching and learning, and additional studies are under way. In this example, and in LEEP faculty's experiences in general, we find that the curiosity about teaching sparked by being online leads to greater benefits from such endeavors, and for teaching in general, than will ever be evident from simple counts of students reached, no matter how important that latter statistic is.

New Questions
Another change we notice after several years of providing online education, is that the kinds of questions that we, and others who provide online learning, are beginning to ask show concern for areas beyond learning outcomes and teaching practice. Questions arise about life beyond the classroom: Will students feel part of a school or university? Will students gain a sense of community or belonging with other students, the school and/or university? How will students (and instructors) adapt to the online environment? What forms of interaction will they adopt?

Addressing such questions has brought new fields of research into the examination of online education. In particular, research on *online community* and *computer-mediated communication* have been integrated into the research and practice agenda for online education (Haythornthwaite, 2003; Palloff & Pratt, 1999; Renninger & Shumar, 2002; Rudestan & Schoenholtz-Read, 2002); business and professional organizations pick up this agenda in their desire to form and support *communities of practice* (Brown & Duguid, 1991; Lave & Wenger, 1991; Wenger, McDermott & Snyder, 2002; for a recent review see Davenport & Hall, 2002). Attention from a computer science perspective has highlighted interest in *affordances* (Gaver, 1996) or what a device, interface, object, or environment permits or leads an individual to be able to do. Closely allied to this, but of more relevance for looking at cooperative and collaborative environments, is Bradner's notion of *social affordances* (Bradner, Erickson, & Kellogg, 1999) which relates technologies to what they enable in terms of group interaction. The concept of affordances is picked up in three of the papers in this volume (Bruce; Haythornthwaite & Bregman; and Robins).

As we use more research perspectives to approach online distance learning environments, we open up even more questions about these environments.

- How do we talk online? (e.g., Herring, in press). What is the nature of *persistent conversations*? (e.g., Erickson, 1999). How does *how we talk* affect how others perceive us and how we perceive others? How do we get students comfortable online? What are their concerns about their online presentation of self? (e.g., Bregman & Haythornthwaite, 2003; Haythornthwaite & Bregman, this volume). How does being online change how we view, interact with, and relate to instructors? (e.g., Ruhleder, this volume). How can we visualize

conversations and participation? (e.g., Donath, Karahalios, & Viégas, 1999; Erickson, Herring, & Sack, 2002).
- How do people share information, experiences, and expertise? How do we provide technology support at a distance? (e.g., Twidale & Ruhleder, this volume). What kinds of interactions are important, and thus what kinds do we need to support? (e.g., Burbules, this volume; Haythornthwaite, 2002b). How do students share information? (e.g., Haythornthwaite, 2000, 2001; Ruhleder, this volume). How do they provide each other with social support? (e.g., Haythornthwaite et al., 2000; Kazmer, 2000).
- How do we—and *do* we—create and maintain interpersonal ties with people who are online and at a distance? (e.g., Haythornthwaite et al., 2000; Hearne & Nielsen, this volume). What happens when we have to leave? (e.g., Kazmer, 2002, and this volume).
- Do elements of offline community, group behavior, and learning show up online? (e.g., in folklore, Hearne & Nielsen, this volume). Where are they the same, where are they something new? (e.g., Bruce; Ruhleder, this volume).
- What else is important to online learners? What is going on in their lives that contributes to their readiness, facility, and/or frustrations with the online environment, and their participation in it? (e.g., Kazmer & Haythornthwaite, 2001, reprinted in this volume).

Future Prospects

Will all education become online, conducted at a distance between faculty and students who never or only rarely meet, and involve students multitasking via video, audio, and text on tasks for home, work, and school? Well, perhaps some education will. The Internet is here to stay, and online education is becoming an integrated part of both distance and on-campus teaching. While we do not expect the online to replace the offline, we do expect online modes to become more available, reaching out to wider audiences and providing increased opportunities for learning and communing online. Thus, we believe it is important to face this challenge and learn as much as we can about how to do it properly.

The body of work presented in this volume is diverse, intentionally so. We want to show the diversity of questions raised about creating and sustaining an online distance-learning environment, as well as show how bringing a diversity of perspectives to bear gives us a more encompassing perspective on what is involved. We balance this diversity with a focus on the LEEP environment we all have been involved with and have studied.

We believe it is important, and of interest to many readers, to bring together in one place these many works. We find that as these kinds of online environments are used more for teaching, learning, and business, they cannot be well understood without considering the many impacts they have on all aspects of life and learning. Indeed, our purpose with this book is to show how important it is to consider the many ways in which adopting and implementing an environment of this sort affects the students, faculty, and administrators involved and the milieu they come to live in.

Acknowledgments

It is hard to compile either a complete or short list of people to acknowledge and thank for this book, and for LEEP. Overall, we thank all students, faculty, office, and administrative staff who have participated in and supported LEEP. We would like to thank in particular Leigh Estabrook and Linda C. Smith, for their roles in creating and maintaining LEEP and for personal support and mentorship. For this book, we thank Pat Lawton and Rae-Anne Montague for the idea and implementation of the August 2002 LEEP retreat that made it apparent what a wealth of work was available on LEEP, which then became the basis of this book. We thank Vince Patone and Jill Gengler for past and current administration of the Information Technology Office, and to them and their graduate assistants for fostering the user-centered technical support outlook that has helped so many to be online. We thank all students for participating in this grand experiment, and in particular we thank those who have taken time to participate in interviews, fill out questionnaires, attend retreats, and help out fellow students with practical and professional advice. Last, but not least, we thank faculty from on- and off-campus, and the teaching assistants who supported their efforts; in particular, we thank Maggie Kimmel, professor of LIS, University of Pittsburgh, and Leigh Estabrook on behalf of LEEP students for the traditions and indelible memories created at boot camp.

Notes

1. Refer to the GSLIS Web site for details on course requirements (www.lis.uiuc.edu). GSLIS offers a traditionally organized on-campus schedule for students who reside locally. Two other options accommodate commuting students. A Fridays Only option provides full program requirements over a two-and-one-half-year period with on-campus attendance necessary only on Fridays; similarly, a Summers Mostly option is designed to make most courses available during the summer.
2. In the first few years, students also had the option of beginning in January. Due to the high demands of the boot camp sessions on faculty and support staff, and the increase in interest in the program, students can now only start once a year.
3. Video streaming was attempted in the first semester of LEEP. However, transmission speeds and the need to support less expensive computing options for students, made the technology inappropriate for at-home and at-work delivery of lectures. At the on-campus location, Web

cameras record still pictures that are taken at regular intervals while the instructor lectures; students can access these during class time.
4. For more on the scholarship of teaching and learning (SoTL), see the annotated bibliography from the Carnegie Foundation available at: http://www.carnegiefoundation.org/elibrary/docs/bibliography.htm

References

Barab, S. A., Kling, R., & Gray, J. H. (Eds.). (2004). *Designing virtual communities in the service of learning.* New York: Cambridge University Press.
Barron, D. D. (2003). *Benchmarks in distance education: The LIS experience.* Westport, CT: Libraries Unlimited.
Bourne, J. & Moore, J. C. (Eds.). (2003). *Elements of quality online education: Practice and direction.* Needham, MA: Sloan Consortium.
Bradner, E., Kellogg, W., & Erickson, T. (1999). *The adoption and use of "Babble": A field study of chat in the workplace.* Proceedings of the 6th European Conference on Computer Supported Cooperative Work (ECSCW '99) (pp. 139–158). Copenhagen, Denmark.
Bregman, A., & Haythornthwaite, C. (2003). Radicals of presentation: Visibility, relation, and co-presence in persistent conversation. *New Media and Society, 5*(1), 117–140.
Brown, J. S., & Duguid, P. (1991). Organizational learning and communities-of-practice: Toward a unified view of working, learning, and innovation. *Organization Science, 2*(1), 40–57.
Davenport, E., & Hall, H. (2002). Organizational knowledge and communities of practice. *Annual Review of Information Science and Technology, 36,* 171–227.
Donath, J., Karahalios, K., & Viégas, F. (1999). Visualizing conversation. *Journal of Computer-Mediated Communication, 4*(4). Retrieved from http://www.ascusc.org/jcmc/vol4/issue4/donath.html.
Eisenstadt, M., & Vincent, T. (2000). *The knowledge web: Learning and collaborating on the Net.* London, UK: Kogan Page.
Erickson, T. (1999). Persistent conversation. *Journal of Computer-Mediated Communication, 4*(4), whole issue. Retrieved from http://www.ascusc.org/jcmc/vol4/issue4.
Erickson, T., Herring, S., & Sack, W. (2002). *Discourse architectures: Designing and visualizing computer-mediated communication.* Workshop at the CHI 2002 Conference, Minneapolis, MN. (Position papers available at http://www.pliant.org/personal/Tom_Erickson/DA_CHI02_WrkShp_Sum.html). Accessed January 2, 2004.
Estabrook, L. (2003). Distance education at the University of Illinois. In D. D. Barron (Ed.), *Benchmarks in distance education: The LIS experience* (pp. 63–73). Westport, CT: Libraries Unlimited.
Gaver, W. (1996). Situating action II: Affordances for interaction: The social is material for design. *Ecological Psychology, 8,* 111–129.
Haythornthwaite, C. (2000). Online personal networks: Size, composition and media use among distance learners. *New Media and Society, 2*(2), 195–226.
Haythornthwaite, C. (2001). Exploring multiplexity: Social network structures in a computer-supported distance learning class. *The Information Society, 17*(3), 211–226.
Haythornthwaite, C. (2002a). Strong, weak and latent ties and the impact of new media. *The Information Society, 18*(5), 385–401.
Haythornthwaite, C. (2002b). Building social networks via computer networks: Creating and sustaining distributed learning communities. In K. A. Renninger & W. Shumar, *Building Virtual Communities: Learning and Change in Cyberspace* (pp. 159–190). Cambridge, UK: Cambridge University Press.

Haythornthwaite, C. (2003). Online communities of learners. In K. Christensen & D. Levinson (Eds.), *The encyclopedia of community* (pp. 1033–1039). Thousand Oaks, CA: Sage.

Haythornthwaite, C., Kazmer, M. M., Robins, J., & Shoemaker, S. (2000). Community development among distance learners: Temporal and technological dimensions. *Journal of Computer-Mediated Communication, 6*(1). Retrieved from http://www.ascusc.org/jcmc/vol6/issue1/haythornthwaite.html. (Reprinted in this volume).

Herring, S. C. (Ed.). (in press). *Computer-mediated conversation*. Cresskill, NJ: Hampton Press.

Hiltz, S. R. (1994). *The virtual classroom: Learning without limits via computer networks*. Norwood, NJ: Ablex.

Kazmer, M. M. (2000). Coping in a distance environment: Sitcoms, chocolate cake, and dinner with a friend. *First Monday, 5*(9). Retrieved from http://www.firstmonday.dk/issues/issue5_9/kazmer/index.html.

Kazmer, M. M. (2002). *Disengagement from intrinsically transient social worlds: The case of a distance learning community*. Unpublished doctoral dissertation. University of Illinois at Urbana-Champaign.

Kazmer, M. M. (2003). *Online learning and community embeddedness: How existing ties transform the growth of relationships between educational and community settings*. Paper presented at the Information, Communication, and Society / Oxford Internet Institute Symposium, September 17–20, Oxford, UK.

Kazmer, M. M., & Haythornthwaite, C. (2001). Juggling multiple social worlds: Distance students on and offline. *American Behavioral Scientist, 45*(3), 510–529. (Reprinted in this volume.)

Ko, S., & Rossen, S. (2001). *Teaching online: A practical guide*. Boston: Houghton Mifflin.

Koschmann, T. (Ed.). (1996). *CSCL: Theory and practice of an emerging paradigm*. Mahwah, NJ: Lawrence Erlbaum.

Koschmann, T., Hall, R., & Miyake, N. (Eds.). (2002). *CSCL 2: Carrying forward the conversation*. Mahwah, NJ: Lawrence Erlbaum.

Lave, J., & Wenger, E. (1991). *Situated learning: Legitimate peripheral participation*. Cambridge, UK: Cambridge University Press.

Lynch, C. (2002). *The afterlives of courses on the network: Information management issues for learning management systems*. EDUCAUSE Center for Applied Research Bulletin. Retrieved November 9, 2003 from http://www.educause.edu/asp/doclib/abstract.asp?ID=ERB0223.

McKinney, K. (in press). The scholarship of teaching and learning: Past lessons, current challenges, and future visions. *To Improve the Academy, 22*.

National Center for Educational Statistics (2003). *Distance education at degree-granting postsecondary institutions: 2000–2001*. U.S. Department of Education. Retrieved November 6, 2003 from http://nces.ed.gov/surveys/peqis/publications/2003017.

Palloff, R.M. & Pratt, K. (1999). *Building Learning Communities in Cyberspace*. San Francisco, CA: Jossey-Bass, Inc.

Pew Internet and American Life Project (2001). *The Internet and education*. Pew Internet and American Life Project. Retrieved October 30, 2003 from http://www.pewinternet.org/reports/toc.asp?Report=39.

Renninger, K. A., & Shumar, W. (2002). *Building virtual communities: Learning and change in cyberspace*. Cambridge, UK: Cambridge University Press.

Robinson, P. A. (Director) (1989). *Field of Dreams*. Universal Studios.

Rudestan, K.E. & Schoenholtz-Read, J. (Eds.) (2002). *Handbook of Online Learning: Innovations in Higher Education and Corporate Training*. Thousand Oaks, CA: Sage.

Russell, T. (1999). *The no significant difference phenomenon*. Raleigh: North Carolina State University. (Associated Web site: http://teleeducation.nb.ca/nosignificantdifference/index.cfm).

Simonson, M. R. (2003). *Teaching and learning at a distance: Foundations of distance education*. Upper Saddle River, NJ: Merrill/Prentice Hall.

Small, R. V., & Paling, S. (2002). The evolution of a distance learning program in library and information science: A follow-up study. *Journal of Education for Library and Information Science, 43*(1), 47–61.

Twigg, C. A. (2001). *Innovations in online learning: Moving beyond no significant difference.* Troy, NY: Rensselaer Polytechnic Institute Center for Academic Transformation.

Wenger, E., McDermott, R., & Snyder, W. M. (2002). *Cultivating communities of practice.* Boston, MA: Harvard Business School.

Education Online

CHAPTER 1

Nicholas C. Burbules

Navigating the Advantages and Disadvantages of Online Pedagogy

The Navigational Metaphor

This essay is framed by a set of ambivalent attitudes in relation to online courses, and indeed toward the broader potential impact of new information and communication technologies on education (Burbules & Callister, 2000). Typical educational reforms constantly promise the new panacea, the Best Way of Teaching, the curricular theory or gimmick that will equalize opportunities, raise standards, lower costs, motivate unmotivated students, and improve the links between education and the wider aims of preparing citizens and workers for adult life. But in my own view, education is more about optimizing than maximizing, confronting trade-offs between competing goods that cannot all be pursued at the same time. It is inherently imperfect, and imperfectible. Every new approach to education gains us some things at the expense of others; every advantage can be seen, from some point of view, as a disadvantage. Hence my guiding metaphor here is Odysseus, guiding his ships between the Scylla and Charybdis, who both threaten to destroy him: *navigating,* finding a path where there is no one right way (Burbules, 2002).

The navigational metaphor is useful here from another standpoint as well. The current generation of Web browsers sport such bold, intrepid names as Navigator and Explorer, connoting movement, journeying, but also the risk of getting lost or sidetracked from one's path. Nevertheless, sometimes we find that in getting lost or sidetracked, we discover something very valuable that we never might have found in a more intentional, linear way. Education is intrinsically like this, and yet the dominant models of efficiency and accountability gaining widespread acceptance today as reform policies in education only recognize and reward the kind of means-ends thinking that regards education as just another engineering problem of fitting methods to desired outcomes. Time off task is wasted time. Anything not on the test is of secondary importance at best; at worst, it is actively discouraged.

And so we turn to the topic of online education. I believe that we are in the midst of two struggles to shape the future possibilities of online pedagogy. The first is whether moving courses online is regarded primarily as a means of expanding access to educational opportunities for those who cannot or will not attend bricks-and-mortar schools (for a variety of reasons), or whether it is regarded primarily as a way of increasing revenue by expanding course offerings, or by offering courses with fewer expenses. These two aims are not in fundamental contradiction (expanding access can also increase revenues), but they are in tension over a number of specific policy decisions, such as how such courses will be priced and to whom they will be marketed.

The other struggle is whether the development of online courses will follow technical instructional design rules (some of them implemented through the constraints of commercial courseware), which have the effect of *standardizing* and *narrowing* the range of educational design options (typically based on the traditional models of classroom teaching and learning), or whether the capabilities of new information and communication technologies will be exploited in ways that support innovative and creative approaches to pedagogy that are *different* from traditional classroom teaching and learning. If we simply transport syllabi, reading lists, lectures, and quizzes from the classroom to a digital format, a tremendous opportunity will have been squandered.

At the outset, then, I want to make my own stance clear. In my view, educational success *entails* the risk of failure, or more precisely, sometimes what appears to be a failure from one standpoint may turn out to be an educational success from another standpoint, and vice versa. Teaching and learning, like navigating, is about *finding a way*—and sometimes *making a way*—in an ill-structured domain. It isn't a matter of "best practices" but of better and worse practices, experimentation, learning from mistakes, and improvement along multiple axes of what constitutes success, one axis of which is maintaining a reflexively critical attitude toward what we are considering to be *success*. (Successful for whom? Successful in relation to what purposes? Successful in relation to short-run payoffs, or in the longer run?) I do not think that any single educational reform tradition, across the political spectrum—from back-to-basics, to progressive education, to critical pedagogy—is entirely safe from the dangers of complacency and One-Best-Way-ism. Each has insights, and each has blind spots. Any intelligent stance is manifold, slippery, and foxlike—like Odysseus himself—pragmatic in the deep sense of trying to find workable approaches without the prejudice of ideological or theoretical barriers that say "you can't do that" or "these two approaches can't be combined." (The Greeks had a term for this: *metis;* Burbules, 2002).

One Example of Online Teaching

For a number of years I have been offering a course as part of the University of Illinois program in Curriculum, Technology, and Educational Reform (CTER), co-taught in the first year with Bertram (Chip) Bruce. This is an almost completely online Masters degree program that is geared toward teachers who use technology in their own schools and classrooms. Because of this broader purpose, the innovative use of technology in our teaching, and promoting critical reflection about the technologies we are using in the program, are part and parcel of the program itself. The technologies are not simply a "delivery system" for course content (a ridiculous conception of teaching in any event, since teaching is not about the *delivery* of information). In the CTER course I teach (a "capstone" course on ethical and policy issues), the mistakes I have made invariably created opportunities to open up unplanned discussions on the capabilities, the limitations, and the dangers of these new information and communication technologies for education. A link on a simulated student Web page (to a site selling racy underwear), which we intended to push the teachers' buttons about what constituted acceptable or unacceptable Web content for students, was changed (without our knowledge) into a pornographic site. The teachers, many of whom were accessing these pages from their school computer labs (with students and colleagues in the vicinity), went into total rebellion. When we tried to explain that we had never intended to push them so far, we received an object lesson in the difficulties of establishing (or reestablishing) trust with class members in the absence of face-to-face contact. In another year's class, streamed audio content proved to be useless to a hearing-impaired student, which opened up group reflections about hidden barriers to access—and about what are the realistic limitations of trying to make an online course fully accessible to *everyone*. In another course, a topic with racially charged associations was on the table, in which some class members had different racial positionings relative to the issue, but in the absence of face-to-face interaction those racial identities were not foregrounded in who was saying what about the issue. Is such information relevant to evaluating what people say? Irrelevant? Would knowing such characteristics qualify them as experts on racial experiences or disqualify them as special pleading for their own group? Such serendipities in the course were virtually a daily experience ("virtually"—I'll come back to that); did they take us off topic from the readings or issue of the day, or were they in fact, at a deeper level, more central to the purpose of the course than much of the intentional content?

In this CTER course I have adopted a few approaches, modified over the years, which play a greater role in the nature of the course experience for students than I had ever planned. The first one I want to mention here is assigning group projects. I have a prejudice that teachers are too isolated in their work roles, and that many do not come to regard fellow teachers as in any deep sense of the term *colleagues*. So I make collaborating together a central requirement in the course; something they need to *learn* how to do, and something that often does not come easily to them. Students work on a final group project together, and they know that they will share the final grade. This grading policy frequently raises a discussion about whether it is fair, and what happens if not all members contribute to the final project "equally" (whatever that means), which in turn opens up discussion about the nature of collaboration and the various ways in which group members can contribute to the effectiveness of an overall effort even when their contributions may not look exactly the same. It also frequently opens up a discussion about the fairness of grading itself. But to be frank, nearly every class section has included at least one team with a member who goes AWOL (absent without leave); and this problem or failure opens up its own opportunities for the students (and for me) to engage in some critical reflection about whether the shared-grade approach really is fair to everyone.

A second example from this CTER course concerns the nature of the team projects themselves. In the very first section of the course Chip Bruce and I told students that their projects would be posted as Web pages; it was an online course so we thought their research and writing should be online as well. This decision has had repercussions beyond anything we ever imagined. First, the teams became very motivated: most class assignments are only ever seen by two people—the student who writes it and the instructor who grades and returns it. Normally, its work is considered to be done at this stage: whether it gets filed, thrown away, or stuck on a refrigerator, the cycle of production/evaluation/feedback has been closed. But when students know that their work will be permanently posted, publicized, and available for hundreds or thousands of other educators to see, the value and purpose of the project (beyond earning a grade or satisfying the instructor) become much more salient to the students working on it. The projects for this course have generally pertained to developing white papers on current educational controversies surrounding the uses of new technologies in education (plagiarism, hacking, filtering, privacy, and so on; Levin, Burbules, & Bruce, 2003). These position papers are, in my view, the best single resources anywhere on the Web synthesizing and explaining these issues for educators: they have been accessed tens of thousands of times, and they are linked to by a variety of general Web sites for K–12 educators. I can't tell you how proud the students are of what they have created.[1]

These projects have had another unexpected benefit. Later cohorts of CTER students have used these Web resources for two kinds of purposes: (1) as curriculum content, in orienting them to the ethical and policy issues my course and other courses in the program want them to think about, and (2) as raw material for their own group projects, evaluating the pages for design and content, updating them (fixing dead links, and so on), developing new appendices to supplement them, and in some cases questioning or going beyond those pages to examine further related concerns that may have arisen since those pages were first created (the Web site contains both the original and the corrected or supplemented versions). Here again, further questions arise about collaboration: Whose names go on which versions? How does a link between A and B create an implied association between them? Can people be held accountable for views that they are associated with, but which may not reflect their own beliefs? When is a class project "finished," and is there any reason to think it needs to be "finished," within and across different sections of the course?

The third course component I want to discuss here is the use of multiple media (I think of them as *channels*) of communication: synchronous, asynchronous, large group, small group, public, private, collective, individual, text-based, and audio. Every section of the class has used different tools to develop a variety of alternative discussion channels. Again, this started originally with my assumption, which has turned out to be fairly well supported by later research, that different class members will feel comfortable with different venues; and that someone who is relatively silent in one venue may be much more voluble in another. This has certainly been my experience, and for a class that stresses *access* as a central theme, the reflection over how apparently open and neutral avenues of communication may in fact inadvertently encourage or discourage different individuals or groups from participating, has proven an invaluable object lesson. But beyond this, what has been most striking is how groups of students, despite my intentions or expectations, develop distinct *uses* for these different channels: what they discuss, how long their postings or comments are, how they engage one another through questions or challenges, how formal or informal their comments are, how bold or assertive or confrontational they are willing to be, all vary depending on the channel they are using—and these vary, as well, in terms of who is using that channel. Why other courses limit the options for class discussion to only one forum (or channel) has always puzzled me, when my experience has been that multiple channels provide complementary, largely nonoverlapping opportunities for class engagement. Indeed, I would say that this is one of the potential advantages of new information and communication technologies for teaching, compared with traditional classroom arrangements.

On this point let me touch briefly on a more recent innovation in this class: *blogging* (short for "we*b logg*ing": using a web page to post personal journal entries or a running commentary on a particular topic). I have now added a requirement that students create blogs (web logs) and post to them at least once a day. I know the addresses but I tell the students I will only check in occasionally. Other students in the class cannot read them at all. These are not graded assignments. It has been interesting to see how variously the students use these resources; some use them as class journals, including regular comments and reflections on the course, the readings, the assignments—and while they know I am reading them, the student comments are often unusually frank and provide the kind of insight and feedback on how the class is going, more or less in real time, that instructors rarely receive (and even then not usually until the course is over). Other students use the blogs as a supplement to class discussions, adding afterthoughts that either did not occur to them during class or that they did not have a chance to express in class. Sometimes, given the time delay, these are much richer and more fully formed ideas than arise in the rapid give-and-take of class exchanges. Still others use the blogs as a notebook or work space, storing quotations, references, Web links, or text pieces for class assignments. And of course, most students use them as some combination of these elements. But given my comments on multiple channels previously, I do find that these blogs have become a non-redundant resource; students use them for all sorts of purposes that do not seem to be covered by other communication channels. Furthermore, their semiprivate nature gives students a chance to express things (as they might during closed-door office hours) that are often quite revealing about their responses to the class or to my methods of teaching—they are surprisingly honest and blunt in these observations. The lack of face-to-face contact, so often regarded as a disadvantage in online teaching, is in this instance a benefit.

The things I do in this CTER class are certainly not meant as a recipe for how to do online teaching; if I have learned anything about teaching over the past twenty-five years, it is that what works for one instructor may not work for another, or even that what works for me with one class or group of students may not work, or may work differently, with another group. I mention these things because they are examples of how I try to take distinct advantage of the online medium to do things differently from my normal classroom. While some of these practices (group projects, for example) could be established in any teaching setting, for me these components (the teamwork, the fact that the teams work largely independently and in a self-directed way, the fact that their projects will be published and used as a resource by others, the multiple channels of within-team and across-team discussions, and so on) fit together as patterns of communication and collaboration that undoubtedly give these online classes a different mood and dynamic from my usual classes. The learning is much more self-directed and self-motivated; and the range of interactions I have with students, and that they have with each other, is wider and more varied than a class in which our interactions are guided mainly by the readings, lectures, or discussion questions that I select for them. To the extent that these reforms could be recreated in my usual teaching, the flow of influence is exactly opposite from the more typical model, discussed earlier, in transferring course content from a classroom into the online curriculum. Increasingly, my regular classroom teaching is being influenced by my online experiences. The fact that online interactions are more *virtual* and less face-to-face becomes in many ways an *advantage* of this type of teaching. Let me turn to this topic next.

Virtuality

The term *virtual reality* (VR) was reputedly first coined by Jaron Lanier, head of Virtual Programming Language, Inc.[2] It is usually taken to refer to a computer-mediated simulation that is three-dimensional, multisensory, and interactive, so that the user's experience is "as if" inhabiting and acting within an external environment. But there are two main characteristics of most conceptions of VR, which, I will argue, inhibit a deeper understanding of *virtuality* or *the virtual* (terms I will prefer here to virtual reality). The first assumption is to put the matter of technology at the forefront: VR is computer generated; it involves the use of goggles, gloves, or head-tracking devices. But the key feature of the virtual is not the particular technology that produces the sense of immersion, but the sense of immersion itself (whatever might bring it about), which gives the virtual its phenomenological quality of "as if."[3] When we think of the virtual in this way, we see that all sorts of things can create this sense of immersion: watching a film, reading a book, listening to music, or just being caught up in a reverie or conversation, for example; all of these can yield engrossing experiences of multisensory worlds which, when we are immersed in them, fill our experiential horizons. But there is nothing necessarily technological (or at least not involving computer technologies) about these immersive experiences.

The second assumption in most of these definitions is to characterize VR as a substitute for reality, as an illusion or a trick. Terms often used in place of virtual reality include *simulated reality* or *artificial reality*. The problem with this view is that it assumes an overly sharp separation between the "virtual" and the "real"—the real seems to be a simple, unproblematic given that we perceive and interact with directly, while the virtual means something more like the imaginary. But this is too simple. We know that any reality we inhabit is to some extent actively filtered, interpreted, constructed, or made; it is not merely an unproblematic given. At the same time, the virtual is not merely imaginary; the virtual is better seen as a *medial* concept, neither real nor imaginary, or even better, as both real and imaginary.

In the context of computers and digital culture, this bifurcation of the synthetic and the real has obscured a deeper understanding of what is changing in the ways that we make and explore our worlds, mediated by and through new technologies. Very rarely, if ever, is there a *direct* perception of anything; we actively observe, select, filter, and interpret our experiences in all sorts of ways that construct distinct and sometimes idiosyncratic versions of the world. Some of these mediations are technological in nature: eyeglasses, cameras, telescopes—or, more subtly, concepts, categories, theories, and assumptions. The world we perceive is always already a world we "make" to some extent (Goodman, 1983). This understanding, then, complicates the picture expressed in quotes like, "the more completely 'virtual,' the more completely 'made' our lives become, the more obsessively we search to rediscover something simply given, something authentic" (Herman & Mandell, 2000, online). There is something to this view, of course; but matters aren't so simple. In my view, the virtual challenges such dichotomies. In this sense the term *virtual reality* is a misnomer.

I don't think I need to review here all the recent theoretical work that challenges the easy distinction between representation and reality.[4] The boundaries of our "real" selves, "real" lives, "real" experiences are already fluid and contingent. An excellent discussion of some of these issues, in the context of new technologies, is Sherry Turkle's book, *Life on the Screen,* published in 1995. For many of the people she interviewed, the Internet is a place they inhabit, not simply a tool they use; some users spend so much of their day working, playing, interacting, exploring, and creating online that this becomes their primary mode of existence—what we call ordinary life or real life is not what is most important or "real" to them. Plugged in, logged on, immersed in what they are doing for hours at a stretch—for these folks it is no exaggeration to say they live in a virtual world. What is most striking in reading these accounts is how these people report their *preference* for the online world; they say it is *more* real to them than their ordinary lives, more important to them, and where they feel their authentic selves get expressed. One important dimension of this change is *how* people inhabit the virtual space; often by constructing online identities that are different—sometimes dramatically different—from their ordinary selves (a man representing himself as a woman; a shy woman representing herself as sexually aggressive; a black person "passing" as white, or vice versa; a soft-spoken geek posing as a heavily muscled superhero). These are not, in any simple sense, substitutes for their real selves—performances, fantasies, or role playing. These people often say that they prefer their online selves, and even say that these avatars are more truly who they are, or feel themselves to be, than their apparent identities. As Turkle notes, this trend is part and parcel of broader social and cultural trends that highlight the constructed and non-essentialist nature of personal identity. Either one can discount these people's views as deluded or pathological, or one must acknowledge that something new and different is happening for them.

It still needs to be explained, however, *how* the virtual sustains the sense of "as if"—what some call telepresence, and what I am calling here immersion (on telepresence, see, for example, Steuer, 1992). I gave several examples previously of experiences that can sustain a sense of immersion, and which are to this extent *virtual experiences:* watching a film, reading a book, listening to music, or being caught up in a reverie or a conversation. What gives virtual experiences this quality of immersion? I define four interrelated factors at work here: interest, involvement, imagination, and interaction.

An experience is *interesting* to us when it is complex enough to allow us to pick out new elements, even with repeated encounters. We can shift focus and notice things we had not noticed before. An interesting experience has to present a kind of puzzle that is challenging enough to engage us in actively trying to work out what is going on. Even rereading a book or hearing a piece of music that is very familiar can have the capacity to interest us anew if there is enough to it that we can pick out something that we hadn't noticed before, allowing us to appreciate it or understand it in a new way. Interest is one of the qualities that can sustain the sort of engrossment that causes us to be immersed in a virtual experience. But of course, interest is not an intrinsic quality of experiences; what is interesting to me may not be interesting to you. Something that lacks interest cannot sustain a truly immersive experience.

An experience is *involving* when we have a reason to care about what we are experiencing; we pay attention to it because it concerns us in some way. Perhaps there is a narrative structure involved, or a goal or aim that matters to us (games can be like this, of course). In some cases there may be an aesthetic component to involvement because we enjoy the experience and this is what makes us care; at other times the experience may not be enjoyable, but it involves us because it seems important for other reasons.

An experience engages our *imagination* when we can interpolate or extrapolate new details and add to the experience through our own contributions. We may be interpreting what is going on, making guesses about things that are not immediately present to us (visualizing the face of a character described to us, wondering what their inner thoughts might be; conjuring an image to go along with a piece of music we are hearing; thinking about what the unseen interior of a house we see in a painting might look like); or we may be anticipating what will happen next in some sequence or development. Actively going beyond the given is part of what engages us in it.

An experience is *interactive* when it provides us with opportunities to participate in it, not only perceptually or intellectually but also through embodied action and responses. Many theorists put interactivity at the forefront of what makes virtual reality so vivid and plausible, when we are able to act upon an environment, see the effects of our actions, and react to them. This deeper engagement of our body's movement, activity, and sensations triggers unconscious responses that make us feel "this is really happening," below the level of conscious analysis (for example, how the perceptual field of a technological VR environment moves as you move your head wearing goggles or a helmet). But again, it is a mistake to think of this as a factor only in such technological VR environments. When watching a film or hearing a story, our posture, body tension, and startle responses—or to take another example, our relaxation, rhythmic movement, and kinesthetic sensations listening to music—are a key dimension of the quality of immersion that makes the virtual seem or feel real to us at the moment it is happening.

These four qualities, as described here, are not meant to be exhaustive of all the factors that constitute the virtual, and they are not entirely discrete from each other—one could consider imagination in the sense defined here as a kind of interactivity; interest and involvement clearly have a lot to do with one another. But I think they are helpful in clarifying the processes through which immersion happens, and they help us understand why immersion can be such a powerful mode of response. They push our understanding of the virtual beyond simply thinking of it in terms of vividness or verisimilitude ("it seems so real!"); and they decouple what makes the virtual, virtual, from the issue of technology and the specific media through which engagement happens. All of these qualities (interest, involvement, imagination, and interactivity) could be true, for example, of an intense conversation with a friend; for long stretches the conversation could sustain an immersive, virtual experience. (Think of a friend recounting a traumatic event, or a humorous anecdote, in which we are not only listening, but actively engaged with what she is telling us. All four of the factors described here could be involved as we identify with the event and even, in some sense, virtually re-experience it with her.)

Most of all, while grounded in characteristics and qualities of the virtual environment, this analysis makes clear that immersion is a consequence of our active response and engagement with them—it is not something that happens *to* us. Nevertheless, it is possible to see some of the ways in which virtuality can be abused: as a method of deception or manipulation, for instance. I have already described people who state that they prefer their virtual experiences and identities, consider them more real, as far as they are concerned. For some of these people it may truly be a concern that they become addicted to virtual experiences, or can no longer differentiate the virtual from other modes of experience. Countless science fiction stories and films (most recently, and perhaps most famously, *The Matrix* series) have been premised on the idea that a person may permanently inhabit the virtual and lose awareness of the context that gives the virtual experience its boundaries. Here the illusion/reality dichotomy seems to reemerge, but in my view it is more accurate to say that these are different kinds of realities, made worlds, some of which are more susceptible to questioning about how and why they are made the way they are (a memory versus a live event; an historical text versus a "truthful" fiction; and so on). It is the lack of an ability to ask such questions, to regard the context of *any* experience as potentially problematic, which is a potential issue. The whole point of "immersion" is that for periods of time we forget that we are watching a film, wearing goggles, sitting in a symphony hall, and so forth. But if we *perpetually* forget this, abuses and dangers can arise.

On the other hand, turning this question around, I would argue that this analysis of immersion, and how it happens, has strong implications for the design of educational environments and experiences. Interest, involvement, imagination, and interactivity, as I have defined them here, are essential educational resources if we mean to engage and motivate active student learning: in this sense, any truly educational experience is immersive, or in other words, *virtual*. Again, I do not mean that it must be technologically mediated and require computers, but I do mean to upset the assumption that face-to-face classroom interactions are necessarily more authentic, more meaningful, or more educationally productive than technologically mediated ones. Under certain circumstances, given the nature of schools and classrooms as we have them today, it may be easier to foster the dimensions of interest, involvement, imagination, and interactivity through computers or other technologies; they do have certain advantages in this regard. Online education (what others call *distance education*) can be just as vivid, meaningful, and dynamic as face-to-face interactions in a classroom—or even more so. Each domain has its own unique qualities and advantages; for this reason, to me, the question is not a matter of which is better or which should substitute for the other, but rather what is the distinct capability of each to support immersive learning experiences. (For example, as I have mentioned, in my online courses there often is more, and more varied, student interaction and participation than in many regular classroom seminars.)

Virtual Teaching and Learning

The virtual classroom, therefore, does not just mean "the computer-mediated classroom" or "online teaching and learning." Nor, given the account I am presenting here, is this the new educational revolution or panacea that will solve all our educational problems—the new Best Way of Teaching. But given the definition of the virtual as immersive, and the four components I identify in that process (interest, involvement, imagination, and interaction), it is not too much of a stretch to say that *all* successful learning environments, of whatever form, partake of the qualities of the virtual to some degree. Computer technologies may or may not be useful in facilitating these qualities; virtual teaching isn't necessarily online, and online teaching isn't necessarily virtual. But in any teaching circumstance, certain "virtual" questions emerge.

What is of interest to the learner? Dewey (1902: 1971) is famous for warning that when we try to find a way to make what we want students to learn interesting to them, we have already taken the wrong path; rather, he advises, we should begin with what *is* interesting to them and work with that resource to get the learning we value off the ground. Good as this may sound, it is not very realistic. While undoubtedly teachers should spend more time respecting and pursuing student interests rather than overriding them because of what the curriculum (or the standardized test) says must be covered, good teaching and project design can elicit interest even with material that is not immediately interesting or of concern to students. Interesting subject matter is engaging and puzzling at a level that poses an attractive challenge to the learner. Too difficult and the student loses interest out of frustration; too simple and it loses its quality as a challenge—an observation that clearly implies that the same material presented the same way cannot be equally interesting to everyone. The key is to allow a degree of individual responsiveness and choice, moving through material in a way that varies in pace and difficulty, and in which students can seek new challenges when they feel ready for them. In this regard certain kinds of technologically mediated environments can have an advantage; and as my colleague Rod Riegle (Illinois State University) once pointed out to me, curriculum designers may be able to learn some useful things from computer game designers in this regard. Problem solving, pacing, and alternative paths of investigation can all help promote interest.

What is involving for the learner? Previously I defined this quality in terms of enjoyment and importance: learners are involved with things that matter to them. Here Dewey is much closer to the truth, I believe: if learning opportunities are not enjoyable or important for the students, one has a major burden in trying to *make* them satisfying or important (usually through extrinsic rewards, or sometimes through the threat of adverse consequences otherwise). Widespread educational success is not possible under such conditions. Dewey's advice that we need to start where students are already motivated and eager to learn, and link our purposes to that engine, is a valuable corrective here.

How do I engage the learner's imagination with this problem? This is perhaps where my examples run most closely to the traditional notion of the virtual: simulations, models, case studies, or narratives that construct a plausible version of reality and allow room for the participant to interpolate or extrapolate new content as they work to make sense of it. But to reiterate the point, these may or may not be computer-generated simulations, models, and so on. In my CTER class, the daily discussions about ethical and policy issues are always generated out of case studies (some totally fictional, some based on actual events) that require the students to analyze and reach conclusions about recognizable choices or dilemmas they may face as educators; indeed, one of the ways they exercise their imaginations is by conceiving parallels or analogies with actual cases with which they have had to struggle. These case studies are also *puzzles,* with more or less recognizable consequences at stake—I try to make them interesting and involving for students. They are often situations in which the teachers have little trouble imagining themselves; this also motivates them to try to think them through. And if I am a successful designer of case studies, they are layered, subtle—they do not exhaust the possibilities or generate a simple answer quickly; the more students think about them, the more dimensions or potential consequences they can imagine, which makes their deliberations more ambiguous and difficult (in the educationally valuable sense of those terms).

How can I facilitate interactions between students and the learning situation, and among students in coping with it? I doubt that I need to belabor this point here; the uses of team projects, multiple channels of communication, opportunities for open deliberation and for private, personal reflection on course activities, all are intended to facilitate such interactivity. To a degree, this factor cuts across and interacts with the others: the interactions with other students often help make the project involving and important to them; their imaginations are sparked through the processes of sharing and building upon one another's ideas; in a group learning project, what one person finds interesting can complement what another student finds less so (and vice versa).

And there is one last point to make about the immersive quality that these four types of experience help constitute: the sense of immersion can be fun; it can be enjoyable to be lost in a reverie or contemplation of what interests and engages us. When people talk about learning as play, this is typically seen as juvenile or unrealistic: serious learning is considered to be too difficult, even stressful, to be fun. But "play" that comprises interest, involvement, imagination, and interaction is perfectly serious, and it is not only compatible with difficulty—at some level it *requires* a degree of difficulty and complexity (on the seriousness of "play," see Chapter 3 in Burbules, 1993). I will put this even more strongly: learning that has lost its sense of connection with play, that is no longer immersive, engaging, and enjoyable, will encounter motivational limits, problems of retention and transferability to other lifelong contexts, and other issues (cheating, for example), to a much higher degree than virtual learning, as I have described it here. Those are empirical questions, I suppose, but they stand as an article of faith for me.

Having argued all this, I return (somewhat perversely, or playfully perhaps) to the theme of navigation. It is almost certainly true that not everything students need to learn can be taught in this way; and what is interesting, involving, and so forth for some students will not be for others. As a consequence, creative teachers need to make a series of compromises between how virtual their teaching can be, and how much of it must be more direct and, even, routine. It may even be that for certain subject matters, a certain amount of direct, routine learning is necessary in order to learn enough for it to begin to become interesting and enjoyable. (On the other hand, this can be, and often is, a handy rationale for forcing students to put up with boring material, taught in a boring way, because we can't think of a better way to do it, or don't want to take the time and effort to. We keep telling ourselves, and the students, that eventually it will become interesting and intrinsically rewarding.) And so we encounter another Scylla and Charybdis: between rethinking a curriculum to support more virtual learning, while acknowledging a boundary or limit—a shifting one—to what can be refigured in this way. Erring in the other direction, instructors can think that what is interesting or important *to them* is necessarily so to learners, or that the way of presenting and organizing information that works for their ways of thinking will necessarily be the way that best engages and challenges diverse learners.

These teaching choices pose a number of dilemmas: how to make a classroom inclusive while recognizing that every choice effectively excludes someone; how far it is possible or desirable to expand access, given scarce resources; how educationally beneficial or how educationally compromising the lack of face-to-face engagement can be; how far to go in accommodating the convenience and scheduling of students, viewed as clients or customers, without becoming overly commercialized and entrepreneurial. Some of these dilemmas may seem exclusively pertinent to online teaching, but in fact they illustrate many crucial dilemmas in teaching of all sorts (think of large amphitheater classes in the university). We often don't recognize these trade-offs any longer in our traditional classroom settings because those contexts are so familiar and taken for granted by us, or because the choices implicit in those arrangements were made and negotiated long ago, whereas in online teaching they are still new and unfamiliar to us. "Virtual" education doesn't solve any of these problems without confronting us with new ones.

But to the extent that we can be successful in making learning experiences more virtual, it is because we are effective in creating or designing environments that facilitate learner interest, involvement, imagination, and interactivity. Such design choices balance questions about what we want students to learn with a reflective exploration of what motivates them and engages them as diverse learners. The possibility of thinking outside traditional classroom patterns of communication and collaboration is part of what is exciting about new information and communication technologies; but we do not *need* new technologies to do so. Navigating these new possibilities and dangers confronts us with an uncertain, challenging time. Yet these new possibilities also can open up a new virtual space for us as educators: one that can be a product of *our own* interest, involvement, imagination, and interactions—and maybe one that can even be fun for us as well.

Acknowledgments

This chapter was originally given as an invited talk at the Library Education Experimental Project (LEEP) Retreat at the University of Illinois, August 2002.

Notes

1. For work produced by these students, see *White Papers on Technology Issues for Educators* (http://lrs.ed.uiuc.edu/wp/).
2. See "Virtual reality: A definition history" http://www.fourthwavegroup.com/fwg/lexicon/1725w1.htm.
3. On this sense of immersion, I have been influenced by exchanges with Alan B. Craig and William R. Sherman, National Center for Supercomputing Applications, University of Illinois.
4. A good overview of this work, focusing especially on the ideas of Baudrillard and Derrida, can be found in Poster (2001).

References

Burbules, N.C. (1993). *Dialogue in teaching: Theory and practice*. New York: Teachers College Press.
Burbules, N.C. (2002). 2001: A philosophical odyssey. In S. Rice (Ed.), *Philosophy of Education 2001* (pp. 1–14). Urbana, IL: Philosophy of Education Society.
Burbules, N. C., & Callister, T. A., Jr. (2000). *Watch IT: The promises and risks of information technologies for education*. Boulder, CO: Westview Press.
Dewey, J. (1902: 1971) *The child and the curriculum,* and *The school and society*. Chicago: University of Chicago Press.
Dreyfus, H. (2001). *On the Internet (Thinking in action)*. New York: Routledge.
Goodman, N. (1983). *Ways of worldmaking*. Cambridge, MA: Hackett Publishing.
Herman, L., & Mandell, A. (2000). The given and the made: Authenticity and nature in virtual education. *First Monday, 5*(10). Retrieved from http://www.firstmonday.dk/issues/issue5_10/herman/index.html.

Levin, J. A., Burbules, N. C., & Bruce, B. C. (2003). *Open publishing of exemplary educational resources: The case of the CTER white papers*. Unpublished manuscript.

Poster, M. (2001). *What's the matter with the Internet?* Minneapolis, MN: University of Minnesota Press.

Steuer, J. (1992). Defining virtual reality: Dimensions determining telepresence. *Journal of Communication, 42*(4), 73–93.

Turkle, S. (1995). *Life on the screen: Identity in the age of the Internet*. New York: Simon and Schuster.

CHAPTER 2

Bertram C. Bruce

Maintaining the Affordances of Traditional Education Long Distance

We learn whenever we attempt to make sense of experiences. Thus, learning occurs alone or in groups; at home, at work, and at play; in face-to-face settings, as well as online and on television; in natural and in constructed settings; with and without books; for toddlers and elders and everyone in between. Yet the word *learning* is often thought to apply to that special set of situations we find in school. School (or college, university, training center, etc.) brackets learning into manageable chunks for purposes of funding, delivery, assessment, and accreditation.

Schooling is thus defined as the activity that occurs within a certain space, the classroom, and a certain time, the school day, or the 50-minute hour. Despite what we may assert about learning beyond the walls of the school and about lifelong learning, it is difficult to avoid the equation of learning with school, and therefore, the equation of learning with sitting at a desk, looking at a blackboard attached to the front wall of the classroom. The center of learning is identified with the classroom, and it seems heretical to challenge the centrality of the school building or the school calendar. Such a challenge is rightly interpreted to imply challenges to other aspects of formal learning: the textbook, the assessment system, and even the teacher. Many now see learning, even fully accredited, formal, certificate-driven learning to be possible anytime and anywhere.

The frame for formal learning consists of practices associated with time, space, knowledge, and participants. Online learning, often conceived as learning anywhere/anytime, promises to radically alter that frame and the associated practices. The advent of the Internet has now led to an exponential growth in the number of distance course offerings. Where once one could point to a few special cases such as the Open University[1] in the United Kingdom, now virtually every institution of higher education is considering, if not implementing, online course offerings. Consider just a few of the claims that are being made about these changes and see what they might mean for education.

The frame for learning first of all defines its *space*. For example, the school building is clearly defined and separate from other structures. It sits in a schoolyard, surrounded by a wall or fence. Often there are signs on the nearby streets warning motorists to slow down. These things serve practical functions, not the least of which is to define the space where learning is to occur. General learning occurs within that space in the classroom or auditorium. Specific forms of learning occur in designated spaces, such as laboratories, libraries, or a playground. Online learning challenges these structures and the assumptions underlying them. It is already leading to significant changes in terms of where one accesses educational resources, especially at the secondary and higher levels. External degrees from open universities are now common and well accepted. These programs are particularly attractive to those living in areas far removed from centers of higher learning. Students with disabilities, and those who work are finding increased opportunities to learn. One's country, even the language one speaks, is becoming much less a barrier to educational access.

The frame also determines *time*. We define programs of study involving multiple courses. A semester-long course comprises units enacted in weeks or days. Lessons are defined as short time segments, with mini-lessons even briefer. The most complex areas of inquiry are ultimately broken down into numbers of minutes of study. Online learning is increasingly attractive even to those geographically near to centers of learning for reasons of time and convenience. As the programs expand, we see the many ways that online education can expand learning opportunities. For many people, who must fit coursework within constraints of family and part-time work, online courses make higher education attainable.

The framing of time and space is associated with other aspects of learning. *Knowledge* itself is typically framed within books, or even the sole textbook. What we do with what we learn is usually framed as well, perhaps as that which is written in a "blue book" or as checkmarks on a multiple-choice quiz. These knowledge practices are now changing. As schooling is tied more to work, we will see the benefit of learning that can be used directly in careers. The ability to remain in one's home community may provide better grounding for educational experiences. We cannot say yet how these changes will affect other goals of education, such as promoting a common understanding, developing capable citizens, and enlarging the individual's capacity to appreciate and contribute to the larger culture.

Participants are framed as well—the teacher and students, administrators, and classroom aides. With online learning, these roles may change in dramatic ways. The lecture may have to be reconceived given the emerging technology for high-speed, low-cost delivery of video, or even virtual reality, on demand.

Schooling as an institution is a framed element, which will undergo fundamental reorganizations in the online environment. The lines between schools, community colleges, technical colleges, universities, museums, nature centers, and workplaces are blurring. As more courses are offered online, students will find it easier to continue full-time work while studying. There will be less need for the local college in each community or region. How many institutions of higher learning will survive? One-half of those in operation today? One-tenth? Will students even continue to study through public institutions or will they turn to corporations or new organizations for coursework? The technological revolution in the workplace is leading to an increased integration of schooling and work. Moreover, just to use the Internet is to enter into the commercial world. Online education is both a reflection of and a stimulus for a blurring of the lines between students as learners, as workers, and as consumers.

Similar claims have been heard before, first with correspondence courses and external degree programs, and later with educational radio and television, videocassettes, teleconferencing, and similar media. But the integration and expansion of all these tools through the Internet, and the increased accessibility of digital media, raises anew questions about the future of education. Many of these changes will be good, and many, not so good; what is clear is that the structures and modes of learning are already undergoing dramatic changes. In this context it is well worth asking: Is anywhere/anytime learning possible? What is lost and what is gained? And, at an even more fundamental level, what has changed?

Some Definitions

Terms such as *online learning* have definite meanings—unfortunately, far too many. Because I want to examine here arguments for and against "online learning," it will be helpful to define a few terms in advance.

Asynchronous communication—the exchange of messages in a medium that does not require the simultaneous presence of the sender and the receiver. By this definition, ordinary postal mail qualifies as asynchronous communication, but the term usually refers to asynchronous electronic communication, such as e-mail.

Synchronous communication—the exchange of messages in a medium that requires the simultaneous presence of the sender and the receiver, for example, in an electronic chat system. The line between synchronous and asynchronous is a function of the sociotechnical system, not just the technologies per se. For example, two conversants could use e-mail in a chat-like, synchronous fashion by agreeing to be online at the same time and sending rapid replies. Another pair might use instant messaging in an asynchronous fashion by leaving messages in the chat window. Or, they could use the *away* function, which is available in most programs, allowing users to leave messages saying what they're doing or when they might be available (Bruce, 2003, pp. 2–5).

Distance learning—distance education provides a unique opportunity for those who wish to study but cannot attend residential institutions because of personal circumstances or occupational obligations. The term was once synonymous with *correspondence course,* and later with educational television, but has increasingly been used to refer to learning through an array of communication technologies, including video, teleconferencing, e-mail, and the Web. These tools have now emerged as integral components of on-campus courses as well, so distance per se, the physical location of the student relative to the class, has become a less defining factor. Thus, the concept of distance learning may fade away as the means by which it is enacted parallels other modes of learning.

We can distinguish four situations for instruction, the first two of which might be considered distance learning. Many courses and programs today are hybrids, with some of each of these modes of learning. The LEEP program is a notable example, with its on-campus sessions, synchronous classes, and bulletin board interactions. But for the purpose of analysis, we can focus on specific learning events, which tend to fall into one or the other of these categories:

Real-time distance learning—students and teachers interacting in real time, but in different locations. They may do this through computer-mediated means, such as chat systems or Web sharing, or through audio or video channels. The key features are that they have simultaneous interactions but are not in the same room.

Asynchronous distance learning—interactions may occur at different times and places. Typically, this case involves bulletin board systems, online assignments, and a Web-based syllabus.

Conventional classroom—students and teachers are co-located; their interactions occur in the same time and place. This is the most familiar case, one in which students occupy the same room at the same time. Although the traditional mode, it embodies in the fullest sense the high-tech concept of synchronous communication.

Asynchronous co-located learning—a fourth logical case, can occur in certain circumstances, but is much less common. This could occur when students interact in the same place at different times. For example, students might check an experiment in progress in a science laboratory and communicate through a lab notebook there.

Binding Time

One way to think about the frames of learning is provided by the concept of *binding time,* a term from computer programming language theory. It refers to the fact that terms in a language can be assigned values early or late in the process of carrying out a computer program. For example, a constant, such as "2" is bound early, whereas a variable, such as "x" is bound later. Wegner (1968, p. 17) defines it this way: "The moment during execution at which a given set of attributes is fixed (bound) is said to be the *binding time* of the given set of attributes." When a program is compiled, attributes are said to be bound early because they are fixed well before they are executed; when a program is interpreted, attributes are bound late. In general, binding early makes the program more efficient but less flexible. Think of planning a vacation. It may be simpler and more efficient to fix the mode of transportation early (one less thing to think about if you buy the tickets now), but doing so is less flexible, and could create a problem should conditions change.

Although the technical term, binding time, applies only to formal languages and interpretations of sentences in those languages, it provides a useful lens for examining the varieties of learning structures made possible with new technologies. Table 2.1 shows some of the major features of instruction and how they are realized in different cases. The first two rows designate the defining characteristics of each mode. Thus, time is bound early in the conventional classroom; the timetable sets when the class is to meet, well in advance. This is also the case for synchronous or real-time distance learning. But for asynchronous distance learning there is learner control over the time of the learning, hence *anytime*. Similarly, space is set or bound early for the conventional classroom. It is often set early for real-time distance learning, especially if learners need to go to a place with special teleconferencing equipment. But again, for asynchronous distance learning, that choice of space is much freer, hence *anywhere*.

The succeeding rows in Table 2.1 refer to various aspects of the instructional process. For each aspect, the designations of *never, early, mid,* and *late* are tendencies given to the affordances of the technologies. Most are sociotechnical, reflecting a combination of social and technical factors. For example, most instructors try to write a syllabus and select readings before a course begins. But the current mechanisms for preparing Web-based courses and the expectations of distance learners make that more imperative for asynchronous distance learning than for the conventional classroom. In the case of LEEP, early syllabus development is promoted as a best practice.

Objects of study and visuals, such as science apparatus, books, maps, archaeological remnants, music players, or technical devices, play a role in many classes. In the conventional classroom, they don't appear to the students until the moment of their use in class, and for the instructor, can be selected close to the time of the class. In the distance cases they are difficult to use at all (i.e., never) or must be chosen well in advance of class (early). Similarly, the form of class activities and dialogue remain less fixed in the conventional classroom case until the moment of enactment (late). In the distance settings, more elements need to be set up ahead of time (early). Teacher response in a conventional classroom can also come late—for example, comments as graded assignments are returned in class. In the distance cases, these responses tend to come earlier, and students often expect early responses (as in "you haven't replied, but I posted my message last night!"). On the other hand, student work can be bound early in synchronous settings (face-to-face or distance), for instance, whenever the instructor says "so, Daniel, what do you think of the author's argument about the effects of the Renaissance?" The next two sections discuss these issues further.

TABLE 2.1. **Binding Time for Key Features of Learning Situations**

Learning Aspect	Conventional Classroom	Real-time Distance Learning	Asynchronous Distance Learning
Time	early (synchronous)	early (synchronous)	late (asynchronous)
Space	early (co-located)	early–mid (distant, but set)	late (distant)
Syllabus, readings	early–late	early–mid	early
Objects, visuals	late	never–early	never–early
Activities	late	early–mid	early
Dialogue	late	late	early
Teacher response	late	early–late	early–late
Student work	early	early	lat

None of the modes of learning stand out as purely early or late binding. It is almost as if there needs to be a balance of flexibility and efficiency. In general, the conventional classroom requires an earlier binding time for place and time, but it allows a later binding time for course elements than do either the real-time or the asynchronous distance learning cases. Thus, a binding time argument says that the conventional classroom is more flexible in terms of learning activities, but less efficient. Similarly, it fixes the meeting place and time quite efficiently, but is inflexible about those.

The Case for Anywhere/Anytime Learning

Proponents of anywhere/anytime learning typically conceive their work as arising from the affordances of new technologies, such as videoconferencing, interactive simulations, the Web, e-mail, or electronic bulletin boards. To a large extent, these tools, especially hypertext, provide a later binding for course content, which can increase flexibility for both students and teachers.[2] The rich information resources of the Web and electronic databases, which are widely accessible, can be designated as part of the class materials if the instructor chooses. Instructors can also add examples, elaborations, extensions, and qualifications, which cannot be included in other media because of space limitations. They can even add them after the class has met, in a very late binding way. Multimedia possibilities are expanded. It is becoming relatively routine now to incorporate video, audio, animations, and a variety of graphical formats.

Rather than being simply readers as they investigate the medium, students can learn through writing as well. They can respond through e-mail and bulletin boards or use Web forms; they can create Web content. Active engagement, which is encouraged through interactive features such as dynamic simulations, online laboratories, and point-and-click interfaces, promises greater opportunities for learners to explore and create.

The case for anywhere/anytime learning can also be explained in terms of other binding-time phenomena. The late binding of time and place for asynchronous distance learning is what gives it the purported anywhere/anytime character. If the time and place of learning do not have to be determined until the moment of interaction, then the learner has the maximum possible flexibility. This breaking of the frame permits the claimed advantages of greater access, and greater connection to community and work.

Educational administrations and commercial organizations are often very intrigued with the idea of distance learning, and especially its realization in Web-based courses, because of its apparent efficiencies. Decide on the syllabus once and for all, and it is no longer necessary to pay people to develop multiple variants.

For students, the early binding of course materials and format actually allows a later binding for student work. For example, in an online course, a lecture is set out early. It may typically be read or viewed long before the designated day or anytime (and anywhere) afterward. The act of student engagement (reading, comprehending, responding) can be relatively late in the process of the course, and relatively much under student control (late binding). This makes it easier for students to adapt the course activities to their own lives. In comparison, in a face-to-face lecture, there is the possibility of that dreaded moment when the professor calls on a particular student. This requires at least the semblance of attention and processing of the course materials (early binding), a requirement that reduces student flexibility.

Teachers, too, appreciate the efficiency of Web-based courses, although many recognize that they lose flexibility, which can hamper their ability to meet learner needs (see next section). Proponents argue that interactive software and multimedia software can address these concerns about flexibility. The Web allows learner control of information access. Students can experience online labs at any time and from any location. It is easier to move around on a Web site and attend to the portions that meet learning needs. The Web thus provides opportunities for self-directed inquiry and for exploring phenomena in depth. Material on the Web is hyperlinked, both within a document to show connections of concepts, and between one document and another. A consequence is that learners can more easily move from one idea to another. The Web also provides greater learner control of the pace of learning. Learners can repeat activities, linger over them, or skip parts they already know.

Anywhere/anytime means that formal learning comes to the student rather than the other way around. It also means that learning may not be so removed from other life experiences: It occurs in the workplace, in the context of immediate problems; it occurs in the home, with family present; it occurs in the community, in the context of the history, values, and needs of that community.

Thus, beyond the technology-driven argument, the energy and appeal of the anywhere/anytime learning idea is also a reprise of the progressive education movement, which sought to remove the separation between formal and informal learning. John

Dewey's idea that all knowledge begins and ends in ordinary experience resonates with current notions that learners need not abandon their home, family, community, or work to extend their learning. Instead, formal learning may be connected to those situated experiences. Dewey saw this as connecting learning to life:

> Thus I have attempted to indicate how the school may be connected with life so that the experience gained by the child in a familiar, commonplace way is carried over and made use of there, and what the child learns in the school is carried back and applied in everyday life, making the school an organic whole, instead of a composite of isolated parts. (Dewey, 1907, p. 106)

The case then for anywhere/anytime learning rests on several arguments. Some pertain to the medium, with its multimedia, hypertextual characteristics. Some pertain to the binding time configuration. Early binding time for course construction leads to greater efficiency, and later binding time for enactment, especially of student activities, provides greater student flexibility. Some build upon an explicit or implicit desire to have learning more deeply connected to life. This is particularly the case for online learning in the workplace environment, where the late binding of student work means that it can be deeply connected to ongoing work. Of course, any particular instantiation of an online course may fall far short of these ideals.

The Case against Anywhere/Anytime Learning

The movement promoting learning anywhere and anytime builds in part upon our recognition that learning in life is much more than what occurs in the confines of a classroom or a designated time period for a class. For example, we see that students graduating from a university often describe opportunities to learn from other students and informal learning experiences derived from the environment of the university as being even more important than their formal coursework.

This acknowledgment of life learning is part of what we think about when we respond positively to the rhetoric about learning beyond the walls of the classroom. And yet an interesting irony emerges. The movement to online learning often means that formal education is then reduced to navigating courses divorced from any shared social context. The online learning community established by a course can be a thin community with strictly limited modes of interaction, shared beliefs, or common purposes (cf. Dewey, 1916: 1966). The concept of learning freed from the constraints of time and space thus curiously reduces to learning confined within a new frame of asynchronous communication without the serendipitous experiences that many of us most value.

In the language of binding time, the conventional setting offers late, and unpredicted, binding of a host of attributes: How does today's history lecture relate to the debate on student government? How does this science topic relate to news of a recent discovery? How does the weather affect our interpretations of a poem? How does the professor's insight from research add to the current class discussion? How does a chance encounter in the hallway provide a new perspective on the themes of a course? Current events, social relations, physical surroundings, and more, ensure that learning in the conventional setting in fact does occur anywhere and anytime. Of course, distance courses can in principle provide much of this late, and hence situated, binding. But the argument against typical realizations of anywhere/anytime learning is twofold. One part is that without the shared time and space it is simply not possible to do some of this late binding. (Imagine a history instructor saying, "The lack of heat in the building today gives us a sense of what life in the middle ages must have sometimes been like.") The second part is that the typical and often recommended early binding of course materials and activities makes those situated linkages less feasible.

This can be seen by examining the key aspects of learning situations shown in Table 2.1. For example, a syllabus and selection of readings are the norm, especially for secondary- and tertiary-level classes. In the conventional classroom these are usually prepared in advance, but a well-known feature is that they can be changed. An instructor may find a new article that fits the course goals or the particular interests of the students. Relevant news items can easily be brought into the discussion of the day. Assignments and lectures are frequently adjusted to fit the questions students ask or ideas the instructor has developed. This last-minute adjustment accounts for the *on-the-fly* experience of teaching, which many instructors admit to sheepishly, but also value as a means to make their classrooms more dynamic. This on-the-fly adjustment depends on a host of factors in the situation: students' facial expressions, the weather, events on campus, availability of materials, the day's colloquium. In a real-time distance learning situation, it is possible to do some of these adjustments, but less easily, because those factors are less accessible to all. In asynchronous distance learning it is even more difficult to adjust on the fly. A terrific idea in a shared temporal and spatial setting may lose its timeliness when enacted over the time span of a week, and without the shared spatial context, it may lose relevance. A newfound article cannot be distributed to the class by photocopying it ten minutes ahead of the session. We can describe these differences by saying that the asynchronous distance learning case requires an earlier binding time; the syllabus and readings are typically set earlier and are less subject to change. The conventional classroom allows the latest possible binding time.

Similarly, we can look at other features of the classroom (objects of study, activities, dialogue, teacher responses) in terms of their binding time. For example, objects of study, such as a book, an image, a device, or a nature specimen, are used often in many classes. In the conventional classroom, an instructor can select such an object or change the selection at the last moment. A photograph or object can simply be held up to the class or passed around. In the two distance cases, one would typically need to digitize the object and post it on the class Web site, with a message ahead of time to class members to examine it. It is possible to arrange for similar objects to be brought in. For example, the Lesley University Science in Education program (http://www.lesley.edu/soe/science/) has students do hands-on science investigations in their homes or wherever they may be taking the course. Using similar materials (one experiment involves a jar, olive oil, a cork, string, and a timer), students are able to experience phenomena and discuss them with other students and instructors. Thus, *hands-on* is not an attribute that clearly distinguishes between face-to-face and distance learning. But though it is possible to achieve hands-on learning in any of the environments, the setup for hands-on learning in the Lesley University program must be done well in advance (early binding), just as the setup for Web-based materials is typically done. Similar problems exist for students making pictures (e.g., workflow diagrams, physical force models) or physical objects (e.g., an electrical circuit) and sending those objects to the instructor. One can imagine ways to do that (send a digital image, send by mail), but it is unlikely to be both as timely and complete as it could be in the conventional classroom.

In the case for anywhere/anytime learning it was noted that students in asynchronous settings experience a later binding time, which gives them a greater sense of control. Not surprisingly, many teachers feel a loss of control of student work directly proportional to the students' increased sense of control. These shifts in binding time for different aspects of the course index other changes in the teacher-student relationship as well, which can be problematic given the institutional expectations of teacher control over course content and grading.

The flexibility of the conventional classroom regarding course content and modes of interaction leads to a potential (though not always realized) richness of the learning experience. It is an *affordance,* not of the chalkboard technology so derided by proponents of new technologies for learning, but of the larger sociotechnical system in which learning is embedded—the system comprising human activity, spaces, artifacts, tools, and communications media. Various approaches, such as information ecologies (Nardi & O'Day, 1999), provide ways of understanding how the lectures, textbooks, and tools of the classroom are only a few of the actors within the network of human and technology actors in the school.

Traditional face-to-face education claims to offer learning specified in syllabi, delivered by instructors, and assessed on tests. Despite these claims, its greatest contribution may be in what it *affords,* rather than what it ostensibly *delivers.* Or, to put it another way, its contribution may be through its invisible elements rather than its visible ones. If that is true, then the new frame offered by online learning may deliver just as well, but in so doing, it excludes the anywhere, anytime learning that in fact characterizes much of the overall traditional experience.

The case then against anywhere/anytime learning rests on several arguments. One is that the very success of online learning has changed the conventional classroom. Thus, the rich media used online are now a part of face-to-face classes as well, and can no longer be used as an argument for online learning per se. What the early binding time for course construction gains in greater efficiency is lost in terms of reduced flexibility, especially if one considers the myriad situated extensions of the classroom. The later binding time for student work provides greater student flexibility, but loses in terms of building a learning community. Finally, the desire to have learning more deeply connected to life may argue even more strongly against the online environment.

Rethinking the Debate

The issues around this debate are crucial ones, but in the final analysis it may be the wrong way to characterize the problem. Both the pro and the con positions, as presented above, follow a media-effects approach. This is a dominant approach to analyzing the effects of technology or new media (see Gauntlett, 1995, 1998). Typically it follows the pattern:

- analyze the technology
- describe its effects
- interpret those effects

Thus, a proponent says the technology does thus-and-so, and therefore it will have such-and-such effects. Are there other ways to understand the role of technologies? I'd like to suggest several approaches, which provide lenses for seeing the phenomena of user appropriation as well as frameworks for interpreting what actually happens when the system is deployed (see also Bruce, 1999, 2003).

The first is to recognize that the online environment is what Roland Barthes (1970: 1974) calls a *writerly text,* one that locates the reader as a site of the production of meaning.[3] Regardless of how well resources have been collected and organized, curricula have been designed, or even training delivered, the power of the reader/user to appropriate the system in ways that make sense within a local context should not be underestimated. Accordingly, how well the online environment supports education depends on how it is distributed, interpreted, and re-created through use. These issues are difficult to predict, as Merkel (2002) shows in a detailed account of technology use in low-resource communities. She details the many disjunctions between well-meaning developers and the situation of community members, which affect what the technology is in practice.

These differences can be extreme. For example, in a recent dissertation, Wang (2003) showed how children collaborated in a first-grade classroom. The teacher had allocated five minutes for each child at the computer. On their own, children developed a system in which one child used the left half of the keyboard, a second used the right half, and a third used the mouse. Thus, they managed to get 15 minutes each at the computer, while achieving greater success in navigation or game playing than any one would have alone. The meaning of the applications, the children's use of time and space while interacting with the computer, and the learning that occurred were only in part determined by the hardware and software design. A similar reinterpretation and redesign of the human-computer system is repeated in many contexts and nearly always underestimated by developers (see Twidale, 2003, for similar examples in adult use).

These are examples of *pragmatic technology*. One sense of that term is the common-language notion of technology that works to meet real human needs, accommodates to users, and is situated in time, place, and setting. A second, related concept, comes from pragmatist theory (e.g., Addams, Dewey, James, Mead, Peirce), in which technology is seen as the outcome of resolving a problematic situation. The latter sees technologies as both means of action and forms of understanding (Dewey, 1938; Hickman, 1990). This is a *constructivist* view of technology itself. Technologies are not seen as fixed objects with predefined functions, but rather as tools that are interpreted and remade into other tools. The incorporation of a technology into social practice is a function of political and economic forces, historical accidents, cultural conceptions, and a host of other factors in addition to any characteristics of the technology as physical object itself. Moreover, the attributes of the technology are themselves shaped by social forces (Bijker, Hughes, & Pinch 1987).

This perspective is helpful for understanding divergent or unintended uses. It also helps in understanding whose problem is being addressed. For example, a problem may be defined by the systems designer as organizing a collection of high-quality resources on biology, whereas the high-school teacher user may be concerned with improving test scores. These two problems may have some overlap, but their difference needs to be understood if we are to make sense of how the system gets used, or not, in that classroom.

Closely related to the pragmatic technology conception is situated evaluation, a framework for understanding innovation and change (Bruce, Peyton, & Batson, 1993). This framework emphasizes contrastive analysis as it seeks to account for differences in use. An underlying assumption is that the object of study is neither the innovation alone nor its effects, but rather the realization of the innovation or the innovation-in-use. It produces hypotheses supported by detailed analyses of actual practices, which make possible informed plans for use and change (cf. Bruce & Rubin, 1993, p. 215).

Use of any new technology is a long-term process of adaptation (DeSanctis & Poole, 1994). This is not just to say that it takes time to learn how to use a new tool; more deeply it is that context determines use and in turn use determines context. The consequence is that we see processes of substitution, enlargement, and reconfiguration. It then becomes crucial to ask where we are in a process whose end is not in sight. The Concerns-Based Adoption Model (Hord, Rutherford, Hiding-Austin, & Hall, 1987), which emphasizes examining the change process rather than a snapshot of use, is one tool that can be used to examine those processes, especially when it is coupled with a dynamic (pragmatic technology) model of the innovation.

Implications for Research and Practice

Taken together, these lenses point toward a critique of online learning that is dynamic, situated, participatory, and open to new possibilities. Rather than conceiving the classroom as a recipient of a finished and tested technology, we might see it instead as an example of a *Community Inquiry Laboratory* (http://inquiry.uiuc.edu/cil), a place where members of a community come together to develop shared capacity and work on common problems (Bruce & Bishop, 2002). *Community* emphasizes support for collaborative activity and for creating knowledge that is connected to people's values, history, and lived experiences. *Inquiry* points to support for open-ended, democratic, participatory engagement. *Laboratory* indicates a space and resources to bring theory and action together in an experimental and critical manner. A community inquiry laboratory is most importantly a concept, not a technology in the narrow sense. Thus, online learning becomes not a thing with determinate consequences, but an environment in which participants create meanings.

When we analyze the attributes of this new environment for learning in relation to those of the conventional classroom, we can see a variety of distinctions with differential effects on participants. Changing the binding time for course attributes offers new possibilities, both positive and negative for all involved. But none of these are determinate for the overall learning experience. Teachers and students can make use of these differences in a variety of ways. Their re-creations of the technology incline us to consider the entire learning experience, rather than the characteristics of one set of tools versus another. The larger question is how those tools can be used to achieve quality learning.

Notes

1. The Open University (http://www.open.ac.uk) is Britain's largest teaching institution, offering distance courses since 1971. Its videos and course modules are used worldwide. The virtual study at http://www-tec.open.ac.uk/systems/st.html is an intriguing vision of what learning spaces could be, revealing both exciting possibilities and inherent limitations of digital technologies.
2. It is important to note that these tools are only incidentally identified with the online course mode. An instructor could (and many do) use online tools in a linear, nonvisual, noninteractive way. Moreover, any of the online tools can also be used in face-to-face settings or to complement face-to-face meetings.
3. This is another example of the binding time issue. Readerly texts, as defined by Barthes, bind meaning earlier than do writerly texts.

References

Barthes, R. (1970: 1974). *S/Z*. Translated by R. Miller. New York: Hill and Wang.

Bijker, W. E., Hughes, T. P., & Pinch, T. (1987). *The social construction of technological systems*. Cambridge, MA: MIT Press.

Bruce, B. C. (1999, March). Challenges for the evaluation of new information and communication technologies. *Journal of Adolescent and Adult Literacy, 42*(6), 450–455.

Bruce, B. C. (Ed.) (2003). *Literacy in the information age: Inquiries into meaning making with new technologies*. Newark, DE: International Reading Association.

Bruce, B. C., & Bishop, A. P. (May 2002). Using the Web to support inquiry-based literacy development. *Journal of Adolescent and Adult Literacy, 45*(8), 706–714.

Bruce, B. C., & Rubin, A. (1993). *Electronic Quills: A situated evaluation of using computers for writing in classrooms*. Hillsdale, NJ: Lawrence Erlbaum Associates.

Bruce, B. C., Peyton, J. K, & Batson, T. W. (Eds.). (1993). *Network-based classrooms: Promises and realities*. New York: Cambridge University Press.

Burbules, N., & Callister, T. (2000). *Watch IT: The risks and promises of information technologies for education*. Boulder, CO: Westview.

DeSanctis, G., & Poole, M. S. (1994). Capturing the complexity in advanced technology use: Adaptive structuration theory. *Organization Science, 5*(2), 121–147.

Dewey, J. (1907). *The school and society*. Chicago, IL: University of Chicago Press.

Dewey, J. (1938). *Logic: The theory of inquiry*. New York: Henry Holt.

Dewey, J. (1916:1966) *Democracy and education. An introduction to the philosophy of education*. New York: Free Press.

Foucault, M. (1972). *The archaeology of knowledge and the discourse on language*. Translated by A. M. S. Smith. New York: Pantheon.

Gauntlett, D. (1995). *Moving experiences: Understanding television's influences and effects*. London: John Libbey.

Gauntlett, D. (1998). Ten things wrong with the "effects model." In R. Dickinson, R. Harindranath, & O. Linné (Eds.). *Approaches to audiences—a reader* (pp. 146–150). London: Arnold.

Gay, J. & Cole, M. (1967). *The new mathematics and an old culture*. New York: Holt, Rinehart & Winston.

Hickman, L. A. (1990). *John Dewey's pragmatic technology*. Bloomington, IN: Indiana University Press.

Hord, S. M., Rutherford, W. L., Hiding-Austin, L., & Hall, G. E. (1987). *Taking charge of change*. Alexandria, VA: Association for Supervision and Curriculum Development.

Merkel, C. (2002). *Uncovering the hidden literacies of "have-nots": A study of computer and Internet use in a low-income community*. Unpublished doctoral dissertation, University of Illinois at Urbana-Champaign.

Nardi, B. A., & O'Day, V. L. (1999). *Information ecologies: Using technology with heart*. Cambridge, MA: MIT Press.

Twidale, M. (2003). *Over-the-shoulder learning*. Retrieved October 28, 2003 from http://alexia.lis.uiuc.edu/~twidale/research/otsl/.

Wang, X. (2003). *Constructing a third space at the computer in a first-grade classroom*. Unpublished doctoral dissertation, University of Illinois at Urbana-Champaign.

Wegner, P. (1968). *Programming languages, information structures and machine organization*. New York: McGraw-Hill.

Exploring Community

CHAPTER 3

Caroline Haythornthwaite,
Michelle M. Kazmer,
Jennifer Robins, Susan Shoemaker

Community Development among Distance Learners: Temporal and Technological Dimensions

Introduction

As Internet-based education programs expand, educators are being challenged to go beyond delivering information to remote learners to building community among them (Bruffee, 1993; Dede, 1990, 1996; Harasim, Hiltz, Teles, & Turoff, 1995; Kaye, 1995; Renniger & Shumar, 2002). These programs are no longer add-ons to on-campus endeavors. Instead, they represent a true alternative to on-campus options, and current programs are merely the beginning of a continuing trend for this type of anywhere, anytime learning (e.g., Beller & Or, 1998). As online programs become accepted replacements for the on-campus experience, there is increasing interest in understanding how interactions among learners are being addressed in the online world. How can we ensure that online programs are more than electronic correspondence courses? Key to overcoming the correspondence model is moving the student from the position of an isolated learner to that of a member of a learning community. Thus, there is a need to understand what community means in these environments so that we can promote them, and support individuals in adding to the critical mass of interaction necessary for their formation and maintenance.

The emphasis on creating community is fueled by research that reveals a number of positive outcomes for individuals and the learning communities to which they belong. The strong interpersonal ties shared by community members increase the willingness to share information and resources, setting the stage for collaborative learning (Haythornthwaite, 2002). Strong communal ties increase the flow of information among all members, the availability of support, commitment to group goals, cooperation among members, and satisfaction with group efforts (Argyle, 1991; Bruffee,

1993; Chidambaram & Bostrom, 1997; Dede, 1996; Gabarro, 1990; Harasim, et al., 1995; McGrath, 1984; Wellman, 1999). Trust in the community fosters contribution and support in times of need (Haines, Hurlbert, & Beggs, 1996). Individuals benefit from community membership by experiencing a greater sense of well-being and happiness, and having a larger and more willing set of others to call on for support in times of need (Hammer, 1981; Haines & Hurlbert, 1992; Haines, Hurlbert, & Beggs, 1996; House, 1981; van der Poel, 1993; Walker, Wasserman, & Wellman, 1994; Wellman & Gulia, 1999b).

Yet when we consider fostering community, we are constrained by a view of community tightly bound to the notion of people living close to each other, interacting face-to-face to share companionship and support of all kinds (Wellman, 1999). So, too, our concept of learning communities is bound up with the notions of university campuses and physical colleges. How can we build community without a physical place and through computer media that are traditionally described as "lean," unable to transmit the full range of verbal and nonverbal cues necessary to support strong interpersonal ties (e.g., Daft & Lengel, 1986)?

Although still considered by many to be outside the realm of *real* community, studies of online environments have already found that we can indeed create community and sustain strong ties through electronic media (e.g., Baym, 1995, 1997; McLaughlin, Osborne, & Smith, 1995; Reid, 1995; Rheingold, 1993; Smith, McLaughlin, & Osborne, 1996). These studies show that when we view community as what activities people do together, rather than where or through what means they do them, we can see that community can exist liberated from geography, physical neighborhoods, and campuses (Wellman, 1979, 1999). We still maintain close ties with others, yet we can do this using e-mail, online chat rooms, telephones, cars, and airplanes. Moreover, we can maintain ties and community with otherwise unreachable others, perhaps predicated on a single interest shared with a small number of other people from around the globe (Wellman & Gulia, 1999a; Wellman, Salaff, Dimitrova, Garton, Gulia, & Haythornthwaite, 1996).

Studies of online communities show that members exhibit behaviors that traditionally identify the presence of community offline. Online participants in e-mail networks, newsgroups, chat rooms, and MUD [multi-user domain] environments support common goals and a strong commitment to the purpose and tone of their community (Baym, 1995; Curtis, 1997; Donath, 1999; King, Grinter, & Pickering, 1997; Reid, 1995; Rheingold, 1993). They recognize boundaries that define who belongs and who does not, establishing their own hierarchies of expertise, their own vocabularies and modes of discourse (Marvin, 1995; Sproull & Kiesler, 1991). Members share a common history and a common meeting place (e.g., the Usenet group or chat room). They socially construct rules and behaviors, and enact community rituals (Bruckman, 1998; Fernback, 1999; Jones, 1995, 1998; Kollock & Smith, 1999; McLaughlin, Osborne, & Smith, 1995; Mynatt, O'Day, Adler, & Ito, 1998; Smith,

McLaughlin, & Osborne, 1996). Rules of behavior and a shared history provide an identity for the group and a way of knowing how to behave and how to anticipate the behavior of others (Donath, 1999; Mynatt, et al., 1998), as well as identifying those who do not belong to the community or who are new to the community (McLaughlin, Osborne, & Smith, 1995).

Established rules of behavior, conduct, and expression help individuals know how to behave in the online space, and how to expect others to behave. This helps them feel comfortable in the environment, allowing them to invest time and trust in their ties with others. As they build stronger, more intimate ties, they gain access to the kind of support and continuity that underpins community, moving the individual from a position of isolation to membership in a known community (for a further elaboration of the role of ties in online learning communities, see Haythornthwaite, in press).

These studies show that it is indeed possible to maintain community online. However, we do not take as a given that it exists in any specific context. Thus, in the context of any specific online environment, it is important first to ask: Do members recognize their environment as a community? Do they feel they belong to it? Then, to determine what characterizes community in that environment:[1] What does *community* mean for members of this environment? What is its membership and boundaries? What are members' common goals? What history do they share? What rules of behavior have they evolved? Finally, if we find community to be a positive construct, we then ask: How can we promote community in this context and gain its benefits for individual members?

This study applies these questions in the context of an online educational environment. Over the last year we have followed 17 computer-supported distance students in the Library Education Experimental Program (LEEP) of the Graduate School of Library and Information Science (GSLIS), at the University of Illinois at Urbana-Champaign.[2] Our goal has been to explore how these students create and maintain interpersonal relations in such an environment, which ties are important for maintaining them through the program, and whether these ties have built a sense of community in this environment. Hence our focus has not been on evaluating courses or course delivery mechanisms. We are also interested in understanding the whole student experience in a distance context, not in carving off instructional interactions from the management of the rest of their lives, and so we have explored what other aspects of work and home compete for their attention during their time in the program.

Although we did not take as a given that community exists among these students, we were immediately gratified to find that the students have a strong sense of community, primarily based on their association with other LEEP students. We also find two other major results from this work. First, that the temporal characteristics of the program are reflected in temporal aspects of attachment to, membership in, and departure from the community. Students enter, exist in, and then exit from the program and from the community, requiring and returning different kinds of support at different stages. Second, we see how the technologies, both the computer technologies and the ways in which the courses are structured, provide opportunities and means for interaction that affect and contribute to support and community among these students.

We begin with a description of the LEEP environment and data collection. The remaining discussion presents results from our analysis of the interview data.

The Research Setting and Data Collection

LEEP is a distance option for the master's degree at GSLIS. Students accepted into this option begin their program in a cohort with approximately 30 to 50 others who attend an intensive on-campus session, known as *boot camp* to the students, where they complete one of the required courses in just two weeks. Following this session, students return home and take their remaining courses via the Internet. They return to campus once a term for a one-day session for each class they are in. Those taking multiple courses and those with more free time may be on campus for several days; others spend as little as a day on campus, coming in just for one class and leaving immediately after. They will always encounter students in their current class, but may not encounter students they met at boot camp or former classmates during these on-campus sessions. Each midterm, on-campus session includes an optional social evening where faculty and students can come together for dinner and conversation.

Courses are conducted using a combination of synchronous and asynchronous interaction. Instructors deliver live lectures using RealAudio along with PowerPoint slides or Web pages. Live sessions have been offered as infrequently as twice a term, and as frequently as once a week by different instructors. During live sessions, all students gather virtually in the class Internet Relay Chat (IRC) room. The names of all attendees are available to class participants. Students use IRC to submit questions during the lecture; text submitted to the class chat room is visible to all members of the class. Separate chat rooms can be used for break-out sessions, and a "chalk board" can be used to present discussion results to others. Lectures and chat from the class chat room are recorded and available for later viewing through the LEEP Web facilities. Students can also use IRC's "whisper" facility to direct a comment to specific others in the class, without the text being recorded or visible to anyone else.

Web boards are used in most classes for discussion and exercises, and there are also Web boards for program-wide announcements and discussion. All students have e-mail accounts. They use e-mail to reach other students, instructors, GSLIS administrators, and the LEEP assistants who provide technical support. They have access to their own telephones and to a toll-free 800 number to call GSLIS instructors or staff. Phone conversations are less common than e-mail communication, but are used to reach the same people.

Homework and assignments are generally submitted via the Internet as Web pages, Web board postings, or attachments to e-mail. Students also send in assignments by fax and sometimes by regular mail. Many courses include group projects; students coordinate their own interactions to complete these projects, calling on instructors as necessary. In-class presentations can be achieved by having students call in to GSLIS and having their phone conversation broadcast via RealAudio. Such presentations are usually accompanied by a Web page or slide display that can be seen by all students. Assignments, grading, and comments are returned to students via regular mail or e-mail.

Data Collection

Students who participated in this study volunteered to be interviewed at length over one year. We endeavored to exclude those who were current participants in other LEEP research studies to avoid overloading the students. Our list was divided alphabetically among three interviewers who contacted students on their list, aiming for five students apiece. In the end we conducted interviews with 17 students; four interviews were conducted with 16 of them, and three interviews with one student. Interviews were conducted by phone and lasted approximately one hour. The four interviews were conducted in midterm fall 1998, near the end of the fall term 1998, midterm spring 1999, and near the end of the spring term 1999. Each interview was tape recorded and then transcribed. Each interviewee has been given a pseudonym, with the names reflecting the gender of the interviewee.

Students were not all first-term students: three began the program in 1996 (from which many of their cohort had already graduated), two in 1997, and the remainder in fall 1998. All students were similar in their high motivation to achieve the degree; and all worked outside the home (16 full-time, one part-time, but full-time by the end of the year), most in library or library-related endeavors (e.g., archives), which provided synergy with their coursework. Experience in these settings ranged from 1 to 20 years. Students were all mature adults, living in their own accommodations, usually with a spouse; three had small children, four had grown children; only two lived alone.

Interview Questions

Community is predicated on exchange and support (Haines, Hurlbert, & Beggs, 1996; Walker, Wasserman, & Wellman, 1994; Wellman & Gulia, 1999b; Wellman & Wortley, 1990) and so our interview questions were directed at exploring issues of support and community development among the LEEP students. Questions focused on who, among other LEEP students, staff, and faculty, and non-LEEP contacts, provided the support that allowed students to complete the program and feel part of the program.

Interview questions focused on interaction patterns: who provided individuals with support and to whom did they give support; what did they feel the LEEP community gave to them and they to it. We explored what made it possible for students to continue in this environment: did major support come from those outside LEEP (e.g., their family, friends, or co-workers), or did major support come from members of LEEP (e.g., other students, technical staff, or faculty members)? Indeed, did they need support and if so, of what kind, or was this just a routine activity for them? We explored what they did with others (e.g., working on class assignments, socializing online or off, exchanging personal news, or giving advice), and what this meant to them in their feelings toward LEEP as a community. We also explored what other obligations (work, family, etc.) or life events competed with their attention to their studies and how this affected their interaction patterns.

We used a grounded theory approach to our questioning and analysis (Strauss, 1987; Strauss & Corbin, 1990). Analysis of each set of interviews was used to formulate hypotheses and areas of questioning for the following interviews. Interviews were semistructured, and interviewers followed the lead of the interviewee in exploring issues of support and community, while still maintaining a focus on our core concerns. Analyzing the data consisted of coding the data looking for themes in student experiences, comparing across students for commonalities and differences, and analyzing the characteristics of the themes that emerged.

We have accumulated a wealth of information, not all of which can be reported on here. While answers to all the questions inform the results presented here, this paper is largely based on a series of questions that probed for students' ideas of what community meant to them. Questions used to lead the interviews included: Do you feel there is a LEEP community that you are part of? How would you characterize that community? What do you feel you get from this community? What do you feel you contribute to the community? Do you think there is enough community? How does this community compare with other communities you belong to now or have in the past?

Community

We explored first whether students actually believe that there is such a thing as a community associated with the distance education program, and whether they feel they belong to it. Indeed, the null hypothesis of "no community" was one we hoped to reject, and we were relieved to be able to do so. All our interviewees report that they perceive a community associated with LEEP, and all but one felt they maintained a strong involvement with that community. Although some acknowledge that lately they have "faded back" from involvement in the community, nevertheless they identify something from which they have receded, which at one time was extremely important to their LEEP experience.

As noted above, researchers of face-to-face and virtual environments have identified a number of characteristics that identify the presence of a community, including recognition of members and nonmembers, a shared history, a common meeting place, commitment to a common purpose, adoption of normative standards of behavior, and emergence of hierarchy and roles. So, too, the distance learners can identify who belongs and does not belong to their community. Early on they make a distinction between themselves as members of the LEEP environment, and non-LEEP others. As Betty states at the end of her first semester as a LEEP student:

> It's a different kind of world that most people aren't used to so they can't really understand it since they're on the outside. [Betty]

They are often called on to describe their community to nonmembers who "don't completely understand how it works" [Alice], and this reinforces for them their difference from others and their similarities with LEEP students. Over time they increase their separation from nonmembers. For example, one student mentioned that the time she spent explaining LEEP to friends and family decreased as the novelty of her own experience decreased. Thus, as members get more embedded in and familiar with their own community, they no longer extend membership even to introducing others to the environment.

While other LEEP students are central to their community, certain important others provide support and fill roles essential for the community. LEEP students include in their wider definition of the community the technical staff who provide essential start-up information, and who help them whenever they are having difficulties; the faculty who deliver the courses and who also provide support; and administrators whom they communicate with via e-mail and meet when on campus.

Yet it is bonds with other students that matter the most, bonds that strengthen because of shared history, "shared survival" particularly from the boot camp experience, but also from finishing the first class at a distance as well as working together toward a common purpose. As Jeff states at the end of his first semester:

> The on-campus session, you know the boot camp, created sort of a shared experience, sort of a history. And the class did the same thing, by the end of the class we all had survived something together. Common purpose. Common professional sort of profile. [Jeff]

During boot camp, and then over their time in the program, they form bonds of friendship and share emotional and practical support with other LEEP students (see below for further details on student-student bonding). They share the common goal of completing the program and graduating with their degree, and joining their chosen profession.

Their common meeting ground is primarily the LEEP computer environment. This consists of: general Web boards used by all LEEP students, faculty, and staff; Web boards for discussions associated with each class; IRC chat rooms used in conjunction with live lectures for classes; and e-mail. Of secondary importance as a common ground is the physical campus where students spend their time during boot camp and again once per semester. Social rules of interaction are built up around the technologies available for communicating and the opportunities for interaction afforded by entrainment (McGrath, 1991) with class activities. For example, students use the whisper facility of the chat technology to socialize during class, and the timing of assignment submission to initiate e-mail conversations with others. In this way students achieve a *virtual proximity* in replacement of the physical proximity they lack (see also Haythornthwaite, 2000).

Thus, there are many characteristics that the LEEP community shares with offline communities, even though separated by distance and restricted to computer-mediated communication (CMC). However, community does not suddenly appear fully formed when students begin the program. There is a learning and adjustment phase that is more difficult for some than for others. Moreover, the degree of, and need for, involvement and embeddedness in the LEEP community varies across individuals and over time. Just as students learn to enter the program, they also learn to exit it as well. Equally important as this temporal dimension of community membership is the way in which the technologies—the Web boards, chat rooms, and class structures—provide means and opportunity for interactions, both synchronous and asynchronous, that make it possible to make connections and create community among these distance learners.

The following sections are organized according to the temporal aspect of community development. Within each section the importance and use of technologies is highlighted to show how these establish the conditions under which community is built.

Joining the Community

Boot camp unites members of each year's cohort and builds a community for them within the overall LEEP program. While later their community will grow to include others associated with LEEP, at first their community is centered on their boot camp cohort. Their common experience provides the shared history that forms strong intra-cohort bonds and initiates many lasting friendships. It is when the students begin the distance portion of their program that they become aware of the distinction between themselves and others, between who is inside and outside their community. Family, work mates, and traditional students are now outsiders who did not share boot camp, nor do they share this new educational environment. As Alice states:

> The community is a unique experience. Not many people are part of an experience like this in education.

The cohort is reinforced at a distance during the student's first semester. Immediately following boot camp, most students take the remaining required course of the program together. Cohort membership sustains individuals through this first semester, as they are in class with those with whom they engaged face-to-face. Their interpersonal ties remain strong, sustained by the memory of names, faces, and shared experiences:

> Even though they would be just a name on the screen in the chat room or on the Web board, you still had the memory of knowing them from boot camp, which was such an intense experience. That gave you a connection. It was almost like they were there. You could imagine them. Since it was just recently, and you had them fresh in your mind, you knew exactly who was saying it and what it sounded like, if they had really said it, and what it would have sounded like. [Alice]

At home they now deal with technical difficulties, coursework load(s), and managing work, home, and school with no one at hand who understands their "different kind of world." But, virtually at hand

> ... there's a group of people out there who know exactly what I'm going through and can help me, that have been there, and have done everything, and they're supportive and caring and kind and even if I have a stupid question it's okay. They'll answer it. And vice versa ... if someone else has a stupid question ... [Rene]

Exchanges with other LEEP students become vital for validating their own experiences and for overcoming isolation:

> I felt it was individual for me at times, when I thought certain assignments were difficult, but then you talk to other students and they're having the same challenges, same difficulties. [Beth]

These descriptions of the strength and importance of association, and identification with cohort members are echoed in the reports from all the interviewees. Students' reports show the strength of the interpersonal ties created among these distance learners, ties built during boot camp and then sustained at a distance (see also Small, 1999 for similar reports from distance learners).

As with offline strong ties, these learners provide each other with multiple resources, including information, social support, and emotional support, and the resources flow both ways as individuals both give and receive these resources (Haythornthwaite, in press, 2000; van der Poel, 1993; Walker, Wasserman, & Wellman, 1994; Wellman, 1999). Moreover, the exchanges need not be immediate or in-kind exchanges. Barbara explained how she repaid extra work by a classmate in one semester by extra work on her part in a different class in the next semester. Bill explains that he receives "moral support" from the community, but gives "fresh ideas"; Rene receives friendship and contributes "comic relief." Such delay of repayment and the more generalized and balanced reciprocity (Wellman, Carrington, & Hall, 1988; Wellman & Gulia, 1999b) demonstrate the trust present in communal relations among these individuals, a key attribute of community.

For those who have just completed boot camp, the circle of willing and helpful others is large, comprising their whole boot camp cohort.[3] They find they have a wealth of people whom they know and can call on for information, and who provide this spontaneously in a supportive atmosphere:

> I'm not a practicing librarian so I had these people helping me out and feeding me information and they were great. We'd just be talking on the Web or in class in the chat room and they'd use all of these acronyms and I'd come back on and say whatever. Then somebody would whisper and give me an explanation. Everybody was so nice and polite. There was never a hint of 'you should know this.' [Beth]

Thus, students find themselves in a safe environment, filled with supportive others, a condition considered essential for collaborative learning (Bruffee, 1993). As Barbara explains:

> I think the other thing that the community has given me is the encouragement, you know in a regular situation to just . . . to speak out and say something . . . to write something in and to have a comment. It doesn't feel like an unsafe environment to say something. It feels like nobody's going to ridicule you for what you say. [Barbara]

But not everyone feels safe to begin with; not everyone is able to mobilize the resources of the cohort or adjust to this strange new world. Those who fail to make community connections, particularly early in the program, are more distressed about their LEEP experience. Here is one student's account of how she felt at the beginning of their first semester.

> I'll have to tell you that it has been one of the most stressful times in my whole life . . . I've had quite a lot of difficulty adjusting to the isolation of being in a nontraditional classroom . . . not being able to talk face-to-face with the other students . . . I started to have a lot of anxiety . . . just wondering if what I was posting sounded okay or if it sounded so bad . . . Finally I just had to take time off work. [Nancy]

Although the stress experienced by this student represents an extreme case, Nancy's feelings of uncertainty are present in other's reports also, particularly in relation to Web board postings. For example:

> At the beginning it was difficult for me because I felt like when I posted something it had to be perfect. All the time all these other people are just talking away . . . I found that difficult to get used to because I felt like I had to be perfect. [Ted]

The reduced cues environment that reduces negative feedback such as ridicule also reduces positive feedback so that individuals do not know if they are doing the right thing. Nancy finally telephoned the instructor to find out how she was doing. Making this connection with the faculty member, and other connections with LEEP students, including a strong personal tie that provided her with social support, greatly increased her comfort level in the program.

Individual Differences

Individuals who feel less comfortable, less safe in the community, are those who also feel they contribute less to the community, those who do not actively engage in reciprocal exchange of resources. For example, Sue explains that she gains most of her support and community needs outside LEEP, thus she feels she has an "extremely slender" attachment to the LEEP community. What she receives from the community is disproportional to what she perceives she contributes. The LEEP community offers support and "it's reaffirming when, if you are really burnt out then you talk to other classmates and that gets you back on track." Yet she feels that she does not return a lot to the community, "I don't feel I give a lot [to the community] to be completely honest. I feel I'm very marginal . . . I don't feel that I put in as much effort as other people."

Sue's case demonstrates an extreme position, but others range in between that and the engagement of highly active and highly immersed community members. For example, Ted, early in his time in LEEP, sees others as highly active in the community— "I swear they must live by the computer. It must be by their bed and they post in their dreams"—but feels his own contribution is not "as adequate as I wish it would be," judging his activity level to be "a little less than halfway of those who never talk and those who talk all the time."

At this stage, Ted is also trying actively to stay fully engaged in the LEEP community, trying not to fade back. His contact with others in his class at the time he made this comment was largely through the Web board postings:

> I feel like every week I have to post something, even if I don't know what I'm doing. So I'll try to put some ideas across. Where in a classroom, there are some days where you don't say anything, you just listen; where there are other days where you are really animated because you have experience maybe. You know what the readings were about and they turned you on and you want to talk about it or you are more conversant in. Sometimes I'm not and I almost feel like I have to [contribute] every week. [Ted]

We can see from Ted's account that there is conscious effort made to stay with the community and not to disappear in the anonymity of cyberspace. This is an important aspect of LEEP students' experience, which we explore next.

Making a Conscious Effort to Maintain Ties

Maintaining ties and community at a distance and via CMC is perceived by students to require more effort than in a face-to-face community. Students feel they need to expend effort beyond what is needed in an on-campus situation in order to remain connected to the community, to be "more purposeful in [their] community development and more strategic" [Holly]. As Doris describes it:

> You have to make more of a point to reinforce things because you're not going to bump into people, you have to make a point of nurturing friendships more so than you do in a neighborhood community or church community or work community where you just bump into people . . . Maybe you do have to work at it more, because it's easier to drop out of it, too . . . you can just kind of fade back if you want and just say, well I'm just going to sit here and do it more like a correspondence course unless the professor has a particular requirement. Whereas maybe it's harder to do that in a face-to-face community. [Doris]

Those who fail to make community connections, particularly early in the program, are more distressed about their LEEP experience. Here, Nancy reflects on her first few months in LEEP:

> I was so stressed out, and that was before I talked to [the instructor] . . . we talked for a long time, maybe an hour and a half, or longer, and I know, I realize I should have done that a couple of weeks into the class . . . I was feeling very isolated and very lonely. [Nancy]

As students become more integrated with other LEEP students, and with faculty and staff, they move from a stressful position of isolation to confident membership in their community. This is in keeping with results of research on social support in other settings. The more other people with whom an individual maintains supportive ties, the more positive the association with measures of happiness, mental health, and well-being (Haines & Hurlbert, 1992; Hammer, 1981; van der Poel, 1993; Walker, Wasserman, & Wellman, 1994; Wellman & Gulia, 1999b). Dynamic and interactive communication has also been associated with increased satisfaction, performance quality, learning, sociability, and cooperation (Rafaeli & Sudweeks, 1997). So, too, these students show more satisfaction and happiness when connected to others.

Regulating Social Distance: Fading Back/Coming Forward

As Doris's comment above indicates, fading back, not participating, treating LEEP as a correspondence course, is relatively easy in this CMC environment. The phrase "fade back" is used in two ways by students: to describe being in the background of a class—somewhat like sitting in the back row in a classroom, but less purposive than deliberately choosing a back seat—and to describe letting go of or "disengaging" from the program. We discuss the first meaning of "fade back" here and disengaging in the following section.

In the LEEP distance environment, you cannot be seen by others, put on the spot, or made to participate. This lack of exposure is facilitated by the reduced cues of the CMC environment, for example, text without voice, voice without body language, class attendance without seating arrangements (Culnan & Markus, 1987; Haythornthwaite, Wellman, & Garton, 1998; Sproull & Kiesler, 1986). Indeed, students can sign in for class so their names appear in the IRC session, yet never be visible so instructors cannot see if they are actually present. This can have a negative impact on the learning community when students let themselves fade back and then fail to contribute to the public good (Connolly & Thorn, 1990; Markus, 1990). It can also have a negative impact on the individual as he or she misses out on the socializing and support given by others and finding that others share his or her trials and tribulations.

However, the reduced cues environment can also act positively to encourage contribution to the community, extending an "open invitation to participate in this online environment" [Barbara], where you are free to ask "stupid" questions.

> You don't have to see the immediate gasping reactions to what you say if you . . . if you say [4] . . . or write something that maybe you think 'Oh, maybe that was too inane . . . or that was too stupid . . . or that was too obvious.' You don't see those eyes rolling. [Barbara]

Another aspect of fading back is how comfortable individuals are with being visible or invisible.[5] Ted expressed a discomfort with being invisible, and so he found ways to overcome that, to come forward and be present in the community. By contrast, Alice says she likes to be able to fade back:

> It's a community where you can fade back really easily, which I like. I'm from a big family where you can fade back if you need to. I like that. [Alice]

But she also notes that this same environment provides little opportunity to "stand out and shine," to be recognized across the program for your work.

Thus, we see that students can bring themselves forward or they can choose to fade back, and some students may be satisfied with either condition, or at least with the option of either condition. Yet those who fade back unwillingly, perhaps because of technical problems (for example, in a class that held only two live sessions, one student was unable to connect for the first one, and described herself midterm as still "waiting to see what it [LEEP] was all about"), or because the social distance was initially too great to bridge (see Nancy's comments above), are not satisfied with this condition. Moreover, a nonparticipant does not contribute to the communal exchange, and diminishes the overall potential for interaction and collaborative learning.

In the same way that face-to-face classes can encourage some and discourage others, so too, the technologies used to support distance classes, can, paradoxically, both increase and decrease active involvement in communal exchanges. The new technologies have neither cured nor caused this paradox, but instead have put a new spin on it. However, perhaps even more than in face-to-face classes, we need to monitor contribution, ensuring that each individual is connected to the class in a manner that serves his or her educational experience, and that also serves the learning community.

Coming Together: The Importance of Synchronous Connection
As students strive to engage with LEEP, we are led to ask what helps them make this connection: What means of communication, what activities, and what support helps them feel part of a community?

There are two means of communication that support classwide interaction at a distance: the synchronous IRC sessions, and the asynchronous Web board posting. Synchronous communication, particularly during the live lecture times, contributes much more to community building than asynchronous communication (although Web board postings have been described as "butter on toast," continuing interaction that is "real thin but still tasty" [Jerry]). While a few students find the live sessions an inconvenience, most express a need for this kind of contact. Live sessions provide both intellectual and emotional content, but more importantly provide simultaneous, many-to-many contact that helps stave off feelings of isolation.

> I seem to get more out of class when we meet live more often . . . It keeps you from feeling isolated . . . The immediacy [is nice], even though you're typing, not speaking to them directly, you're typing with them. [Janet]

> I need to hear my professor's voice. I need the stimulation of you know, comments, and you know, I need my other classmates to respond to me, or I need to respond to my other classmates in the chat, when we're having a class. I mean I just need that feedback from them. [Nancy]

Small (1999) reports similar comments from computer-supported distance students as they "bemoaned the lack of frequent, face-to-face contact with faculty" (p. 36).

Face-to-face communication, although considered by the students as essential for building community, nevertheless takes a second place to the use of communication technologies because of their distance from each other. Students who save up their social interactions for face-to-face midterm sessions remain isolated and dissatisfied with the meager contact they have. When the face-to-face contact supplements ongoing relations it "enhanced the program. It enhanced enjoying what you were doing because you had personal relationships with people" [Beth], and also has a powerful effect on their sense of community. However, it is not so much the face-to-face contact that they share, but the opportunity to come together with "a bunch of people who all know what this is about" [Doris].

Along with the public, classwide communication, private communication is also important for students. E-mail, IRC whispering, and the telephone fill an important niche for students, providing private, person-to-person contact. This helps sustain stronger interpersonal ties, allowing those in crisis to communicate with their closest friends (via e-mail or phone), and allowing small subgroups to socialize around class activities and class times (via e-mail and IRC whispering). We notice also that the structure of the classes also structures interaction time. Poole & DeSanctis (1990) coined the term *adaptive structuration* to refer to the way in which use of media is determined by group use. Here we see how the structure of the class also sets conditions that lead to the way in which individuals make use of the media (see also Haythornthwaite, 2000). Students engage in near-synchronous e-mail sessions that are entrained with regular class activities, such as weekly Web board posting or assignment due dates. For example:

> A lot of times last semester when I was working late at night, and then I would post my assignments, we found out that a lot of our—well, both of us were working late at night. We were both working late at night; so even now, sometimes, I'll—if I'm finishing up something, and I'll just send her a quick note. I'll say '. . . are you there?' And she'll write me back, 'Yes, I'm here.' So, yeah I really feel very close to her, even though she's in [another state]. [Nancy]

Thus, we see that the way the course is structured creates opportunities for media to be used to maintain contact with others. This is an important point to consider when designing such classes because the opportunities for interaction support not only the class content, but also the invisible social community that makes it possible and fun to engage in this sort of learning community.

Disengaging from the Community

As students progress through the program, the desperate need to make contact diminishes. They become familiar with class routines, the technologies and norms for their use, and their distanced companions and fellow travelers. It is no longer all new, and even when new versions of software are introduced, such changes are seen as minor. Yet change is happening.

First, their cohort becomes diluted. Members of previous and following cohorts join their classes and their in-class connection to members of their own cohort fades.

As the immediacy of boot camp fades, making and sustaining connections to LEEP students becomes harder, particularly when making new connections to non-cohort class members.

Early in their program, most students strive to maintain connections to the LEEP community, making new contacts through classes and particularly through group projects. Over time, students taking fewer classes per semester see the possibility of being left behind while everyone they know finishes without them. Some increase their pace in the program in order to remain with their cohort or close friends (e.g., by increasing from one to two courses per semester). Yet the cohort still dissipates, and so does their attachment to the community. Fellow cohort members and others students with whom they have been close throughout the program fail to end up in the same classes or may have already graduated. Sue, who is nearing completion of her degree, describes how this affects her in-class interactions:

> Now I am in a class where there is no one in there that I really have any kind of connection with and I actually have to e-mail someone today and ask if they will provide me with some information and it's a little awkward because I don't have any kind of relationship with that person. [Sue]

As students approach the end of their time in the LEEP program, they go through a process of disengaging from the program, allowing nature to take its course, fading back from the community, reluctantly watching it and their membership in it recede in time. Here is Holly's account of this phenomenon:

> I feel a sense of loss because that real close community that I had with those folks isn't there any more, and I think [it's] because you have that on-campus time with those people, and you really develop a bond with them. [Holly]

And, although other opportunities have presented themselves for getting together with other LEEP students (most notably an online "technical know-how session" which many students mentioned), Holly says:

> I'll see those opportunities and then I say, it's just hard to fit more things in and so you start, you know you have to make choices, yeah I want to be a part of a LEEP community but on the other hand I'm graduating in one semester, I have a job, I have a family, I can only give so much. So I think sometimes, something like an online community . . . I don't know, you just have to make your choices, and sometimes it's easier to say 'no' to an online community because it's not right there in front of your face all the time. [Holly]

Once again, the reduced cues environment makes it easier to fade back and allow the community, and one's contribution to the community, to slip away.

At the same time that students are going through a process of disengaging from LEEP, they are simultaneously engaging or reengaging with the "outside world." Students about to leave the program stop making the effort to maintain ties with other LEEP students, as Holly's comment shows. They turn their attention instead to their work and home communities, reengaging with the people and activities that received less attention while they were completing the degree. Some LEEP graduates are starting new jobs and need to develop ties with a new work community; others are reconnecting with the jobs they held throughout their time in the program. We see their focus changing from being overwhelmingly (in fact often stressfully so) engaged with LEEP, to largely engaged, and then to only marginally engaged with LEEP. As an extreme example, when one of the interviewees was asked to participate in an interview only a few months after she had graduated, her response was, "I've totally put all of that out of my mind."

Overall we see that the tight formation of community that begins during boot camp sustains students through the early portions of their program. By the middle of the program, they are accomplished LEEPers, able to introduce newbies to the environment, but also like old dogs occasionally annoyed at the puppies biting at their toes. By the end of the program, they are consciously disengaging from the LEEP community now that their friends have left, and turning their attention to the next new world to conquer.

Supporting Virtual Distance-Learning Communities

This paper has focused on the community aspects of computer-supported distance learners' experiences, and the temporal aspects of joining, existing in, and exiting from the program. We are pleased to find a strong sense of community, initiated by the boot camp, and sustained at a distance via computer media. We also hear that the distance experience can be trying, particularly at the beginning, as students cope with new technologies and new ways of interacting in a world no one understands (including the students themselves in their early months in the program). Interviews show how students, interacting from a distance and starting from a position of isolation, make connections with fellow students and recognize and live with members of a virtual community. The existence of the community is felt by all participants, enforced in part by their differences from outsiders, and in part by their shared trials and experiences with insiders. Our interviews also show that this sense of community and the social support received from other students helps make it possible to share and learn in this environment.

We also note several aspects of the CMC community that have an impact on supporting a distanced learning community. Although we recognize that we have examined only one distanced environment, the LEEP program has evolved over three years and we have heard from students in cohorts from each year. Thus, we believe that these observations will be useful for other online distance education programs. While it is possible that just by bringing students together into the program they may achieve a sense of community, we believe that without attention to community characteristics we would be providing an impoverished environment, or one in which community is recognized only as students near completion of their program. In time-limited groups such as our distance-learning environment, we need to bootstrap community and augment the bonds that make it worthwhile and rewarding to make the extra effort to stay in contact. Thus, we provide the following as suggestions on how to accelerate a process that might occur on its own, given enough time.[6]

Promote Initial Bonding
We note the importance of the initial bonding experience and the stressfulness of the first semester off campus. It takes more effort to maintain ties, and during early semesters individuals are still unsure of how to go about maintaining a presence in the virtual community. Our interviews suggest that it is necessary to provide opportunities for group interaction and to focus on encouraging and making possible individual participation, particularly in the first off-campus course. Our interviews also suggest that synchronous activity is likely to help more than asynchronous because it provides a common meeting ground and at least temporal proximity, elements important for building community. Regular meetings may help more than irregular ones since they help establish a routine on which students can piggyback their social interactions. This extends to assignments and weekly work as well, as students establish routines of work submission followed by social interaction. It also appears to be important for instructors of first semester students to give feedback on the quality and appropriateness of postings, so that individuals may gain a sense of what is right and wrong in this new environment.

Monitor and Support Continued Interaction and Participation
Where the goal is to support collaborative learning, we also need to support and encourage participation. When students fade back they fail to contribute to the pool of resources that should be available to all students. Thus, we need to be aware of where and when fading back occurs and take steps to pull students back in, not only to the educational experience, but also to the social experience of the program. Although we are not likely to monitor person-to-person activity, we can monitor contribution to class Web boards and to chat sessions. Even a simple count of who contributed would quickly highlight those having problems engaging in the class and allow instructors to plan their next steps accordingly.

Building community requires more than just work activity. Moreover, socializing eases work relations. Thus, it is important to provide means and opportunities for students to become engaged in both the educational and social experience of the program.

Provide Multiple Means of Communication
These interviews and other studies show the importance of multiple means of communication: public and private, synchronous and asynchronous, multiparty and one-on-one, distanced and face-to-face for sustaining group interaction (Haythornthwaite, 2000; Haythornthwaite & Wellman, 1998; Dennis & Valacich, 1999). Whether seen as directly relevant to the educational experience or not, students need these multiple ways of interacting in order to support their need to engage in class, task, social, support, emotional, and intellectual exchanges.

Conclusion

Overall, we see many positive outcomes with these students that bode well for distance programs. We see tangible results such as students' receiving increased job responsibilities and access to special opportunities because of their participation in this type of environment long before they complete the program. We see intangible results as stressed, fearful, and/or timid individuals gain confidence and take on leadership roles in LEEP. We also see people who could not otherwise achieve this degree becoming full-fledged members of their chosen profession. Lastly, we see something unique from this kind of distance program—that students receive a dual education. They learn to use new technology and gain experience in distanced interaction as well as learn the subject matter for the program. We believe this is an important addition to the repertoire of any educational program, and one well worth pursuing.

Acknowledgments

This paper is reprinted with permission from the *Journal of Computer-Mediated Communication*. It appeared originally in September 2000 (volume 6, issue 1), and is available online at: http://www.ascusc.org/jcmc/vol6/issue1/haythornthwaite.html. It is presented as printed originally, but references have been updated where relevant.

Our thanks go to the 17 individuals who gave generously of their time for the interviews that provide the data for this paper. This work was supported by a grant from the University of Illinois Campus Research Board. An earlier version of this paper was presented at the Association for Library and Information Science Educators conference, January 2000, San Antonio, TX.

Notes

1. See McLaughlin, Osborne, & Smith (1995), who state, "what constitutes virtual community?" is the "unexplored territory" in CMC research (p. 93).
2. For details on the GSLIS LEEP program, see http://www.lis.uiuc.edu/gslis/degrees/leep.html and http://leep.lis.uiuc.edu.
3. The boot camp bonding is so strong that one cohort referred to themselves as "3.2" for the second session boot camp that started students in the third year of the program, separating themselves from the others who started in the same year.
4. It is interesting to note how students refer to their e-mail and Web board postings as if a conversation had occurred in the normal manner of a traditional classroom. They say "if I say" when it is something they write. We have noticed this extensively in our interviews, and we believe it reflects their attention to the act they are engaged in rather than to the technology through which it is achieved. Over time, the technology disappears into the background, becoming the means and not the end of their endeavors (see also Bruce & Hogan, 1999).
5. For further discussion of students' concerns regarding visibility, see Bregman and Haythornthwaite (2001).
6. For students' advice to students, see Kazmer (2000).

References

Argyle, M. (1991). Cooperation in working groups. In *Cooperation: The basis of sociability* (pp. 115–131). London: Routledge.

Baym, N. K. (1995). The emergence of community in computer-mediated communication. In S. Jones (Ed.), *CyberSociety: Computer-mediated communication and community* (pp. 138–63). Thousand Oaks, CA: Sage.

Baym, N. K. (1997). Interpreting soap operas and creating community: Inside an electronic fan culture. In S. Kiesler, (Ed.), *Culture of the Internet* (pp. 103–120). Mahwah, NJ: Lawrence Erlbaum.

Beller, M., & Or, E. (1998). The crossroads between lifelong learning and information technology: A challenge facing leading universities. *Journal of Computer-Mediated Communication, 4(2)*. Retrieved from http://www.ascusc.org/jcmc/vol4/issue2/beller.html.

Bregman, A., & Haythornthwaite, C. (2001). Radicals of presentation in persistent conversation. Proceedings of the 34th Hawaii International Conference on System Sciences. Los Alamitos, CA: IEEE Computer Society Press. Retrieved from http://www.hicss.hawaii.edu/HICSS_34/PDFs/DDPTC01.pdf.

Bruce, B. C., & Hogan, M. P. (1999). The disappearance of technology: Toward an ecological model of literacy. In D. Reinking, M. McKenna, L. Labbo, & R. Kieffer (Eds.), *Handbook of literacy and technology: Transformations in a post-typographical world* (pp. 269–281). Hillsdale, NJ: Erlbaum.

Bruckman, A. (1998). Community support for constructionist learning. *CSCW: The Journal of Collaborative Computing, 7,* 47–86.

Bruffee, K. A. (1993). *Collaborative learning: Higher education, interdependence, and the authority of knowledge.* Baltimore: John Hopkins University Press.

Chidambaram, L., & Bostrom, R. P. (1997). Group development (I): A review and synthesis of developmental models. *Group Decision and Negotiation, 6*(2), 159–187.

Connolly, T., & Thorn, B. K. (1990) Discretionary data bases: Theory, data and implications. In J. Fulk & C. W. Steinfeld. (Eds.), *Organizations and communication technology* (pp. 219–234). Newbury Park, CA: Sage.

Culnan, M. J., & Markus, M. L. (1987). Information technologies. In F. M. Jablin, L. L. Putnam, K. H. Roberts, & L. W. Porter (Eds.), *Handbook of organizational communication: An interdisciplinary perspective* (pp. 420–443). Newbury Park, CA: Sage.

Curtis, P. (1997). MUDDING: Social phenomena in text-based virtual realities. In Kiesler, S. (Ed.), *Culture of the Internet* (pp. 121–142). Mahwah, NJ: Lawrence Erlbaum.

Daft, R. L., & Lengel, R. H. (1986). Organizational information requirements, media richness and structural design. *Management Science, 32*(5), 554–571.

Dede, C. J. (1990). The evolution of distance learning: Technology-mediated interactive learning. *Journal of Research on Computers in Education, 22,* 247–264.

Dede, C. (1996). The evolution of distance education: Emerging technologies and distributed learning. *American Journal of Distance Education, 10*(2), 4–36.

Dennis, A. R., & Valacich, J. S. (1999). *Rethinking media richness: Toward a theory of media synchronicity.* Proceedings of the 32nd Hawaii International Conference on System Sciences. Los Alamitos, CA: IEEE Computer Society Press. Retrieved from http://www.computer.org/proceedings/hicss/0001/00011/00011017.PDF.

Donath, J. S. (1999). Identity and deception in the virtual community. In M. A. Smith, & P. Kollock (Eds.), *Communities in cyberspace* (pp. 29–59). New York: Routledge.

Fernback, J. (1999). There is a there there: Notes toward a definition of cyberspace. In S. G. Jones (Ed.), *Doing Internet research.* Thousand Oaks, CA: Sage.

Gabarro, J. J. (1990). The development of working relationships. In J. Galegher, R. E. Kraut, & C. Egido (Eds.), *Intellectual teamwork: Social and technological foundations of cooperative work* (pp. 79–110). Hillsdale: Lawrence Erlbaum.

Haines, V., & Hurlbert, J. (1992). Network range and health. *Journal of Health and Social Behavior, 33,* 254–266.

Haines, V. A., Hurlbert, J. S., & Beggs, J. J. (1996). Exploring the determinants of support provision: Provider characteristics, personal networks, community contexts, and support following life events, *Journal of Health & Social Behavior, 37*(3), 252–64.

Hammer, M. (1981). Social supports, social networks, and schizophrenia. *Schizophrenia Bulletin, 7,* 45–57.

Harasim, L., Hiltz, S. R., Teles, L., & Turoff, M. (1995). *Learning networks: A field guide to teaching and learning online.* Cambridge, MA: The MIT Press.

Haythornthwaite, C. (2002). Building social networks via computer networks: Creating and sustaining distributed learning communities. In K. A. Renninger & W. Shumar, *Building Virtual Communities: Learning and Change in Cyberspace* (pp. 159–109). Cambridge: Cambridge University Press.

Haythornthwaite, C. (2000). Online personal networks: Size, composition and media use among distance learners. *New Media and Society, 2*(2), 195–226.

Haythornthwaite, C., & Wellman, B. (1998). Work, friendship and media use for information exchange in a networked organization. *Journal of the American Society for Information Science, 46*(12), 1101–1114.

Haythornthwaite, C., Wellman, B. & Garton, L. (1998). Work and community via computer-mediated communication. In J. Gackenbach (Ed.) *Psychology of the Internet* (pp. 199–226). San Diego, CA: Academic Press.

House, J. S. (1981). *Work stress and social support.* Reading, MA: Addison-Wesley.

Jones, S. G. (Ed.) (1995). *CyberSociety: Computer-mediated communication and community.* Thousand Oaks, CA: Sage.

Jones, S. G. (Ed) (1998). *CyberSociety 2.0: Revisiting computer-mediated communication and community.* Thousand Oaks, CA: Sage.

Kaye, A. (1995). Computer supported collaborative learning. In N. Heap, R. Thomas, G. Einon, R. Mason, & H. MacKay, *Information technology and society* (pp. 192–210). London: Sage.

Kazmer, M. M. (2000). Coping in a distance environment: Sitcoms, chocolate cake, and dinner with a friend. *First Monday, 5*(9). Retrieved from http://www.firstmonday.dk/issues/issue5_9/kazmer/index.html

King, J. L, Grinter, R. E., & Pickering, J. M. (1997). The rise and fall of Netville: The saga of a cyberspace construction boomtown in the great divide. In S. Kiesler (Ed.), *Culture of the Internet* (pp. 3–33). Mahwah, NJ: Lawrence Erlbaum.

Kollock, P., & Smith, M. A. (1999). Communities in cyberspace. In M. A. Smith & P. Kollock (Eds.), *Communities in cyberspace* (pp. 3–25). New York: Routledge.

Markus, M. L. (1990). Toward a "critical mass" theory of interactive media. In J. Fulk & C. W. Steinfield (Eds.), *Organizations and communication technology* (pp. 194–218). Newbury Park, CA: Sage.

Marvin, L. (1995). Spoof, spam, lurk and lag: The aesthetics of text-based virtual realities. *Journal of Computer-Mediated Communication, 1*(2). Retrieved from http://www.ascusc.org/jcmc/vol1/issue2/marvin.html.

McGrath, J. E. (1984). *Groups, interaction and performance.* Englewood Cliffs, NJ: Prentice Hall.

McGrath, J. E. (1991). Time, interaction and performance (TIP): A theory of groups. *Small Group Research, 22*(2), 147–174.

McLaughlin, M. L., Osborne, K. K., & Smith, C. B. (1995). Standards of conduct on Usenet. In S. G. Jones (Ed.), *CyberSociety: Computer-mediated communication and community* (pp. 90–111). Thousand Oaks, CA: Sage.

Mynatt, E. D., O'Day, V. L., Adler, A., & Ito, M. (1998). Network communities: Something old, something new, something borrowed . . . *CSCW, 7,* 123–156.

Poole, M. S., & DeSanctis, G. (1990). Understanding the use of group decision support systems: The theory of adaptive structuration. In J. Fulk & C. W. Steinfield (Eds.), *Organizations and communication technology* (pp. 173–193). Newbury Park, CA: Sage.

Rafaeli, S., & Sudweeks, F. (1997). Networked interactivity. *Journal of Computer-Mediated Communication, 2*(4). Available at: http://www.ascusc.org/jcmc/vol2/issue4/rafaeli.sudweeks.html.

Reid, E. (1995). Virtual worlds: Culture and imagination. In S. G. Jones (Ed.), *CyberSociety: Computer-mediated communication and community* (pp. 164–183). Thousand Oaks, CA: Sage.

Renniger, A., & Shumar, W. (Eds.)(2002). *Building virtual communities: Learning and change in cyberspace.* Cambridge: Cambridge University Press.

Rheingold, H. (1993). *The virtual community: Homesteading on the electronic frontier.* Reading, MA: Addison-Wesley.

Small, R. (1999). A comparison of the resident and distance learning experience in library and information science graduate education. *Journal of Education for Library and Information Science, 40*(1), 27–47.

Smith, C. B., McLaughlin, M. L., & Osborne, K. K. (1996). Conduct control on Usenet. *Journal of Computer-Mediated Communication, 2*(4). Retrieved from http:/www.ascusc.org/jcmc/vol2/issue4/smith.html.

Sproull, L., & Kiesler, S. (1986). Reducing social context cues: Electronic mail in organizational computing. *Management Science, 32*(11), 1492–1512.

Sproull, L., & Kiesler, S. (1991). *Connections: New ways of working in the networked organization.* Cambridge, MA: MIT Press.

Strauss, A. L. (1987). *Qualitative analysis for social scientists.* Cambridge: Cambridge University Press.

Strauss, A. L., & Corbin, J. (1990). *Basics of qualitative research: Grounded theory procedures and techniques.* Newbury Park, CA: Sage.

van der Poel, M. (1993). *Personal networks: A rational-choice explanation of their size and composition.* Lisse, Netherlands: Swets & Zeitlinger.

Walker, J., Wasserman, S., & Wellman, B. (1994). Statistical models for social support networks. In S. Wasserman & J. Galaskiewicz (Eds.), *Advances in social network analysis* (pp. 53–78). Thousand Oaks, CA: Sage.

Wellman, B. (1979). The community question. *American Journal of Sociology, 84,* 1201–1231.

Wellman, B. (1999). The network community: An introduction to networks in the global village. In B. Wellman (Ed.), *Networks in the global village* (pp. 1–48). Boulder, CO: Westview Press.

Wellman, B., Carrington, P., & Hall, A. (1988). Networks as personal communities. In B. Wellman & S. D. Berkowitz (Eds.), *Social structures: A network approach* (pp. 130–84). Cambridge: Cambridge University Press.

Wellman, B., & Gulia M. (1999a). Net surfers don't ride alone: Virtual communities as communities. In M. Smith & P. Kollock (Eds.) *Communities in cyberspace* (pp. 167–194). London: Routledge.

Wellman, B., & Gulia, M. (1999b). The network basis of social support: A network is more than the sum of its ties. In B. Wellman (Ed.). *Networks in the global village* (pp. 83–118). Boulder, CO: Westview Press.

Wellman, B., Salaff, J., Dimitrova, D., Garton, L., Gulia, M., & Haythornthwaite, C. (1996). Computer networks as social networks: Collaborative work, telework, and virtual community. *Annual Review of Sociology, 22,* 213–238.

Wellman, B., & Wortley, S. (1990). Different strokes from different folks: Community ties and social support. *American Journal of Sociology, 96,* 558–588.

CHAPTER 4

Betsy Hearne
Anna L. Nielsen

Catch a Cyber by the Tale: Online Orality and the Lore of a Distributed Learning Community

Introduction

"To catch a tiger by the tail" is a bit of proverbial folklore that suggests imminent problems and possibilities. That tiger is a good metaphor for online education. Given the potential for both positive and negative effects, the prospect of harnessing technology to build a learning community across boundaries of geographical space, as well as boundaries of culture and personality, can be intimidating. In fact, one of the most frequent concerns about online education is that students will not form in cyberspace the kind of communities that they do in the physical proximity of an on-campus classroom. One distance education student, recalling some radio coverage of distributed learning programs, commented:

> Most folks—even fair-minded and balanced reporters from NPR—seem to have preconceived notions about distance ed that any amount of discussion and demonstration won't dispel. How many of us have had the experience of hearing some mistaken notion about distance ed ("Oh, I could *never* do that! I would miss the collegiality" or—my personal favorite— "Distance education will never work because the students don't learn to interact with others") and when we try to explain how fabulous LEEP is the eyes glaze over or the disbelieving smirk begins to play about the lips. . . . (hendrsn1 22 May 09:21:55)

To examine this issue, we spearheaded a project of collecting stories from students in our distributed learning program to see if they shared a common lore, which is characteristic of all true folk communities and would validate the LEEP (Library Education Experimental Program) program as an authentic community.

The LEEPlore project involved the electronic collection of stories about the Graduate School of Library and Information Science (GSLIS) online graduate program. Stories were posted on Web boards open to all students, faculty, and staff in the general GSLIS population. These stories formed a richly thematic online exchange or "story swap." Contrary to popular perceptions that online education programs isolate students, the LEEPlore project provides evidence of true community in the virtual environment and reflects the nature of that community. As another student posted to the Web boards where we collected LEEP stories:

> I truly can't wait until the day that LEEPlore and LEEPculture disperse across the country to such a degree that we will not have to counter graduates from on-campus library schools who commonly retort, 'Oh, I could never do an online program—I need too much community.' (weisz 27 May 2002 08:58:33)

In fact, if there is one theme paramount in our collection of electronic stories, it is the strong bonding among students in the distributed learning community.

Background and Context

The process of collecting electronic stories is innovative in folklore, as is applying folkloristic methodology to analyzing electronic communities. Oral lore has long been acknowledged to reveal much about a group's codes, beliefs, and values, and online communication offers many parallels to the oral tradition even though technically it is written. Like the oral tradition, online communication tends to be more informal and ephemeral than print tradition; people "talk" into their computers via e-mail, text chat, and Web board posts. Often the audience is clearly defined and verbally responsive, unlike the audience for published writing. And often, one story leads to another in a fluid form of dialogue. Moreover, in an online community, electronic "telling" is the natural format for expression and exchange, just as speech is the natural format for expression and exchange in an oral community.

Most general users of the Internet are already familiar with the way urban legends spread electronically, as stories are forwarded from one person to another (about computer viruses, for instance) until the original source is lost in the mists of virtual reality. Like all urban legends, a few of these stories are based in truth and others are hoaxes with enough plausibility to convince us to keep passing them on. This process mirrors the way folktales, myths, and legends have passed through the oral tradition for centuries. Of course there are differences. For instance, Internet legends can be longer (though often they are not), can contain more details and print-mode wordplay, and can be archived (though they are frequently deleted or dumped, disappearing into the air like spoken words). Yet the similarities between oral and electronic lore suggest that many types of lore do circulate via the Internet and are worth collecting and examining as reflections of common values and connections in geographically distributed communities.

The rules for our electronic collection and subsequent analysis have followed standard fieldwork procedure, which has recently started reflecting attention to online data collection (Ruhleder, 2000). We had the advantage of being both "insiders" and "outsiders," one of us a teacher outside the student circle, the other a student outside the faculty/staff circle, but both of us are part of the LEEP experience. (Hearne teaches online and on-campus classes; Nielsen migrated from LEEP to on-campus and then entered the doctoral program.)

Without leading our informants with any directives, we solicited stories via the mode most accessible to them, an announcement on the LEEP home page that allowed them to click on a URL and "tell." Students could respond either publicly by Web board or privately by e-mail. Later, after each of us had sent one e-mail urging a different student to submit a story, we realized that this might represent undue pressure on the part of a teacher or classmate and discontinued the practice, at least for the first "open-floor" stage of the research. We had some ideas about what we might find, but imposed no preconceived theories on analysis of the data. And while precedents existed in the form of studies investigating the culture of onsite academic communities (Toelken, 1968; Baker, 1983; Lau, 1998), online academic communities (Hsu & Bruce, 1998; Sherry, 1996), other kinds of online communities (Jones, 1995; Rheingold, 1993; Sapienza, 1996, Kollock & Smith, 1999), and LEEP itself (Haythornthwaite, Kazmer, Robins, & Shoemaker, 2000), no one to our knowledge has collected stories reflecting the folklore of an online distributed learning community.

We organized our electronic bulletin board by cohort—a group that enters the program together in an initial two-week, on-campus training that students call "boot camp." We were curious to know whether stories from different cohorts would reveal varied themes of experience, and most important, what overall themes would emerge across boundaries of time and space in this distributed learning community. Like all research, the LEEPlore project was a leap of faith. We hypothesized (or suspected, bet, guessed—depending on whether your folk group comprises academics, detectives, bookies, or kids) that:

1. LEEPers, whether they had graduated or were currently enrolled, would respond from wherever they were located around the country/world and share their stories of the LEEP experience.
2. Their lore would reveal the values, codes, and beliefs of a folk group.
3. LEEP folklore would parallel that of onsite programs that have already been studied for their academic folklore, justifying claims that a virtual program can generate a strong sense of community.

62 • Exploring Community

As the project matured, both of us acted as participant observers of the storytelling, occasionally responding with comments to show that we were listening attentively. (Online communities rely on verbal cues and graphic symbols, or emoticons, in lieu of eye contact and other physical expressions.) In addition, as members of the community, we each posted a story that was important to us, independently selecting themes of birth and rebirth that turned out to be related. Partial quotes from these show our styles and perspectives:

> On my watch (303LE and 309LE), there have been three babies born so far, the last one closest to online labor. It was Wednesday evening, Feb. 13, 2002, when Tracy Ducksworth text-chatted that she was not feeling too well but would try to get through class. Between contractions and tech problems we helpfully suggested names such as Leeper and Webby. Somehow she did get through the class and the next thing I heard was a phone message from her husband, Otis, saying that Tracy had had a baby. Nothing about gender, weight, name, or health of mother and child, BUT, said Otis, Tracy would make up the assignments she missed! (hearne 19 Apr 2002 15:11:56)

> My birthday fell in the first week of bootcamp, the eve before a major assignment was due. I stayed awake the day before until 4 A.M. to finish my paper and give myself my birthday as freetime. I remember going to computer labtime on Oregon [Ave.], and sitting there singing softly to myself, "Happy Birthday to me! Happy Birthday to me! . . ." And it was a happy moment because it was, in fact, a happy birthday. I had busted a [trip] across the country to do something I really wanted to do, against the better judgement of many back home. "Correspondence school? Why don't you get a real education . . ." You all know the types of comments I mean. So I felt good, and I felt proud. I loved being with people who cared as much as I did about LIS. (anielsen 28 Apr 2002 23:12:30)

The Stories and Tellers

During the pilot stage of this study, we collected and analyzed four months worth of posts. The announcement was posted to Web boards on April 11, 2002. By August 16, our cutoff date for presenting the analysis at a LEEP retreat, the LEEPlore Web boards featured 375 posts. Over the next three months, 180 more accrued, tapering to a final post on November 18 when we closed the boards. Some are stories, some variants of the same story, and some comments or conversational exchanges about the stories and variants. The gender ratio of tellers—85 female to 6 male—reflects the high percentage of women in the program and in the profession at large. In fact, the many stories by women who chose the distance education program because it would not uproot them from families, jobs, and/or locations suggests that an inclination to develop online community may be inherent in a self-selected group of students already so committed to community that they will not move. Their formation of a new community in addition to the old may reveal community "longings" that are place and space independent.

As happens in physical storytelling communities, the virtual community reveals a small core of designated and self-designated storytellers who speak up while others remain silent, a process that always affects the selection of stories and emphasis of themes. However, the number of responses to high-profile storytellers, whether in the form of variants or commentaries, suggests that such tellers often represent experiences common to others.

Some stories, we suspect, were simply not told. Although the rate of students who stay in the program and graduate is extraordinarily high, a few drop out during boot camp and we obviously do not hear from them. "Lurkers" often "listen" without contributing stories themselves, another parallel to the oral tradition, though it is interesting to contrast the rather negative online term of "lurker" to its more positive offline equivalent of "audience." Some experiences of death, divorce, and hostility are too personal to expose online, while other traumas require the humorous perspective gained with time to divulge (more on this later). In addition to self-censorship there is selective memory: what we forget shapes our history as much as what we remember. For instance, Nielsen cites examples of her own forgetting of a "whisper incident" (students can click on one another's names during class and "whisper" something that no one else can hear, resulting in disasters when whispers accidentally get sent to the whole class) during her LEEP masters-degree student days; and she only vaguely remembered the mothership story (analyzed below), which others recalled as important. A few tellers did take advantage of e-mail to either Hearne or Nielsen to communicate private stories.

What the Stories Tell

Like tigers and online education, stories can get wildly out of control. Once you've caught a tiger by the tail—or a cyber by the tale—a pressing question follows: Now what? Collecting tales is only the first step toward analyzing, classifying, and interpreting them. The same story means different things to different people, depending on age, gender, experience, occasion, cultural background, and many other factors. Throw in different tellers and variants, and soon it becomes difficult to apply any interpretive theory. However, we can better understand what stories tell us by identifying patterns of commonality and difference. This process has long been formalized in traditional folklore with the Motif and Tale Type indexes. The Motif Index (Thompson, 1956) classifies and numbers the smallest elements of character, symbol, or action identifiable across a broad range of stories; the Tale Type Index (Aarne, 1961, Rev. and Trans., Thompson) classifies and numbers story patterns based on combinations of these elements. Of course, classification schemes are made to be broken, and there is great overlap and blurring of distinctions among the new motifs and types we have identified in LEEPlore. Basically, however, motifs and types do emerge and lead us to a clearer understanding of cultural patterns in the LEEP community culture.

A surprising number of stories follow the traditional journey quest pattern that Joseph Campbell (1973) outlined: the hero/ine answers a call, undertakes a literal journey with tests along the way reflecting an allegorical journey of maturation, and returns with newly acquired wisdom to his/her home. Campbell's theory of an "ur-tale"—and indeed the entire structural study of folklore texts—has been called into question by the school of contextualized performance studies (Dundes, 1964; Bauman, 1977, 1986; Ben-Amos, 1993). But ironically, our experimental ethnography of online stories adapts well to old-fashioned structural identification, especially in the absence of a physical performance context in the electronic environment. In LEEPlore certain contemporary themes permeate the stories, especially the theme of balance: balance of family, work, and school; balance of stress and humor; balance of physical and virtual realities. LEEPers often use the same phrases, references, metaphorical images, and graphic icons, a common lexicon of informal knowledge characteristic of folk groups. More similarities of experience emerge than differences, further testimony to a bonded community. The following story types were the most pronounced, and examples of them all will appear in our analysis.

- Destiny stories (so named by students who recalled when/why/how they "joined up")
- Boot camp stories (accounts of the intensive two-week on-campus orientation for each new cohort)
- Bonding stories (about friends, support, community, camaraderie)
- Superhuman guide/helper stories (about faculty or staff viewed as heroic or "omnipotent")
- Teacher stories (faculty not necessarily seen as heroic!)
- Family and pet stories (stories about the home life of online students)
- Travel stories (to and from on-campus sessions)
- Technology stories (dealing with electronic complexities and disasters)
- Food stories (in both on-campus and online sessions)
- Setting/location stories (access points for students online; temporary headquarters on campus)
- Disaster, breakdown, and survival stories (about stress and crisis in the life of an online student)
- Hidden identities, multiple identities, folk doubles, doppelgangers (online "masks")
- Creation stories (the beginning and early days of LEEP)

In the process of our narrative research, we read and reread the posts; underlined and identified every important element or motif of a story or story fragment; categorized these motifs into patterns that emerged; organized the categories into a framework for presentation; and returned to the marked passages yet again to pick out the most striking examples of each category. We have chosen three methods of presenting our LEEPlore work. The first is a story thread selected for in-depth examination; the second is an exploration of the pervasive theme of humor that permeates the entire collection of stories and functions strongly in the LEEP students' survival of stress; and the third is an experiment in creative analysis that we have called a narrative collage.

A Mothership Story

All communities have folklore that serves as a common reference point for their creation and/or value system. The form of such folklore may vary from myth to legend, from *pourquoi* tale to corporate anecdote. One story in particular emerged as important to the LEEP community and became what some students called a "family story" and others called, apropos of the Star Wars imagery frequently evoked by technology-oriented LEEP students, a "mothership story" (graduate Gwen Evans coined the phrase). This story, which I've entitled "The Magic Circle," is a tale within a tale within a tale within a tale, mostly generated by the voluble summer-2000 Cohort 5 (102 posts compared to the next most numerous posts of 39 from summer-2001 Cohort 6.2), and mostly related in a thread called "The garbage can in the big room," though references to the story continue in other threads as well. Almost all of the LEEP students are familiar with this story because it was told by someone who has regularly taught a required course during LEEP boot camp. Dr. Margaret Mary Kimmel (aka Maggie) is a noted LIS educator and storyteller on the faculty of the Department of Library and Information Science at the University of Pittsburgh. She also co-teaches every summer—with a GSLIS faculty member, Leigh Estabrook, who was dean of GSLIS for 15 years—an introductory LEEP core course called "Libraries, Information, and Society" (LIS390) about professional issues, values, and ethics of information specialists. During the last session of every boot camp, Professor Kimmel tells each new cohort a story about a story called "Sody Salyratus," an Appalachian Jack tale collected by Richard Chase in *Grandfather Tales* (Chase, 1948).

In the course of multiple posts, in which a number of students struggled to remember the occasion and stumbled on an unfamiliar phrase at the heart of the story, two students posted cohesive variants including multiple layers of the story. Even some of the fragmented posts related to the story are worth reading in sequence, however, since they reveal much about the process of constructing a group memory. Quoted below are eight selections in the Magic Circle thread, which consisted overall of 20 posts, some consecutive and others appearing as occasional references.

. . . was there anyone who WASN'T in tears at the end of Maggie's story at the last class of bootcamp? I remember her starting the story, and we were all filling out our evaluation form thing, and she repeated in that bootcamp voice "put your hands in your lap" (or whatever she said) because we weren't paying attention, and then in 10 minutes there was nothing but sobbing to be heard. I remember people still crying outside the building 15 minutes later. There's a storytelling story. (evans1 25 Apr 2002 19:43:39)

Gwen, I have a feeling this may be another LEEP family story. If it's the story of Solie Soleradus (sp?), we also heard it in 6.1, and had a similar communal response. Does anyone remember enough of it to post it? (ksantama 26 Apr 2002 10:09:34)

All I remember was it was about a little boy who, I think, was taught by a storyteller that drawing a magic circle would keep you safe—and that they found him, unharmed, next to a dead man, and he had drawn a magic circle. I can't remember much more, but it's making me cry right now to write this. (evans1 26 Apr 2002 12:39:09)

And it was Maggie who had given the boy the story. She had gone into a classroom and had told the story about the magic circle and in the telling sang a song, which I think had a refrain something like "suli suli" (sorry I'm not quite sure), and I think the man was a relative that the boy stayed with—my weak memory says that the boy was pretty disadvantaged and this was his caregiver. He had disappeared from school for a couple of days, and when he was found, he [was] next to the dead man, singing the "suli suli" song in his magic circle. I think the teacher then called Maggie to let her know what had happened.

Can anyone else fill in the blanks? Anyone have Maggie's e-mail so we can ask her? (ikens 26 Apr 2002 13:01:30)

I think the words are "sody saleratus". Saleratus is an old term for baking soda and I think the story had a magic powder in it that was used in baking, too, as well as the magic ring of powder. Interesting how everyone remembers how the story made them feel but we're so unclear on the details! (rgraham 26 Apr 2002 14:22:48)

You're right, Rebecca!

It was sody, sody, sody saleratus!!!

I vividly remember the boy sitting in his magic circle singing Maggie's song, and then, Maggie just finishing the story and leaving. It was very powerful. (ikens 26 Apr 2002 14:31:29)

No one can tell the story like Maggie can but she had wrapped the class in a magic circle and then told the story with the song that goes something like "sody, sody sody something". There was a little boy in the class that was driven to school each day by a neighbor man/caretaker. Apparently, that same day Maggie told the story, the man died. When the boy didn't show up for school after a couple days, they found him next to the man. He had wrapped himself in a magic circle and was singing the sody song. It was a powerful story about the power of storytelling. (dmenning 28 Apr 2002 10:47:22)

Okay, okay. I know Slugo's coming late to this party, but I'm one of those who was still weeping 30 mins after we left that session with Maggie. Like Sean, I remembered "Sody, Sody" but dubbed over the next word with something that was more meaningful in my lexicon (no, it didn't rhyme with "Chee.tos"—by the way, for all you trans fatty acid lovers, please note the correct spelling of this LEEP favorite; see also, http://www.fritolay.com/consumer.html and click on "Dietary Information"—now there's a misnomer!).

What I remember most, though, was that Maggie had me hooked from the get go. Before she even began her story, she shared with our cohort how she had quieted her roomful of young listeners.

Maggie had announced she was going to tell a story, but that in order to listen to the story and understand it, everyone needed a little bit of magic. Luckily, she had some magic in her pocket, but when she polled the storytime listeners, she discovered to her dismay that no one else had thought to bring any magic with them. She described how she carefully reached into her pocket and then, with a gentle puff of breath across her opened fist, she dispensed a generous portion of "magic" to everyone in the room, cautioning them to capture it quickly in their hands before it flew away. Then, with each child clutching their invisible but very personal treasure hoard, she asked each of the children in the room to save half of their magic—"because you never know when you may need it" (a prelude to the story to be told, of course). The way I remember it, she then asked the children to share the other half of their magic by releasing it in the room for storytime. And then, within the protection of the magic circle, Maggie proceeded to tell her story.

That day, I was sitting toward the upper reaches of the auditorium-style lecture room in Gregory Hall and the effect of Maggie's words were not lost on me nor on my other LEEP cohort members as I surveyed the room from my vantage point. In the space of Maggie's sigh, we became her encircled storytime class. As listeners we reached into the air above us with our imaginations, never doubting that Maggie's magic could be captured and shared among us, even in the graduate realities of LEEP life. And, suddenly, but oh so subtly, we were engaged by and entered into Maggie's story. Some of us were touched so deeply because it became our story: Oh, what a great Glinda The Good Witch of the South power it must be to touch lives so deeply as Maggie did with her storytelling. What magic indeed. That power—that responsibility—to make a positive difference in the lives of others through the telling and encircling of our stories is something that was indelibly imprinted on me that day. But, more than that: I remember thinking that Maggie's story was such an emotional experience because its message to me was that the power of such magic is only fully realized when it is meaningfully shared.

If ever there was a defining LEEP principle for me, it would be this. I didn't fully realize it then, but I no longer was learning to be about competition, about being the best among others, constantly seeking out learning opportunities and ideas as if somehow by claiming them first they also could not be claimed by others. What I began to realize over the next couple of months was that LEEP-learning was a dynamic process that was all about verbalizing, intellectual risk-taking, sharing—not competing—with others.

Information was not something to be hoarded—to inform it needs to be released. LEEP was about releasing and spreading the magic. LEEP has provided a remarkable learning template that I am now applying to my workplace, my volunteer efforts and my personal life.

I know that if I had taken the same courses of LIS graduate study in a traditional classroom setting, perhaps my grades would not have been significantly different, and even my level of measurable achievement may have been the same. But there is no doubt in my mind that the abiding depth and meaningfulness of my learning experience would have been much less. It is the shared relationships and bonds forged with my virtual classmates and professors and deans in LEEP that truly have been magical and already are missed. (trevista 24 May 2002 00:13:37)

About halfway through the posts, we e-mailed Kimmel (per request by "ikens") to relate *her* version of the story she told, which she promptly e-mailed to us and which proved that the students had collaboratively reconstructed an accurate retelling:

[T]he story was concerned with a telling of "Sody Sallyratus." "Sody" is the story I told a 3rd grade class on a day before a literature conference where I was a speaker. I used a magic circle and told Sody to these kids. I had a night class the Monday I got back and the phone was ringing when I got in. The voice at the other end asked if I had been in her city's schools the Friday before and told a story and there was something about magic and music. Seems a 3rd grader usually got a ride to school with the neighbor who dropped him off on the way to work. The little boy never made it to school and when they found him he was inside a magic circle singing "sody, sody, sody sallyratus" and holding the hand of the neighbor who had overdosed and died.

I use it to make the point that you may never know the impact you have—but no matter where you work, we have the power of the information and the great gift of being able to give it away. (Kimmel e-mail)

There are multiple layers to "The Magic Circle" narrative. The first is "Sody Salyratus" itself, about a mountain family—a woman, a man, their little boy, their little girl, and a pet squirrel. When the woman runs out of baking soda for biscuits ("sody salyratus" is an archaic term for baking soda), she sends the little boy to the store. He gets the sody salyratus and walks back home over a bridge where he encounters a bear that eats him and his sody salyratus. To investigate the delay, the woman next sends her little girl, who meets the same fate, and her husband, ditto. She herself goes to check on the situation and gets eaten in turn. Finally the pet squirrel becomes impatient, waiting for his biscuits, and ventures forth. He meets the bear, clambers up a tree, and climbs out on a limb, where the bear follows him and falls off, splitting in two. In this circular narrative, all the family members who have journeyed away from safety survive their trials, return home, and share their biscuits generously with the heroic little squirrel.

None of the LEEP students is familiar with the story and Maggie does not tell it in detail. Rather, she describes telling it to a class of third graders in a strange city where she has journeyed to make a speech. First she prepares the graduate students, who have themselves journeyed to a strange place with many trials to overcome, in the same way as she always prepares young children who are about to journey into the strange world of story.

Next, Maggie tells the story of returning home and receiving a phone call about a young boy who has survived via the power of her story. She then reminds these information-specialist-initiates that they will never know how the power of the information they distribute will enable people to survive. Thus, in telling them a story within a story, she is also encircling them with a story about their own capabilities (1) to help others survive through knowledge; (2) to survive the terrors of boot camp themselves by virtue of the magic of knowledge; and (3) to value their interdependence with the least member of the knowledge community for survival.

Here, then, is a tale within a tale within a tale within a tale. Imagine an onion. The innermost layer, or core, is the Appalachian survival tale itself, involving a journey. The second layer is a survival tale about the results of telling a survival tale, in the course of the storyteller's journey, to a young audience that included the boy who survived by invoking the story in a crisis. (Yet another layer, nonverbal but visually apparent, is implied here: Maggie is physically disabled and dependent on a wheelchair to the extent that any journey becomes a test of survival). The third layer is Maggie's telling of both survival tales to an audience of graduate students surviving a journey involving severe trials. The fourth layer of this metanarrative is the LEEP students' collective telling of all three tales on the LEEPlore Web board, where they communally construct (and reconstruct) their own emotionally and intellectually resonant stories of Maggie's stories and share interpretations of what it all means. Adding yet another layer is the story (of all the stories) as it is being told in this research paper, highlighting the power of knowledge that is the founding myth of all research communities. (The word "myth" here reflects its folkloristic meaning as a cultural founding story, rather than the popularized pejorative sense of an untruth.)

As folklore, this multilayered narrative reveals the intricate way in which selective memory operates in the creation of variants. Two dimensionally, the onion layers of story might be better envisioned as abstract circles—magic circles of protective knowledge. All communities have folklore that reflects shared values and reaches initiates via elders or mentors, often through stories that have mythological resonance. "The Magic Circle" is certainly a kind of founding myth, coming as it does at the beginning of LEEP students' community experience, bonding new community members together in a ritual passage, highlighting the importance of community itself, and surviving as a remembered community experience. Many other stories (about the rite of the "valuing assignment," for instance, a project that kept students up all night) also reflect a shared customary lore that enables LEEP students to identify (and identify with) their online learning community in the face of outsiders' ignorance, employers' suspicion, or even graduates' self-doubt about the new program's value.

Despite the serious focus of "The Magic Circle," students often told more stories of mischief than of the hard work they did. Folklore reveals the underside of a culture, the trickster, fool, and clown—as well as the hero—in us all. Folklore often suggests, too, that humor is a basic element of survival. LEEPlore showed just how important humor is to the survival of both individuals and the LEEP community.

Humor and Survival

Of the many patterns and motifs that LEEPlore revealed, it was often the interpersonal humorous stories that evinced and convinced us of the presence of community. Humor depends on a shared cultural code that is both defining and binding. Like other folkloric elements of esoteric knowledge that verify group membership in traditional settings (Jensen, 1965), humor verifies group membership in virtual settings, as well. Marvin (1995) cites the shared jargon of "spoof, spam, lurk, and lag" in "text-based virtual realities." In Sapienza's (1996) discussion of hacker folklore on Usenet, he analyzes a trickster narrative representative of the hacker subculture, which is noted for insider jokes about non-hackers. Baym's (1995) study of computer-mediated communication finds that humor is "embedded in shared knowledge, shared codes, and shared emotional significances" (p. 3). To some extent, shared humor is proof of community, and the computer-mediated communication space of LEEPlore proves fertile ground for exchanging humor that creates and sustains community.

We identified patterns of humor that functioned in several distinct ways, including conquering adversity and strengthening social ties. Students remembered and humorously reflected on potentially traumatizing moments of stress, defusing negative effects and creating a mechanism to cope with the collective trials and tribulations of LEEP. Embarking on a master's program is challenging enough; adding the new and strange environs of the virtual lends a further dimension to the rites of educational experience, effectively providing the LEEP students with a rich field of material from which to make jokes. Interestingly, results of a 1992 study on the effects of humor and stress find that humor, especially for women, can modify the negative effects of stress into a more positive experience (White & Winzelberg, 1992). Perhaps the high percentage of women coping with stress in the program accounts for the humor that permeates LEEPlore!

When students shared difficult moments, others' humorous responses included stories of similar experience, all of which then resounded as community moments. Thus stories of humorous response to stress and challenge reflected, created, and strengthened a sense of the LEEP community. As Terrion and Ashforth (2002) affirm, "humor can be used to foster learning and community, a sense of what the group or organization represents, and a sense of cohesion" (p. 60). Humorous stories, then, are particularly applicable and useful in a geographically distributed online learning environment. In fact, a comparison of stories recollected about the on-campus boot camp and online virtual classrooms shows that humor functions in virtual environments just as effectively as in physical environments.

Boot Camp Humor

Commentary from Freud (1960) to Henman (2001) suggests that we use humor to stabilize our perspective, detaching ourselves from an oppressive reality, and we see this clearly in stories about boot camp:

> During bootcamp we had received some complementary meals at the Ilini Tower cafeteria as a reward for being stuck in the "condemned" tower our first days in Chambana [nickname for Champaign-Urbana, the location of the graduate school]. Remember that! While a table of us was enjoying the comforts provided by our cafeteria ice-cream cones and reminiscing about the psychotic nature of days past and what creatures might lurk ahead, Sean Scott surprised us all by a rendition of the Blair Witch Project's "I'm so scaaarrred!" We all needed a good laugh and that one brought me to tears. You just may have saved my life, Sean! It was smooth sailing after that wake-up to reality. :) Thanks, Sean!! Forever your biggest fan! (clpeters 13 Apr 2002 14:38:54)

The humorous story lightened everybody's mood, diminishing "the psychotic nature of days past" into a spoof, effectively transforming this into an inside story that is still laughed over two years later online. The accidental substandard housing, through humor, turned into a bonding moment that built up the group. The humor diminished the effect of the trauma by releasing the tension of the trauma. De Koning and Weiss (2002) say that "the positive effect of humor comes from a 'cognitive shift,' which leads to a change in affect" (pp. 2–3). Through a joke shared among LEEPers, the negative experience took on a new and less threatening meaning.

Upping the ante, humorous stories are also used to carry each other and ourselves through potentially breaking moments (Henman, 2001). When it works, we take pride in our ability to overcome. "Humor is not resigned; it is rebellious. It signifies the triumph not only of the ego, but also of the pleasure principle, which is strong enough to assert itself here in the face of the adverse real circumstances" (Freud, 1928, p. 217). Two LEEPers attest to this:

> Where else [but our community] could you hear the heavy breathing of your colleagues, discover their nervous habits, and gasp with amazement at the way some churned out papers in an hour? I nearly rented a laptop for bootcamp, but I'm glad I didn't. Now I

know who bites her nails and who laughs under stress. People I stood laughing with, soda in hand, at 2 A.M., outside the LIS computer lab, are the ones who are dear to me. (sphillps 14 May 2002 17:48:08).

Everyone giggled and then it happened. Jill and I slowly but surely lost control, spiraling ever deeper into such helpless laughter that we actually ended up crying. Every time one of us got part way in control, we would see the other and start off again. I felt like I was about 7 years old. (smessina 19 Apr 2002 18:47:00)

These stories evince the obvious connection between humor and community: the LEEPers were in a crisis ameliorated by a humorous view of their shared reality. We even mock our fears with humor, to hold the negatives at bay.

Just a quick recollection about waiting in line the first day at Illini Towers to check in before the march to Bromley. Although I knew there had been a change of plans and that the LEEPers were being relocated, I did not know that all the people registering were not in the LEEP program. The gentleman in front of me was sporting multiple tattoos and his beer belly was protruding from his black Megadeth-type t-shirt, and I remember thinking how impressive it was that this program was really going for diversity! (sullivan 25 Apr 2002 18:43:37)

This LEEPer can joke about her anxieties because they are over and were actually unfounded. She has survived LEEP, and she has fellow LEEPers to joke with online. The story defines insiders and outsiders as well, and not just by contrasting LEEP students with steelworkers. Who else but a LEEP community member would even know about the steelworkers who won the best room reservations during boot camp? The joke is successful because it moderates fears and establishes membership in a community through references only an insider would mention and understand (Toelken 1996). For a joke to work, it needs to reflect a group's social norms (Matte 2001).

Finally, we use humor to express relief when the negatives are successfully and communally navigated. We even grow fond of our miseries, as our handling of them brings the connectedness of joint resolution.

Future bootcamp generations may flay me for saying so, but I would never propose dropping the valuing assignment from the bootcamp curriculum. For me, at least, it inspired confidence, camaraderie, and a delirium of laughter that comes only from sleeplessness and a walk on the edge of academic destruction (sphillps 11 May 2002 16:50:03)

The tensions of the negative experiences are over, and the LEEPers expel them with pleasure and joy in accomplishment. That they choose to do this together, with their own jocular folklore, makes them a community.

Online Humor

Following boot camp, humor continues to sustain the community online. From the very first cohort:

> . . . after we went home, all those hours spent trying to get that beta version audio software to work . . . I can't even remember the NAME of it now, and it seemed so important at the time. Anyway, remember the night a bunch of us were online saying, "Hal, I can hear you. Can you hear me?" It was so scratchy and faint that it felt like we were part of the WWII resistance. . . . And then, loud and clear out of my speakers comes Becky Robinson talking to some sixth grader she'd gotten to help her with it. "DO YOU THINK THEY CAN HEAR US? I WONDER IF THIS IS WORKING?" How that kid got it transmitting so well remains a mystery. . . . (lewis 22 April 2002 20:02:30)

Another student from the same cohort responded in kind:

> Here I was, a Young People's Services librarian getting ready for our library Halloween program. The thought occurred to me that since we could change our aspects in the MUD [multi-user domain], that the LEEP students could have a Halloween Party. So we all showed up in costume. Everyone from J. Edgar Hoover (in drag) to Bunny Watson (from the movie Desk Set) was there—some people changed costume 3 times. Here we all were working like fiends trying new technologies, getting back in to the routine of school, learning our technical ropes and we discovered that we could make the technology fun. I think that was the moment when I realized that I could do this, that I would make it through this because we were able to have fun together. The humor on the student bulletin boards kept many of us going when we were at our most stressed. (anielsen posting jhalsall e-mail)

LEEP members created their own terminologies to relate their humorous experiences much like the MOO (multi-user domain, object-oriented) members Marvin examined (1995). One common mistake entailed incorrect use of the whisper function. When a student clicks on a name, a red box appears, and the LEEPer is able to "talk" to only the person whose name is inside the red box, a virtual whisper. Every cohort has a story about failing to keep that red box clicked and inadvertently turning a whisper into a shout.

> A bunch of us were whispering in Doc D's class about what we were drinking and/or what we wished we were drinking, and Paul Mottola typed to the entire class "Brass Monkey. It's sold in all the best bodegas in New York." (evans1 25 Apr 2002 08:48:54)

These incidents could lead to code words that were known and used without some students even understanding or remembering the source:

Cohort 5.0 people referred to such a transgression as a 'brass monkey.' I have no idea where that came from, but I love it. Nothing beat someone slipping up on the whisper, and then everyone whispering to everyone else 'BRASS MONKEY'! . . . (rcmcgowa 25 Apr 2002 01:50:06)

I used to whisper with my friend Simone in Gov. Pubs, Marilyn Moody's class. I was telling her about my trip to a bar in Champaign, but i couldn't recall the name. It was the 'Rose Bowl' (interesting place, to say the least), but she misspelled it as 'Rose Bowel'. Then she wrote 'I meant Bowl'. THEN she wrote 'not bowel', which was accidentally posted to the whole class during a discussion. Completely busted. She refused to whisper to me after that. At the end of the next class to make up for what she saw as *my* fault for starting the whole thing, I also wrote 'bowel' during class. It's the only b. monkey I've been involved in. (rcmcgowa 7 May 2002 12:07:57)

Here *brass monkey* has become a term only LEEP members understand as a code word for CMC protocol error. Moreover, in talking about a mood-altering substance, they are also playing at altering a work space—already altered from physical to virtual—into a play space.

Humor "about problems allows a group to see these problems in perspective and to get on with its work" (Morreal, 1991, p. 371). Humor, by means of its mood-altering nature, can turn potentially unbearable moments into stories to share later. "Humor is our collective adaptation to our situation" (Palmer, 1994, p. 57). Together, we resist stress and transgression, trials and tribulations, fear and terror. We use humor to cope with stress and turn the stress into pleasure. We grow from a group of individuals under duress to a community taking control. Humorous stories helped LEEP become and sustain a community.

A Narrative Collage

Our close reading of the "Magic Circle" mothership story and our thematic analysis of the way humorous stories function in LEEP communities rely on conventional analytic methods. We turn now to a more experimental mode, a presentation of online LEEPlore in the form of a narrative collage that combines stories from many tellers into one cohesive tale. In creating this collage, we put together our experience with analyzing text and our experience with storytelling. We drew not only on the LEEPlore tellers' story-making powers, but also on our own.

The narrative collage is voiced by a prototypical LEEP student who is in fact collectively reconstructed from many of the stories put together. Every detail is true to the stories—we made none of it up—but we collaged selected passages into one narrative, drawing on the narrators' own words, phrases, and occasionally entire posts. Because this narrative incorporates so many quotes from the collected stories, it gives a strong sense of the storytellers' voices, experiences, and thematic concerns. The commonalities that underwrote such an ur-tale were many: the protagonist/hero; her call to destiny; her guides and helpers; her journeys and fellow travelers; her trials, tests, and triumphs along the way; classroom settings both on campus and in the virtual environment; themes of experience and evolving knowledge; and some happily-ever-afters. Besides including elements of character, action, and theme lifted directly from the posts, we were careful to identify and incorporate the words, references, in-jokes, and metaphorical images that testify to LEEP as a strong virtual folk community with a common language.

For instance, the students started telling what they eventually identified as "LEEP destiny stories" in several threads ("Getting in," "Getting to LEEP," "My LEEP destiny story," "My destiny story," "Long time comin'," "destiny stories," "My LEEP experience"). To begin our LEEPtale, we took eleven typical posts ranging from one- to two-page stories and incorporated them, as an archetypal pattern with a few individual details, into the first paragraph. In the case of the "destiny thread," the stories came from Cohorts 2, 4, 5, 6.1, 6.2, and on-campus students (who also can take LEEP courses if there is class space after the LEEP students have completed registration). As in the "Magic Circle" mothership story, these posts also show how students respond to each other in building a communal memory of shared experience through story. Here are a few excerpts from some very long posts to demonstrate the basis for only one paragraph in the "LEEPtale," a paragraph about the call to adventure that is represented by the "destiny" thread:

> In the late spring of 1999, after several years working as an elementary teacher at a bilingual school in Mexico, I had a revelation about the importance of school libraries. Much of this was the influence of . . . a veteran librarian of 30 years with whom I had frequent conversations. The library at our school was okay, but lack of support from administration and staff turnover were taking their toll on service. I went to our principal to ask what he thought about me going to library school for an endorsement and his response was that I was to be the elementary librarian next term. Apparently, the recruitment efforts hadn't been going so well. Somewhat overwhelmed, I went back to [the librarian] for advice. How can I prepare for this? As always, [she] gave me some great tips. (Her Alma Mater is Wisc-Madison.) A link on the ALA directory led me to LEEP. It sounded perfect—Internet-based, independent learning . . . I quickly got an application together and sent it in—mostly by fax. It was June by the time I finished applying and by then I was back in my hometown—Halifax, Nova Scotia (Canada) for summer break. My acceptance came quickly . . . (rmontagu 23 Apr 2002 21:59:20)

> . . . I had been working away at [a manufacturing company]. I ended up being their competitive intelligence guru (ha!) and managing a library of competitive info. It was all by the seat of my pants and using my common sense (i.e. why don't we alphabetize the info by company name and put it where people can find it and use it.) . . . My company

ha[d] taken to ravaging its staff with insane layoffs. They abruptly let go my boss whom I would have slaved for interminably because she was the best. That night I went home and said, "Okay, Kathleen, are you going to just talk about it or are you going to do it." That's the night I started to seriously researching library school. (I mentioned that fact in my exit interview a year later.) Later I came across the following Portugese proverb which only served to underscore my intentions: "A ship that doesn't sail, never reaches port." It's still hanging up in my kitchen. So I took up sailing. I talked to my friends . . . both life long librarians. They bought me coffee and shared their lives. I didn't want to move to San Jose or L.A. for their MLS programs, so . . . I went to the ALA site and looked only at those programs that were offered via distance ed. Of course LEEP came up. I called. I collected info. I researched. . . . I applied in January 2000 and was accepted . . . June rolled around and I can tell you I was pretty excited to give my notice. I bought a new outfit for the occasion including my "quitting [the company]" underwear. I took my book club's advice and chose the blue pair. So with 6 weeks off before boot camp, I gathered my energies and prepared to start this new adventure. That's my LEEP destiny story. I can't *imagine* going anywhere else or doing it any other way! (ksmith8 24 Apr 2002 19:54:38)

. . . While volunteering at a neighborhood school library a couple of years ago, I kept experiencing flashbacks and fond memories of my own elementary school library. . . . This librarian told me about an article she read in School Library Journal about different distance learning programs around the country. I borrowed the article and, for various reasons, ended up applying only to LEEP. Having five-year-old triplets at the time was the biggest consideration for me. I had been a stay-at-home mom their whole lives, but it was because they were about to start school that I decided I might as well too. . . . Sorry this has been so long, but I'm glad to have finally shared it. The upshot is I finally feel like I'm doing what I was meant to do. At age 42, that feels great! (ksantama 25 Apr 2002 07:07:05)

When I thought about getting a library degree, I wrote to the American Library Association trying to locate a school that offered any type of correspondence courses, etc. That was in the late 1980s, probably a decade preLEEP. There were a few courses here and there, I think, but no programs. As a 30-something, working mother I was trying to stay at home. Well, actually I needed to get the undergrad first anyhow. . . . In 1998, a friend of mine . . . was finishing LEEP and wanted me to sign on. . . . I'm here now and I can't believe I'm almost halfway finished already!! When I think of correspondence courses compared to LEEP, I shiver. : { I can't imagine being cut off from everybody, not being able to whisper and ask the really stupid questions. LEEP was a long time comin' for me . . . . (ramillr1 21 May 2002 22:57:22)

My sentiments (sort of) exactly! I had wanted to go to library school since the late 80s but couldn't see my way toward paying private school tuition or making a long drive once or twice a week for class (assuming that I would have been able to leave work on time, which in those days, was *highly* unlikely). When I heard about the LEEP program, I leapt! It met all my criteria: excellent program, in-state tuition, and class from any location that allow loggin' on! As I said to my hubby when I started, "It's like a dream come true!" He looked at me for a moment and replied, "It *is* a dream come true . . . a *funny* sort of dream." <grin> And he's right! The GSLIS staff and faculty and my fellow students have run way past any expectation I ever had. Interestingly enough, one of the things I remember from bootcamp was our introductions on the first day. About half of the people mentioned some variation on the phrase "I've been wanting to go to library school for about 10 years. . ." So it seems as though LEEP is a funny sort of dream come true for lots of folks! (hendrsn1 22 May 2002 09:12:14)

. . . I thought I'd throw in my destiny story. I was trying to get pregnant for years on end (3+ to be exact) and after almost 20 disappointments and one miscarriage, I decided that I needed another focus in my life. If I wasn't going to be a parent, I sure didn't want to have everything else in my life be status quo. I started thinking and library school came to mind. My mom's a school librarian and of course, like all of you, I love books, research, and libraries. . . . I casually mentioned my interest in library school to a college classmate who herself has a J.D. (Temple) and M.L.S. (Rutgers). She sent me the link for the LEEP homepage. Within minutes, I was sure this was the right program. I emailed my partner . . . about it, and within several hours she emailed back and told me that one of her coworkers had gone to GSLIS and was good friends with Curt McKay. I think that it wasn't 24 hours later that Curt was emailing me back with answers to my questions. The best part of this whole story is that I got it all: I delivered my daughter, Clare in November of 2000 and started LEEP last summer. . . . I echo what others have said about the amazing richness of this program and the vitality of the online community. I feel remarkably blessed to be part of it. (smessina 28 Apr 2002 10:44:28)

Thanks for sharing your story, Susan! I hope others chime in here! When I discovered LEEP I was starting my 8th year at a job I didn't really like. I was stressed out and ticked off every single day. My daughter had just turned one and I hated leaving her every day to go do something I found no joy in. I was unable to quit, and I felt trapped. My u.g. degree was in French and International Business. I had toyed with the ideas of earning a teaching certificate in French. I had also toyed with the idea of pursuing an MLS degree, but no local universities offered the program. Then, one day my company's intranet had a link to some distance learning programs sponsored by the company for information technology degrees.

I copied down the link and went home and told my husband that I wanted to look into pursuing an I.T. degree, even if it wasn't exactly what I was looking for, at least it would be a change. He agreed, and when I clicked on the link taking me to the UIUC distance learning web page, the first thing I saw was the library science program. I shouted for my husband. "This is it! This is a sign! This is what I want to do!" He agreed. Then I read more closely and realized the deadline for application was about a week away! I had always had a tendency to come up with great ideas and never follow through, but I dived right into this and miraculously got the application requirements together. I applied without doing any research into the program at all! I had no idea that GSLIS was so highly regarded!

My letter of acceptance arrived one day when I was tired, angry about something that happened at work, and also very sick. I held the letter for a long time before I opened it, not sure if I could handle another bad thing that day. When I saw the words "We are happy to inform you..." I just shouted with joy.

Since that day, I have found the courage and resources to make other changes in my life. I found a way to quit that job I hated. I started working for what I actually wanted in life instead of feeling sorry for myself about the way things were. I feel like I'm setting an example for my children that you can be happy doing what you love, instead of just working to bring home the bacon. Since then, my daughter has turned three and I have a newborn son (LEEP on-campus in bitter winter weather at 7 months pregnant is an experience I don't care to repeat!). My kids have a happy mom working towards a fulfilling career, so LEEP is much more to me than a course of study! (lagregor 28 Aug 2002 19:04:42)

A minimum of fourteen pages of these kinds of LEEPlore posts (only a few fragments are represented here) was incorporated into the first paragraph of the LEEPtale below. For each phase of the LEEP experience described in multiple posts, from the call to destiny, through traveling to boot camp, attending online classes experienced in physically diverse settings, and mentoring new members of the community, we continued to select the most typical stories and synthesize them in the same way. Thus the following narrative collage serves as both an analysis and a way to convey the pattern and power of LEEP stories—and the experience of LEEPers themselves—without quoting hundreds of pages of data. Aspects such as women's issues in relation to education show up as clearly as they would in any other kind of analytic method. Unlike many experimental formats for folklore analysis (see, for instance, Lau, 2002), the narrative collage assumes a rather lighthearted tone that reflects our informants' humorous strategies for negotiating the intense demands of online education. Deeply embedded in this LEEPtale, however, are various tellers' accounts of mental and physical journeys that reflect journeys of maturation: heroes who set out from home, undergo trials, overcome adversity with the intervention of superheroes and helpers, and return to their societies enriched by new knowledge.

LEEPtale

Once there was a woman who had wanted for years to go back to school for a degree in Library and Information Science. Fortunately or unfortunately, she had several children and/or a job and couldn't just up and go wherever and whenever she wanted to. Then one day, by accident, encounter, or persistent design she discovered a way to pursue her quest. She heard it as a call to destiny, as her fate. We will let her tell you the story herself.

It begins during a lunchtime conversation with a friendly librarian after my discovery that neither Chicago nor Las Vegas will hire me as a teacher, that the crummy job with which I support myself and my family will not give me a leave of absence, and that my partner can't leave his/her ailing parents in their long-standing community. My triplets have just turned five years old. Having already applied to several programs that lose my transcripts, fail to answer e-mails—and insist I take the GRE [Graduate Record Examination] and provide community college course transcripts from my high school years, although I have already completed a Ph.D. in a research 1 university—I finally, in desperation, at the very last minute, on the advice of the lunchtime librarian, call GSLIS. A professor returns my phone call on a Sunday evening, answers all my questions, and suggests a good time to visit. This is my first signal that LEEP faculty members are not ordinary people. I apply online, am accepted immediately, and embark on my educational journey with a used computer and a new set of underwear, which I've bought to celebrate the adventure.

My first stop is a mandatory two-week, on-campus session popularly known as Boot Camp. Having actually been through military boot camp, I'm curious to find out the academic version. There are, I will discover, certain similarities of bonding through trials, tests, triumphs, and deprivations of shelter, food, sleep, and clothing. I chart a complex travel schedule from Alaska, Argentina, France, Hawaii, Mexico, or other sites in the United States and abroad. In one airport, I recognize another LEEPer by the infamous Richard Rubin textbook she is reading. We bond immediately and will even become roommates, but meanwhile my airline cancels the next leg of my flight. Overhearing my plight, a stranger offers me a ride from Indianapolis to Champaign. I decide he's safe and arrive—without my luggage. Well, I can always buy another pair of sweats, and from the looks of the syllabus I've studied along the way, I may not have time for that bathing suit I brought along for swimming in my spare time. I see others alighting from various vehicles, including a camper and an oversized truck named Bubba. Bubba is from Texas and does not fit into his parking garage. Some students have been picked up at the bus or train stations by no less than the head of the program. Others are wheeling suitcases along on foot. One smells suspiciously like a brewery, but she quickly explains that this is courtesy of an accidental dousing by celebratory fraternity members whom she passed on her way to the dorm.

My children cry when they see where I'm staying. I have, after all, lived in a developing country, but here I expected electricity, a working toilet, a door that locks, a telephone, a bed with pillows and blankets, corners free of mold and mildew, windows that go up and down, and air-conditioning to counteract the 98-degree heat. But I bid children and partner goodbye and meet the steelworkers who are having a conference next door. Then I try to track down some food. All the restaurants in the area seem to be closed for different reasons. I find a small shop and stock up on ramen noodles, crackers, cookies, and Pop Tarts. A siege mentality takes hold.

In five minutes of the first class, I'm lost and ready to go home. I knew I'd need some technical tutoring, but this is beyond me. I've never been on the Internet. I've never touched a mouse except for the cute mammalian kind. The ITO [Instructional

Technology Office] saves the day. They teach me how to go to class, use a virtual chalkboard, text chat, post to Web boards, give a live group presentation, send slides, and they don't make me feel stupid for not knowing it all to begin with. They teach me to back everything up in case of lightning storms. There are no classes on how to clean an M-16 or throw a grenade, but I learn how to build killer Web pages and use a close tag or my Web page won't even appear. And now I have to *use* the technology. I look over the assignments and see that I will be writing three comprehensive papers in three days. A valuing assignment? What is that? Can cost-benefit analysis really be fundamental to librarianship? Perhaps the hundreds of pages of articles using unfamiliar concepts and library terminology I've never heard of will tell me. Doesn't OPAC [online public access catalog] have something to do with gasoline prices?

I work nonstop and don't sleep for several days. All of this feels like an emotional roller coaster. I cry and wait in line for a pay phone to tell my partner I'm coming home. He/she tells me to sleep on it, which inspires me to insane laughter. He/she will support whatever I decide, which sobers me right up. I go back to my room and find my roommate crying. The woman down the hall is throwing papers around saying there's no way she can do this. Complaints are allowed, but no whining, so she gets on with it. We eat Cheetos and finish our papers as the sun comes up. We don't quit. We're friends. As I make my way into class next morning, I notice a large waste basket overflowing with empty coffee cups and try to stay alert as Dean Estabrook and Professor Kimmel negotiate topics.

The night of the valuing assignment arrives. I sit down with a sheaf of statistics and reports, articles I've skimmed, a general idea for a topic, and absolutely no clue whether the proposal I've written will reveal itself to be a financial disaster or a thrifty bit of cleverness. Having never taken statistics, and having a strained relationship with mathematics in general, I launch directly into writing a report, feeling like I'm driving a car into a dark tunnel at a high rate of speed. I suddenly realize that the tryptophan in the turkey sandwich I've just eaten may foil my all-nighter. I try not to glance at the other monitors around me, which appear to hold sleek tables and complicated formulas. As I click at the keyboard, the hours pass, and some of my boot camp colleagues get up and go to bed. I feel a wave of envy, and then look around as the remaining group reorganizes itself into a little clump of solidarity. As each of us encounters a terrible problem with our logic or our numbers, we tell the others. Someone announces, despairingly, that they have found their proposal is a fiscal wipeout. Several of us wail with laughter. Soon, someone else speaks up and we fall apart again. I have to get up and leave the room when I nearly wet my pants at my colleagues' impending disasters.

We obsess about the warning that the LRL [Learning Resources Laboratory] computers reboot automatically at 4:00 A.M. At 3:35 A.M. we start warning each other, calling out every 25 minutes, and then try to figure out why the reboot mysteriously never happens. The clock ticks, the numbers thin, and each time, the group congratulates the lucky one who has finished and earned a few hours of sleep before the final class.

In between the occasional bursts of laughter, the room grows silent and I discover how to build a table in Microsoft Word. Quietly, in the early morning, my budget falls into line. Next, a conclusion dawns upon me as the sun rises. Sometime after 5 A.M., my moment of glory arrives and I log off and walk through the early morning cool to take a shower and sleep. The inebriated steelworkers cheer a welcome as each student who has finished the valuing assignment stumbles back to the dorm. The best thing about the valuing assignment is that we get through it and nothing else is as bad after it's over.

Leaving boot camp, we laugh and tell the next class not to worry. Drink some wine, walk to the dairy barns, take up knitting, try a nude drawing class that is available in a local church sanctuary, catch a movie on the Quad. Whatever it takes to breathe a break—and then go back to work and you'll be fine. They look at us like we're crazy, and thank us later. We sit outside the dorm and wait for our rides. We collectively bawl at the site of a family welcoming one of ours home. We keep crying as planes, trains, and automobiles roll away. We can't wait to see each other again.

But back home at the computer I can't get into my first online class. I panic. The virtually angelic Information Technology Office staff summons me to the electronic tech room and guides me into class. Then I'm kicked off the network. I get back into class and try to figure out what I've missed and when it will be available in the archived session. The sound is scratchy and I feel as if I'm in a World War II resistance movement, crouching in front of a defective radio. While I'm trying to keep up with typing my thoughts in text chat, my oldest child walks into the room and asks when dinner will be ready. "Not now," I say, "I'm in class." Suddenly I hear the professor on live audio from her own house say to one of her children, "Not now, I'm in class." It is a leveling moment. After the lecture we hear heavy breathing like a phone stalker or Darth Vader invading the network, but it is the professor not quite attuned to her sensitive microphone. We are on edge but also awed by the experience of connecting across continents, from Caesar's Palace in Las Vegas, to somebody's beach house on the east or west coast, to a school in Japan. A pastor's wife ducks prayer sessions of a ministerial retreat so she can log into class. From bedrooms, kitchens, offices, rare book rooms, we are dialing in, logging on, learning about LIS and each other.

The next classes are easier. The professors and the students get used to creating continuity across sudden silences of a system gone down. Some of the professors may even suspect that we are multitasking: to attend class is also to bake, eat, clean, do taxes, have multiple computer screens running to start research on homework, talk on the phone, do dishes, plant bulbs, take a quick shower, practice yoga, write poetry, fix the toilet, treat the Halloween tricksters ringing the doorbell. But of course this is not possible, is it? Not all at the same time, anyway. No, we are always completely focused on text chat, group work, audio lectures, slides, guest speakers, database searching, and interface analyzing. The ITO staff tries to calm our frantic nerves with strange musical interludes of Duran Duran and other noise art. But audio issues are only half the story. Visual effects can be the real problem. There's a little red box that allows us to whisper privately to each other or to the professor about our most personal and/or ridiculous thoughts. The trouble is, if we forget to click on the red box, or we leave the room to join a group, our private whisper becomes very public. So a bunch of us are whispering about what we'd like to be drinking, and somebody forgets to click the red box and types the name of a New York bodega drink, "Brass Monkey," to the whole class. After the initial confusion, brass monkey becomes a class synonym for misguided whispers. A private conversation about the Rose Bowl gets mistyped to a whole class as "bowel" during a lecture on government documents. This leads to further confusion. It's a good thing blushes don't show online. We notice that sometimes a student drops out of whisper sessions and we tease her for trying to get her money's worth from the out-of-state tuition rate.

In addition to whispers, gossip is also rampant. One of the professors, Doc D, defends a ghastly, required paper, and gossip begins on e-mail and ends up on a private group bulletin board (BB), that the author is his wife, a rumor he quashes by busting the board. We learn that group BBs are not as private as we thought and start to wonder about the mysterious "zscriptors" who appear in text chat and class attendance lists. They turn out to be automatic chat-logging software, but virtual reality is full of unidentified strangers, some of them camouflaged by frequently changing identities. Once, for instance, all the students in a class suddenly log on with an S in front of their names. They sound like Swedish terms for various diseases—sgwen, smeighan. Sometimes if we're at the end of the alphabet, the list gets too long for the box on the screen. We can't scroll down in that box, so we fall off the class list and we can't click the box to whisper. Then we add an A to our names—asean, apete—to be head of the class and make sure we can play. We assume Halloween identities, from J. Edgar Hoover in drag to Bunny Watson from the movie *Desk Set*. We throw virtual spitballs and realize that having fun technologically is going to get us through the stress of the program—and get us through together. We go to the same movies, miles apart, and swap notes. Oddly enough, *Patton* is a favorite. We meet for real and virtual beer after class.

Common references and stories prove to us that we understand the language of the group and the group is ours. Everyone who hears the word "antelope" leaps to the same experience of the aforementioned Doc D's core course, where the drill is "clear, clean, concise, correct, cogent!" The antelope is none of these, but part of an article about classification that all of us have to read. There are subgroup terminologies from *Star Trek, Harry Potter,* the YaYa sisters, the Digisleepers, and frogs as metaphorical amphibians of the LEEP experience, living in and switching between two very different environments. There is verse, both comical and lyrical. In deconstructing a corporate Web site for the information architecture course, one group member posts an original in-group rap:

T-Dawg rocks the info to the R-K-tecture

> The Land's End suckas go away on a stretcher
> She'll pop a cap on every bad label
> And drink Jakob Nielsen under the table
> She's got a posse called the Oregonian Army
> To help her enforce labelling synonomy
> Call her tough, call her bad, call her pugh-gilistic
> Cuz she's library-information-scientific.

Nobody can decode this except us—we're a team!

Physical experience, too, binds us together even across long distances. Labor starts online; babies are born. Babies are nursed during class, and unattended toddlers deconstruct our households. A hurricane causes electrical blackouts in the midst of a student's presentation; a nor'easter roars outside another's living room window; a class in the GSLIS basement is interrupted by tornado warning sirens full blast; work and family interruptions intrude on every student's class time. On September 11 the Web boards fall silent while we worry and miss each other in a way that proves how deep our sense of community has become. Routine on-campus sessions lead to debauchery as we cram a semester's worth of socializing into one weekend.

We learn from each other as well as the professors. These are students with years of experience working at jobs and life itself. I am not, as I feared, old enough to be everyone else's mother. There's striking diversity of age, background, and learning styles. Students who would never talk out loud in a physical classroom find themselves fluent in text chat. And some who are naturally oral fall silent in print but shine in audio presentations. In on-campus sessions, we recognize our professors by voice rather than appearance. And always, we give each other advice. Take Professor Smith's class, no matter what else you do. Not only is Professor Smith the Goddess of Information Science, but her legendary kindness to students extends to animals. She has a gift for virtual faith healing. My long-haired Siamese cat, deformed both physically and emotionally and hostile to my partner, my dog, any other cat, and all strangers, purrs on my lap throughout all of Linda's lectures and is permanently cured of a nasty disposition by that gentle but persistent voice. Other guides ease the journey as well: superheroes, humble helpers, jesters, prophetesses, and always fellow travelers from our own and other cohorts.

When I reflect on my LEEP experience, I realize how much more I learned than library and information science—the kindness of strangers and of strangers turned friends; the ethic of cooperation, teamwork, sharing, trust; and above all, perseverance. As one LEEPer said, in preparing the next cohort, "there will come a moment when it will take all your willpower not to flee from here." Because of that, I stood firm and stayed. Someone has posted that "a cohort is like a home, it's wherever your heart is." I remember, then, the old saying that a house is not a home until it has seen a birth, a marriage, and a death. We've seen those and wherever we are, when we log onto LEEP, we're home.

And beyond LEEP? Because we're used to long-distance relationships, many of us keep them up. Sometimes we go out of our way to meet in physical space, as well. We swap mothership stories, introduce our significant others, arrange and photograph mini-reunions to send to missing companions across the Web. We initiate new LEEPers with our lore. We bristle when critics of long-distance education call it isolating. LEEPers are everywhere. The day will come when LEEPlore is library lore.

Conclusion

The end of this LEEPtale is just the start of understanding the way computer technology both changes education and at the same time continues its best traditions, including social bonding. Each of us belongs to many different folk groups. One of those is our educational community. In it, consciously or not, we collect verbal, material, and customary lore that tells us who to be and how to behave. Our initial study of online education stories has shown that:

1. LEEPlore is folklore, with variants in a dynamic pattern of tradition and innovation.
2. LEEPlore *as* folklore is proof of a distributed learning community with deep commonalities of experience, values, and language.
3. LEEPlore can function as initiation and community builder. (One important aspect of the study is that it has actually increased an awareness and sense of community, unlike studies where outsiders' observations sometimes intrude on a community to detrimental effect.)
4. LEEPlore features traditional narrative aspects as reflected in the analysis of a central story, the examination of humor as tonally thematic, and the assemblage of a prototypical LEEPtale.

The implications for other distributed learning programs are many, including the importance of periodic face-to-face group sessions to generate and support the bonding that continues to thrive online. Given the evidence that students learn deeply from each other, especially in professional programs where many are working in the field already, this kind of community bonding is crucial. Online education becomes professional collaboration. As education relies more and more heavily on distance programs, students can enter with faith that they can form close, lasting bonds. One

LEEP student was perusing the Web for associations to our leap frog motif when she came upon an epithet coined by the author Julia Cameron. Meant as advice for writers, it's even more apt for future online student relationships: "Leap and the Net Will Appear!"

We will end this study by letting one of the LEEP students give us a slice-of-life rendition of her online experience:

> My first class was last fall . . . and was Reference 404 . . . Actually, my daughter took LIS 404 LEB with me. She was four to seven months old at the time, and spent each class with me. Most of the time, she'd spend the first half in her little chair with me typing with one hand, and stuffing rice cereal in her maw with the other. When she'd get tired of that, I'd hold her on my lap, and she'd watch the text scroll up the screen. Many days we'd end up with her nursing until she fell asleep in my lap, all while I worked in room 'k' with my group.
>
> She was still pretty young during my all-day session, so she ended up in the A & I database searching lecture so she could nurse while [the instructor] talked! I was so appreciative of [the instructor's] and the rest of the class's flexibility in that regard. I didn't experience that in too many of my on campus classes.
>
> And let me tell you about what happened last week! I'm in my 405LE class, and my husband says, "I have to run a quick errand. I'll be back" and then left Lila to her own devices in the living room. I'd run back and forth between my study and the living room (which is baby-safer than my study), but not often enough to stop her from eating dirt from my plants, eating cactus seedings, pulling books and CD's off shelves, removing pillows and linen from the futon, spreading a thin layer of her toys all over, and just DESTROYING Jeremy's grade book! His papers and ungraded exams were everywhere! She crunched up (and ate!) pages out of his book. He came home and was a little surprised, I'd say. So, I'd say that Lila has enjoyed my LEEP classes, too!
>
> Seriously, though, I got so much out of those LEEP classes, and not just from the instructors. I appreciated that so many of my LEEP classmates were working in the real world, and had such VALUABLE experience to share! Reading everyone's ideas and comments could've been a class in itself! That was the most beneficial aspect of my LEEP experience. I'd happily take more LEEP classes if I could, and I wish that GSLIS would offer a continuing ed type deal via LEEP for LIS professionals in the field. It's a great learning experience, and an awesome way to collaborate with librarians across the nation. I'm honored to have been a participant in such an incredible learning experience, and to have met so many wonderful people, and I'm proud of it. Thanks for the memories, guys! (jezmynne 6 May 2002 02:05:05)

References

Aarne, A. (1961). *The types of the folktale: A classification and bibliography*. (S. Thompson, Rev. and Trans.). Folklore Fellows Communications, no.184. Helsinki: Academia Scientiarum Fennica.

Baker, R. L. (1983). The folklore of students. In Dorson, Richard M. (Ed.), *Handbook of American folklore* (pp. 106–114). Bloomington: Indiana University Press.

Bauman, R. (1977). *Verbal arts as performance*. Rowley, MA: Newbury House Publishers.

Bauman, R. (1986). *Story, performance, and event: Contextual studies of oral narrative*. Cambridge: Cambridge University Press.

Baym, N. (1995) The performance of humor in computer-mediated communication. *Journal of Computer-Mediated Communication, 1*(2). Retrieved from http://www.ascusc.org/jcmc/vol1/issue2/baym.html.

Ben-Amos, D. (1993). 'Context' in context. *Western Folklore, 52*, 209–226.

Campbell, J. (1973). *The hero with a thousand faces*. NY: Princeton University Press.

Chase, R. (1948). *Grandfather tales*. Boston: Houghton Mifflin.

De Koning, E., & Weiss, R. I. (2002). The relational humor inventory: Functions of humor in close relationships. *The American Journal of Family Therapy, 30*, 1–18.

Dundes, A. (1964). Texture, text, and context. *Southern Folklore Quarterly, 28*, 261–265.

Freud, S. (1928). Humor. In J. Strachey (Ed. and Trans.), *Collected papers, volume V* (pp. 215–221). London: Hogarth Press.

Freud, S. (1960). *Jokes and their relation to the unconscious*. J. Strachey (Ed. and Trans.) New York: W. W. Norton & Company.

Haythornthwaite, C., Kazmer, M. M., Robins, J., & Shoemaker, S. (2000). Community development among distance learners: Temporal and technological dimensions. *Journal of Computer-Mediated Communication, 6*(1). Retrieved from http://www.ascusc.org/jcmc/vol6/issue1/haythornthwaite.html (Reprinted in this volume).

Henman, L. D. (2001). Humor as a coping mechanism: Lessons from POWS. *Humor International Journal of Humor Research, 14*(1), 83–94.

Hsu, S., & Bruce, B. C. (1998). The missing borders: Pedagogical reflections from distance education. *Teaching Education, 10*(1), 47–54.

Jensen, W. M. (1965). The esoteric-exoteric factor in folklore. In A. Dundes (Ed.), *The study of folklore*. Eaglewood Cliffs, NJ: Prentice-Hall, Inc.

Jones, S. G. (Ed.). (1995). *Cybersociety: Computer-mediated communication and community*. Thousand Oaks, CA: Sage.

Kollock, P., & Smith, M. A. (1999). Communities in cyberspace. In M. A. Smith, & P. Kollock (Eds.), *Communities in cyberspace* (pp. 3–25). New York: Routledge.

Lau, K. (1998). On the rhetorical use of legend: U.C. Berkeley campus lore as a strategy for coded protest. *Contemporary Legend: The Journal of the International Society for Contemporary Legend Research*, n.s. *1*, 1–20.

Lau, K. J. (2002). This text which is not one: Dialectics of self and culture in experimental autoethnography. *Journal of Folklore Research, 39*(2/3), 243–259.

Lefcourt, H. M. (2001). *Humor: the psychology of living buoyantly*, New York: Kluwer Academic.

Lefcourt, H. M., & Martin, R. (1986). *Humor and life stress: Antidote to adversity*. New York: Springer-Verlag.

Marvin, L. (1995). Spoof, spam, lurk, and lag: The aesthetics of text-based virtual realities. *Journal of Computer-Mediated Communication, 1*(2). Retrieved from http://www.ascusc.org/jcmc/vol1/issue2/marvin.html

Matte, G. (2001). A psychoanalytical perspective of humor. *Humor: International Journal of Humor Research, 14*(3), 223–241.

Morreall, J. (1991) Humor and work. *Humor: International Journal of Humor Research.* 4(3–4) 1991, 359–373.

Nezlek, J. B., & Derks, P. (2001). Use of humor as a coping mechanism, psychological adjustment, and social interaction. *Humor: International Journal of Humor Research, 14*(4), 395–413.

Palmer, J. (1994). *Taking humour seriously.* London & New York: Routledge.

Rheingold, H. (1993). *The virtual community: Homesteading on the electronic frontier.* Reading, MA: Addison-Wesley.

Ruhleder, K. (2000). The virtual ethnographer: Fieldwork in distributed electronic environments. *Field Methods, 12*(1), 3–17.

Sapienza, F. (1996). Hacker folklore on Usenet: A rhetorical approach to hacker subculture. *EJournal, 6*(2). Retrieved from http://www.ucalgary.ca/ejournal/archive/ej-6-2.txt.

Sherry, L. (1996) Issues in distance learning. *International Journal of Educational Telecommunications, 1*(4), 337–365.

Terrion, J. L., & Ashforth, B. E. (2002). From 'I' to 'we': The role of putdown humor and identity in the development of a temporary group. *Human Relations, 55*(1), 55–88.

Thompson, S. (1956). *Motif-Index of folk-literature: A classification of narrative elements in folktales, ballads, myths, fables, mediaeval romances, exempla, fabliaux, jest-books, and local legends.* 6 vols. Bloomington: Indiana University Press.

Toelken, B. (1968). The folklore of academe. In J. H. Brunvand (Ed.), *The study of American folklore* (pp. 317–337). New York: W. W. Norton & Company.

Toelken, B. (1996). *The dynamics of folklore.* Logan: Utah State University Press.

Trice, H. M., & Beyer, J. M. (1993). *The cultures of work organizations.* Englewood Cliffs, NJ: Prentice Hall.

Whites, S., & Winzelberg, A. (1992). Laughter and stress. *Humor: International Journal of Humor Research, 5*(4), 343–355.

CHAPTER 5

Michelle M. Kazmer
Caroline Haythornthwaite

Juggling Multiple Social Worlds: Distance Students Online and Offline

Using the Internet means bringing into our offline lives yet another social world, one in which we operate through media, communicating and maintaining ties with people who live at a distance and who we may rarely or never meet. How successfully do we manage integration of this new world into our existing world? Do worlds collide or seamlessly integrate into a cohesive whole? For one year, the authors followed 17 students as they engaged in a distance-learning program. The authors explored their involvement with the online learning community and how this affected their relationships with family, work, volunteer, and peer groups. Students' satisfaction with the program increased, and anxiety about operating in the online world decreased, with increased involvement with the learning community. This was realized at the expense of offline communities and activities. However, the authors also found a reverse trend when students reengaged with offline life as they neared the end of their program. This work highlights the importance of temporal aspects of involvement in online worlds and provides some insight into the priorities, needs, and rewards involved with managing multiple worlds.

As the Internet becomes integrated with our lives, we bring into our offline lives another social world (Strauss, 1978) where we operate through media, often at a distance, and with people we may rarely or never meet (Wellman & Gulia, 1999; Wellman, et al., 1996). Despite increasing use of Internet technology, most of those who add an online world to their existing worlds enter a new domain. In doing so, they add new norms and conventions for interaction; expand networks of friends, coworkers, and co-learners; and accept new ways of maintaining ties with others. When a new online world is added, how do participants manage relations among worlds? Do worlds collide or are they seamlessly integrated into a cohesive whole? Are we faced with a competitive process where time in one world is stolen from another or a collaborative process whereby conduct and content in one world aid and influence that of another?

One increasingly popular arena of online life is Internet-based distance education (Harasim, Hiltz, Teles, & Turoff, 1995; Renninger & Shumar, 2001). This has extended the reach of universities and other educational organizations and increased opportunities for students to pursue degrees. Yet little is known about the impact of this form of education on students' lives. How do students manage their lives with the addition of this online world? How is the online experience more than just adding the educational component to their lives? How do they prioritize different aspects of their lives? Answering such questions and understanding the burdens and challenges associated with online education is important for preparing students entering and coping with such programs. Thus, we are interested in the social phenomena associated with balancing or even juggling online and offline commitments, and in using this understanding to enhance the overall experience of students.

To explore the character and impact of Internet-based distance education, we have been studying the experiences of distance students in a graduate degree program at the Graduate School of Library and Information Science (GSLIS), University of Illinois, known as LEEP (Library Education Experimental Program).[1] In this article, we present results from a qualitative analysis of longitudinal interviews with 17 students that describe how students' online and offline worlds overlap and how they manage and juggle their multiple world responsibilities.

A Social Worlds Perspective

A social world consists of people who share activities, space, and technology and who communicate with one another (for a full explanation of this concept, see Strauss, 1978). Each world is coordinated around a primary activity (e.g., learning, tending family, earning a living) and is usually associated with one site (e.g., the university, the home, the workplace), and yet these worlds intersect. It is this interaction that is of interest. As Strauss (1978) noted, "A major analytic task is to discover such intersecting and to trace the associated processes, strategies and consequences" (p. 123). Here we explore the intersection of online learning with other worlds that students inhabit. We find this perspective useful because it "makes a strong contribution to understanding the complexities of human social organization by aiming to grasp rather than deny them" (Clarke, 1991, p. 119). It promotes exploration of all aspects of an individual's experience, recognizing that social worlds emerge from the way that individuals allocate time and resources. It also lacks the affective baggage of the often imprecise term *community* and allows description of spheres of individual activity without necessitating the attainment of intangible, group-oriented experience. A number of recent studies have found this approach useful for understanding how individual involvement in multiple worlds affects perceptions and use of technology. Covi (1996) described how scientific researchers' multiple social world memberships interact to affect the way they use digital libraries; Fitzpatrick, Kaplan, and Mansfield (1996) found that systems administrators' involvement in multiple worlds affected their perceptions and use of their work space; and Star, Bowker, and Neumann (2003) showed how involvement in multiple worlds affected the use of information systems. In the Internet context, the social worlds perspective leads us to consider all of an individual's worlds, not just online ones, and the way in which online and offline life intersect and interact with each other. This is in contrast to approaches that tend to classify the Internet as a social world in itself. For example, a number of articles about the HomeNet project discussed how using the Internet affects other aspects of people's lives (Kiesler & Kraut, 1999; Kraut, Kiesler, Mukhopadhyay, Scherilis, & Patterson, 1998; Kraut, Patterson, et al., 1998), and Nie and Erbring (2000) discussed the social consequences of innovation and how the Internet affects personal interactions.

Treating the Internet as one social world is not without consequences. Examining time spent on the Internet tends to obscure the use of technology for a specific social purpose. The approach implies that when people begin a new activity, such as Internet use, all the time spent doing the new activity is subtracted from other activities. This hides the way that activities overlap and how time spent online can benefit offline relationships. Such a priori definitions of what constitutes a world fail to acknowledge the way in which individuals spread their social relations across multiple means of communication and social contexts, blurring locational and medium-specific definitions of worlds (Haythornthwaite, 2000; Haythornthwaite & Wellman, 1998; Wellman & Hampton, 1999; Wellman, et al., 1996). Executives conduct business on the golf course, we receive family phone calls at work and business calls at home, and we use the Internet to maintain local and distant ties with those who share common interests. The Internet defies designation as maintainer of one social world—it is instead a medium through which we have the opportunity to maintain multiple social worlds.

The social world perspective is a particularly useful way to frame examination of distance education students because they are involved in many spheres of activity and must cope with what at first seem separate worlds of online and offline commitments. We turn now to the multiple worlds of these distance learners, beginning with an overview of their educational environment and proceeding to the results of our analysis.

The Distance Education Environment and Data Collection

The distance education program option known as LEEP allows students to complete a master's degree in library and information science (LIS) at a distance through courses conducted via the Internet. Students begin their program with a two-week intensive on-campus session (*boot camp*). All remaining courses are taken from home via the Internet, with students required to come to campus once a semester. Distance courses are conducted using a combination of synchronous and asynchronous interaction. Live lectures (given from twice a semester to weekly, depending on the class) are delivered via RealAudio and use Internet Relay Chat (IRC) for student questions and discussion. Web boards (Web-based bulletin boards) are used for class discussions and exercises and for program-wide announcements and discussion. All students have e-mail accounts, and a toll-free phone number is available for calls to campus. Assignments, which may include group projects, are submitted as Web pages, Web board postings, or attachments to e-mails, and less frequently by fax and regular mail. Grading and comments are returned to students via regular mail or e-mail.

For one academic year, we followed 17 students as they began and progressed through their distance education experience. Four one-hour phone interviews were conducted with each student in midterm fall 1998, near the end of the fall 1998 term, midterm spring 1999, and near the end of the spring 1999 term. Interviews were tape recorded and transcribed. Names used below are pseudonyms, with the names reflecting the gender of the interviewee.

The interviewees were at various stages in their degree program: Of the group, three began the program in 1996, two in 1997, and the remainder in 1998. All were new to this type of program and to distance education. Each student worked outside the home (16 full-time and 1 part-time, but full-time by the end of the year), and most (12 of 17) in library or library-related endeavors (e.g., archives), with 1 to 20 years' experience. Students were all mature adults living in their own accommodations, usually with a spouse or significant other; three had small children and four had grown children; and only two lived alone.

Our interviews explored students' involvement with the online learning community and how this affected and was affected by their relationships with family, work, volunteer, and peer groups. Analysis of each set of interviews was used to formulate hypotheses and areas of questioning for the following interviews. Analysis consisted of coding the data for themes in student experiences, comparing for commonalities and differences, and analyzing the themes that emerged (for details, see Haythornthwaite, Kazmer, Robins, & Shoemaker, 2000). Questions focused on the exchange of resources between the interviewee and people in their personal social network (Haythornthwaite, 2000, 2002; Wasserman & Faust, 1994; Wellman, 1997). We explored involvement with and obligations toward fellow students, family, friends, parents, coworkers, and so forth; who provided social, technical, and other support; who helped students manage classwork, child care, household chores, and so forth; and what kinds of online and offline activities students engaged in and with whom. An earlier article described how students strongly perceived LEEP to be a community, one primarily founded on interactions among students (Haythornthwaite, et al., 2000; see also Kazmer, 2000). They provided each other with social support, companionship, major emotional support, and sociability. At first this environment is unknown territory; norms and conventions are sought but little understood. Writing publicly through Web board postings combines the agony of self-exposure with the self-doubts of the returning student (for an examination of concerns about self-presentation, see Bregman & Haythornthwaite, 2001). However, it is not long before students are old hands at online exchanges, carrying on conversations according to the norms of this environment.

The Multiple Worlds of Distance Learners

Involvement in any intensive program can be expected to affect other aspects of students' lives, and here we focus on how involvement in an intensive online experience interacts with obligations and commitments in other domains. Our attention to the management of different social worlds derives from a desire to prepare new students as they enter the program and to make recommendations for the program. We wanted to know what helps students to work through and complete this program. Other research has pointed to a loss of real-life engagement with increasing online engagement (e.g., Kraut, Patterson, et al., 1998; Nie & Erbring, 2000). A program that takes too much from offline life may become unmanageable for students. Thus, we are interested in the extent to which LEEP interferes with offline involvement, what impact this has on students' lives, and where that impact becomes critical for remaining in the program. At present, the program has a very high retention and completion rate, a situation we want to maintain.

The first step in understanding the interaction of worlds is to identify the separate worlds in which students are involved. Our interviews reveal three mandatory worlds that individuals dwell in and rotate through on a daily basis: LEEP, work, and home. Obligations in each cannot be shirked, although occasionally they can be delayed. There are also other optional worlds: extended family and friends, volunteer work, and the LIS profession.

The LEEP Distance Learning World

LEEP is inhabited by instructors, administrators, support staff, and students. Among these inhabitants we can distinguish social circles within the LEEP world, such as cohort members who shared the same boot camp, students who have been or who are in the same class, circles of close friends, students who have worked on group projects together, and administrator-student and instructor-student combinations. However, when students refer to their LEEP world, they are usually referring to time spent with other students: Their bonding and sense of a LEEP community comes from interaction with other students while grappling with technology, discovering communication norms, progressing into the LIS profession, and sharing a world that no one in their local world understands (for details see Haythornthwaite, et al., 2000). Because our examination is taken from the perspective of the student, our discussion of the LEEP world generally refers to the student-student LEEP community.

Work World

Work encompasses where students earn their living, their job, and the people with whom they work. Work world members include supervisors, coworkers, and others who work within the same organization. Supervisors have often been instrumental in helping individuals enter the program, and their support makes it easier for students to reconcile their LEEP and work worlds. Whether work is in the same domain as LEEP also makes a difference for students. Synergy between what is learned and experienced in LEEP and what is valued and rewarded at work plays an important part in integrating these worlds. Those in unrelated work fields express a craving for contact with the profession that increases as they continue through the program, whereas those in related work fields find immediate applications for knowledge gained in LEEP. Working in a common domain provides students with access to willing and informed coworkers, and through them with access to further remote coworkers. Moreover, their coworkers' familiarity with the program confers immediate prestige on the student and acceptance of the student's goals. Those outside the profession find it harder to gain this recognition or understanding.

Home World

Home primarily comprises immediate family—spouses, significant others, and children below college age. Young children occupy a central position in this world. They require attention at home, and parents are involved with their school and extracurricular activities. Although spouses and significant others are highly important to the LEEP students' personal worlds, it is children who take first place in their attention and prioritizing.

Optional Worlds

The optional worlds include, in decreasing order of obligation, other family and close friends, remote family and old friends, and volunteer groups (e.g., parent-teacher organizations, church, civic organizations). Although geographically close others tend to get less attention while an individual is involved in LEEP, students report increased contact with remote relatives and old friends as a result of e-mail connectivity and the students' new and growing presence on the Internet.

The professional library and information science world is another optional world, but one that becomes more significant to students over time. As they progress through the program, they increasingly identify with the profession and are identified by others as members of the profession; they become aware of the principles behind the rules applied in local practice. This world is enacted through a mix of membership in professional associations, participation in association meetings, interactions at work, and interactions within libraries and with librarians.

Juggling Multiple Worlds

> Enrico Rastelli, the most legendary juggler of the twentieth century . . . stands, ostrichlike, on one leg, with a large ball balanced on the top of each foot, one on his bent knee, one in each hand, and one on top of his head. A stick extends from his mouth, and a ball perches on the end of the stick, balancing yet another stick, which is balancing yet another ball. The juggler looks like a human house of cards. (Levine, 1998, p. 76)

Juggling—a term offered by several students—is an apt metaphor for students' mode of operation. Students juggle, as well as handle, decide, rearrange, or accommodate LEEP and their other obligations. For example, Holly feels that "anybody who's a mom and who's juggling work, family, and this LEEP program" will understand her experience. Like Enrico Rastelli, they balance multiple responsibilities in a continuous state of precariousness.

The juggling image also accords with Strauss's (1978) comment that "most social world and sub-world entries involve *orbiting* processes; i.e., moving from one to another, retaining both or dropping the original, plus simultaneous memberships" (p. 124). Students enter the LEEP world, but the LEEP world also enters their array of orbiting worlds. Although in principle adding LEEP is the same as adding any new social world, the online environment offers extra challenges. Students must learn how to handle LEEP, including how to operate the technology, how to communicate online, what the rules and protocols are, and how long tasks will take. They add not just an extra world but one with new rules of entry, exit, and engagement.

Juggling LEEP with ongoing activities requires active management and conscious attention. Strategies for juggling include integrating LEEP into the orbit, accomplished consciously by prioritizing and scheduling time and effort, and isolating LEEP for attention, often by carving out personal space for LEEP work. Over time, the process of switching between and juggling obligations in multiple worlds gives way to synergy, in which what is learned in one world helps in another. The next sections examine managing strategies for successful LEEP engagement, then examine how juggling evolves into synergy for many students.

Let the Juggling Begin

Ted, like Holly quoted before, is adept at juggling. He manages work, school, family, travel, and professional writing responsibilities. In his first year, Ted had to apply extra effort to build a schedule that would enable him to stay involved with his family and still get some sleep. He made a conscious decision to put off tasks, such as gardening, that could be done when he was less busy, and to add tasks that supported his LEEP work, such as implementing changes to technology at home (including adding a telephone line). He prioritized his children's activities as number one, even if that meant missing a LEEP class or taking a lower grade in a course.

Ted, and many like him, bring LEEP into their lives as an extra world. Unlike on-campus students, who generally are pursuing the degree full-time and have often pre-planned by leaving work, LEEP students drop very little. In this sense they are similar to on-campus students who take the degree part-time while holding full-time jobs. However, the LEEP student's load is different because of the newness of the computer-based distance environment. They integrate not only the world of education but also the world of computer-mediated communication into their lives.[2] Students remarked that they are getting a dual education—one in the subject area and one in the social and technical use of communication technologies.

Students prioritize and schedule their time and effort. Most students report that more effort is needed to maintain a presence in the virtual LEEP environment than they believe would be needed in an on-campus setting (Haythornthwaite, et al., 2000). This adds to their overall load; newer students like Jeff often say that assignments "took a lot longer than I expected" and that they feel compelled to work harder to project a good image online (e.g., in their Web board postings) (see Bregman & Haythornthwaite, 2001; Haythornthwaite, et al., 2000). At first, students focus on managing additional time demands within the 24-hour day by engaging in an ongoing process of assessing what has to be done and what can wait, letting go of things that are reparable (such as close family relationships) or expendable (like watching television), cramming what has to be done into the remaining hours of the day during the semester, and using breaks as opportunities to catch up on delayed activities and relationships. Managing strategies include prioritizing and planning, scheduling and appropriating time and space, and calculated neglect and repair of specific activities.

Prioritizing and Planning

In allocating time and effort, students balance emotional needs (e.g., with family and children) with task needs (e.g., schoolwork), and accomplishing tasks (paid work, dinner, and homework) with managing relationships with inhabitants of their worlds (children, spouses, bosses, coworkers, friends, and family). They decide which of their worlds is more important and then which tasks and relationships are most important within the world. They identify first the expendable tasks, then the reparable ones, and finally the crucial ones. Although prioritizing revolves around LEEP (a strange new constant that has a high priority associated with students' lifelong goals), it is not the top priority at all times. Work and home, particularly children, compete equally for time and attention, so each is prioritized and reprioritized over time. Some students plan ahead for the semester. They decide how many worlds to juggle and, like Holly, drop optional activities before they begin LEEP or, like Beth, decide that LEEP must be balanced with demands of other worlds:

> Before I started LEEP I was real involved in [a particular civic organization] here in my town, and I was on the board and real active, and I pretty much had to just forgo that completely. (Holly)

> My rate is only one course a semester because I have to do all the [children's] sports and the academic [LEEP work] and maintain my family. (Beth)

Others, such as Barbara, demonstrate more day-to-day planning:

> As far as family activities . . . what typically would happen is you know if there was a family activity that was going to take place, say, over the weekend when I was going to be doing some studying, I would do as much of the activities then as I could and then . . . maybe if I could stay up later that night you know to do the work.

Although Ted deals with more minute-to-minute planning,

> I still have not been able to teach my kids not to disturb me when I'm working. It's hard to do when they come up with a math problem they don't understand or a fight. . . . You have to stop and quell that.

Holly and others find they have "had to say 'no' to a lot more activities: involvement in church, involvement in my kids' school, socially." They say "no" because they have responsibilities in other worlds, which have to be managed by planning:

> I have a family, I have to look at my time and say, 'Oops!' I've got a couple of hours block on Saturday to do this, I can't plan to do other things. So I've really found over the last year especially that I'd had to be much more of a manager of my time. (Holly)

> Rather than being able to say, 'Okay, well, yes, I can just put some laundry in and then run out the door and spend the rest of the afternoon [with extended family] doing whatever.' . . . I have to say things like, 'No, I've got to at least spend a few hours today working on this' or 'Six hours today doing this and then maybe tomorrow we'll see.' (Barbara)

Although according to Beth, adding the LEEP world "cramps your time," successful planners—such as Holly, Barbara, and Beth—are active planners who can say, "I know what to do and how to allocate my time." At the other end of the managing continuum are those who manage on the fly—cramming, losing sleep, or skipping meals rather than saying no to activities and relationships. Ellen admits that "sometimes my recreational activities interfere with when I need to be sitting alone doing my homework." She attributes this in part to the lack of synchronous time for class, that "there's no set time to sit down." The immediacy of the real world of friends overshadows, for her, the call of the virtual world. Many, even those who are in control of their planning, steal time from sleep for LEEP work:

> Sometimes I don't get to my work until 9 o'clock, so by the end of the week I'm desperately needing sleep. (Ted)

> I'm up until 1 o'clock or 2 o'clock . . . not just one at a time, or once a week, but a few nights a week to do the work because that's when it could be done. (Barbara)

Setting priorities is not done once and for all. Although some students do make firm decisions on priorities before beginning the program (e.g., Beth), all must at times make choices about what to complete and what to let slide. Those who drop activities before beginning the program often see time-consuming participation in the LEEP world as temporary and have a longer view of when reparation can be made. Barbara talks about trade-offs in terms of these short- and long-term effects. After some 1 and 2 o'clock bedtimes, she admits:

> I might not be 100 percent as productive at work [after late night studying], but for me that is a short-term situation. I know that the long-term effect of me being involved in this program and getting the knowledge I think is going to . . . outweigh those drowsy moments.

Students in their first semester often make on-the-fly decisions. They may be aware of the need to prioritize, but have not yet developed strategies for doing so. Doris, in her first year as a LEEP student, explains:

> Part of my problem, why I'm writing the paper at night and things like that, is because I don't set priorities, I don't forgo enough, and maybe I should just sort of accept that I should.

Similarly, Ted found out the hard way about the importance of setting priorities:

> I remember from my first assignment I did an all-nighter, then went to work the next day. At my age I can't do that any more.

As students prioritize on the fly, they follow a consistent hierarchy of dispensing with activities. First to go are solitary leisure activities such as television, reading, needlework, and gardening. Next are social leisure activities with friends such as going to the movies or out to dinner. Volunteer work, if not dropped before beginning LEEP, is dropped or reduced at this stage. Next, classes, work, sleep, and even eating are compromised.[3] Students may begin to use class time for other homework, work time for LEEP, and sleep time for anything else—prioritizing has given way to cramming. The clean separation of worlds fragments as one world intrudes on another and time and energy are borrowed from one world with a promise of repayment in the future. Last to go are time with family, particularly children, and schoolwork itself. But even these can give way: Family has to "understand that [Mommy or Daddy] is doing work now and can't be disturbed" and expectations for grades can be reduced. The new demands on students' time are not simply schoolwork in a traditional sense. Social associations with other students take time and include socialization into the profession. Learning includes not just subject content but also how to implement and use the technology, how to function socially in a virtual learning environment, and how to juggle priorities in multiple worlds. We should not see on-the-fly prioritizing as a failure to prioritize, schedule, and stick to a plan, but rather as the reason for success. As Mark Levine (1998) remarked:

> It isn't simply that jugglers can do things that other people can't, I thought, but that jugglers are a peculiarly apt embodiment of the human effort to cope gracefully with more demands, from more directions, than one person can reasonably be expected to manage. (p. 76)

We note that the ability to cope gracefully, or even to cope at all, may distinguish these students from others who try to juggle multiple worlds. Both deliberate planning and coping with change on the fly are important for balancing worlds. Although we believe that other populations may also function in this way, it is possible that such coping strategies are a function of the maturity and higher educational attainment of these students. Involvement in online worlds may overwhelm less accomplished users, creating the kind of withdrawing from real-world activity observed in other studies.

Scheduling and Appropriating

Claiming Time and Territory for the LEEP World

Although students juggle multiple worlds, they occasionally need to exist in one world, separated from the others. One priority is to concentrate on LEEP work without interruptions.[4] Even students who prioritize cannot succeed without creating time and space to accomplish prioritized activities. Allotting fixed periods of time for tasks in LEEP is initially difficult for students. They are unfamiliar with the technologies, norms, and protocols of the online environment; unable to determine how long schoolwork will take; and unable to find the time needed for LEEP work.

One technique is to leverage the benefits of the asynchronous portions of the program. Doris, for example, prefers to work at night; she discovered that she could do LEEP work then, leaving her daytime schedule fairly intact. Other students, like Clarissa, may not prefer to work at night, but that is the time most open in their schedules and is therefore when many LEEP tasks get done. Holly leverages the ability to work asynchronously to do her LEEP work in small chunks throughout the day. The interleaving and wedging of LEEP into nonreserved time becomes so important to these students that they can come to resent actual meeting times, for example, live classes and on-campus sessions. This can result in tension between synchronous and asynchronous operations in LEEP, reflecting a split between those who crave synchronous interaction and those who resent the imposition on their schedules.

Another technique used by students is to create territory in the home world where they can carry out LEEP work. Students have mixed success in this. Beth found herself moving to various locations in her house as family members needed each workspace for other purposes; Ted tried locations around his house to find a quiet space where he could work. Clarissa, after one year of distance education, was still wrestling with creating private space for herself and her schoolwork. Even when physical space can be claimed, family members, especially children, often have difficulties accepting these boundaries between worlds as barriers to interaction. As Barbara mentioned, young children don't understand that "if Mommy has the door to her office closed you're not supposed to be bothering her." Clarissa does different kinds of work in her room, some of which is interruptible and some of which is not, and family members cannot tell the difference. Even when they have claimed space, students still split their attention between the LEEP and home worlds. Because managing multiple worlds includes prioritizing on the fly, some interruptions take precedence over LEEP work. Maintaining relationships is part of multiple world management, and availability, especially for children, is often more important than completing school tasks.

Students often create LEEP space in their work worlds; they use computers at work to do their LEEP work (often with the consent of employers). Jerry, a first-year LEEP student, has a home office but sometimes does LEEP at work, despite the threat of interruptions:

> Every once in a while something will come up at work and I can't get away for the synchronous session at home so I'll be at work so I'll do it at work, but I try to do it at home so I can participate without getting phone calls and interruptions.

Thus, work, like home, often places the student in two worlds simultaneously, with people and activities from these environments interfering with attention to the LEEP world.

Another world separation technique is to keep involvement in LEEP away from the people in their other worlds—hoarding LEEP to themselves. Thus, Ellen says:

> As far as bringing someone else or a significant other to the on-campus,[5] I'm not ready to do that. I've heard other people say that too. 'I'm not ready to mix that up just yet.'

Many also become fatigued at explaining LEEP to others. Although eager to demonstrate it when they first begin, they soon do not want to have to explain it to outsiders anymore. Thus, whereas juggling is important in managing multiple worlds, so too is concentrating exclusively on particular worlds at particular times. Although this section has discussed how to give attention to the LEEP world, the following section describes how individuals pay back other worlds, creating the needed balance over time.

Neglect and Repair

As students prioritize their multiple world activities, they decide that responsibilities in some worlds can be neglected with the promise of future repair. Relationships with spouses and partners, close and extended family, and friends most often require repair. Students depend on semester breaks and summers to nurture interpersonal relations neglected during academic semesters. Alice shared with us her experiences in prioritizing and repairing some interpersonal relationships. She maintained close touch with her family, but found that involvement in LEEP reduced her visits with friends from once a month to once every two months, and involved shifting visits to the summer when she did not take classes. To stem the potential impact of neglect on interpersonal relationships, some students do frequent "temperature taking," thinking about and discussing how both partners can continue to nurture the relationship. A common solution is to schedule time together, setting up dates to watch movies or just hang out (Kazmer, 2000).

Others find that the work world must be neglected, if not wholly given up. Barbara feels that the short-term loss of attentiveness to work will be repaid later with her increased knowledge. Sue, however, found no alternative but to change work worlds to accommodate her LEEP world:

> What I did was quit that job, because the director didn't want to be more flexible with more time off. I didn't want to ask her. I could see that she wasn't going to be flexible with it. So I quit that job and now I have a job with less hours. Now I have more time to do my homework and I did that on purpose, because I don't feel I need that extra stress.

However, like any other world, sometimes it is LEEP that must be neglected and revisited later. Doris, having a difficult semester personally, shared that after the loss of a good friend:

> It just seemed like a monkey wrench kept being thrown into my plan to be methodical about this, so I was kind of proud of myself for getting that assignment out of the way and just begin like, okay, now the crises have all past and I'm going to make more of a plan and stick to it.

Thus, a rounded view of students' lives considers not just the day-to-day rhythm of home, work, and school, but also the way in which individuals use the rhythm of the semesters to balance worlds.

From Juggling to Synergy

Juggling requires constant attention, and students must be responsive to changes in each world for the next throw to be successful. For example, Clarissa rearranges her own activities to accommodate LEEP, but those rearrangements affect her husband, who had to miss activities to do child care; her work, where she had to take days to complete LEEP work; and her meeting schedules for other groups. Although students begin with multiple adjustments to separate worlds, soon they notice ways in which their multiple worlds blend together and help one another. Janet sums this up best:

> More than being an educational program, it's more a life program. I think in order to be in LEEP we have a sense of where you are and where you're going at home and at work and at school. In my past experience in graduate and undergraduate programs when you focus on school it's school and when you focus on home it's home. But here the lines are all very fuzzy. I didn't anticipate that, that the lines would be so fuzzy between work and school and home.

Cross-World Synergy

Where lines between LEEP and work, home, and other worlds begin to blend, students experience opportunities for mutual benefit. Instead of collisions, synergy develops between what they are doing and learning in LEEP and what they are doing in other worlds. Positive synergies have been seen primarily between LEEP and work, but also with all other worlds. These include the transfer of knowledge from one domain to another and access to a network of others on whom to call for expertise and advice (see also Nardi, Whittaker, & Schwarz, 2000).

Benefits flow from LEEP to the workplace as students gain course content and technical expertise that they can apply at work. They may be able to assume additional work duties or do projects for LEEP that can be used in the workplace. Barbara was given an extra opportunity at work specifically because of LEEP:

> Because of my involvement in the program, one of my colleagues said, 'Oh you'd be a good person to do this . . . you should do the demo for this because she's a librarian and you're in the library school.' . . . That was kind of nice. That was one where being involved with the program . . . made something happen that wouldn't have otherwise happened.

Course content can help students understand ongoing work practices. For instance, Alice, who had been working in libraries for several years before she entered the LEEP program, tells of understanding the "bigger picture" related to local policies:

> One of the rules in circulation in the library I'm working in now, you can't give out titles over the telephone. . . . People will call . . . and you have to do this kind of guessing game where you say, 'Tell me the possible titles and I can tell you which one it is.' . . . Since I've been doing the LEEP program, I understand that a library has a burden to protect peoples' privacy. . . . So the LEEP thing made me think more about that. Censorship issues and stuff like that that I haven't really thought about. Those kind of things are bigger picture, things that I would kind of think about every once in a while.

LEEP also provides students with access to a network of instructors and practitioners in various areas of LIS. They can marshal that collective knowledge to help solve problems in their own workplaces.

Whereas workplaces benefit from students' LEEP involvement, they support the students in many ways. Often students are given time and access to computers at work for LEEP. Students rely on resources at work, including library materials and knowledgeable coworkers. And just as LEEP course content can help workplace practices, the converse is true: Students often have a large body of experience on which to draw that helps them understand the material better and, when shared, helps other LEEP students. Jeff explains quite vividly these beneficial interconnections:

> Working at work is a lab for me to do library stuff. I mean for example we're talking about copyright or whatever, I mean that's a part of my job is to come up with a copyright policy. So it's like a place for me to apply everything that I'm learning . . . it's like a mutual benefit, what I'm learning helps me in my job, and having my job to work out the kinks and apply actually what I'm learning, mutually reinforces.

LEEP and the LIS Profession

As students find increasing positive overlap between their school and work worlds, they begin to see that involvement in LEEP also interacts with their involvement in the LIS profession. Many students report feeling increased ties with the profession and greater understanding of its philosophy and practices. This helps them feel more competent and confident at work. Personal contact with members of the profession at conferences and other workplaces leads to a sense of personal belonging and helps in moving from a paraprofessional to a professional position. It helps in the LEEP world, too. For example, students who rely on the network of public librarians when they travel find that they can get permission to use public library Internet connections and other computer resources more easily because they are becoming members of the profession through LEEP.

Students also realize that the friends they make within LEEP will make up a portion of their professional cohort after graduation, and that maintaining those relationships will help them as they complete LEEP courses and long afterward. Holly, who has already seen several LEEP friends graduate, explains this multifaceted benefit. She sees the LEEP community as

> a support system: an emotional support system, an intellectual support system, people you could ask questions, get information from. I also feel professionally it's a network. It's been interesting as I've been in it longer and I've seen people graduate and get jobs, that there are people that I have connections with professionally that here in LEEP that are in areas in work the same as mine.

LEEP and Home, Friend Worlds

The worlds of home, extended family, and friends can also coexist beneficially with LEEP. These worlds often provide the emotionally supportive interpersonal contact that students say helps keep them going in LEEP. Home and friend worlds often provide technical equipment and support and are repaid with the technical expertise that students gain from LEEP. Students leverage their new comfort with electronic communication to reestablish and strengthen ties with far away family and friends and to introduce technologies into their volunteer organizations. For example, Beth found that the expertise with technology she gained in LEEP allowed her to plan her family's vacations using the Internet; help her college-age daughter with information retrieval; and carry out banking, word processing, and scheduling online. Because of her example and her help, more of her geographically remote family has come online and she keeps in touch with friends and family all over the world. Another student helped establish a used-computer distribution program to benefit low-income users. Thus, we see increased social contact associated with learning and using online technologies; however, we note that this effect is not seen until students have gained confidence with the technologies and have become familiar with them over time.

Collisions

Although synergies demonstrate the best of all worlds, not all overlaps between LEEP and other worlds are so smooth. Where lines remain hard and fixed, worlds cannot combine synergistically and may collide uncomfortably. Collisions occur when two or more worlds are competing for resources of attention or time; for example, a collision can occur between LEEP and the family when a LEEP class is scheduled during the dinner hour, when family members resent time taken away from other activities, or when new routines collide with old ones.

Sometimes LEEP and work are not synergistic. Sue, quoted above, changed jobs to manage LEEP. Others see no synergy between their current work and what they hope will be their future work. Doris works in a profession that she thinks is removed from LIS but hopes to move into an LIS job after graduating. To support herself, she continues to work in her first profession but feels keenly the absence of the synergy that she sees other students experiencing and wishes she did not feel such a disconnect between LEEP and her daily work. Real life can also interfere with LEEP. Life events can become so overwhelming that LEEP falls by the wayside: Hospitalization, ill children, deaths of friends, family, and pets are all causes of collisions in which the LEEP world must be handled later. LEEP students praise instructors for their flexibility on course completion schedules in the face of such real-world interference.

Discussion

We learn from these students that these many communication technologies provide a medium rather than a world—LEEP is a world, the Internet is not—and that the important issues in their lives revolve around managing multiple world relationships rather than managing online/offline dichotomies. Although it is easy for an outsider to consider LEEP students' worlds as divided between online and offline, dichotomizing their lives in that way does not accord with their experiences. When they talk about LEEP, they do not discuss it as a separate online activity. Instead, they talk about it in terms of the people, experiences, and tasks it comprises and how it interacts with home, work, and friends. The issue that emerges is not how students' manage online involvement, but instead how they integrate this new world into their array of existing worlds. Juggling and synergy result from students taking an active approach to managing their multiple worlds, where one of those worlds just happens to include heavy use of Internet communications technologies.

Increasing involvement in an online environment is more complicated than a simple, unconscious transfer of attention from offline time. Students actively manage time, activities, and relationships; prioritizing what and who needs to be dealt with first, what can be dropped, and what can be left aside and repaired later. Children get high priority, but spouses, parents, and friends have to wait. Personal entertainment (television, needlework, and gardening) are dropped, and household chores are left until later. It is in the voluntary world that most activities are dropped (see also Putnam, 2000). Work—paid work—fades to the background if not compatible with LEEP, but it provides increasing synergy when compatible. These students' patterns of interaction suggest that adding an online world can increase and decrease social involvement, depending on the individuals' skills at multiple-world management, their familiarity with the technologies, or with the way they prioritize and enact cycles of neglect and repair of relationships.

Although we believe that other populations and online environments are likely to function in similar ways, we note that the way in which LEEP has emerged for its members as a community (see Haythornthwaite, et al., 2000) and not just an educational program may create a social world more completely than other online endeavors. Also, as noted above, LEEP involves graduate students selected because of their ability to succeed in such an intensive educational option. Their success in actively managing multiple worlds and experiencing beneficial overlap may result from their particular talents in organizing. However, this in itself is also an important factor to recognize. Not everyone may be able to juggle these multiple worlds, nor does everyone know how to do it at first. Online worlds may indeed displace offline worlds in a form of neglect without repair, or with repair so far in the future that it cannot be recognized today. As involvement in the program increases, students do withdraw from offline responsibilities, trying to create their own mental and physical space so that they can concentrate on LEEP work. They increasingly depend on social interactions with LEEP students who understand what one student called their "different kind of world." Yet involvement in LEEP increases opportunities at work, and experience with the technological environment provides many with synergy that allows them to help children with their schoolwork and increase contact with distant friends and relatives. Time stolen from family and other extracurricular activities is often only borrowed. Experiences gained in LEEP are paid back to other worlds as students become increasingly technologically and professionally savvy.

Using the social worlds perspective, we see the impact of online education or of the Internet as a complex interaction among multiple, sometimes competing, social arenas. We have seen, in some literature on the interactions between online and offline life, a way of discussing Internet use in fairly broad strokes (e.g., Kraut, Kiesler, et al.,

1998; Kraut, Patterson, et al., 1998; Nie & Erbring, 2000). Our students' reports suggest that to evaluate the impact of the Internet it is important to understand the social worlds brought into play when people go online and how these social worlds are juggled, integrated, and/or collide with other worlds, offline or on.

Acknowledgments

This paper is reprinted with permission from November 2001, *American Behavioral Scientist, 45*(3), 510–529. © 2001 Sage Publications.

Authors' Note: Our thanks go to the 17 individuals who gave generously of their time for the interviews that provide the data for this article, to Jenny Robins and Susan Shoemaker who participated in interviewing and earlier analyses, and to Jeff Boase for helpful comments. This work was supported by a grant from the University of Illinois Campus Research Board.

Notes

1. For details on the Graduate School of Library and Information Science (GSLIS) Library Education Experimental Program (LEEP), see http://alexia.lis.uiuc.edu/gslis/leep3, and http://leep.lis.uiuc.edu.
2. One of the students was able to compare the experience of taking a degree by driving to a campus after work versus taking a degree via LEEP. This student felt that LEEP provided a great relief from the previous routine of driving to campus and very much enjoyed being able to be in the home when taking classes.
3. See also Putnam (1996), who reported, "harried souls do spend less time eating, sleeping, reading books, engaging in hobbies, and just doing nothing" (p. 6). Putnam went on to note that such people forgo these activities but still maintain their involvement in volunteer organizational activity. Here we find students drop volunteer work to maintain engagement in their important organizational activity, that is, LEEP. It is possible that LEEP fits the same niche in an individual's life as a volunteer group membership. Further research would be necessary to explore this possibility.
4. We can expect that there are also times when the students want to exist in the work or home worlds without interruption from LEEP. Because our interviews were about LEEP, we can only comment here on techniques for corralling time for work in that world.
5. Referring to the mid-semester on-campus day for each course being taken.

References

Bregman, A., & Haythornthwaite, C. (2001). Radicals of presentation in persistent conversation. In *Proceedings of the Hawai'i International Conference on System Sciences*. Los Alamitos, CA: IEEE Computer Society Press. Retrieved from http://www.hicss.hawaii.edu/HICSS_34/PDFs/DDPTC01.pdf.

Clarke, A. (1991). Social worlds/arenas theory as organizational theory. In D. Maines (Ed.), *Social organization and social process: Essays in honor of Anselm Strauss* (pp. 119–158). New York: Aldine de Gruyter.

Covi, L. (1996). Social worlds of knowledge work: Why researchers fail to effectively use digital libraries. In *Proceedings of ASIS Mid-Year Conference*. San Diego, CA: Information Today.

Fitzpatrick, G., Kaplan, S., & Mansfield, T. (1996). Physical spaces, virtual places and social worlds: A study of work in the virtual. In *Proceedings of the ACM 1996 Conference on Computer Supported Cooperative Work* (pp. 334–343). Boston: Association for Computing Machinery.

Harasim, L., Hiltz, S. R., Teles, L., & Turoff, M. (1995). *Learning networks: A field guide to teaching and learning online*. Cambridge, MA: MIT Press.

Haythornthwaite, C. (2000). Online personal networks: Size, composition and media use among distance learners. *New Media and Society, 2*(2), 195–226.

Haythornthwaite, C. (2002). Building social networks via computer networks: Creating and sustaining distributed learning communities. In K. A. Renninger & W. Shumar, *Building Virtual Communities: Learning and Change in Cyberspace* (pp. 159–109). Cambridge: Cambridge University Press.

Haythornthwaite, C., Kazmer, M. M., Robins, J., & Shoemaker, S. (2000). Community development among distance learners: Temporal and technological dimensions. *Journal of Computer-Mediated Communication, 6*(1). Retrieved from http://www.ascusc.org/jcmc/vol6/issue1/haythornthwaite.html. (Reprinted in this volume.)

Haythornthwaite, C., & Wellman, B. (1998). Work, friendship and media use for information exchange in a networked organization. *Journal of the American Society for Information Science, 46*(12), 1101–1114.

Kazmer, M. M. (2000). Coping in a distance environment: Sitcoms, chocolate cake, and dinner with a friend. *First Monday, 5*(9). Retrieved from http://www.firstmonday.dk/issues/issue5_9/kazmer/index.html.

Kiesler, S., & Kraut, R. (1999). Internet use and ties that bind. *American Psychologist, 54*(9), 783–784.

Kraut, R., Kiesler, S., Mukhopadhyay, T., Scherilis, W., & Patterson, M. (1998). Social impact of the Internet. *Communications of the ACM, 41*(12), 21–22.

Kraut, R., Patterson, M., Lundmark, V., Kiesler, S., Mukhopadhyay, T., & Scherlis, W. (1998). Internet paradox: A social technology that reduces social involvement and psychological well-being? *American Psychologist, 53*(9), 1017–1031.

Levine, M. (1998, December 7–14). The juggler. *The New Yorker,* 72–80.

Nardi, B. A., Whittaker, S., & Schwarz, H. (2000). It's not what you know, it's who you know: Work in the information age. *First Monday, 5*(5). Retrieved from http://www.firstmonday.dk/issues/issue5_5/nardi/.

Nie, N. H., & Erbring, L. (2000). *Internet and society: A preliminary report*. Stanford, CA: Stanford Institute for the Quantitative Study of Society.

Putnam, R. D. (1996). The strange disappearance of civic America. *American Prospec, 24*. Retrieved from http://www.prospect.org/archives/24/24putn.html.

Putnam, R. D. (2000). *Bowling alone: The collapse and revival of American community*. New York: Simon & Schuster.

Renniger, A., & Shumar, W. (Eds.). (2001). *Building virtual communities: Learning and change in cyberspace*. Cambridge: Cambridge University Press.

Star, S. L., Bowker, G. C., & Neumann, L. J. (2003). Transparency beyond the individual level of scale: Convergence between information artifacts and communities of practice. In A. Bishop, N. Van House, & B. Buttenfield (Eds.), *Digital library use: Social practice in design and evaluation* (pp. 241–270). Cambridge, MA: MIT Press.

Strauss, A. (1978). A social world perspective. *Studies in Symbolic Interaction, 1,* 119–128.

Wasserman, S., & Faust, K. (1994). *Social network analysis.* Cambridge, MA: Cambridge University Press.

Wellman, B. (1997). Structural analysis: From method and metaphor to theory and substance. In B. Wellman & S. D. Berkowitz (Eds.), *Social structures: A network approach* (pp. 19–61). Greenwich, CT: JAI Press.

Wellman, B., & Gulia, M. (1999). Net surfers don't ride alone: Virtual communities as communities. In M. Smith & P. Kollock (Eds.), *Communities in cyberspace* (pp. 167–194). London: Routledge.

Wellman, B., & Hampton, K. (1999). Living networked on and offline. *Contemporary Sociology, 28*(6), 648–654.

Wellman, B., Salaff, J., Dimitrova, D., Garton, L., Gulia, M., & Haythornthwaite, C. (1996). Computer networks as social networks: Collaborative work, telework, and virtual community. *Annual Review of Sociology, 22,* 213–238.

CHAPTER 6 Michelle M. Kazmer

Disengaging from Online Community

Other chapters in this book show in a variety of ways that when students are involved in the LEEP (Library Education Experimental Program) program, it is an extremely important part of their lives. This chapter shows how students handle the several months before and after graduation when LEEP becomes less important to them, and when their energies and attention turn back to other aspects of their lives. While the community and culture of the program are often primary for students during the beginning and middle of their time in it, the importance of LEEP in the life of a student after they have graduated can fade quickly. A graduate named "Violet" explains how this shift occurred for her:

> I really don't give it a whole lot of thought anymore, like I said. I really don't think too much about it. [. . .] you do feel like you're a part of something when you're in it, but then when you go back to your own life, you look back and . . . You had all those friends you thought you'd keep in contact with, and then a year down the road, you've all separated and grown differently and have other priorities. And the priorities that you had prior to going into LEEP have resurfaced again and taken the important place in your life where they were in the beginning. They were sort of swept under the rug for a year or two. [Violet, three months after graduating from LEEP][1]

The Transience of Online Learning Worlds

Online learning communities have one major characteristic that distinguishes them from many other online worlds and online communities—they are temporary. Students taking courses or degrees come into the community only for a limited time, and they know from the beginning that it is limited. Like transient workers, they know that they will make friends, share confidences, work together, and support one another, but that when the degree is earned and the work is finished, everyone will move on to the next job (Adler & Adler, 1999).

These learning communities are thus *intrinsically transient*, that is, they are by definition temporary. Because of this intrinsic transience, even as the members build a community together, they also understand that their community will be dismantled as each member *disengages* when it is time to graduate. Examination of this disengagement process is a key addition to the study of online communities, which has thus far focused primarily on the building and maintenance stages. This chapter describes results from interviews with 30 students about their experiences as they prepare to graduate and actually disengage from the intensive online learning experience of LEEP. We discuss the 12 dimensions associated with the disengagement process as identified from the interviews, and the implications of this process for online learning and virtual communities.

Social Worlds, Engagement, and Disengagement

We have chosen to take a *social world* perspective (Strauss, 1978) rather than continuing to use the term *community* to refer to the online learning environment. A social world consists of people who share activities, space, and technology, and who communicate with one another (Strauss, 1978). Using the social world perspective lets us explore all aspects of each individual's experience, and describe spheres of individual activity without needing to focus on a group-oriented community (see also Kazmer & Haythornthwaite, 2001).

As described above, the social world that is created and occupied by distance learners is temporary by its definition, and thus intrinsically transient. We use the term *intrinsically transient social world*, or ITSW, to refer to the temporary shared experience of online learners. In an ITSW, all of the members understand that their shared experience will come to an end. Even so, the learners in this environment engage with each other from the beginning of their time in the program. They create strong bonds of friendship and provide one another with emotional support. They also create intensive working relationships that involve frequent communication (see also Haythornthwaite, Kazmer, Robins, & Shoemaker, 2000, for more details). In addition, LEEP takes a position of primary importance in the lives of students while they are in the program.

The social world of distance learners is intrinsically transient, and thus will come to a predictable end, but the participants in the LEEP program definitely make emotional and functional commitments to one another and to the program itself. What happens, then, to participants' shared relationships and their intense focus on the program when the time comes to graduate? Looking at the community building that occurs among distance learners, Haythornthwaite, et al. (2000) made it clear that near the end of their time in the program, students were disengaging from the shared social world, separating themselves from their relationships within it and decreasing their focus on it. After they spent a few semesters building community, LEEP students dismantled their shared learning worlds. Also, individual students disengaged from their involvement in the LEEP community. However, at that time, we had not interviewed enough graduating students to let us understand or describe this disengagement process in detail.

Moreover, the act of departing or disengaging from online social worlds has received little attention in the literature (but see Bruckman & Jensen, 2002; Jablin, 2001; and Kolko & Reid, 1998, for related work), despite its obvious importance in educational environments for passing on the word about programs. Much of the literature about online community has focused on the description, building, and maintenance of such communities (e.g., Babbie, 1996; Baker & Ward, 2002; Blanchard & Horan, 1998; Dickinson, 2002; Fox & Roberts, 1999; Haythornthwaite, 1998; Kennedy, 2000; Ridings, Gefen, & Arinze, 2002; Rojo & Ragsdale, 1997; Smith, 1999; Weedman, 1999; Wellman & Gulia, 1999). Studies of the communications media, virtual community participants, special interest newsgroups, text-chat environments, and even *emoticons* contribute to our understanding of how humans develop and maintain relationships online.

Finding out more about disengagement processes necessitated examining the literature in other fields of study. One such area is migration preparation, the study of groups and individuals who are getting ready to leave their country of residence permanently or semipermanently (Rousseau, Drapeau, & Corin, 1997; Rousseau, Said, Gagne, & Bibeau, 1998). Studies in this area indicate that people's experiences while they are preparing to depart one place affect their success in achieving a stable, successful situation after their migration. This idea, that a departure from one social world might affect a person's success in subsequent social worlds, is particularly important in online learning. This is because people earning a degree online are usually expected to join what we have called a *logical next world*. For example, students earning a master's degree in library and information science might be expected to join the social world of information professionals. That would be their logical next world. It is possible, also, to have more than one logical next world. These students might also be expected to join the social world of alumni who graduated from the same program.

Another area of research related to disengagement is gerosociology (Cumming & Henry, 1961; Newman & Newman, 1999; Quinnan, 1997). Aging people may prepare for many types of departure, and for different types of relationships to end. They may move from a large house to a small one, or from a familiar neighborhood to a care facility. They may also be separated from family, friends, and their spouses. Studies of these transitions highlight an important feature of disengagement as a process. Not only do people actively disengage themselves, they are also sometimes encouraged by other people or by society to disengage. Being aware of these multiple motivations for disengagement prevents us from viewing it as a process that individuals complete by themselves.

A final helpful area of research was that of transient groups (Arrow, McGrath, & Berdahl, 2000; Gersick, 1988; Tuckman & Jensen, 1977). Although the intrinsically transient social world of distance learners is larger than a *group* and also lasts longer (years instead of hours, weeks, or months for a transient group), there are elements from the studies of transient groups that relate to disengagement. Tuckman and Jensen added an *adjourning* stage to their group process model, one of the earliest acknowledgments in the literature that the ending processes of transient groups are of interest. Arrow et al. and Gersick developed further models of group processes that not only recognize the importance of a phase similar to disengagement, but also indicate that the disengagement process begins much earlier than the last days of a group's existence. Knowing that students may begin to disengage some time before they graduate helped us to capture the whole process as we collected data.

The remainder of this chapter focuses on the process students go through as they disengage from the online, distributed, intrinsically transient social world of distance education. We provide a description of disengagement, illustrated by quotes from a number of students.

Disengagement from, and beyond, LEEP

The LEEP program served as an exemplar of an ITSW for this exploration of the process of disengaging from online worlds. Interviews with 30 LEEP students near the time of their graduation reveal multiple dimensions of the (often complex) disengagement process. The disengagement process helps to shape the future relationships that online learning graduates have with one another, socially and in their shared profession. Disengagement affects the relationships that graduates have with the institution they have left behind. Disengagement also affects how graduates continue to use the various technologies they used for online learning, and how they transfer their technological expertise into new arenas.

Understanding disengagement has implications beyond the LEEP program. Online learning is an increasingly common arena for the creation and dissolution of transient virtual communities. Educators and researchers have begun to explore the relationships that graduates of distance learning programs have with each other and with the educational institutions from which they have graduated (Pennsylvania State University, 1996; Lesht & Schejbal, 2000; Levy, 1999). Continuing personal and professional relationships among graduates, continuing professional development by further education and training, and recruitment of new students provide specific examples of postgraduate activity. Distance learning programs can better support each of these activities if they better understand students' departure processes.

The next section provides a very brief description of the data collection and analysis methods that were used for this study. The following section provides details about the disengagement process itself, including quotes from some of the students. The final section explores some of the implications for disengagement on the practice of online learning and virtual community.

Research Participants, Data Collection, and Grounded Theory Analysis

Data for this study were collected via semistructured interviews with 30 LEEP students. Questions guided participants to talk about their experiences at the end of their time in LEEP. In keeping with grounded theory methodology (Strauss & Corbin, 1998), findings from the previous study by Haythornthwaite, et al. were used to build questions for this study. Participants were master's degree distance students enrolled in LEEP who were within two semesters of graduation. Fifty-five interviews were conducted over the telephone, tape-recorded, and transcribed. Eighteen students were interviewed twice, before and after they graduated. These interviews allowed us to examine disengagement activities that occurred while students were still in the program and those that occurred afterward. Six students were interviewed twice after graduation, allowing us to focus on postdeparture disengagement activities. The remaining interviews took place with students before graduation.

The interviews were analyzed using the techniques and procedures of grounded theory outlined by Strauss and Corbin (1998). This qualitative method uses the basic techniques of questioning and making comparisons within the context of a close examination of the interview data. The analysis is interactive and ongoing throughout data collection; that is, each interview and round of interviews is analyzed beginning as soon as it is completed and continuing throughout the project data analysis. This continuous analysis is used to design the further data collection instruments, which then act as a feedback loop with more focused exploration of emerging important ideas. These techniques are then used throughout the processes of coding and memoing to build up the overall analytic narrative and the specific concepts and subprocesses that are characteristic of the process being studied. The analysis indicated that disengagement is a twelve-step process. The 12 steps are explained in the following section.

How Disengagement Proceeds

The disengagement process really begins just as students are beginning their program, long before they are thinking about graduating and moving on to their next job or personal goal. More specifically, the disengagement that is going to happen near the end of their time as distance learners is shaped by the community-building that happens near the beginning, and by the social/working relationships students form with one another. In other words, it is precisely because students build ongoing supportive relationships while they are in the online learning program that they have to disengage at the end. Those relationships are important to students' success in the program, but the more involved the students are in their shared learning community, the more they will have to disengage from at the end. Fortunately for the students, as will be explained below, some of the dimensions associated with disengagement are also associated with success in the logical next world of the information profession.

Most of the disengagement process happens, as might be expected, during the last few months before graduation. At that time, disengaging students are most active about breaking ties with friends from the program, renewing friendships elsewhere, and making sure they have established a position in the logical next world. A small amount of disengagement occurs during and after graduation, when the students say their farewells to each other and relinquish their last ties to the online world of students.

The following discussion of disengagement describes the 12 dimensions in approximate chronological order as participants experience them through their disengagement. The students interviewed for this study provided hours of rich interview data, all of which contributed to the model of disengagement. The quotes from their interviews that are included in this section demonstrate how actual participants spoke about their LEEP experiences, and were selected because they exemplify sentiments expressed by other participants as well.

Early Steps in the Disengagement Process

The first two dimensions of disengagement actually start to occur long before the students are ready to graduate, as mentioned above. The first of these is that students actually *experience intrinsic transience*. Students are always aware that their LEEP social world is going to come to an end, and that awareness affects how they develop relationships with other students. The awareness of intrinsic transience also provides students with a way to support themselves emotionally during their time in the program. It gives them a way to reassure themselves that their "real" lives and relationships will be back to normal soon. Experiencing intrinsic transience also allows students to minimize the impact of their membership in the social world on their outside relationships and leisure activities, because they can suspend involvement with them for a finite amount of time.

After graduation, Jennifer reflects on her intense focus on LEEP and her knowledge that it would only be for a two-year period. She explains her experience of intrinsic transience:

What worked for me was saying, I'm cutting these two years out, and I'm really going to, you know, I'm going to do it, I'm going to do it well, and it's going to be over, and then it's going to be a part of me, you know, that will function like, you know, anything else that you do has become a part of you so that you don't have to focus on it constantly all the time. [Jennifer, one month after graduating from LEEP]

The second early step of disengagement occurs as students *become members of their cohort,* the group of students who enter the program together each July. Membership in this social world begins with a shared face-to-face experience with the cohort, and each participant's experience throughout his or her time in the program is heavily influenced by the cohort. Participants share a two-week, face-to-face experience during which they build relationships that endure throughout participation. In addition, the progress of the cohort provides a reference by which participants gauge their own progress through the program. At the end, then, participants must disengage from the cohort as well as the larger social world of LEEP.

Before she graduates, Edith reflects on how she bonded with her boot camp friends by sharing two weeks with them on campus:

You always seem to bond most with the people that you start your original cohort with because, um, you're there for two weeks with them. Versus one or two days, or just a classroom day for any other groups. And a lot of times there were people that have started in my cohort that would be in other classes. And so, I had a roommate that was, I think she was assigned to me when we started, and her and I ended up staying roommates each time we came back to campus, until she graduated earlier than I did. [Edith, one month before graduating from LEEP]

Active Disengagement near the Time of Graduation

We now fast-forward in the disengagement process. Students have been working with their cohort for several semesters, taking courses, maintaining friendships among their online classmates, and looking forward to earning their degrees. In the last few months of their time in the program, students realize that the their time is running short and start to disengage actively from the LEEP social world in a variety of ways, explained here.

First, the *length of time* spent in the social world, as well as the pacing of progress and the allocation of resources (such as money) during membership, becomes acutely important to students as they prepare to disengage. Near their departure from LEEP, students develop keen awareness of the amount of time they spent in the program and awareness that the end is very near. This newly acute awareness motivates participants toward disengagement, and also leads them to allocate carefully resources of time and money in anticipation of imminent departure.

Also near the time of departure, students start to *shift their focus* to relationships and activities outside the social world of school. During the final semester, students pay less attention to LEEP, both to their relationships with others in the program and also to their schoolwork. Instead, they focus on outside activities, from the routine (such as gardening) to the eventful (such as family gatherings). In addition, because of expertise developed during membership, participants do not need to focus as intently on their activities in LEEP in order to perform them well. Finding that the technology finally runs smoothly and that creating a Web page for an assignment is no longer an arduous process frees the students to pay attention to other things.

Martha, a recent graduate, explains that her focus has shifted from LEEP, and also from her family and friends, to professional activities:

> I'm kind of really focused on my job right now, because I want to do a good job, and I want to learn things. That doesn't mean that my family and my friends are unimportant to me, but I kind of feel like I've got a handle on that, so I'm pretty much really constantly thinking about what sort of professional activities I need to engage in. Should I publish, you know, what should I be doing next? You know, I do a monthly personal activities report, so I guess that's kind of my latest preoccupation, is just making sure that I'm a really good [. . .] librarian. [Martha, one month after graduating from LEEP]

This quote also shows Martha adapting her role to match what she is expected to do as a member of the logical next world of the profession after she departs LEEP. Both of these aspects of disengagement are explained further, below.

The third major shift that students go through as they get close to graduation involves a change in their *goals and motivations*. Within the LEEP social world, students change their goals from successful participation to successful disengagement. While they may still want to perform well academically, many students admit that their primary goal is simply to be done. Students also find motivation in the immediacy of their move into their logical next world. They begin to seek the goal of higher status in other social worlds, especially the professional world they are joining by earning the degree.

Hank indicates during his last semester as a student that he is less focused on schoolwork because, though he is determined to complete the degree and knows he must earn grades high enough to fulfill requirements, the drive he felt at the beginning of the program to excel in every class has faded. This change of goals is part of disengagement:

> [T]he work I do for LEEP, I would say that it has, it started out fairly strong and then it probably peaked in that one [. . .] semester and it has dwindled somewhat just because now it's just sort of a matter of keeping up. Whereas there was a while when [. . .] I was willing to put in much more time than was necessary, to get things done just because I really wanted to get things right, or I really wanted to describe something more fully

[. . .], I would really try to go into some depth. And I would try to make things look really nice, that I turned in in the form of Web pages. And [. . .] just having been through it for over a year at this point, I just don't have the same kind of motivation. [Hank, one month before graduating from LEEP]

At this point in disengagement, students realize that time has run short, and in their excitement to be finished they begin to focus away from LEEP, toward goals outside the degree program. As they do so, they begin to take on the *new identities and roles* that are associated with graduation and with moving into the logical next world of the information profession. Students' roles change within the program, as they become experts within the social world and also prepare to be ex-participants. For example some students take the lead on group homework projects while earlier in the program they did not do so. Other students go so far as to ask to be excused from group projects, because they are so focused on finishing and are no longer interested in the role of team player. Disengaging students also start to take on their future identities as professionals and as graduates of the program.

In changing their role from that of a contributing team player within the learning social world to that of an individual student wanting to finish the program expeditiously, students find themselves *changing their locus of support*. Rather than interacting frequently with and relying on other students for emotional and functional (e.g., with schoolwork) support, the disengaging student turns instead to people who are physically near, such as family, friends, and coworkers. One particular kind of support that is very likely to shift is that of mentoring. Disengaging students who have developed a mentoring relationship with a faculty member from LEEP often develop new mentoring relationships with someone from their workplace.

Not all relationships from within the social world are forsaken in favor of local ties. Some of the relationships that students developed inside the social world change *footing*, as frequent interaction and shared activities give way to infrequent contact and remote professional networks. To put it simply, friends who shared the emotional hardships of a demanding academic program become colleagues who share coffee at conferences and meetings. This is not a thoughtless process. Disengaging students work to understand how their relationships will continue after membership, when the shared activities and technology of the LEEP social world are gone. A fairly obvious finding is that disengaging students lose touch with one another and decrease the frequency of their interaction.

For example, Evelyn finds that her relationships with her LEEP friends have changed as they have all disengaged from LEEP. She hopes that infrequent e-mails will suffice to maintain these friendships:

I suppose that I don't feel like I have to have a whole lot of contact to still consider these people my friends and colleagues. You know, I don't think it's the quantity of contact that we have, but the quality that we'll have later on that will keep us, you know, in touch with each other. [Evelyn, three months after graduating from LEEP]

Many of the changes associated with disengagement are predicated on the student being successful in *joining the logical next world* by landing a position as an information professional or librarian. This is a goal on which disengaging students focus quite intently. They will not have a place in which to practice their new role as a professional with a master's degree if they do not have an appropriate job. Graduates who do not find a professional position also do not have a new workplace to provide support as they shift away from their LEEP classmates.

Many students already have a job in an information setting. Their preparation for joining the profession is primarily smoothing the transition from the LEEP social world to the professional world. Disengaging students who do not already have a job in the professional world work primarily on securing such a position. Only then can they look toward smoothing their transition out of one social world and into another.

Here, for example, Vivian must decide whether to look for a job in the new town before she moves there and while she is taking four classes in LEEP. She elects instead to wait until she finishes the degree and moves to her new home, thus separating the job-seeking part of disengagement from the degree-completion part:

And what I wanted to do was go ahead and finish up so that I could find a job in this area in my profession as a professional. So I could either have taken two classes this semester and two classes in the spring, finished up next spring, and looked for a job again, because I would have had to have looked for a job this last fall. Or I could just do a blitz, finish up in a few months, just live on his salary, and then find a professional position. [. . .] I'm going to take some time, probably about a month, because that'll be holidays and I'll just take that time off, just to kind of regroup, and then just really start looking for a job. And in the area that I'm in. (Interviewer: So you're not job hunting now then?) No, not with four classes. There's no way. [Vivian, two months before graduating from LEEP]

This quote from Vivian also demonstrates other aspects of disengagement: managing time, as she adjusts her course schedules to accord with successful disengagement; and closing membership, as she indicates her plan to end participation, take a break, and then move on her next tasks.

Completing Disengagement

By the time of the actual graduation date, most students have almost completed their own disengagement from the LEEP social world. Graduating provides a ritual to mark the end of participation in the program. Though the disengagement process takes time, graduation is a definite moment of ending. Near the time of graduation,

LEEP students *say their final farewells* to one another, and they prefer to do so face-to-face. Indeed, this reflects the fact that each student's experience is shaped by his or her cohort experience. The cohorts met and bonded face-to-face at the beginning of the program, and most students want to say farewell in the same way.

Some students do not feel ready to leave. This is especially common for students who have not secured a job in a professional setting, but that is not the only reason for reluctance. For example, graduates of this program who have never before worked in a library may not feel ready to do so even upon completion of their required coursework. Whatever the reason, such students purposely delay their graduation date (e.g., by taking additional classes) in order to give themselves more time in LEEP.

Dolly describes seeing her cohort friends and taking leave of them during their final on-campus visit. This quote also shows the intrinsic transience of each cohort's LEEP social world, as Dolly reacts to the changing population of the LEEP program as a whole:

> I suppose it was a little bit poignant but we didn't really dwell on that. You know, like the dinner that we went out to. Because we all knew it would be, we didn't know when we're going to be together again. But really we didn't play that up. Because most of the time we're not together at all. And then we did go to the LEEP dinner, which I always go, but I didn't go this time. Because, we kind of stopped by, before, 'cause that was the night we were going to go out to dinner to a real restaurant. [W]e kind of looked around and to tell you the truth I didn't really recognize too many people, and so it wasn't like oh, I want to be here so I can see people. Cause I didn't really, you know what I mean, this was like a later in time thing, whereas the first on-campus was really wonderful cause you were like, oh my gosh, I get to see everybody again and this is fun and I can talk to people. [Dolly, two months before graduating from LEEP]

A major part of becoming a member of the LEEP social world was joining the cohort at the beginning of the program. Now, at the very end of disengagement, students take the step of *disengaging from the cohort*. This occurs when students stop thinking of themselves as cohort members and of their cohort as the primary reference of progress toward graduation. Instead, disengaging participants begin to think of themselves as individuals earning a degree and securing a position in the profession.

After graduation, former students are very quick to *fill in* time that was taken with participation in the LEEP world and *close up* their memories of that participation. Students rapidly forget details of their membership (see the quote from Violet at the beginning of this chapter). Just as quickly, they fill in the time left open in their schedules by the absence of LEEP activities. Only one aspect of the last step of disengagement keeps them tied to LEEP for a little while longer: the new graduates often find that they need to tie up any final loose ends of membership by doing things such as forwarding their e-mail and requesting last-minute job references.

These twelve steps of disengagement, and the overall process that comprises them, indicate how members of an intrinsically transient social world disengage from that world when their time of necessary departure is near. The specific details about each of the 12 steps demonstrate some of the activities and items that are particularly important to people who are disengaging from such a world. The next section includes a discussion about why disengagement is important, and the implications of the disengagement process for practice and for research.

Significance of Findings and Implications for Research and Practice

First, this section highlights a few aspects of disengagement that might help other online education programs, faculty, and administrators, to support and guide distance learners through their final semesters and graduation. Two general observations are followed by several specific suggestions for practice. These are in turn followed by some implications for further study.

The first general observation indicated by these findings is that the timing of how we provide support for people preparing to leave online social worlds is important. By identifying a process that has steps that tend to occur before and after the point of departure, we are able to understand better what support needs to occur and when. Understanding the process also highlights those instances where individuals have difficulties at particular steps. Even more, now it is possible to observe where there are differences in the process for different kinds of participants. In turn, that allows for more focused assistance to be provided.

The second general observation is that disengagement is not confined to the point of departure (e.g., graduation day). Instead, disengagement is shaped by events in the social world from the day people join. Events that happen early on, such as bonding experiences and the way people first meet, will determine how they ritualize their departure. Because events that happen earlier than the last month or so also shape the disengagement process, we know that there is need to intervene early and even plan the process.

This study of disengagement focused on students. As members of the learning social world, students are the primary shapers of disengagement: Students are the ones who select their course loads, apply for jobs, and adjust their relationships. However, faculty and technical staff in online learning programs also play important roles in shaping disengagement. Faculty members provide job references and help students decide what classes to take and what jobs to apply for. Faculty members also decide whether to remain available to students after graduation, which in turn affects how quickly the student finishes disengaging. Technical support staff and other administrators control access to the technology that is used within the online learning social world, and are responsible for keeping students aware of procedures for technology transitions such as e-mail forwarding. Faculty and administrators also determine when students have completed the requirements for graduation, and negotiate with students to enable them to earn the degree even when things go wrong. Understanding what students are trying to accomplish during disengagement can help faculty and staff to make decisions and best support the disengagement process.

Three other opportunities for faculty and staff to help disengaging students were suggested by this study. First, students who were slower in proceeding through the program and were thus left behind by their cohorts felt isolated during their last semester. Perhaps being aware of this isolation will encourage faculty or staff to create ways to ease this isolation for such students. Second, by the time students reach the stage of disengaging, they have many ideas about what they believe works in distance learning. Distance learning programs might find it useful to ask their graduates what they thought worked, and consider those suggestions for improvement. Third, graduates say that they use school resources as sources of information. They not only rely on class project Web sites, archived audio lectures, and course reading lists as information resources; they also start to use the group discussion mechanisms as an information resource rather than a communication medium. Understanding how alumni are likely to use such things might help guide procedures for archiving access.

Additionally, students who do not already work in the profession or field they are studying may benefit from help in their transition to the logical next world of work. Such help should go beyond aiding them in identifying available jobs and providing letters of reference. These students also could benefit from help in implementing their learning at work. Before graduation, that could be accomplished by arranging practica or other work experiences and specifically guiding students in implementing learning in those settings. After graduation, help in implementation might have two forms. First, course materials should remain available to graduates so that they can revisit assignments, readings, and lectures once they are working. Second, extended mentoring allows novice workers to ask questions about implementation in a safe environment, and of a trusted adviser.

Focus on the professional world should not completely overshadow the other logical next world of online education: the world of past participants (alumni). Disengaging participants in this study also emphasized that they would appreciate help from the program in maintaining contact with the alumni world. They do not want to be left alone to keep in contact with one another, but they recognize such contact as an important part of their professional networking. Alumni of online education would appreciate events sponsored by the school to give them an excuse and a motivation to get together again.

The concept of disengagement from online community in general and from learning communities in particular is still in need of further exploration, and this study has provided a framework to guide such study. For example, the disengagement process provides a new lens for the study of learning outcomes in distance learning. How does the disengagement process shape the retention of materials learned? In addition it has repercussions specifically for professional programs, in which the networks made for future knowledge sharing on the job are an important outcome of the educational process.

Because this project focused on LEEP, and because it spanned a fairly short period of time, some future areas of study are also readily apparent. The first is that disengagement needs to be studied in other online education programs, ones that are at other education levels, and that use different cohort models and different course delivery mechanisms. More longitudinal study is also needed. When participants are interviewed within two or three months of departure, as they were in this study, they are still adjusting to new jobs, discovering how their friendships will change over time, and recovering from the tiring experience of being in LEEP! Interviewing participants after another six months, another year, and another two years should provide a better picture of how the activities of disengagement affect future activities and relationships.

Conclusion

An attention to disengagement will allow degree-oriented distance education programs to improve alumni relations, new student recruitment, professional success of alumni, and emotional and instrumental support for graduating students. Supporting students through disengagement leaves them feeling confident in their jobs, willing to reach out to prospective students, and looking forward to continuing professional relationships. People who work to develop, or participate in, many types of intrinsically transient online social worlds should be able to use the results of this study to work on supporting their members as they leave, both instrumentally and emotionally, and supporting the disengagement process in a way to facilitate desirable future results. As well, disengagement may have implications and provide further explanation for the success or failure of future knowledge sharing.

Acknowledgments

Many thanks to the LEEP students and graduates who participated in these interviews and without whom this research would not have been possible. Data collection for this project was supported by a University of Illinois at Urbana-Champaign Graduate College Dissertation Research Grant.

Note

1. Quotes are identified by the pseudonym of the participant who made the statement. Pseudonyms reflect the gender of the participant. Some quotes contain the mark [. . .], which means that identifying details have been removed from the quote in order to protect the anonymity of participants.

References

Adler, P. A., & Adler, P. (1999). Transience and the postmodern self: The geographic mobility of resort workers. *Sociological Quarterly, 40*(1), 31–58.

Arrow, H., McGrath, J. E., & Berdahl, J. L. (2000). *Small groups as complex systems: Formation, coordination, development, and adaptation.* Thousand Oaks, CA: Sage.

Babbie, E. (1996). 'We Am a Virtual Community.' *The American Sociologist, 27*(1), 65–71.

Baker, P. M. A., & Ward, A. C. (2002). Bridging temporal and spatial 'gaps': The role of information and communication technologies in defining communities. *Information, Communication & Society, 5*(2), 207–224.

Blanchard, A., & Horan, T. (1998). Virtual communities and social capital. *Social Science Computer Review, 16*(3), 293–307.

Bruckman, A., & Jensen, C. (2002). The mystery of the death of MediaMOO: Seven years of evolution of an online community. In K. A. Renninger & W. Shumar (Eds.), *Building virtual communities: Learning and change in cyberspace* (pp. 21–33). NY: Cambridge University Press.

Cumming, E., & Henry, W. E. (1961). *Growing old: The process of disengagement.* New York: Basic Books.

Dickinson, A. M. (2002). Knowledge sharing in cyberspace: Virtual knowledge communities. In D. Karagiannis & U. Reimer (Eds.), *Proceedings of Practical Aspects of Knowledge Management 4th International Conference* (pp. 457–471). Berlin: Springer-Verlag.

Fox, N., & Roberts, C. (1999). GPs in cyberspace: The sociology of a 'virtual community'. *The Sociological Review, 47*(4), 643–671.

Gersick, C. J. G. (1988). Time and transition in work teams: Toward a new model of group development. *Academy of Management Journal, 31*(1), 9–41.

Haythornthwaite, C. (1998). A social network study of the growth of community among distance learners. IRISS '98 Conference, March 25–27, 1998, Bristol, UK.

Haythornthwaite, C., Kazmer, M. M., Robins, J. & Shoemaker, S. (2000). Community development among distance learners: Temporal and technological dimensions. *Journal of Computer-Mediated Communication, 6*(1). Retrieved from http://www.ascusc.org/jcmc/vol6/issue1/haythornthwaite.html. (Reprinted in this volume)

Jablin, F. M. (2001). Organizational entry, assimilation, and disengagement/exit. In F. M. Jablin & L. L. Putnam (Eds.), *The new handbook of organizational communication: Advances in theory, research, and methods* (pp. 732–818). Thousand Oaks, CA: Sage Publications, Inc.

Kazmer, M. M., & Haythornthwaite, C. (2001). Juggling multiple social worlds: Distance students on and offline. *American Behavioral Scientist, 45*(3), 510–529. (Reprinted in this volume)

Kennedy, T. L. M. (2000). *Virtual communities: An exploratory study of feminist experiences in cyberspace.* Unpublished Honours B.A., Brock University, St. Catharines, Ontario, Canada.

Kolko, B., & Reid, E. (1998). Dissolution and fragmentation: Problems in on-line communities. In S. G. Jones (Ed.), *CyberSociety 2.0: Revisiting computer-mediated communication and community* (pp. 212–229). Thousand Oaks, CA: Sage.

Lesht, F., & Schejbal, D. (2000). *Alumni giving: Does distance education affect alumni giving?* Toronto, Canada: 18th Annual NUTN Conference.

Levy, P. (1999). An example of Internet-based continuing professional development: Perspectives on course design and participation. *Education for Information, 17,* 45–58.

Newman, B. M., & Newman, P. R. (1999). *Development through life: A psychosocial approach* (7th ed.). Belmont, CA: Brooks/Cole.

Pennsylvania State University. (1996). *Distance education at Penn State: Vision, principles, and policies.* University Park, PA: Pennsylvania State University.

Quinnan, E. J. (1997). Connection and autonomy in the lives of elderly male celibates: Degrees of disengagement. *Journal of Aging Studies, 11*(2), 115–130.

Ridings, C. M., Gefen, D., & Arinze, B. (2002). Some antecedents and effects of trust in virtual communities. *Journal of Strategic Information Systems, 11*(3–4), 271–295.

Rojo, A., & Ragsdale, R. G. (1997). A process perspective on participation in scholarly electronic forums. *Science Communication, 18*(4), 320–341.

Rousseau, C., Drapeau, A., & Corin, E. (1997). The influence of culture and context on the pre- and post-migration experience of school-aged refugees from Central America and Southeast Asia in Canada. *Social Science and Medicine, 44*(8), 1115–1127.

Rousseau, C., Said, T. M., Gagne, M.-J., & Bibeau, G. (1998). Between myth and madness: The premigration dream of leaving among young Somali refugees. *Culture, Medicine and Psychiatry, 22,* 385–411.

Smith, M. J. (1999). Strands in the Web: Community-building strategies in online fanzines. *Journal of Popular Culture, 33*(2), 87–99.

Strauss, A. (1978). A social world perspective. *Studies in Symbolic Interaction, 1,* 119–128.

Strauss, A., & Corbin, J. (1998). *Basics of qualitative research* (2nd ed.). Thousand Oaks, CA: Sage.

Tuckman, B. W., & Jensen, M. A. C. (1977). Stages of small-group development revisited. *Group and Organizational Studies, 2,* 419–427.

Weedman, J. (1999). Conversation and community: The potential of electronic conferences for creating intellectual proximity in distributed learning environments. *Journal of the American Society for Information Science, 50*(10), 907–928.

Wellman, B., & Gulia, M. (1999). Net surfers don't ride alone: Virtual communities as communities. In M. Smith & P. Kollock (Eds.), *Communities in Cyberspace* (pp. 167–194). London: Routledge.

New Challenges and New Features in Online Settings

CHAPTER 7

Caroline Haythornthwaite
Alvan Bregman

Affordances of Persistent Conversation: Promoting Communities That Work

Collaborative activity, whether conducted face-to-face or in online spaces, whether for work, learning, and/or the development of a community, requires contribution to the group endeavor in the form of exchange of ideas, opinions, thoughts, and resources. Yet we find two related problems when trying to get people working or learning together, at a distance, and via computer media. Online participation requires that individuals express their thoughts *and* present themselves. In an earlier paper we explored root concerns of users in becoming participants online as revealed in longitudinal interviews with students in the LEEP (Library Education Experimental Program) distance education program (Bregman & Haythornthwaite, 2003). We review these concerns below, but take the argument further to shift the emphasis from the theoretical aspects discussed in that paper to the more practical aspects of promoting participation and community.

Collaborative activity is group activity, and as such it requires getting to know and be known by others. Online participants have to initiate and then sustain successful working relations with others, as well as contribute to keeping the whole group going.[1] Interaction and conversation are needed to develop trust about the reliability of others and the quality of their contributions, and so they can develop trust in you. People get to know who knows what in a group, and use that as a means of both allocating and retrieving information and tasks.[2]

Although futuristic images suggest distributed coworkers meeting and deliberating in cyberspace just as they would "in real life," current reality involves a lot of text-based electronic communication, where participants are neither seen nor heard.[3] Distributed participants more often than not have to express their thoughts and present themselves through text—by writing in chat rooms, on bulletin boards, on Web pages, via e-mail, and in word-processed documents that end up as attachments to e-mail.[4]

Thus, we find one unintended consequence[5] of computer-mediated activity is its high emphasis on writing (and thus also reading) and the ability to express oneself through writing. Moreover, it is more than just expression of thoughts. It is also presentation of an image of self—a persona—that represents you to others as you wish to be seen (see also Turkle, 1995; Rheingold, 2003). Thus, a second unintended consequence of computer-mediated collaboration is that even the presentation of self has to be done through writing. And now let's add a third dimension: not only must thoughts and personae be constructed through text, but how you do that persists over time. Whatever you write now reveals your thoughts and personality for as long as the logs exist, and to whomever has access to those logs both now and in the future.

Pity the poor naïve users who enter this domain—needing to write, but cognizant of both the meaning it gives to them as actors in this collaborative space and the persistence of the image they present. Thus, it is not surprising to find that new users have difficulty crossing the threshold into collaborative activity, taking steps to contribute, and understanding how to balance old ways of working, writing, or being educated with the strangeness of the new online environment.

The importance of these aspects of new user behavior became apparent to us in analyzing a series of longitudinal interviews with seventeen master's students in the LEEP distance program (see the Introduction to this volume for details on the program). A series of longitudinal interviews that explored the notion of community among these individuals (see Haythornthwaite, Kazmer, Robins & Shoemaker, 2000) showed that when students begin the program, writing is their *entrée* to and explanation of the community.[6] Students report how they learn about others through their writing, consciously watching what and how others post, and using these observations to evaluate themselves and their own postings. Together, students co-construct norms about acceptable styles, and quantity and quality of communications for each of the available media.[7] Yet this is all difficult for them at first. The lack of understanding of communication norms engenders anxiety about their writing and often also about themselves. Thus, it is important to understand the dual challenge facing participation in online environments: getting new users active in online spaces, and getting them comfortable expressing and presenting themselves online.

We have been exploring the particular concerns of new users as they come to join the LEEP online collaborative and community experience. We have learned that a sense of community exists in LEEP primarily derived from student-to-student interaction, and that this contact is important for satisfaction in the online program (see Haythornthwaite, Kazmer, Robins & Shoemaker, 2000). To make contact online, and to build a satisfying community, it is imperative that individuals contribute— that their voices be heard and that they can hear others. Yet this is more difficult online, where you don't have the casual encounter in the hallway, and where ways of communicating are new and strange. And it is more difficult when you have yet to learn the conventions—or *genres*—of online conversations.

The kind of conversation that supports an online environment combines elements and traditions of both speech and writing. Online conversation, whether conducted via e-mail, chat, online bulletin boards, or other means, is not only carried on through written text, but text that remains as a record of the conversation. "Previously ephemeral in-class discussions persist and remain available for later review. Every opinion, however well expressed, every joke, turn of phrase, and typographical error remains preserved, leaving a written legacy of an individual's persona and style" (Bregman & Haythornthwaite, 2003, p. 124). Interaction by such means constitutes a *persistent conversation*, a term originated by Tom Erickson and Susan Herring (see Erickson, 1999a; 2003). The persistent nature of such conversation, and the way it "may be searched, browsed, replayed, annotated, visualized, restructured, and recontextualized" (Erickson, 1999b) means that participants draw on the genres of both speech and writing when composing and interpreting messages. Thus, in analyzing the conditions that face new users in LEEP, and to understand how such text-based interaction plays out in any online spaces, we have looked to the literature on genre in writing and in speech for clues to understanding genres of persistent conversation.

Genres are important for online collaborative activity because, as Miller (1984) has pointed out, such shared, rule-based, and conventional means of communication help members of discourse communities accomplish social goals, such as getting work done, learning, making friends, and sustaining community. We find that in introducing new users to the environment, the task "becomes one of how to help community members identify and use genres associated with *persistent conversation*" (Bregman & Haythornthwaite, 2001, np; see also Miller, 1984, 1994).

In looking at these new users and making sense of their struggle to learn the communication norms of this environment, the work of genre theorists in speech and writing helped us identify three dimensions of interactivity that suggest root concerns for all users of persistent conversation. Elsewhere, we have described at more length our proposed *three radicals of presentation in persistent conversation* (Bregman & Haythornthwaite, 2001, 2003). We suggest these radicals as root concerns for new users of any online space, but illustrate them here with examples from the LEEP distance-learning environment. From their accounts, we can see how concerns about writing and self-presentation through persistent textual interfaces affected their ability to contribute, create, and belong to their community. We find that these dimensions revolve around speaker-audience relations. In accepting the importance of speaker-audience relations in forming genres we follow Bakhtin (1953:1986, 1975:1981); and in searching for root, or *radical* concerns of users we follow Frye (1957:1969), from whom we have adapted the phrase "radicals of presentation." The three radicals are:

Visibility: relating to the means, methods, and opportunities individuals use for presentation

Relation: relating to the nature of the tie between speaker and audience, *and* the ties among audience co-participants

Co-Presence: relating to the temporal, virtual, and/or physical co-presence of speaking and listening participants

We revisit the three radicals here, explaining them briefly, and then drawing particular attention to how each affects new users. We add here descriptions of the ways in which technologies, both social and computer-based, can help new users through the initial trial period. We examine for each radical the social and technical affordances that promote or hinder new users, in other words, what features of the social and technical infrastructures allow adjustment to visibility, awareness of others, and co-presence with others. The term *affordance* originated in psychology in the work of Gibson (1979). It has been adopted in referring to technical artifacts by both Norman (1988) regarding physical objects, and Gaver (1996) for computer systems. From these views, an environment, physical device (e.g., a doorknob, a chair), or computer representation (an icon, a window) each affords (i.e., allows for the possibility of) specific kinds of action by the individual.

More recently, a social dimension has been added to the concept of affordance by Bradner and colleagues (Bradner, Kellogg & Erickson, 1999). Their working definition of a *social affordance* is "the relationship between the properties of an object and the social characteristics of a group that enable particular kinds of interaction among members of that group" (p. 154). The environment, device, or representation is considered in terms of what it allows or makes happen to others as well as to the individual. As they explain:

> . . . consider a door that opens out into a busy hallway. If a person opens the door quickly, it may strike someone entering from the other direction. One possible solution is to put a glass window in the door. The glass window addresses the problem at two levels. At the level of individual perception, the glass makes a person on the other side visible (i.e., the window affords seeing through it to a sighted person). At the social level, since people are socialized to not strike others with doors, they will refrain from doing so if given the chance. Furthermore, not only can the potential door opener see through the window, but the person on the other side can see as well, and thus there is shared knowledge of the situation (e.g., 'I know that you know that I know'). As a consequence, the door opener will be held accountable for her actions. This accountability, which arises from the optical properties of glass, human perceptual abilities, and the social rules of the culture, is an example of what we call a social affordance. (Bradner, Kellogg & Erickson, 1999, p. 154)

Social affordances are an integral part of collaborative environments. Since the purpose is to engage and encourage participants, to "open the door" to others, it is particularly important to consider the social aspects of technologies and the way technologies are appropriated to afford social interaction.

Three Radicals of Presentation in Persistent Conversation

Visibility

To be visible in a traditional environment, it is sufficient to show up—to be seen in the common space. This is not so online. Being present requires active presentation of self in the online space, and as we have already noted, this is most likely to be through text in contemporary online environments. *Visibility* requires that participants *choose a medium* from among the available means of communication, through which they want to be "seen." For example, they must choose between e-mail or chat, weighing their familiarity with the conventions of the medium and the visibility it provides or imposes (e.g., through private or public conversation, to one person, or to the whole class). Or they might choose phone over e-mail, seeking the visibility of voice cues over the text of e-mail. Choice of medium may also depend on what is socially acceptable for communication from one person to another within the group (e.g., from a low-ranking employee to the owner of the company), or what the group or organization has either socially sanctioned (see Markus, 1994; Yates, Orlikowski, & Okamura, 1999) or technically sanctioned by including or excluding as an option for members of the online environment.

Second, they choose the occasion or *timing* of the communication (e.g., during a synchronous class session or asynchronously at their own convenience). They may also choose a timing that takes advantage of known social patterns among participants. Students in these classes often choose the timing of assignment submission (e.g., the night before class) as an opportunity for conversation with others. They use e-mail in a near synchronous manner by choosing to send e-mail soon after submitting assignments. This "entrainment" of group members to the timing of assignment submission (McGrath, 1984) affords the opportunity for a social interaction; and the technical capabilities allowing rapid delivery of e-mail affords the use of an asynchronous medium as a synchronous one.

Third, when they come to compose their communication, they choose a *method* of expressing themselves, including the form, style, and tone of the communication, and whether to conform to observed communication conventions (e.g., using a salutation and signature) or the norms of group expression and behavior. For example, e-mail format originally followed the tradition of office memos. Users have the option of choosing to follow those conventions or ignoring them (see Yates & Orlikowski, 1992, on reproducing the conventions of the formal business letter). Rules and conventions may have arisen from the community itself, evolving through use and positive reinforcement garnered for following those conventions (DeSanctis & Poole, 1994). Thus, players in a limerick game adhere to the rules or are corrected in their behavior (Erickson, 1999c); members of a Usenet group discussing soap operas make conventional uses of e-mail headers to signify message content in a manner established by the group (e.g., those that reveal plot details; Baym, 1995, 2000; see also McLaughlin, Osborne, & Smith, 1995, for discussion of status cues, signatures, roles, etc., in CMC [computer-mediated communication] discourse.)

When they begin, new online participants know none of the local norms. The new distance students do not know how to post appropriately to class Web boards, class chat, and even e-mail. They do not know how to craft their words to express themselves in a way that shows them as they wish to be seen. With this uncertainty comes anxiety, perfectionism, and self-doubt.

> I started to have a lot of anxiety and you know just wondering you know if what I was posting was . . . uh . . . you know . . . was . . . sounded okay or if it sounded so bad . . . I was really beginning to have a lot of self-doubts. [Nancy, in her first distance class][8]

> At the beginning it was difficult for me because I felt like when I posted something it had to be perfect . . . It takes me a lot of time just to post on the Web board just because of the idea that it has to be perfect. [Ted]

To learn the norms, they watch the quality and quantity of others' posts, and judge their own contribution from that.

> When I read everybody else's postings they sound so much more intelligent than mine. [Nancy]

> There seem to be those in the community that are very active. I swear they must live by the computer. It must be by their bed and they post in their dreams. Then there are some of us, and I might be one, I won't say you never hear from, but in that fringe a little less than halfway of those who never talk and those who talk all the time. [Ted]

These results show how important the start-up phase is for individuals and for collaborative groups. Unchecked anxiety about self-presentation can prevent individuals from contributing, creating a barrier to overall participation. Thus it is important to pay attention to start-up and initiation when getting collaborative activity up and running.

While most students become comfortable with the local norms and their contribution to them by their second semester, contributing online still requires effort. Students feel that it continues to take more effort to stay visible online that it would face-to-face (see Haythornthwaite et al., 2000). Thus, to keep continued participation requires commitment on the part of participants, or intervention from instructors, sufficient to maintain contributions even in the face of this extra effort.

Social and Technical Affordances for Visibility
Individuals can increase or manage their visibility both socially and technically. Choosing and using a medium inherently involves a choice about visibility. Media technically afford different degrees of visibility as part of the constitution of the medium: writing and conversation styles are made visible via text; and voice and speaking style via audio streaming, telephone, and teleconferencing. Media also afford different choices for the visibility of co-participants in a conversation, for example, by choosing between BCC (blind carbon copy) and CC (carbon copy) e-mail options. Similarly, a list of the individuals signed into a chat room shows who and how many are present, and e-mail "To" and "From" lists show who else is included in the conversation. Conversations may be enhanced or curtailed by the way in which media make the individual visible.

Providing means for posted pictures and biographies, and archives of postings to Web boards, and so forth, can enhance the visibility of the individual. As a social affordance, the visibility offered by an online picture gallery (e.g., uploaded to a common site) or picture-posting norm (e.g., on personal home sites) goes both ways. Enhancing visibility in this way allows the individual to reveal more about him- or herself, and affords the opportunity to learn more about others by looking at their pictures. Similarly, archived postings allow a longer time for retrieval and review of postings, increasing the visibility of all contributors.

New users and new groups may face particular problems in getting the conversation going. A critical mass of contributions is usually needed to start discussion, picture posting, etc. Moreover, without some posting, new users will not have a corpus to examine to determine norms. It often falls to the continuing leadership or administration to bootstrap such interaction and contribution (Connelly & Thorn, 1990; Markus, 1990). The visibility of participants can be encouraged through interventions such as leading by example (e.g., in setting the tone of conversation style online and speed of response to queries), reward mechanisms (e.g., recognition or awards to members of the community for contributions), and establishing norms or requirements for posting biographies, participating on Web boards, or other such activities.

Why should we spend time enhancing visibility? A key side effect of the presentation of self is that the personal disclosures build stronger interpersonal ties among participants, which generally enhances satisfaction with group endeavors. Encouraging recurrent communication behaviors helps create and reintroduce the genres that contribute to community. As participants use and see use of a common set of genres, it becomes clearer to them how to act and behave in the online space, thereby reducing their uncertainty and reticence to post.

Lurking, fading back, and being invisible *do not* contribute to conversations, community, or collaborations: "one cannot subscribe to a community, one must participate interactively" (Doheny-Farina, p. 37). This does not mean that one must be visible at all times to be a member of the community. Differentiation of functions or roles within the community means that, at different times, it will be appropriate for different people to be visible. If such visibility is effected, community is enhanced; if expected participation does not materialize, community is diminished and may dissipate entirely (Rafaeli & Sudweeks, 1997).

Relation

In participating online, students make different choices of media and expression according to their relation with their audience, and according to who they know is with them in the audience. The less well they know others in the class, the more anxious they are about communicating, and the more careful they are in what they write. The weight of the written word exceeds that of other types of communication[9] and increases concerns about exposure.

> When I see things written down they seem to have more weight, so when you pretty much communicate with other people through writing I think holy cow these people are so smart. I'll look dumb if I ask them. [Alice]

Concerns about exposure are moderated by relations among participants. The better they know others, the easier it is to ask "dumb questions," the more they feel they exist in a safe environment, a condition considered essential for collaborative learning (Bruffee, 1993), and indeed for collaboration of any kind. The better they know others, the more likely they are to add extra communication with them through a medium that provides a more private exchange (Haythornthwaite, 2000). The private interaction makes the environment safer because exposure can be limited to known and trusted others. Thus, many of the distance students report how they use IRC's (Internet Relay Chat) whisper facility to socialize with friends during class sessions, and to gain clarification of class content. This private exchange makes them feel part of the group and yet not excluded or ridiculed for not knowing everything.

> I'm not a practicing librarian so I had these people helping me out and feeding me information and they were great. We'd just be talking on the Web or in class in the chat room and they'd use all of these acronyms and I'd come back on and say whatever. Then somebody would whisper [via IRC] and give me an explanation. Everybody was so nice and polite. There was never a hint of "you should know this." [Beth]

The radical of *relation* suggests two things for building participation. First, that the environment needs to provide facilities whereby participants get to know others, thereby reducing anxiety about exposure. Second, some means of communication are better suited to some kinds of communication than others. The backchannels of IRC whispering and private e-mails provide a much-needed second channel for certain kinds of communication among a certain subset of the overall group (Cogdill, Fanderclai, Kilborn & Williams, 2001; Haythornthwaite et al., 2000). Thus, it is important when supporting collaborative activity to provide multiple means of communication so that individuals and subgroups within the full set of participants can use means that suit their needs and preferences (see also Haythornthwaite, 2000; Dennis & Valacich, 1999).

Social and Technical Affordances for Relation
Technical design and social conventions can both promote getting to know others. As noted above, posting biographies or personal statements provides disclosure about others, as does seeing who is signed in online, how many are participating, and whether these others are friends or strangers. Socially, having longer-term, continued associations rather than rotating groupings enhances getting to know others and their style. Excluding lurkers can ensure that everyone knows something about the participants with whom they are interacting.

Conversely, design can also be used to limit getting to know others. This can be useful, as in the way that anonymity in group decision and support systems can promote idea generation. Other designs to limit familiarity include having revolving groupings, limiting the identification of others (e.g., using names or pseudonyms but no other information), and allowing large groups of unknown size and composition that include lurkers.

While anonymous participation and rotating groups may promote the purpose and the provision of ideas, limiting the activity of getting to know others runs counter to notions of building online community. Instrumental exchanges that get work done do not in themselves build community; interpersonal bonding is also needed to build a community. Hence, the goals of the group need to be considered when making such technical choices. However, even for groups aiming to form closer online ties, new users may enjoy the ability to remain anonymous until they get the feel of the environment. For example, a trial period of nonpersistent conversation may help users get familiar with the technical features of the environment and provide beginners with a safe environment for play that can later promote participation. Similarly, although anonymity may not be the goal of the group, it may be a useful tool to use on occasion to bootstrap idea generation.

A further consideration in looking at affordances and the root concerns about relations is the way the composition of a group may constrain or enhance access to particular kinds of information. While a strongly tied community of users may be motivated to share information, this information may be limited in extent or homogeneous in kind. Thus, the advantages of motivated participation and communication among strongly tied members need to be balanced with the new information and perspectives that come through weak ties (Granovetter, 1973). Studies of LEEP distance learners have shown that the media chosen by instructors as the main means of contact for the class play an important role in connecting all members, whether strongly or weakly tied. More strongly tied pairs add on to that base communication via other means (see Haythornthwaite, 2000, 2001, 2002, 2003). Thus, choices made about media by instructors have impact on access to information by all members of the class.

Thus, whether the goal is for a strong community of known colleagues, an anonymous, wide-ranging exchange, or some combination, relational ties are a root consideration. We are not saying that knowing everyone is the best plan, nor that anonymity is. We emphasize that *relation* is a root characteristic of online communication that affects interaction and can be addressed in both social and technical design to promote either outcome.

Co-presence

The third radical, *co-presence*, has to do with bringing people together in a shared space. Our interviews revealed that co-presence was important for creating the kind of group feeling that helps build relationships and contributions, and that elusive thing known as community.

Presence is a familiar theme in discussions of CMC (e.g., Short, Williams & Christie, 1976; Heeter, 1992; Lombard & Ditton, 1997). Early work described how media that conveyed multiple cues (e.g., voice, dress, appearance, body language) provided a higher degree of "social presence." The design of new media has often been aimed at recreating the multiple cues of real life in an attempt to make the individual feel more like they are in a real environment. However, our interviews revealed that a key attribute of presence for the distance students is co-presence—being there with others (see also Heeter, 1992). In this way, presence reveals itself as relational, in other words, dependent on ties between participants, not just a property of individual participants' interactions with the technology. It can be enhanced by bringing speaker and audience together—virtually and temporally—by using synchronous communication in a common virtual space.

Being co-present with the speaker and with fellow students fills an emotional need for some participants.

> I need to hear my professor's voice. I need the stimulation of comments . . . I need my other classmates to respond to me, or I need to respond to my other classmates in the chat, when we're having a class. I mean I just need that feedback from them. [Nancy]

Not only does it provide immediate feedback and thus a more interactive collaborative exchange, it also contributes to an enhanced feeling of community among students.

> The second thing that really helps is the IRC just because it is spontaneous, real-time. They are there at the same time you are. It's not like they answer at two o'clock in the morning in their bathrobe or from work. Wherever they are, they are online right now. I think the IRC really helps. Nothing else really feels like a community. I need the synchronous stuff. [Jerry]

Thus, like Miller (1994), we see co-presence as tying consideration of presentation to community maintenance, and addressing how to support community rather than just communication.

Social and Technical Affordances for Co-presence
Co-presence is enhanced by a number of social and technical affordances. The immediacy afforded by synchronous communication media, and the greater number of physical cues offered by synchronous video over audio over text each contribute to a greater sense of being there with others. However, synchronicity needs to be managed, particularly for large groups. Thus, a regularly scheduled, synchronous chat session is needed to afford the opportunities for people to gather in the same virtual place at the same real time. Students also report that a little face-to-face time adds immensely to their subsequent feelings of being there with others when online. They have a "face to go with the name on the screen" after they have met face-to-face (e.g., in the mid-semester on-campus session). Both of these—synchronous meetings times and face-to-face meetings—are interventions that fall to instructors and/or administrators to implement.

Students also find that knowing more about others (the *relation* radical) also contributes to enhanced feelings of co-presence. Knowing more about what others' home situations are when online helps ground their own experience and makes them feel they have more in common with others, such as knowing that others are dealing with the same at-home interferences such as children who want attention, or that others also spend time folding laundry while listening to lectures. Co-presence is also enhanced by the use of backchannels to talk with other members of the audience (e.g., during an online, real-time lecture). By whispering to others, they know there is an audience that is co-present and following the lecture in the same way they are. The technical feature of whispering affords augmentation of feelings of co-presence.

At the community level, co-presence addresses the way in which we look for the online equivalent of (or substitute for) shared physical space: the commonality of shared landmarks (the computer on the desk at home; landmarks on the computer desktop such as those found in a common interface); the identification of known external landmarks in the online space or place (common hyperlinks); shared experiences (e.g., knowing that others also have children bothering them while working); and shared time schedules. Our interviews indicate that these subtle aspects of co-presence are significant to how online participants come together—how they "commune."

Summary

We reviewed briefly here the three radicals of visibility, relation, and co-presence, which we find are root concerns of users of online spaces. Analysis of interviews led us to believe that while these are important and relevant for understanding the genres of persistent conversation, they stand out in sharp relief for new users. Attention to these radicals suggests a way of looking at the concerns facing new users and adjusting social and technical features to afford the appropriate visibility of themselves and others, the nature and extent of others in the environment, and the way these bring people together.

We find that getting new users active in shared space involves getting comfortable with the environment through trusting others and their own self-representation. The online students need to trust that they are operating in a safe environment—one in which it is permitted to ask "dumb questions," where it is safe to put themselves out there and be visible. They also need to trust that the way they represent themselves through persistent conversation reflects the persona they wanted to project. To trust requires getting to know their audience (i.e., those to whom they posted messages), including what others are like, how many there are, how perfect their personas are, and how tolerant they are of missteps. Getting to know others also means finding a place in this audience or community, whether as peer, guru, or newbie, and then how to present themselves to that audience. Moreover, finding a place also involves creating a place by using conventions, and creating and sustaining norms and conventions of expression via each medium within the community.

We emphasize again that the radicals show us root characteristics that concern online users. We have presented here how attention to these three radicals allows us to approach new users' concerns in a way that lets us see what social and technical affordances can strike at the root of their concerns, with the hope that attention in this direction will ameliorate their transition into and participation in their online endeavors.

Notes

1. For more on group activity and group functions, see McGrath, 1984; Argote, Gruenfeld, & Naquin, 2001.
2. This kind of knowledge about the group is known as *transactive memory*. See Wegner, 1987; Brandon & Hollingshead, 1999; Monge & Contractor, 2003.
3. Attention to bandwidth, equipment costs, learning costs, and the reach across regions, tends to leave us working substantially in text. Even when meetings are augmented by video or audio conferencing, the need for temporal co-presence often leaves much communication to flow outside formal meeting times, through text-based electronic media.
4. For descriptions of the media see Curtis, 1997; Sproull, 1991 regarding e-mail; Werry, 1996 regarding Internet relay chat (IRC); Marvin, 1995 regarding MUDs.

5. See also Rogers, 1995, and Sproull & Kiesler, 1991 for more on unintended consequences of innovations.
6. For more on conversation and its relation to community, see Cherny, 1999; Miller, 1984, 1994; Munro, 1998.
7. See also DeSanctis & Poole, 1994, on how norms and uses emerge from group use, a process they call *adaptive structuration;* and McLaughlin, Osborne, & Smith, 1995, on the introduction of norms to CMC environments.
8. Quotations from participants are included to illustrate the more general findings.
9. This persists even if the instructors try to make a more conversational use of the media.

References

Argote, L. Gruenfeld, D., & Naquin, C. (2001). Group learning in organizations. In M. E. Turner, *Groups at work: Theory and research* (pp. 369–411). Mahwah, NJ: Lawrence Erlbaum.

Bakhtin, M. M. (1953:1986). The problem of speech genres. In C. Emerson & M. Holquist (Eds.), *Speech genres and other late essays* (pp. 60–102). Austin, TX: University of Texas Press.

Bakhtin, M. M. (1975:1981) *The dialogic imagination: Four essays.* Edited by M. Holquist. Austin, TX: University of Texas Press.

Baym, N.K. (1995) From practice to culture on Usenet. In S.L. Star (Ed.) *The cultures of computing* (pp. 29–52). Oxford: Blackwell.

Baym, N. K. (2000). *Tune in, log on: Soaps, fandom and online community.* Thousand Oaks, CA: Sage.

Bradner, E., Kellogg, W., & Erickson, T. (1999). *The adoption and use of "Babble": A field study of chat in the workplace.* Proceedings of the 6th European Conference on Computer Supported Cooperative Work (ECSCW '99) (pp. 139–158). Copenhagen, Denmark.

Brandon, D., & Hollingshead, A. (1999). Collaborative learning and computer-supported groups. *Communication Education, 48*(2), 109–126.

Bregman, A., & Haythornthwaite, C. (2001). Radicals of presentation in persistent conversation. *Proceedings of the 34th Hawaii International Conference on System Sciences.* Los Alamitos, CA: IEEE Computer Society. Retrieved from http://www.hicss.hawaii.edu/HICSS_34/PDFs/DDPTC01.pdf.

Bregman, A., & Haythornthwaite, C. (2003). Radicals of presentation: Visibility, relation, and co-presence in persistent conversation. *New Media and Society, 5*(1), 117–140.

Bruffee, K. A. (1993). *Collaborative Learning: Higher Education, Interdependence, and the Authority of Knowledge.* Baltimore: John Hopkins University Press.

Cherny, L. (1999). *Conversation and community: Chat in a virtual world.* Stanford, CA: CSLI Publications.

Cogdill, S., Fanderclai, T., Kilborn J., and Williams, M. (2001). Backchannel: Whispering in digital conversation. *Proceedings of the 34th Hawaii International Conference on System Sciences.* Los Alamitos, CA: IEEE Computer Society.

Connolly, T., & Thorn, B. K. (1990) Discretionary data bases: Theory, data and implications. In J. Fulk & C. W. Steinfield. (Eds.), *Organizations and communication technology* (pp. 219–234). Newbury Park, CA: Sage.

Curtis, P. (1997). MUDDING: Social phenomena in text-based virtual realities. In Kiesler, S. (Ed.), *Culture of the Internet* (pp. 121–142). Mahwah, NJ: Lawrence Erlbaum.

Dennis, A. R., & Valacich, J. S. (1999). Rethinking media richness: Toward a theory of media synchronicity. *Proceedings of the 32nd Hawaii International Conference on System Sciences.* Los Alamitos, CA: IEEE Computer Society Press. Retrieved from http://www.computer.org/proceedings/hicss/0001/00011/00011017.PDF.

DeSanctis, G., & Poole, M. S. (1994). Capturing the complexity in advanced technology use: Adaptive structuration theory. *Organization Science, 5*(2), 121–147.

Doheny-Farina, S. (1996). *The wired neighborhood.* New Haven, Conn. Yale University Press.

Erickson, T. (1999a). Persistent conversation. *Journal of Computer-Mediated Communication, 4*(4), whole issue. http://www.ascusc.org/jcmc/vol4/issue4.

Erickson, T. (1999b). Persistent conversation: An introduction. *Journal of Computer-Mediated Communication, 4*(4). Retrieved from http://www.ascusc.org/jcmc/vol4/issue4/ericksonintro.html.

Erickson, T. (1999c). Rhyme and punishment: The creation and enforcement of conventions in an on-line participatory limerick genre. *Proceedings of the 32nd Hawaii International Conference on System Sciences.* Los Alamitos, CA: IEEE Computer Society Press.

Erickson, T. (2003) *The persistent conversation minitrack: History.* Retrieved October 28, 2003 from http://www.pliant.org/personal/Tom_Erickson/HICSS_PC_History.html.

Fish, R., Kraut, R., Root, R., & Rice, R. (1993). Video as a technology for informal communication. *Communications of the ACM, 36*(1), 48–61.

Frye, N. (1957: 1969) *Anatomy of Criticism: Four Essays.* New York: Athaneum.

Gaver, W. (1996). Situating action II: Affordances for interaction: The social is material for design. *Ecological Psychology, 8*(2): 111–129.

Gibson, J. J. (1979). *The ecological approach to visual perception.* Boston: Houghton Mifflin.

Granovetter, M. S. (1973). The strength of weak ties. *American Journal of Sociology, 78,* 1360–1380.

Haythornthwaite, C. (2000). Online personal networks: Size, composition and media use among distance learners. *New Media and Society, 2*(2), 195–226.

Haythornthwaite, C. (2001). Exploring multiplexity: Social network structures in a computer-supported distance learning class. *The Information Society, 17*(3), 211–226.

Haythornthwaite, C. (2002). Strong, weak and latent ties and the impact of new media. *The Information Society, 18*(5), 385–401.

Haythornthwaite, C. (2003). Supporting distributed relationships: Social networks of relations and media use over time. *Electronic Journal of Communication, 13*(1). Retrieved from http://www.cios.org/getfile/haythorn_v13n1.

Haythornthwaite, C., Kazmer, M. M., Robins, J., & Shoemaker, S. (2000). Community development among distance learners: Temporal and technological dimensions. *Journal of Computer-Mediated Communication, 6*(1). Retrieved from http://www.ascusc.org/jcmc/vol6/issue1/haythornthwaite.html. (Reprinted in this volume)

Heeter, C. (1992). Being there: The subjective experience of presence. *Presence: Teleoperators and Virtual Environments, 1*(2): 262–271.

Lombard, M., and Ditton, T. (1997). At the heart of it all: The concept of presence. *Journal of Computer-Mediated Communication, 3*(2). Retrieved from http://www.ascusc.org/jcmc/vol3/issue2/lombard.html.

Markus, M. L. (1990). Toward a "critical mass" theory of interactive media. In J. Fulk & C. W. Steinfield (Eds.), *Organizations and Communication Technology* (pp. 194–218). Newbury Park, CA: Sage.

Markus, M. L. (1994). Electronic mail as the medium of managerial choice. *Organization Science, 5,* 502–527.

Marvin, L. (1995). Spoof, spam, lurk and lag: The aesthetics of text-based virtual realities. *Journal of Computer-Mediated Communication, 1*(2). Retrieved from http://www.ascusc.org/jcmc/vol1/issue2/marvin.html

McGrath, J. E. (1984). *Groups, interaction and performance.* Englewood Cliffs, NJ: Prentice Hall.

McLaughlin, M. L., Osborne, K. K., & Smith, C. B. (1995). Standards of conduct on Usenet. In S. G. Jones (Ed.), *CyberSociety: Computer-mediated communication and community* (pp. 90–111). Thousand Oaks, CA: Sage.

Miller, C. (1984). Genre as social action. *Quarterly Journal of Speech, 70*(2), 151–167.

Miller, C. (1994). Rhetorical community: The cultural basis of genre. In A. Freedman & P. Medway (Eds.), *Genre and the new rhetoric* (pp. 67–78). Basingstoke, UK: Taylor & Francis.
Monge, P. R., & Contractor, N. S. (2003). *Theories of communication networks.* Oxford: Oxford University Press.
Munro, J. S. (1998). *Presence at a distance: The educator-learner relationship in distance learning.* University Park, PA: American Center for the Study of Distance Education.
Norman, D. (1988). *The design of everyday things.* NY: Basic Books.
Rafaeli, S., & Sudweeks, F. (1997). Networked interactivity. *Journal of Computer-Mediated Communication, 2*(4). Retrieved from http://www.ascusc.org/jcmc/vol2/issue4/rafaeli.sudweeks.html.
Rheingold, H. (2003). *Smart mobs: The next social revolution.* Cambridge, MA: Perseus.
Rogers, E. M (1995). *Diffusion of innovations.* Fourth Edition. New York: The Free Press.
Short, J., Williams, E. & Christie, B. (1976). *The social psychology of telecommunications.* London: John Wiley & Sons.
Sproull, R. (1991). A lesson in electronic mail. In L. Sproull & S. Kiesler (Eds.) *Connections: New ways of working in the networked organization* (pp. 177–184). Cambridge, MA: MIT Press.
Sproull, L., & Kiesler, S. (1986). Reducing social context cues: Electronic mail in organizational computing. *Management Science, 32*(11), 1492–1512.
Sproull, L. & Kiesler, S. (1991). *Connections: New ways of working in the networked organization.* Cambridge, MA: MIT Press.
Turkle, S. (1995). *Life on the screen: Identity in the age of the Internet.* New York: Simon & Schuster.
Wegner, D. (1987). Transactive memory: A contemporary analysis of the group mind. In B. Mullen & G. Goethals (Eds.), *Theories of group behavior* (pp. 185–208). New York: Springer-Verlag.
Werry, C. C. (1996). Linguistic and interactional features of Internet Relay Chat. In S. Herring (Ed.), *Computer-mediated communication* (pp. 47–63). Amsterdam: John Benjamins.
Yates, J., & Orlikowski, W. J. (1992) Genres of organizational communication: A structurational approach to studying communication and media. *Academy of Management Journal, 17*(2), 299–326.
Yates, J., Orlikowski, W. J., & Okamura, K. (1999). Explicit and implicit structuring of genres in electronic communication: Reinforcement and change in social interaction. *Organization Science, 10*(1), 83–103.

CHAPTER 8　　　　　　　　　　　　　　　　　　*Jennifer Robins*

Affording a Place: The Persistent Structures of LEEP

Introduction

> ... what attracts people is people ... (Munro, Hook, & Benyon, 1999)

Persistent structures are the landmarks that distinguish and characterize a location in both physical and virtual space. They are built into an environment providing a durability and stability that supports social behavior. When behaviors are recurring, a history is accumulated that is inextricably bound to the persistent structures, giving them a symbolic meaning in a community. The aggregate of meanings attached to persistent structures is what transforms a space or location into a *place* (Dourish, 1999; Gieryn, 2000). By identifying and analyzing the relationship between persistent structures and patterned social behaviors, an understanding of this transformation is gained that can inform the design of more meaningful physical and virtual environments (Gaver, 1996).

This research describes the relationship between the persistent structures and patterned behaviors that emerged from a study of a community formed by students in the Library Education Experimental Program (LEEP), a distance education program at the Graduate School of Library and Information Science at the University of Illinois at Urbana-Champaign. In an earlier paper (Robins, 2002), I determined that patterned behaviors observed in LEEP involved forms of social navigation.

Social navigation, a term coined by Dourish and Chalmers (1994) refers to the way people find their way around by observing the activities of others (Dieberger, et al. 2000). Social navigation in cyberspace operates in much the same way as it does in the physical world. In the physical world people make recommendations about places to visit. In cyberspace, Web pages offer lists of recommended sites. In the physical world, people ask for advice from experts. On the Web, there are pages that provide answers to frequently asked questions (FAQs). People also use forms of social navigation that are less direct. For example, if the parking lot of a restaurant is full at dinnertime, people might assume the food there is good. Computer systems can provide a similar means of awareness by displaying indications of *read-wear* on Web pages, which show how many times a page has been visited (Hill & Hollan, 1994). A fourth method of social navigation in both worlds involves the use of guides, tours, and tutorials, all of which are drawn from models outside of cyberspace (Dieberger, 1999; Dourish, 1999; Munro, Hook, & Benyon, 1999). Because of the parallels, behaviors learned in the physical realm can serve as models of behaviors in computer-mediated environments.

In my earlier study, seven social navigation behaviors that distinguish LEEP as a virtual place are identified: *recommender, tutoring, orienting, netiquette, anarchistic, affirming,* and *inclusive* behaviors. Many of these are prosocial behaviors, meaning they are aimed at promoting the well-being of others. Prosocial behaviors are contagious. As people witness acts of kindness, they are prompted to behave the same way. When the action occurs in a virtual place, the acts are more public, and thus more likely to be imitated (Brief and Motowidlo, 1986; Constant, Kiesler, & Sproull, 1996). Some of social navigation behaviors in LEEP occurred by design. Others emerged spontaneously from the activities of students.

In this study, the persistent structures in LEEP are analyzed more closely than in the previous study. The social navigation behaviors supported by each structure are identified. In this way, the role of the structures can be seen more clearly making the transformation from space to place apparent.

Social Navigation in LEEP

For the purposes of simplification, clarity, and verb tense consistency, the labels for the social navigation behaviors in LEEP have been refined in this paper. *Recommender* behaviors and *tutoring* behaviors are combined in the category of *guiding* behavior. *Netiquette* is now referred to as *acculturating* behavior and includes behaviors that reinforce the social mores of the community. *Anarchistic* behavior is referred to as *appropriating* behavior. *Inclusive* behaviors are combined with and labeled after *affirming* behaviors. With this simplification, more attention can be given to the role of the persistent structures in LEEP. By drawing attention to the way these structures support behavior, this study demonstrates the essential role they play in the LEEP virtual community. The five categories of social navigation behaviors are defined next, followed by a description of the seven, key persistent structures of LEEP. The behaviors are: orienting, acculturating, guiding, appropriating, and affirming.

Orienting: Heidegger noted that we act responsively to stimuli in our lives because a response is called for, not because we have used reason to determine an appropriate action. Heidegger labeled this behavior "thrownness." Many thrown behaviors are acts of language that "flow with the situation" during social interaction (Winograd & Flores, 1986). In the virtual environment, this responsive thrown communication lingers in textual form where it can be embarrassing for the program initiate, who lacks confidence in this new medium. Over time, however, occupants develop a better understanding of the role of text in a virtual place. Orienting behaviors are those that characterize this process.

Acculturating: A hallmark that distinguishes a place from a space is the presence of norms for accepted behaviors. Acculturating involves the reproduction and reinforcement of acceptable behaviors and shared values in a community. For example, good manners and etiquette in the physical world are mirrored in the netiquette of the virtual world. There are conversations and expressions that are considered acceptable and violations often meet with reprisals. Acculturation can be more difficult in the virtual realm because of the equivocality of speech when it appears in textual form. Without hearing voice inflections or seeing gestures and facial expressions, meaning can be misinterpreted (Baym, 1995a; Daft & Lengel, 1986; Franco, et al., 1995). Still, culture can be created and maintained in the virtual realm (Baym, 1995b; Jones, 1995; King, Grinter, & Pickering, 1997; Franco, et al., 1995; Hiltner & Walker, 1997).

Guiding: Giving help in the form of instruction or advice is a common prosocial behavior. Efforts that support this activity in cyberspace include the use of recommender engines, like the one used by Amazon.com that tells customers "Here are our recommendations for you." But guiding can also be done by people. Members of cyber communities can offer a rich supply of help and opinions, if this guiding behavior is encouraged (Constant, Kiesler, & Sproull, 1996).

Appropriating: There is a limit to the degree that human behaviors in public places can be controlled. In public cyber places, structures can easily be appropriated by the people they support (Baym, 1995b). Because the medium is largely textual, authority is harder to represent. For example, in chat rooms and on Web boards in LEEP, posts from administrators appear in a form that is identical to that of the students. Therefore, in a busy textual discussion, voices of those in authority are obscured. Rather than a hindrance, appropriating structures can be an affordance in a virtual place because it gives members a sense of ownership and control.

Affirming: Behaviors that arise from the need for approval and belonging are forms of social navigation. Recognizing the impact of affective states in cyberspace, some Web sites greet returning visitors by name, indicating that the site has personalized its accommodations to better meet their needs. In a virtual place, as in a physical place, these affirming behaviors can convey the sense of caring and being cared for, which are hallmarks of a good community (Lyons, 1987, p. 247). They are a response to fundamental human desires for "living together, working together, experiencing together, being together" (Nisbet, 1960, p. 83).

Social navigation behaviors are joint activities that require both signalers and receivers in order to occur (Clark, 1996). To illustrate, in order for guiding behaviors to occur, there must be at least one person seeking guidance and one person giving it. In this analysis, no attempt has been made to separate signalers from receivers.

The Persistent Structures

Studying human activity in relation to persistent structures is a perspective borrowed from activity theory, which explores the ways structures like artifacts, rules, and the division of labor affect human activity (Engeström, 1990; Leont'ev, 1978; Nardi, 1996). Hutchins's work in distributed cognition extends this theory by exploring ways that behavior depends on knowledge that is embedded and distributed through mediating structures (1994). The persistent structures of LEEP are built into the LEEP environment by the program designers. They are the scaffolds that support human activity in this virtual place. There are four types of structures in LEEP: educational, ritual, technological, and administrative. However, in this report, educational structures like classes and instructors are not discussed because they are unique to a distance education environment and do not necessarily apply to the design of other virtual places.

Ritual Structures

The two ritual persistent structures involve face-to-face events: the introductory, two-week, on-campus, summer session that students refer to as *boot camp,* and the mid-semester, on-campus session required for all classes. Boot camp combines a condensed introductory course in information science with workshops where students learn to use various program technologies. Boot camp requires students to work in groups that perform under a series of tight deadlines. Beginning the second semester, students also attend one, full-day, on-campus session for each course they take.

It may seem unusual to include face-to-face activities in a study of behavior in cyberspace, but there is no inherent reason to create a boundary between the two worlds, unless the attraction of a virtual place is to keep the identity of the inhabitants private (Curtis, 1997; Turkle, 1997). Arranging ways for people to interact in both spheres can enrich relationships. In the physical realm, communication is enhanced by the use of gestures, expressions, and the ease with which speech repairs can be made as shared meaning is constructed, simplifying highly equivocal communication (Clark, 1996;). In the virtual realm, communication difficulties related to separation by time and/or distance are overcome. Having face-to-face rituals in a virtual place can combine advantages from both worlds.

Technological Structures

The virtual component of LEEP takes place over the Internet. Classes are conducted using a combination of synchronous and asynchronous communication. The technological persistent structures of LEEP are the computer applications that serve as mediums of communication. The three that are discussed here are the Internet Relay Chat (IRC), the IRC whisper feature, and the Web boards. Students participate in classes using IRC. Instructors' lectures are narrowcast using live audio, while students type in questions and responses to questions. Both the lecture and a log of the IRC session are archived and can be accessed after the class section. The whisper feature is operational during class sessions. Students use this technology to communicate privately with the instructor or teaching assistant. But they also use it to communicate with other students, which makes it a popular feature. The Web board is the most public technology. Each class has its own Web board. Discussions there are stored permanently in the class archive and can be revisited in future years.

Administrative Structures

Two of the persistent structures described here are administrative roles: the technical staff and the moderator of the LEEP virtual environment. These administrators model behaviors that are replicated in the community. The technical staff is available to answer student questions around the clock and on weekends. They can be reached by phone or through a dedicated chat room, which makes it possible for students with dial-up modems to obtain technical assistance. The staff offers training with the LEEP technology and support with technical problems as they arise.

The role of moderator has been filled in LEEP by the associate dean, Linda Smith, who had particular responsibility for oversight of LEEP (for more on administrative roles, see Estabrook, this volume). The moderator is the most visible leader in the community (Kim, 2000), and the associate dean certainly fits that description (see below).

These persistent structures afford and orchestrate the social navigation that occurs in LEEP. The face-to-face activities afford richer communication and work to create a shared history among the students. The technological structures are more than a medium for communication; they are a way for students to achieve a sense of presence in the community. The administrative roles are the government in this virtual world.

Studying LEEP

These findings are from a longitudinal, ethnographic study of LEEP. During 1998 and 1999, seventeen LEEP students participated in four telephone interviews. Transcripts were analyzed after each round of interviews. Each analysis led to the creation of the next question set administered. The four interviews resulted in 750 transcribed pages, which were analyzed again using open coding, a grounded theory method where the codes arise from the data, rather than from a predefined scheme (Strauss & Corbin, 1998). From this analysis, the persistent structures of the program were identified. Data related to these structures were extracted and reanalyzed in order to determine how the structures orchestrate activity. All data quoted in the findings come from these interview transcripts. The respondents are referred to by a pseudonym that reflects their gender.

The Role of the Persistent Structures in LEEP

The matrix presented in Table 8.1 below maps the persistent structures of LEEP to the patterned social navigation behaviors that occur in this community. The matrix illustrates the relationship between the persistent structures in the program and the five social navigation behaviors discussed above: orienting, acculturating, guiding, appropriating, and affirming. The behaviors form the columns of the matrix. The seven persistent structures form the row headings. The first two rows present the ritual structures—boot camp and the on-campus weekend. The next three rows present the technologies; IRC, the IRC whisper feature, and the Web board. The last two rows present the administrative structures—the technical staff and the moderator. An X is used to show that a structure is providing support for a behavior.

The matrix is well populated, suggesting the way that the persistent structures cumulatively reinforce the social navigation behaviors. The empty cells are also informative. For example, during the LEEP boot camp, appropriating behaviors were not evident. This could be due to the intensity of the schedule during those two weeks. Guiding behaviors occur during class sessions in IRC, but they are almost exclusively related to the educational content of the class and are not included in this report. Because of the moderator's authority in the community, appropriating behaviors relative to this role do not occur.

TABLE 8.1. **The Social Navigation Matrix**

Persistent Structures	Orienting	Acculturating	Guiding	Appropriating	Affirming
Boot Camp	X	X	X		X
On-Campus	X	X		X	X
IRC	X	X		X	X
IRC Whisper	X	X	X	X	X
Web Board	X	X	X	X	X
Technical Staff	X	X	X	X	X
Moderator	X	X	X		X

Boot Camp

Social navigation in LEEP begins in boot camp, the face-to-face ritual that transforms incoming students into a cohort. Students arrive on campus as strangers, but during a two-week, condensed course they learn to work together to learn unfamiliar technologies and to complete course assignments. To succeed, they learn how to depend on one another. "We knew what our strong points were and how to blend ourselves well . . ." [Beth]. Through these common activities, relationships are formed that last throughout students' time in LEEP.

Orienting socially in virtual space is challenging because ". . . it is difficult to get to know somebody just in an online environment . . ." [Barbara]; but the LEEP boot camp overcomes this difficulty by creating opportunities for students to form the relationships in the physical world that transfer to the virtual world. "Even though they would be just a name on the screen . . . you still had the memory of knowing them from boot camp, which was such an intense experience" [Alice]. When students see familiar names on screen they recognize that "These are people I know and these are people I don't know" [Barbara]. In this way, the social world of LEEP is modeled after the social world created at boot camp.

> After the first couple of days there was really a sense that we were all in this together, . . . we were all trying to figure this out . . . We were feeling our way both in the course work and in the locality. [Barbara]

Boot Camp helps students in *acculturating* to the online community, by developing "sort of a shared history" [Jeff]. The difficulties students experience help them bond; "boot camp forms you into a group" [Beth]. The difficulties also create patterns of *guiding* behavior:

> . . .because of boot camp and the intensity of it, you help each other with your areas of expertise. So you felt very comfortable e-mailing anybody and saying, "I don't know anything about this and I think you do, can you explain this?" [Beth]

Boot Camp also instills a sense of belonging; "after boot camp you really feel like you're an integral part [of the community]" [Alice]. This *affirming* experience added intensity to the social bonds created between students; "I was so familiar with them, and I was so comfortable with them . . . quite like family" [Clarissa]. Many respondents reported that these bonds were the basis of the LEEP community.

The On-Campus Session

The ritual on-campus weekend, when students meet face-to-face, provides an opportunity to coordinate group projects that require extensive articulation work in order to coordinate the strategies, perspectives, and goals (Schmidt & Simone, 1996). This once-a-semester weekend also reinforces the social networks created at boot camp: "That was just wonderful. To go back to school and find a group of people that I actually clicked with" [Rene]. It also provides an *orienting* opportunity where students "put names with faces" of comrades they meet in the virtual environment, so "You can imagine what they look like and what they talk about . . . You can get a mental picture that helps" [Alice].

The on-campus session is *acculturating*, because it provides a chance to verify impressions that were formed online. Students can "come back and see if the interaction has changed any way from online" [Barbara]. The session can also change the impressions students have of one another:

> When I see things written down they seem to have more weight, so when you pretty much communicate with other people through writing, I think 'Holy cow these people are so smart.' . . . Then I go on campus and I go 'Well!' [Alice]

It also provides an opportunity to vent in a non-textual way. Written complaints are considered poor netiquette; but the weekend spent face-to-face allows for the casual, noncommittal, nonpublished faultfinding.

The weekend session also provides an opportunity for *guiding* behaviors such as exchanging information about courses: "Every professor has his own idea of what the work load should be . . . You also get word-of-mouth when you're on campus" [Ellen]. *Appropriating* also occurs during the on-campus session where friends reunite in an "old home week" [Jan]. Time is made for the type of ". . . very personal conversations" [Clarissa] that are difficult to conduct online.

In addition, the on-campus session gives students a chance to see where they fit into the community: "It was so great just to know that some other people were not really on top of everything." [Nancy]. This type of *affirming* behavior helps students maintain their relationships: "We all had a lot in common, it was wonderful to be able to fall back on that [during the on-campus session]" [Rene].

Internet Relay Chat

The patterns of social behavior learned in the physical world are models used to navigate socially in cyberspace, where behaviors are mediated by technology. In LEEP, Internet Relay Chat (IRC) is used during online class sessions by groups working on projects, and for communicating with the technical staff. IRC offers an immediacy that makes students feel included and connected to each other: "Even though you're typing, not speaking to them directly, you're typing with them" [Jan].

Orienting in IRC, students soon learn that the medium is ephemeral, much like speech, "If you say something silly in the IRC, it is up there for a while, then it will move up there over the top of the screen" [Alice]. By observing the behavior of others in their classes they see that, in this medium, communication has "more heart . . . and a lot less thought" [Bill].

In *acculturating*, students come to enjoy the experience of "working with other people on the same stuff" [Alice]. It is in the chat where netiquette in the virtual community begins to emerge and violations are noticed. For example, attempts at humor sometimes fail, particularly attempts at sarcasm, which can appear cruel, or self-deprecating humor, which can look like self-pity. "It's interesting how you negotiate that sensitivity without facial expressions" [Jerry]. "I feel that you have to be much more careful in responding because they don't know my sense of humor." [Barbara]. Students compensate by adding explanatory text and emoticons.

Students find that *appropriating* the IRC rooms enhances social navigation in LEEP. Just as in the physical world, students socialize when meet in these virtual rooms.

> People would just kind of hang around and talk, chat, either people would come early or stay a little bit later. And people would just talk and stuff, and I felt like that helped, cause you had the chance to talk with people on a less formal level. [Holly]

However, because IRC is a text medium, students find their collective presence is as commanding as that of the instructor. This makes it easier for them to take control of discussions. Because text and names move quickly in IRC, it is possible to follow threads that are off from authorized topics. Occupants become intent on playing off each other's comments. A tangent develops and continues until the theme is played out or the instructor regains control. While this detracts from efficient communication, it strengthens the bond between the students. "It's just a little anarchy. The instructors are still in control . . . but everyone is getting goofy" [Alice].

The immediacy of IRC also supports *affirming* behaviors, because the medium gives students the opportunity to interact together:

> I need the stimulation of comments. I need my other classmates to respond to me, or I need to respond to my other classmates in the chat, when we're having a class. I just need that feedback from them. [Nancy]

The IRC Whisper Feature

The LEEP IRC has a feature that makes it possible for students to talk to one another privately during class time. The feature was meant as a way for students to ask instructors questions privately. However, in LEEP this feature has become a key structure supporting social navigation. When *orienting* to the LEEP environment, students are introduced to the feature:

> A friend of mine . . . she knew people who ended up putting me on their list. I was like "Oh, okay. I'll get a whisper from you. I'll put you all on my list." It ended up being that most of the class was talking to people. [Ellen]

Whispering also plays a main role in *acculturating* in the virtual environment. Most students discover that they are able to split their attention between an audio lecture, the textual class discussion, and whispered conversations with their friends. Whispering provides an extra channel of activity when students are online together:

> So you can still follow along and follow a conversation with someone else. When I whisper I don't feel like I am neglecting listening. I can still listen at the same time. I don't know what it is, but the classes move very slowly. They are not fast paced . . . Not that they are not interesting, [it's] just that they are not speeding along. [Alice]

According to the respondents in this study, whispering is a common behavior in LEEP: "It's like the electronic equivalent of passing notes, but it's the only time you ever see these people" [Doris]. Rules of netiquette in public discussions are relaxed when students whisper. Topics range from the mundane, "I'm going to make a sandwich" [Doris] to the sociable, "How was your ski trip?" [Shannon]. Whispered conversation is also a good way to "blow off steam." [Rene]. Humor is prevalent and while cynical humor is avoided on the Web board and the IRC, it is common in whispers. "You've got the people who are going, 'What does she think she's talking about?'" [Doris]. Occasionally a class is scheduled at the same time as a popular TV show. Some respondents will attempt to balance listening to the lecture, keeping up with the TV plot, and contributing to their whisper groups. But this balancing act has resulted in "failed whispers" that have entered into LEEP lore. A failed whisper is a comment that is meant to be private but is accidentally posted to the entire synchronous population.

Students also use this persistent structure in *guiding* one another: " A lot of [the whispering] does pertain to either clarifying terms the instructor uses, or, if you have to step away for a second and come back, 'What did I miss?' That sort of thing." [Bill]. Whispering is clearly a way of *appropriating* LEEP structures. Students are often unaware of how instructors and administrators feel about the activity. The lack of official reaction to whispers lends surreptitiousness to the activity, reinforcing the anarchistic feel of whispered conversation and reinforcing the students' sense of control in the virtual community.

> I always think it's funny, because I can't decide whether it drives the professor nuts, "Oh, they're paying no attention to me!" or if it gives them a good feeling of, "Wow, my class is so tight." I always wonder. [Doris]

Whispering also supports *affirming* behaviors: "I think that's invaluable in pulling the group together, or, feeling connected with people" [Doris]; "We're all talking among ourselves so it definitely builds a bond between students" [Rene]. Students also encourage one another in whispers, "They are like, 'Go! Go! Go!' You get all these comments on your behalf when you are giving your presentation." [Ellen]. "Almost everybody talked about how whispering was an important part of the social network" [Deb].

The Web Boards

The Web boards are the primary means for establishing the tone at LEEP. Each class has its own boards. In addition, there are Web boards for new students, job announcements, professional associations, and for general discussions. The Web boards are the most public medium of expression in LEEP. Postings to the class Web boards are visible to all students. Their public nature is intimidating to *orienting* students, who are particularly concerned about their postings in class, "I'll look dumb if I ask them this question" [Alice] or "Oh, what are other people thinking about my posting? Oh, gosh, why do my postings sound so shallow, and everyone else's sound so great?" [Nancy]. However, after a period of time of *acculturating,* students find: "Everybody saw everybody's comments, including the professors. We just had to get over feeling self-conscious about it. We've just had to get over it. It was a great experience" [Shannon]. The class Web boards also provide a level of accountability in the community, "You're judged by your peers, because it is all out there and they can see" [Ellen].

Students discover that the Web boards are ideal for sharing help and ideas. These public, prosocial behaviors establish LEEP as a supportive community. Students are comfortable *guiding* one another in a variety of ways and students with more expertise gain recognition as authorities: "with all his postings and stuff you can just tell he knows what he's talking about." [Alice]. In this climate, students turn to one another for help:

> Usually, if [the question] is something I think everyone might have a problem with, I post it to the Web board. [Alice]

> I don't have the library experience some of my classmates do. I wait to see what they're talking about and many times that will help a lot to cause me to think about what the lesson is about and how it applies. [Ted]

Students also begin *appropriating* the technology for personal purposes, "I have all these people who just love to sit on Web boards and give their opinion about stuff. Why don't I post [a job related question] and see what comes back" [Ellen].

The Web boards afford *affirming* behaviors, as well. When students offer each other approval in a public way, it reinforces the sense of community.

> The Web board is where you can throw something out even if you don't know which way you're heading with it or you feel you might of missed something. Then you get a lot of positive feedback. In a general way, it's nice. [Sue]

> It made me check the Web boards much quicker in the morning to see what other people had to say about [my posting] . . . So, I was more personally invested, because it's my project on display. [Jeff]

The Technical Staff

Roles can be considered persistent structures in a virtual place when they appear in a consistent and dependable manner, particularly if they are dedicated to the support of the community. While this might be expected of instructors in a distance education program, LEEP provides two additional roles that act as persistent structures: the technical staff and the moderator. The technical staff helps students with the program's technological components.

The support begins with the technology workshops offered during boot camp. The technical skills of the students who enter the program range from novice to expert. In *orienting* to a virtual place, novices encounter problems using the technology, but the technical support is personalized to meet their needs, "I think a large part of it, the technological part of it [is] making us all feel comfortable with the technology" [Beth]. But mastering the technology is a rite of passage for all LEEP students:

> So, I called the LEEP [technical staff member on duty], he just walked me through everything. It was like he was holding my hand. He said "O.K., do you see up here; look at the top of your screen. Do you see this? O.K. Click on this. Now do you see the pull-down menu? O.K. Now, . . . you need to send your file to the LEEP server." I mean that's what he did. He just walked me through it. . . . I kept thinking, "Oh, gosh, they probably think I'm so dumb, and so stupid, and I can't stand it. It's just not coming and coming." But [he] kept encouraging me, "You can do it; you can do it. Don't worry about it; just do it." So, I remember the very first time that I [did] it all myself. I just screamed, because I could do it by myself. [Nancy]

In *acculturating*, students find they are not alone with this type of experience and even come to argue over who was the staff's "worst nightmare" [Nancy]. But students find that the support is consistent in LEEP: "[It was] 11 p.m. on Saturday night, and he was actually there answering his phone . . . He was like, 'Go to bed. Stop crying. Go to bed. It's taken care of.'" [Rene].

Guiding by the technical staff in LEEP sometimes takes the form of tutorials. Technical support staff post instructions: "'This is how it works.' . . . and it's really all laid out, one, two, three." [Doris]. This level of support leads students to say LEEP is "More than an educational program. It's more a life program" [Jan]. This is also demonstrated in the way students can be seen *appropriating* staff for non-LEEP purposes: "I sent them a couple of totally unrelated, work, computer questions and I feel bad for burdening them with whatever; but, they are generally very, very helpful" [Jeff].

In addition, the prompt, personal service provided by members of the technology staff produces an *affirming* effect, "[He] knows me and what I know and what I don't know and [he knows] my system. . . . He has been so good, so good about answering all the questions promptly, never getting exasperated with ignorance or goof ups" [Beth]. This is another example of how "The program works hard to make you not feel isolated" [Jan].

The Moderator

Having an authority structure in an online community can serve many purposes, and the moderator has played a major role in promoting social navigation. While *orienting*, students first discover that the moderator is active in the community:

> I knew before I'd decided for sure to [join LEEP]. I had a question and I thought of her to e-mail it to. "Does this make sense? Have other people done this kind of thing?" And I e-mailed it to her, she's so responsive . . . [Doris]

In *acculturating*, students find the moderator "seems to know everything" [Ellen]. "Her turnaround on answering questions and concerns is just unbelievable" [Jan]. Because of the way the moderator behaves in the virtual domain, LEEP resembles a benevolent monarchy:

> It's nurturing. I think [the moderator's] personality on the Web board is certainly 're-sponsible.' The double sense of that is that she does respond immediately, and that she takes responsibility. It's very nurturing. It builds a certain amount of security. [Jerry]

Being involved in the community and acting as the ultimate authority, the moderator also models the *guiding* behavior that permeates LEEP: "You know if you have any question, [she] can probably fix it" [Jerry]. Because she is responsive to student inquiries and requests, the moderator lets students know that someone is looking out for their needs. This *affirming* behavior makes students feel like valued members of the LEEP community:

The fact that I had the screw up . . . and she said 'don't worry, let's work it out.' That didn't make me feel like a special case. It made me feel like 'Your just part of the family, we'll work this out.' [Jerry]

The students' admiration for the moderator's responsiveness is a binding force in the community: "I appreciate her. She is something. I wonder she has an e-mail terminal in her ear" [Clarissa]. It is "Another thing that makes me feel like part of the community" [Alice]. "To feel connected, you need that quick response time." [Shannon]

Discussion

In identifying and analyzing the impact of the persistent structures in LEEP, it is possible to see how recurring social navigation behaviors create meaning in a virtual place in much the same way as they do in physical space. This is not surprising since the behaviors originate in boot camp and are reinforced face-to-face during the on-campus session each semester. Other behaviors change their manifestations in the virtual world. For instance, synchronous activities made students feel connected when working at a distance. Reasons for this include an awareness of the presence of others engaged in the same activity. Also, real-time responses make students aware that others are listening to them. Asynchronous feedback is also important in LEEP. A quick response instead of an instantaneous response still makes students feel connected. Feedback from others helps students feel that their behavior and performance is appropriate in the community.

The very persistence of the structures proved important in this study as well. In the physical world and virtual world, consistency conveys meanings related to dependability, accountability, and responsibility. For example, the moderator's role in LEEP simulates the role of government, giving students a sense that they are being cared for. Knowing that a government is present and that someone is in charge reinforces the similarity between a physical and virtual place, while it makes students feel safe and secure.

This analysis also revealed differences between the physical and the virtual worlds. The two text channels, the IRC and the Web boards, allow for different types of expression. The IRC is informal and personal, while Web board exchanges are generally more formal and professional. In the physical world, there is not always an arena where one's professionalism remains on display. The continual presence of this arena in the virtual world caused some students confusion as they discovered that it was not always easy to match the professional, formal demeanors displayed on the Web boards to the ones created through casual exchanges in the IRC or during the on-campus weekend.

Also, in a virtual world, those in control have the power to establish and reinforce the tone of the environment. Social navigation in the virtual realm can be self-reinforcing. Because the behaviors of the technical staff and the moderator are public, they are models for others in the environment. For example, when these leaders respond quickly to students and offer them reassurance and affirmation, it prompts students to reciprocate by behaving the same way to each other. These behaviors set the tone at LEEP.

Conclusion

As evidenced by the well-populated matrix in Table 8.1, the relationship between the persistent structures and the social navigation behaviors in LEEP is mutually reinforcing. Each of the structures supports many of the behaviors, so each of the behaviors is supported by many structures. The persistent structures lend stability to the virtual community while the social navigation behaviors add meaning to the structures. By identifying and describing how this occurs in LEEP, it is possible to explain how a virtual space becomes a virtual place.

In LEEP, relationships and behaviors are established in boot camp: "In a way, we've had this ongoing conversation" [Jan]. The on-campus session fuels the conversation by reinforcing the relationships built in boot camp and online. Using the technical structures that underpin the community, reading takes the place of hearing and typing replaces talking, but the conversation continues. Administrators, in the roles played by the technical staff and the moderator, model the behaviors of the community, being helpful, prompt, personal, professional, and affirming. In this way, LEEP is experienced as a safe and supportive environment.

Students discover that behaviors that occur in a virtual place are similar to those that occur in the physical realm and that they can navigate by drawing on those past experiences. The virtual experience might begin with a sense of uncertainty, but students soon discover familiar friends and a supportive staff. Chat rooms, whispers, and Web boards are transformed into "a continual stream of consciousness" [Beth]. The conversation continues across time and distance. As students become acclimated, they reinforce the social mores of the community and find occasion to appropriate structures for personal as well as professional exchanges. Students also adopt the affirming behaviors of the staff, propagating the prosocial behaviors that occur in LEEP. Through these acts, they assert ownership of the community.

These are the ways that the recurring behaviors and the LEEP rituals, technologies, and administrative staff interact to create the place called LEEP. Considered individually, the persistent structures scaffold behaviors. Taken in the aggregate, the place is imbued with meaning.

References

Baym, N. K. (1995a). The performance of humor in computer-mediated communication. *Journal of Computer-Mediated Communication, 1*(2). Retrieved from http://www.ascusc.org/jcmc/vol1/issue2/baym.html.

Baym, N. K. (1995b). The emergence of community in computer-mediated communication. In S. G. Jones (Ed.), *CyberSociety: Computer-mediated communication and community* (pp. 138–163). Thousand Oaks, CA: Sage.

Brief, A. P., & Motowidlo, S. J. (1986). Prosocial organizational behaviors. *Academy of Management Review, 11*(4), 710–725.

Clark, H. H. (1996). *Using language.* Cambridge: Cambridge University Press.

Constant, D., Kiesler, S. B., & Sproull, L. S. (1996). The kindness of strangers: The usefulness of electronic weak ties for technical advice. *Organizational Science 7*(2), 119–135.

Curtis, P. (1997). MUDDING: Social phenomena in text-based virtual realities. In S. Kiesler (Ed.) *Culture of the Internet* (pp. 121–142). Mahwah, NJ: Lawrence Erlbaum.

Daft, R. L., & Lengel, R. H. (1986). Organizational information requirements, media richness and structural design. *Management Science 32*(5), 554–571.

Dieberger, A. (1999). Social connotations of space in the design for virtual communities and social navigation. In: A. J. Munro, K. Hook, & D. Benyon (Eds.), *Social navigation of information space* (pp. 35–54). London: Springer.

Dieberger, A., Dourish, P., Hook, K., Resnick, P., & Wexelblat, A. (2000). Social navigation: Techniques for building more usable systems. *Interactions, 7*(6), 36–45.

Dourish, P. (1999). Where the footprints lead: Tracking down other roles for social navigation. In A. J. Munro, K. Hook, & D. Benyon (Eds.), *Social navigation of information space* (pp. 15–34). London: Springer.

Dourish, P., & Chalmers, M. (1994). *Running out of space: Navigating in information spaces.* Adjunct Proceedings (Short Papers), Human Computer Interaction Conference, Glasgow.

Engeström, Y. (1990). When is a tool? Multiple meanings of artifacts in human activity. In Y. Engeström (Ed.), *Learning, working and imagining* (pp. 171–195). Helsinki: Orienta-Konsutit.

Estabrook, L. E. (this volume). The distance education program from the management perspective. In C. Haythornthwaite, & M. M., Kazmer, *Learning, Culture, and Community in Online Education: Research and Practice.*

Franco V., Piirto, R., Hu, H., & Lewenstein, B. (1995). Anatomy of a flame: Conflict and community building on the Internet. *IEEE Technology and Society Magazine,* summer, 12–21.

Gaver, W. W. (1996). Affordances for interaction: The social is material for design. *Ecological Psychology, 8*(2), 111–129.

Gieryn, T. F. (2000). A space for place in sociology. *Annual Review of Sociology, 26,* 463–493.

Haythornthwaite, C., Kazmer, M., Robins, J., & Shoemaker, S. (2000). Community development among distance learners: Temporal and technological dimensions. *Journal of Computer-Mediated Communications, 6*(1). Retrieved from http://www.ascusc.org/jcmc/vol6/issue1/haythornthwaite.html. (Reprinted in this volume)

Hill, W., & Hollan, J. (1994). History-enriched digital objects: Prototypes and policy issues. *The Information Society, 10*(2), 139–145.

Hiltner, J., & Walker J. (1996). Super frustration Sunday: The day Prodigy's Fantasy Baseball died; An analysis of the dynamics of electronic communication. *Journal of Popular Culture, 30*(3), 103–118.

Hutchins, E. (1995). *Cognition in the wild.* Cambridge, MA: MIT Press.

Kim, A. J. (2000). *Community building on the Web: Secret strategies for successful online communities.* Berkeley, CA: Peachpit Press.

King, J., Grinter, R., & Pickering, J. (1997). The rise and fall of Netville: The saga of a cyberspace construction boomtown in the great divide. In S. Kiesler (Ed.) *Culture of the Internet* (pp. 3–34). Mahwah, NJ: Lawrence Erlbaum.

Jones, S. G. (1995). Understanding community in the information age. In S. G. Jones (Ed.) *Cybersociety: Computer-Mediated Communication and Community* (pp. 10–35). Thousand Oaks, CA: Sage.

Leont'ev, A. N. (1978). *Activity, consciousness, and personality*. Hillsdale, NJ: Prentice Hall.

Lyons, L. (1987). *The community in urban society*. Lexington, MA: Lexington Books, 247.

Munro, A., Hook, K., & Benyon, D. (1999). Footprints in the snow. In A. J. Munro, K. Hook, & D. Benyon (Eds.) *Social navigation of information space* (pp. 1–14). London: Springer.

Nardi, B. A. (1996). Studying context: A comparison of activity theory, situated action models, and distributed cognition. In B. A. Nardi (Ed.) Context and consciousness: Activity theory and human-computer interaction (pp. 69–102). Cambridge, MA: MIT Press.

Nisbet, R. (1960). Moral values and community. *International Review of Community Development, 5*, 77–85.

Robins, J. (2002). Affording a place: The role of persistent structures in social navigation. *Information Research, 7*(3). Retrieved from http://informationr.net/ir/7-3/infres73.html.

Schmidt, K., and Simone, C. (1996). Coordination mechanisms: Towards a conceptual foundation of CSCW systems design. *Computer Supported Cooperative Work, 5*, 155–200.

Strauss, A., & Corbin, J. (1998). *Basics of qualitative research*. Thousand Oaks, Sage.

Turkle, S. (1997). Constructions and reconstructions of self in virtual reality: Playing in the MUDs. In S. Kiesler (Ed.) *Culture of the Internet* (pp. 143–156). Mahwah, NJ: Lawrence Erlbaum.

Winograd, T., & Flores, F. (1986). *Understanding computers and cognition: A new foundation for design*. Norwood, NJ: Ablex.

CHAPTER 9   *Karen Ruhleder*

Changing Patterns of Participation: Interactions in a Synchronous Audio+Chat Classroom

Introduction

The LEEP (Library Education Experimental Program) Live Sessions provide students and instructors with an important *same time, same place* experience as a regular part of a LEEP class. The technologies allow for many modes of interaction. The instructor can present information via the audio channel with the chat room available for students to ask questions or post comments related to the instructor's broadcast. They can also post messages to each other while the audio broadcast continues. This is where a potential shift in roles may occur. In a traditional classroom, the instructor generally controls the agenda, the resources, and the mode of interaction. In the LEEP environment, students can use the chat room to share their own experiences, answer other students' questions, offer explanations, or interpret the lecture. The instructor now faces the need to accomplish the pedagogical goal of the class session while also monitoring and reacting to chat room activity. This chapter draws on excerpts from audio+chat transcripts to illustrate this phenomenon.

Studying the Online Classroom

The data used in this chapter come from a larger study in which several graduate students and I interviewed faculty, students, and staff involved in the LEEP program. This project was part of a stream of research carried out at GSLIS (Graduate School of Library and Information Science) that is well represented in this book. For my own part, I became very interested in the kinds of interactions that took place during the live audio+chat class sessions. These sessions demonstrate elements of traditional classroom instruction, and of guided discussion (with many opportunities for digression), but also support new patterns of interaction not common to either (see also Ruhleder, 2004).

To look at this more closely, I collected data from two classes offered in summer 2000 and four in summer 2001 (the classes covered topics in business reference, indexing and abstracting, library administration, and grant writing). Using the recorded audio broadcasts of the instructors' lectures and the main class chat room logs of student and instructor comments, I was able to reconstruct the class session in terms of both what students heard via the audio link and what they saw in the chat room (whispers are not represented here, only statements posted to the main chat room and thus visible to the class as a whole).

I turned to Interaction Analysis (Jordan and Henderson, 1995) and Conversation Analysis (Sacks, et al., 1974) to help frame and interpret my observations. Conversation Analysis looks at the nuances of verbal interaction. For example, small interjections (uh huh) let a speaker know that the listener is following what is being said; lengthening a vowel can imply mistrust (she saaays she looked it up. . .). Even silence conveys meaning; a pause after a question or statement ("that was a great class") implies that the listener does not agree and the speaker might respond by weakening their original position accordingly ("well, if you're into subject X"). Interaction Analysis includes these kinds of issues but also looks more broadly at other aspects of interaction, such as the structure of an event, the spatial and temporal organization of an activity, how participation in these activities is determined, and how authority is established.

These frameworks offer a useful way of exploring issues raised by the application of new forms of technology to distance education. LEEP certainly changes the spatial and temporal organization of a class: there is no fixed classroom, no desks facing the front of a room. The disjunct nature of postings and multiple threads on the Web boards and in the chat room are fundamentally different from the standard small group discussion. But I am particularly interested in how the chat component of the live online classroom changes the traditional relationship between instructor and student. Students can pursue topics tangential to the class discussion, they can provide links to additional resources, and they can continue threads as long as there is interest in the topic. The instructor still sets the agenda and develops the overall structure of the course, but online participation gives students a venue to present their own perspectives and assert their own authority.

The availability of a separate forum—the chat room—that runs simultaneously with the instructor's broadcast is particularly fitting for the kind of students who have selected the LEEP option. These students often come with extensive professional experience in LIS (library information science) or other areas and may already hold an advanced degree in another area. This knowledge and experience does not always have a place in the traditional classroom. With the audio+chat arrangement, students don't have to raise their hand and hope to get called on in order to participate in the discussion; they can also pose questions to each other or supply an answer to someone else's question. Conversely, those *not* interested in a particular exchange do not have to sit and listen politely ("uh oh, so-and-so is going to bring up X again") because the broadcast and other conversational threads continue at the same time.

Before moving on to some more extensive examples of how students become part of the audio-chat classroom *multilogue* (Ruhleder, 2000), we begin with a simple example to illustrate how interactions will be represented (see Figure 9.1). In this example, the highlighted boxes show how one particular thread is demonstrated across the audio and the chat portions of the class. Note that the text in the chat room has not been cleaned up: any abbreviations, emoticons, lack of adherence to common rules of capitalization or punctuation, etc., are part of this kind of online forum and correspond to the use of informal language in everyday speech.

FIGURE 9.1. **Sample Representation of Audio-chat Interaction**

Time	Paraphrase of Audio Broadcast	Actual Chat Log
19:17:58	Instructor uses the 1997 economic census as an example of a government database organized around NIAC numbers.	
19:18:21	Instructor talks about search strategies for commercial online databases and refers to a class reading by Jan Tudor.	
19:19:30	Instructor continues to talk about strategies for getting information on specific industries.	S1: I spoke to someone at the census bureau a few weeks ago and they are still working on getting the complete 1997 Economic census online. End of the year
19:20:05	Instructor responds to S1's post: "I did not know that, S1. Thank you for letting us know."	
19:20:25	Instructor continues lecturing	S2: as an aside, i was amazed at how many us govt agencies had booths at the ALA conference with some great information on searching
19:20:29	Instructor starts talking about useful Web sites.	S3: I enjoyed Tudor most. She offers additional tips for gathering information like job announcements.
19:20:51	Instructor experiences some technical problems.	S4: Th econ census is available via cd-rom at government depository libraries. (ideally)

In this example, we can see that the instructor is still the primary presenter, speaking via the audio link. The chat room, however, provides a channel for students to share their own bits of information without interrupting the lecturer. Not only do S1 and S4 contribute information that is useful to the class, but two other students post as well. S2 adds a comment about a conference he attended and S3 picks up on the instructor's discussion of a reading for that week—not bad for three minutes of class time.

Examples of Chat-Participation: Class Excerpts

In the excerpts below, student contributions increasingly become a focal point of overall class activity. They illustrate ways in which the chat and audio threads can be interrelated and their impact on instructor-student and student-student interactions.

1. In the first example, a student asks a question that the instructor misunderstands. Other students in the chat room work to clarify the question.
2. In the second example, the instructor is lecturing on a complex topic. In response to a student's question, another student in the class offers to post some examples to the Web board.
3. Finally, in the third example, a student asks for the definition of a term. The instructor explains, but then loses control of the definition through multiple posts made by a student.

Names are omitted to preserve confidentiality. The chat dialogue is presented as it appeared in the chat room, complete with misspellings, grammatical errors, abbreviations, and so forth.

Excerpt 1: Reframing a Question

In a traditional, face-to-face classroom setting, raising one's hand and asking a question can be daunting. Students new to a subject may not always know the correct terminology to use or the best way to frame their question. As a result, the instructor may not interpret it correctly or may not understand it at all. This happens in LEEP, too, of course. However, the chat room offers students a way to help each other figure out how to reinterpret, reframe, and maybe even answer the question while the instructor moves in and out of speaking to other topics. The following example illustrates how this works. S5 posts a question at 20:00:53 that the instructor answers (20:01:07). S5 tries to reframe it herself at 20:04:18, to which the instructor replies (20:04:25) that he does not understand what she is asking. In a face-to-face class, S5 might not pursue the point any further. In the LEEP example, other students pick up the thread at 20:06:00 and 20:06:02, trying to narrow down what the real question is and keeping the thread going.

FIGURE 9.2. **Reframing a Question**

Time	Paraphrase of Audio Broadcast	Postings in the Chat Room
20:00:53	Instructor is lecturing about index construction, using an example that cross-references the terms *lawyer* and *attorney*.	S5: In regard to omnibus references—would it be taboo to include those Native American groups right under that heading, even though the heading has no locator?
20:01:07	Instructor answers: "It would be if you put a page number..." Instructor continues lecture.	
20:03:08	Instructor answers S6: "Right, thank you. S6, for putting it much clearer than I did..."	
20:04:18	Instructor finishes his answer to S6.	S5: I guess what I really mean is, Can you make up a heading for a list of common entries even through it does not have its own locator in order to minimize cross referencing and achieve better co-location?
20:04:25	Instructor answers: "I'm not sure if I get the gist of that, S5..."	
20:05:43	Instructor continues coal/acid rain example. Instructor sees S7's question and reads it aloud.	S7: Going back to Coal—would you include the acid rain alphbetically under coal with the pages acid rain, 152–153
*20:05:59	Instructor continues to read S7's question aloud.	S8: So acid rain under Heading 'envirment' with other page numbers than found under coal?
20:06:00	Instructor continues to read S7's question aloud.	S9: S5, are you suggesting indexing several specifics under a broader term for better collocation, the point from the specifics to the BT? For example, you'd put the locators under Native Americans with see references from Hopi, Iroquis, and Seminole?
20:06:02	Instructor addresses S7 and S8: "OK, what I'm going to do, I'm sending acid rain to its own heading..."	S10: S5, do you mean can you have a heading without a locator but with subheadings that DO have locators?
20:06:54	Instructor reads S9's question aloud. Instructor starts to read S10's question aloud.	
20:07:29	Instructor finishes reading S10's question.	S8: sorry! [no apparent reason for the apology]
20:07:40	Instructor addresses S9 and S5's questions: 'I think an answer is, it's better to have them underneath a heading...'	

continued on next page

FIGURE 9.2. *continued*

Time	Paraphrase of Audio Broadcast	Postings in the Chat Room
20:08:26	Instructor finishes addressing S9 and S5's questions.	S7: With malocclusion, there are no pages listed. Why not?
20:08:28	Instructor starts to read S7's question aloud.	S11: malocclusion is a heading without a locator, but the subheadings have locators . . . ??? that's OK?
	Instructor uses an example using coal and acid rain.	S6: So if lawyer had several subheadings, it would be better to use Attorney—see lawyer instead of using the double entry?
	Instructor answers S7 and S11: 'Thank you, S7 and S11, let me get back to that malocclusion . . . .'	
20:09:33	Instructor continues to answer the questions on malocclusion.	S5: Right, S10—I'm sort of begging the question of why you would want to employ an omnibus heading—that is, if you can gather Hopi, Sioux, etc. under Native American (even though there are no references in the text to Native Americans in general), why not? Why make the reader go look up each tribe individually? But you may have already answered by question by saying that you do always need a locator.
20:09:48	Silence for 5 seconds.	S11: thank you
20:09:53	Instructor responds to S5: "OK, ominibus heading is not something to use . . ."	

Again, this example highlights some of the work students can do to help each other figure out what it is that they are really asking—what they really don't understand. When S5 did not get a satisfactory answer, other students jumped in to help reinterpret and refine it. The work of figuring out and answering the question took about nine minutes in this example and the process took place concurrently with the lecture and with questions on other topics in the chat room. The instructor monitored the process by keeping an eye on the chat window and remained part of the process with periodic responses.

Excerpt 2: Creating an Online Handout

Software such as WebCT or Blackboard are designed to help instructors provide electronic versions of their syllabi, course packets, handouts, and other materials. These packages are designed on the assumption that the instructor is the primary author of course materials. LEEP technologies allow students to create and share resources of their own construction with other students in the class.

In the previous example we saw how students helped each other refine a question and construct an answer. This example goes one step further. The instructor is lecturing on Boolean searching, a topic that students often find confusing. S7 brings up a simple example at 19:21:27. After a response from the instructor, S9 adds a lengthy comment (19:24:00) and, in response to another student's post, offers to post a more detailed explanation to the Web board (19:29:01)—an electronic handout.

FIGURE 9.3. **Creating an Electronic Handout**

Time	Paraphrase of Audio Broadcast	Postings in the Chat Room
19:19:59	Instructor lectures on the use of uni-terms instead of compound terms in thesaurus construction, using the words *library* and *science* as an example.	
19:21:27	Instructor continues lecturing.	S7: But, can't you limit the unitary terms to 'library and science' not 'science library'
19:21:35	Instructor answers S7: "... that's something you can do when you see a lot of false drops and the system that you are using has the facility to handle adjacency..."	
19:24:00	Silence for 3 seconds.	S9: Actually, I don't think this will work as [another student] wrote it because the Boolean AND is commutative (order doesn't matter). If the terms are unitary, they'll be in different fields, so adjacency won't work. (You could use quotes for string searches in free text, but that would miss those articles where the terms don't appear in text.)
19:24:03	Instructor reads S9's comment and responds: "I think, you know, it's going to be a question of how the strings are parsed when the data for the inverted file is created ..." Instructor moves to new topic and lectures on the use of compound terms.	
19:26:53	Silence for 5 seconds. Instructor chuckles. Silence for 5 seconds	S12: How many rpms are you running on S9? I can't keep up. What was that question all about

continued on next page

FIGURE 9.3. *continued*

Time	Paraphrase of Audio Broadcast	Postings in the Chat Room
19:27:04	Instructor responds: ". . . I think what S9 was saying was [gives an example using Boolean terms] . . . I'm not sure I'm communicating this clearly or not, so others feel free to chime in through the chat and explain it some more . . ."	
19:28:12	Instructor continues: "Meanwhile, I'll go on . . ."	
19:29:01	Silence for 3 seconds.	S9: How 'bout if I put something on the Webboard tonight so I can go into some detail?
19:29:04	Instructor thanks S9 and reiterates that S9 will be posting something on the Web board.	
19:29:09	Instructor adds, "that'll clarify it for us, that'll be a big help." Instructor returns to S7's original post about using uniterms	S12: I think I understand it better. (library and science) not 'science library'
19:29:32	Silence for 2 seconds.	S7: Then why does MESH invert so often?
19:29:37	Instructor responds to S7: "That's a good question. . . . when you look at the beginning of Index Medicus . . ."	S13: Thanks S9. I am finally back. Net congestion.
19:29:49	Instructor continues answering S7.	S12: Thanks S9
19:30:06	Instructor offers another example relating to S7's question.	S8: great! thanks S9

In this example we see how S9, a student who is well versed in the current topic, can be a great resource for the class and for the instructor. S9 not only elaborates on the instructor's answer but also promises to post a more detailed explanation—in short, an online handout—for which the instructor thanks him. In this way, tasks for which the instructor alone was responsible can be picked up by students of their own free will. Of course, this also means that there is more for the instructor to keep track of and verify for accuracy of content and appropriate presentation.

Excerpt 3: Shift in Authority

The two examples above both illustrate some of the positive roles of chat. The instructor can continue presenting material and answering other questions while a student's poorly expressed question is reinterpreted and refined with the help of classmates. A student with special technical knowledge can draw on that knowledge to create a resource that will assist other class members.

There are also drawbacks to such broad student participation in that the instructor may lose control of the discussion. This is illustrated in the example below and centers around the definition of the term *slanted* within the context of abstracting. The excerpt starts with a question from S14. The instructor replies and, in a follow-up message, S14 refers to the practice of slanting in a way that suggests potential ulterior motives. The instructor immediately clarifies that the term *slanted abstracts* is not to be seen in a pejorative light but rather that the term means that an abstract will be slanted to a specific audience. S14, however, interprets the instructor's comment in a completely opposite way (20:21:33); after that, the instructor never quite gets back control over the meaning or use of the term.

FIGURE 9.4. **Shifting Authority**

Time	Instructor Audio Lecture	Chat Room Dialogue
20:18:17	Instructor is lecturing on abstract construction. Silence for 5 seconds.	S14: Instructor [instructor], I'm curious. Authors in cell/molecular biology are required to submit an abstract with the manuscript and when it's published, the author's abstract appears with the article. Do abstracting services use that abstract, or do they write a second one for the databases?
20:18:25	Instructor reads S14's question aloud. Instructor answers S14: "That's going to be completely dependent on the database it goes to . . ." Instructor lectures on the use of abbreviations. Instructor lectures on judging the intended audience.	
20:21:33	Instructor introduces the term *findings-oriented abstracts*. Silence for 4 seconds.	S14: thanks Instructor—of course us authors are not skilled abstractors and we write them for different reasons and with different slants than a professional abstractor would.
20:21:37	Instructor clarifies that *slanted abstracts* is not pejorative, but means slanted to a specific audience. Instructor lectures on selection of verb tense.	
20:21:33	Instructor encourages people to look at some sample abstracts and see if they find a pattern. Instructor laughs and says he'll take it that way.	S14: I probably should have used 'prejudices' than slants—

continued on next page

FIGURE 9.4. continued

Time	Instructor Audio Lecture	Chat Room Dialogue
20:23:57	Instructor starts moving on to the next point on his overhead. Silence for 6 seconds.	S15: Are you saying an abstractor would slant it to make it more understandable to a particular audience while the author would slant it to make it appear to be a more scholarly article than it is
20:24:03	Instructor responds to S15: "I'm looking at it a little bit differently than that . . ."	
20:24:52	Instructor talks about writing at different levels for different user populations.	S14: I think Instructor hit it on the head S15—authors often talk of what they would have liked to have done or obtained in results.
20:25:00	Instructor continues.	S7: Aren't some abstracts submitted prior to the article—so, if all research has not been finished, the abstract might not completely reflect the paper, or might say what is expected to be discovered, but, at the end of the research, the conclusion isn't quite the same as the abstract says. (Hope this makes sense)
20:25:12	Silence for 1 second; says "um." Silence for 3 seconds.	
20:25:16	Instructor responds to S14: "And S14 is mentioning this information, too, . . ." Instructor responds to S7: "I think that would be true if we're talking about meeting abstracts . . ."	S10: slanting=emphasizing?
20:26:19	Instructor explains that those abstracts aren't going into an abstracting and indexing service directly.	S14: in the natural sciences S7, you have to submit the abstract with the completed manuscript and the research has to be complete prior to submitting the paper for peer review.
20:27:41	Instructor responds to S10 saying that slanting is emphasizing, but in a non-pejorative way.	
20:28:01	Instructor says: "Thank you, S14, for putting in the real story. . . . That put it in a much clearer way than I did."	
20:28:38	Instructor continues: "If we move along here . . ."	S15: Is the author's slanting of an abstract considered bad or just par for the course?
	Instructor repeats S15's question, laughs and says, "I'll let S14 handle that one."	

continued on next page

FIGURE 9.4. *continued*

Time	Instructor Audio Lecture	Chat Room Dialogue
20:29:21	Instructor continues lecture. Silence for 2 seconds.	S16: Passing the buck Instructor
20:29:23	Instructor laughs and says, "I am passing the buck because, you know, I open up my MedLine and I take the abstracts as they are . . ." Instructor returns to lecture: "But since I'm talking about the writing of them . . . as opposed to the reading of them . . ." Instructor continues lecture.	
20:31:11	Instructor returns to earlier topic: "Now, I go back to the possibility of a modular or slanted abstract . . ."	
20:32:20	Instructor refers to a page in an article the class read on indexing vs. abstracting skills.	S14: Yes—it's bad S15 if it's done deliberately, which it is. Those of us in the field know who does this—others out of the field may not know. But it happens unconsciously, no matter how hard all of us try to be critical of our own studies—we often (including me) would send the manuscript with the abstract to our peers and competitors asking for a critical evaluation and how the manuscript was written. Many do not do this though--i
20:32:25	Silence for 6 seconds.	
20:32:31	Instructor says he'll wait while people read S14's post. Silence for 5 seconds.	
20:32:39	Instructor starts to continue the lecture.	
20:32:54	Instructor stops mid-sentence. Silence for 5 seconds.	S14: That's why I asked the question of Instructor in the first place
20:32:59	Instructor reads aloud S14's earlier post (at 20:32:20), thanks S14.	

The discussion of slanted abstracts began to get out of hand at 20:21:33. Had the instructor known how the dialogue might progress, he might have stepped in more aggressively. Instead, he dismissed S14's comment with a laugh in order to move on. Unfortunately, other students start to pick up on the meaning S14 proposed. By the time S14 posts a lengthy response citing personal experience to convey authority (20: 32:20, "those of us in the field . . ."), the instructor has lost control of this discussion and lets the incorrect interpretation go unchallenged in order to keep on track with the presentation of material. While it is not impossible for this kind of exchange to take place in a face-to-face classroom, its likelihood is increased by the openness of the online forum, which lets S14 continue to press the point even as the instructor is engaged elsewhere with the course material.

Some Final Observations

These examples show that audio+chat sessions are not just an extension of the traditional face-to-face classroom. Instead, as illustrated above, new forms of class participation are supported by the audio+chat technology, which change the relationships among the participants.

Students become active participants in class presentations, responding to posts made in the chat room, providing answers and explanations to other students, drawing on and sharing their knowledge and experience. They can do this contemporaneously with other class activities and can continue the thread offline, as illustrated by the example in which a student promises to post more information on a topic on one of the class Web boards.

This can be both a help and a hindrance to the instructor. On the one hand, the instructor no longer has the sole responsibility of clarifying a question or illustrating a point. Other students can help with these tasks while the instructor moves on. On the other hand, the instructor must now spend time monitoring and reacting to chat room activity while trying to follow the agenda for the day. Instructors may minimize distractions by not watching the chat room during the lecture or monitoring it only at specific intervals ("I will take some time for questions after I have explained X."). However, ignoring the chat for too long opens up the possibility that inaccurate information will be posted, circulated, and discussed among students.

Traditionally, the relationship between instructor and student has been that of expert and novice. The expert guides the novice through complex territory. In the open forum of the chat room, many potential guides are available, and some of these may know parts of the trail better than the instructor. This is what makes LEEP attractive to students who have professional experience to share and who wish to learn from both their instructors and their peers. The philosophy behind LEEP encourages this form of engagement and the implementation of the LEEP technologies support it. The audio+chat excerpts used in this paper present an initial look at how students and instructors are exploring and experiencing the possibilities and problems of this new engagement and these new technologies.

Acknowledgments

I wish to thank the students, faculty, and staff of the LEEP program for giving me access to their classes. I also wish to thank Brigitte Jordan of Xerox Palo Alto Research Center for her helpful comments on an earlier draft of this paper. This research was supported by National Science Foundation grant #9712421 and by the Graduate School of Library and Information Science, University of Illinois at Urbana-Champaign.

References

Beller, M., & Or, E. (1998). The crossroads between lifelong learning and information technology: A challenge facing leading universities. *Journal of Computer-Mediated Communication, 4*(2). Retrieved from http://www.ascusc.org/jcmc/vol4/issue2/beller.html.

Bruckman, A. (1998). Community support for constructionist learning, *Computer Supported Cooperative Work: The Journal of Collaborative Computing, 7*(1–2), 47–86.

Estabrook, L. (1999). *New Forms of distance education: Opportunities for students, threats to institutions.* Paper presented at *ACRL [Association of College and Research Libraries] National Conference,* Detroit, MI. Retrieved October 27, 2003 from http://www.ala.org/Content/Navigation Menu/ACRL/Events_and_Conferences/estabrook99.pdf.

Goodwin, C. (1981). *Conversational organization: Interaction between speakers and hearers.* New York: Academic Press.

Haythornthwaite, C. (1998). A social network study of the growth of community among distance learners. *Information Research, 4*(1). Retrieved from http://www.shef.ac.uk/~is/publications/infres/paper49.html.

Haythornthwaite, C. (2000). Online personal networks: Size, composition and media use among distance learners. *New Media and Society, 2*(2), 195–226.

Haythornthwaite, C., Kazmer, M. M., Robins, J., & Shoemaker, S. (2000). Community development among distance learners: Temporal and technological dimensions. *Journal of Computer-Mediated Communication, 6*(1). Retrieved from http://www.ascusc.org/jcmc/vol6/issue1/haythornthwaite.html.

Jordan, B., & Henderson, A. (1995). Interaction analysis: Foundations and practice. *The Journal of the Learning Sciences, 4*(1), 39–103.

Kazmer, M. M. (2000). Coping in a distance environment: Sitcoms, chocolate cake, and dinner with a friend. *First Monday, 5*(9). Retrieved from http://www.firstmonday.dk/issues/issue5_9/index.html.

Koschmann, T. (1996). *CSCL: Theory and practice of an emerging paradigm.* Mahwah, NJ: Lawrence Erlbaum.

Levin, J., & Waugh, M. (1998). Teaching teleapprenticeships: Frameworks for integrating technology into teacher education. *Interactive Learning Environments, 6*(1–2), 39–58.

Lombard, M., & Ditton, T. (1997). At the heart of it all: The concept of presence, *Journal of Computer Mediated Communication, 3*(2). Retrieved from http://www.ascusc.org/jcmc/vol3/issue2/.

Mynatt, E., O'Day, V., Adler, A,. & Ito, M. (1998). Network communities: Something old, something new, something borrowed . . . *Computer Supported Cooperative Work: The Journal of Collaborative Computing, 7*(1–2), 123–156.

O'Day, V., Bobrow, D., Bobrow, K., Shirley, M., Hughes, B., & Walters, J. (1998). Moving practice: From classrooms to MOO rooms. *Computer Supported Cooperative Work: The Journal of Collaborative Computing, 7*(1–2), 9–45.

Ruhleder, K. (1999). On the edge: Learning through sidework and peripheral participation. In M. Easterby-Smith, L. Araujo, & J. Burgoyne (Eds.), *Proceedings of the 3rd International Conference on Organizational Learning* (pp. 862–876). Lancaster, UK: Lancaster University.

Ruhleder, K. (2000). The virtual ethnographer: Fieldwork in distributed electronic environments. *Field Methods, 12*(1), 3–17.

Ruhleder, K. (2004). Interaction and engagement in LEEP: Undistancing 'distance' education at the graduate level. In T. Duffy, Thomas & J. R. Kirkley (Eds.), *Learner-Centered Theory and Practice in Distance Education* (pp. 71–90). Mahwah, NJ: Lawrence Erlbaum.

Ruhleder, K. & Jordan, B. (1997). Capturing complex, distributed activities: Video-based interaction analysis as a component of workplace ethnography. In A. S. Lee, J. Liebenau, & J. I. De Gross, *Information systems and qualitative research* (pp. 246–275). London: Chapman and Hall.

Ruhleder, K., & Jordan, B. (1999). Meaning-making across remote sites: How delays in transmission affect interaction. In S. Bodker, M. Kyng, & K. Schmidt (Eds.), *Proceedings of the Sixth European Conference on Computer-Supported Cooperative Work* (pp. 411–427), Cophenhagen, Denmark. Dordrecht, The Netherlands: Kluwer Academic Publishers.

Ruhleder, K., & Twidale, M. (2000). Reflective collaborative learning on the Web: Drawing on the master class. *First Monday, 5*(5). Retrieved from http://www.firstmonday.org/issues/issue5_5/ruhleder/index.html.

Sacks, H., Schegloff, E., & Jefferson, G. (1974). A simplest semantics for the organization of turn-taking for conversation. *Language, 50,* 696–735.

Sproull, L., & Kiesler, S. (1991). *Connections: New ways of working in the networked organization.* Cambridge, MA: MIT Press.

Visser, J. A. (2000). Faculty work in developing and teaching Web-based distance courses: A case study of time and effort. *American Journal of Distance Education, 14*(3), 21–32.

CHAPTER 10

Michael B. Twidale
Karen Ruhleder

Over-the-Shoulder Learning in a Distance Education Environment

One of the greatest challenges inherent in any distance education environment is the development of a support infrastructure that offers sustained, high quality support to all members of the distributed community. LEEP (Library Education Experimental Program) students receive extensive support from staff and other students via e-mail, Web boards, and phone conversations. Students and alumni cite this support as something that sets the program apart from others, making it valuable not only for the technical help offered but also for moral support so students do not feel that they are out there alone with a problem (Kazmer, 2000). The extensive personalized support is crucial. Although students use a standard set of LEEP technologies and are required to conform to some hardware and software standards, the problem of technical support is complicated by all the factors that neither students nor technology people can access, much less control. Students doing coursework from home often share their computers with others and rely on Internet service providers of variable quality; others do all or some of their class work at a workplace where they depend on internal networks and gateways to reach the Internet.

We would like to use this chapter to highlight some of the technological challenges. The LEEP program has met many of these challenges by tailoring existing technologies or developing in-house software to make sure that the technical infrastructure supports the goals of the underlying pedagogy (Gengler, this volume). The LEEP staff offers an extensive set of workshops during the initial on-campus orientation to make sure all students have a common base of understanding of the applications they will be using. Faculty are given a great deal of support in redesigning courses for an online environment (Smith, this volume), and the LEEP staff are there throughout the semester to handle technical problems, especially during live lecture sessions.

Yet programs such as LEEP are challenged beyond traditional expectations by the need to provide high-quality technical support under the following conditions:

- *Distributed instructors as well as students.* The distributed nature of the program means that practitioners with special expertise can be invited to teach in the program. Technical support must thus encompass their needs as well from course development to delivery.
- *Diverse technical settings and support.* Because of the diversity of settings in which students participate in class, they may have other forms of technical support available to them. They may be able to draw on local coworkers or employers' technical staff for help with problems. Technical support at home may come from a partner or children.[1]
- *Multiapplication environment:* LEEP is a multiapplication environment in which support must be able to address problems at that cross applications. Incorporating images into documents, creating a group-accessible space on someone's server, streaming video for a group presentation—all are legitimate activities that can require assistance.

The complexity of this environment places great demands on the support infrastructure. This is true not only for LEEP, but for any distributed work or learning setting with these characteristics. We believe that the whole range of problem solving, from personal attempts, to asking colleagues, to drawing on technical support staff, needs to be understood better in order to facilitate the problem-solving process. In the work we report in this chapter, we observed how people helped each other solve computing problems in face-to-face settings in order to see what lessons we might apply to help-giving at a distance.

Over-the-Shoulder Learning

How do people solve technical problems as they arise? Online help functions, tutorials, and so forth, imply that help-giving or problem solving is a straightforward exercise in knowledge transfer: One person encountering a problem looks up the answer in the online help index; another sends e-mail to the help desk and the return e-mail solves the problem. But is the process always so clear-cut? Consider the following example, which is based on a real episode we observed (as are other examples below):[2]

> Arthur's[3] office just got a new printer that can print double-sided pages. He wants to print out a memo using this new feature, but he does not know how to do it. Bertha walks by and he asks if she knows. She has never done it either, but overheard someone else saying that there was 'a box you can click so it will do two-sided.'

In the process of figuring it out together, Arthur mentions that he hopes he will remember this when he prints the monthly report. Bertha looks at him and says, 'Did you know that there's a new format they want us to use for that?' Cristobal overhears the comment and says that he just got a memo with instructions for the new format.

Cristobal hands Bertha the memo. She skims it and says, 'So we have to do different margins for it, too?' Cristobal answers, 'Yes, for odd and even pages so they can put it in a binder.' Arthur says, 'I think I just saw something like that while we were looking for the box for the printing.'

We term this kind of collaborative problem solving *Over-the-Shoulder Learning* (OTSL). This kind of problem solving takes place in response to a computer problem that arises while trying to get work done. Help can come from a designated technical support person, from a technically adept coworker, or even coworkers who do not perceive themselves as "techies." Working and learning are merged, and knowledge about the task and the broader context in which it is being carried out is as important as technical knowledge.

This certainly describes the case above. Arthur had a real memo he wanted to print double-sided. He and a coworker sat down to pool their information about this feature and printing in general in order to figure out how to do it. A call to technical support might have done just as well. The importance of context, however, comes in the second paragraph when Arthur mentions the monthly report. The technical problem was really a work problem in disguise. And although Bertha's comment about the new format and Cristobal's provision of the instruction memo may spawn other technical questions, they will arise in a work context in which getting the report out is the primary goal.

OTSL can also propagate knowledge within an organization. In fact, LEEP offers us an example of cyber-OTSL. One now famous feature of the chat room is that students can *whisper* to each other. On the right side of the screen, a list of names shows who is logged in to the chat room at that time. Anyone logged in to the chat room can click on an individual name, highlighting it, and send a message—a *whisper*—that will be seen only by the selected person. This feature was discovered by one student who had used it in another chat application. He tried it, it worked, and knowledge of the feature disseminated throughout the LEEP population.

Help-giving and peer support for information technology problems has already been studied extensively (see Twidale, 1999, for an overview). However, most studies have concentrated on whom the help-seeker chooses to ask for help, why that person is chosen, and the details of their physical, social, and organizational proximity. In our work we focus on the interactions themselves, such as the help-giving episode portrayed above. Our goal is to draw conclusions about the nature of OTSL and develop interfaces that will facilitate collaborative learning (Eales & Welsh, 1995). The next section provides more detail about the study we carried out.

OTSL in Context

We undertook a series of field studies in a variety of different contexts in order to develop a data set of help-giving interactions. The primary sites, where we made multiple observations over many months, included:[4]

- A university library reference desk
- A university library help line for recalls, billing questions, etc.
- A corporate research lab in which interns worked on engineering design projects
- A technical support team of large academic outreach department
- Three groups at the headquarters of a large financial services company: one doing *in-house systems development,* one responsible for *technical training,* and one providing *long-distance phone support* for branch managers

While our studies examined informal learning in workplaces, there are many parallels between these sites and LEEP. The activities at the financial services company, for example, sound very much like the work the LEEP staff does, particularly the real-time response that groups like the one providing long-distance phone support must provide. Interns in the corporate research lab ran into problems that involved settings and configurations at the application or system level. The technical support team dealt with problems involving servers and networks over which they had no control. At all of these sites, people had to cope with multiple applications, short- and long-term deadlines, and incomplete understanding of the system as a whole due to its complexity and the dynamic nature of computing.

There are also many similarities between LEEP and the workplaces we studied in the nature of the people we observed. Most participants had many years of work experience and were often highly proficient in using computing to carry out a set of work tasks and routines. This was true of their coworkers and supervisors as well. Many had access to training through their workplace and were motivated to share tips and talk about problems. In short, they had all the makings of willing learners and problem solvers. Similarly, most LEEP students are also holding full-time jobs in contemporary workplaces where computing is a requirement.

Our primary method of data collection was observational. Corporate sites, particularly those engaged in research and development (R&D), were generally willing to let us observe but not willing to allow us to do video- or audiotaping. With the help of graduate and undergraduate assistants,[5] one or two people would spend several hours at a time at a particular site taking notes on any help-giving events they observed and talking briefly with the participants afterward if possible. Outside the corporate settings, we were able to audiotape technology help interactions by users in an academic department over a period of about six weeks as they were happening. In addition, we opportunistically studied ourselves and our colleagues engaging in OTSL, with some episodes captured on videotape.

OTSL occurred in all the contexts we observed. In fact, despite limitations and biases, disparities in terms of organizational size, users' level of technical training, sophistication of available computing equipment, the short- or long-term nature of the work, or any other set of factors, the *commonalities* were most striking. We discuss these commonalities, and their implications for technical support in distance environments, in the following sections.

Locating the Problem

Although computer problems may already be brewing under the surface, they become apparent when something looks wrong (e.g., a printout, a screen layout) or when an application or device responds in an unexpected way. Sometimes the fix will be simple. To return to the example of Arthur and his coworkers, he might have forgotten to click the correct box for double-sided or to unclick the box for a document he wants printed single-sided. But what if the problem goes beyond your understanding of the system or the application? How do you locate the problem when you see something is wrong but the potential cause is hidden from you?

We observed two common categories of problems at all of our field sites. In the first category, the problem arose when something didn't look right to the user (e.g., a document, or a three-dimensional rendering using a CAD system), and the source of the problem lay somewhere in what we call the *substrate* (i.e., the many options, configurations, preferences, and exceptions available under various menu headings). In the second category, problems arose when the system or network didn't act according to the user's expectations (e.g., a Web page was suddenly inaccessible, or an e-mail disappeared mysteriously), and the source of the problem lay not at the level of the application but in how that application fit within the broader architecture of systems and networks within the organization. We call this level the *superstructure*. Two examples of superstructure and substrate follow.

The Invisible Superstructure: "Where am I?"

Users encounter two kinds of location problems that often overlap. First, they often have little sense of how different applications fit together in the work process; and second, they can be unsure about where they are within a broader computing infrastructure. For example, users accustomed to thinking about computing in terms of the applications they use on their desktop computer may have trouble sorting out what is on their computer, what is on the server or the network, and how these interact with each other. For example:

Dolly is a professor with strong computer skills who has promised to show her less-skilled colleague, Edouardo, how to 'put a document on the Web.' Edouardo uses an HTML editor to take an existing document on his own computer and turn it into an HTML file. Then Dolly guides him though the process of transferring that file from his computer to his account on the local server so that others may view it. Once Edouardo has carried out that step, he and Dolly look at the file using a standard Web browser.

Now Edouardo wants to modify something. He makes the change in the editor and saves the new version, but sees that the change hasn't appeared in the browser window. Dolly explains that every time he makes a change he must transfer the new version into his account on the server. Edouardo follows her instructions again but the change still doesn't appear. Dolly explains that he also has to click on the Refresh button on the browser so that the latest version of his document will be displayed.

To Edouardo, the two documents he sees—one in the HTML editor and one in the browser window—look the same and appear on the same screen in front of him. To Dolly, they may look the same and appear in the same place, but her greater knowledge enables her to place them into a broader context, invisible to Edouardo, in which they reside in two places. We return to this issue later in the paper.

The Invisible Substrate: "Why is it doing that?"

Another kind of invisibility entails the many configurations, options, preferences, characteristics, and customizations that users may not even be aware of, but that shape the way applications function. For instance, there are system configurations that determine the availability of access to networks, peripheral devices, and so forth. There are printer settings that may override document settings. Applications give users the means to tailor the look of a single document or to customize it in a way that affects subsequent documents as well. An example of this follows:

Fay is writing a proposal using Microsoft Word.[6] She adds page numbers by pulling down the Insert menu, dragging the cursor down two lines to Page Numbers . . . and selecting the position and alignment she wants.

Now Fay decides that she also wants to insert a header. She goes back to the Insert menu but doesn't see a menu item for adding a header. Under AutoText, however, she spots something to do with headers and footers and tries out the first option it lists:—Page—; the text "- 1 -" appears where her cursor was located, in the middle of the first page of the document.

Surprised, Fay seeks out Gustav, one of the technical staff, who goes to her office with her. He tells her to delete the text that she accidentally inserted and to go to the View menu instead. Fay clicks on View, pulls down the cursor until it highlights Header and Footer, and clicks again. Dark dotted boxes appear at the top and bottom of each page, the text of her document has dimmed, and a tool bar has appeared. Gustav explains to Fay that she can type into the boxes, but in order to return to editing her document she has to close the header/footer view from the tool bar.

Fay's confusion stems from the (very reasonable) assumption that she cannot view something she has not yet put into the document. If she has used footnotes in the past, for example, she would have gone to the Insert menu to enter a new footnote, then used the View menu to view and edit the footnote text. At any rate, Fay now has another set of steps to follow even if they don't seem logical to her.[7]

Gustav's technical training, however, has given him a different perspective on how an application might structure a document internally. For instance, a Word file has some inherent properties that the user cannot change but can ignore or modify to some extent. Gustav knew that all Word documents have headers and footers even though they are not visible unless the user edits them.

Collaborative Problem Solving

Despite the complexities outlined above, people do cope with the breakdowns that occur in their use of computers. We outline here some of the mechanisms that enable this coping. Pervading all the mechanisms of collaborative technical problem solving is the importance of understanding the local context.

Active Participants

We have observed that people asking for help have generally attempted to solve the problem themselves first. They then try to explain their earlier attempts at the outset of any help-giving interaction. This explanation seems to be in part to justify why they deserve to ask for help, and also to give the help-giver some clues about the nature of the problem in order to speed up the process. Even in the simplest case where the help-giver knows the solution, help seekers are usually very active participants in the conversation, trying to clarify their own understanding. However, in cases where the solution is not immediately apparent, it is particularly noticeable how collaborative the problem solving is, with the help-seeker volunteering information on things that they have tried, giving more background on the overall goal, and/or discussing the suitability of alternative work-around solutions. This two-way process of discussion, shared computer operation, and gesturing at the computer, is a way of trying to make visible those invisible layers described above. Viewing the interaction as provision of a simple fix by a help-giver, or as knowledge transfer, misses the point: help-giving episodes need to be understood as collaborative, interactive processes where both sides learn something.

Acknowledging active participants carries implications for the underlying ethos of the community as one that encourages asking for and giving help and an open exploration of technologies, and indeed encourages openness about one's own confusion (Gengler, this volume). For example, if students are to be encouraged to try and solve problems themselves before asking for help, we must be willing to deal with those attempts appropriately. Sometimes their attempts will worsen the problem. If students feel they are being blamed for their prior attempts in the problem-solving interaction, next time they encounter a problem they may not try themselves, resorting first to technical support or even just giving up. Given the interactive nature of technical problem solving, interpersonal skills can be at least as important as technical skills in determining successful efficient interactions that contribute to overall effectiveness (a solution that demoralizes the help-seeker may be effective in the short term but have severe long-term consequences).

Understanding the Real Goals

While a person may ask for help in using a particular feature of an application (e.g., a desktop publishing application), if the help-giver can determine why they actually want to use this feature (e.g., to produce a certain effect for a particular assignment), then an alternative feature may be proposed or even a way of achieving the desired result by a using a combination of applications. These are ingenious *workarounds* (Gasser, 1986) that can be much more efficient than trying to solve the initial problem as described. For a successful workaround to be possible, the help-giver needs to understand the person's real goals. Only then can the two participants work together toward the best solution. This is why asking a colleague for help can be so powerful, even in cases where the help seeker also has access to a more remote but more skilled source of purely technical expertise. The conversation with the colleague can be carried out in terms of the work to be done (e.g., producing and formatting a report in the appropriate way for a particular recipient), and proceeding from there to look at different technological solutions or workarounds. Thus, the technical problem should not be viewed just as a technical problem, but as one that also includes the larger work context.

Solutions Often Involve Multiple Applications

One finding that particularly surprised us in our observations was how often people's work tasks involved using more than one application, and how often the solutions to problems also involved more than one application. For example, one task involved copying a discussion from a live text chat discussion into a word-processing package, editing it into a summary, and then posting that text to a bulletin board.

It appears that one of the strengths of the modern personal computer is that it involves the ingenious composition of functionality from multiple applications in order to fulfill a higher-level work goal. Multiple application composition can be seen in the careful development of the LEEP technology infrastructure (Gengler, this volume). Technologies are composed to create particular learning experiences to fulfill the pedagogical goals of a professor. Similarly, students compose applications to produce innovative pieces of work to fulfill the requirements of an assignment.

This is highly desirable and to be encouraged. It creates substantial robustness in practice: if the needs of teaching or learning change in a small way (e.g., application to a new, more meaningful context for a student to apply a theory, and hence test their understanding) or in a big way (a new kind of course is offered), people can recombine their applications. Similarly, if a new useful functionality appears in a currently used or brand-new application, it can be incorporated into the overall activity by changing the way that applications are combined to achieve the same main goal.

The significance of this for help-giving is that conventional application help (online help manuals and other support infrastructures) discuss only that one application. Unfortunately, if many work tasks involve using several applications together to get the work done, the help system is unlikely to describe how to do such multiapplication tasks. Furthermore, the tasks are likely to involve many context-specific aspects. Thus, even an integrated suite of applications (such as Microsoft Office that might include examples of multiapplication activities within the suite) is unlikely to describe how to do the desired context-specific task. It is only by drawing on local expertise that local solutions can be developed and propagated.

Technical Problem Solving in Distance Education

Distance learning presents a slightly different context for technical help giving and problem solving than face-to-face settings. We will consider the distance education technical support issue from the perspective of the GSLIS LEEP program, which we are familiar with (one of us having taught in it for the last six years, and both of us having done research on the program).

Many aspects of LEEP are typical of the workplaces we studied. The use of the various applications is a means to an end. Students must learn about getting online, using e-mail, chat, audio, bulletin boards, Web pages, and databases, in order to take classes and obtain their professional degree as a way of furthering their career. As well as studying and participating synchronously and asynchronously in class, students must learn how to use various bibliographic databases, specialist applications, and more standard applications in order to produce documents such as reports, term papers, and Web pages. All this implies acquiring a substantial amount of technological skill, and by some people who, although intrepid enough to be pioneers in distance education, would not describe themselves as particularly technology oriented.

Remote technical help and problem solving entails all the issues outlined above, along with certain additional complexities due to the geographic distribution of the participants.

Establishing and Maintaining Context

Technical problem solving between staff and user at a distance requires extra effort. First, help-givers must determine what the remote user is seeing on the computer screen. They must also determine the wider context and infrastructure layers that may have an impact on understanding the underlying problem and routes to a resolution. These can range from understanding the underlying work goal to knowing about the particular hardware setup, operating system, modem used, ISP, local peculiarities, and so forth. Furthermore, context can change over time. A student may be using a home computer, or a work computer behind a firewall, and need to switch easily between the two.

Impoverished Resources for Supporting Conversation

Remote help giving is usually accomplished via telephone or text chat if synchronous, or e-mail or bulletin board if asynchronous. All these modes of interaction are verbal and/or textual in nature, which may be fine for certain kinds of discussions, but at the least is a limitation compared to the multiple cues available in a face-to-face interaction. In the latter we see much pointing and gesturing at the screen with fingers, pens, and the mouse cursor. For example, talking a person through the operation of a graphical user interface is much easier if one can point to the icons and active areas on the screen as they are discussed. Discussion becomes much more fiddly if one has to use words to refer to graphical elements, particularly in cases where the help seeker does not know the name or meaning of that element. In addition, in face-to-face interaction nearby artifacts may be used to support discussion, such as paper printouts, manuals, work documents, or sketches on paper. All these can be used to help to illustrate what is wanted or has already been tried. Problem-solving conversations are about trying to make visible relevant aspects of the invisible substrate and superstructure. The computer screen and other resources can all help in that process.

Barriers to Turn-Taking in Computer Operation

As well as difficulties in seeing the same screen and what is pointed to on it, it is either difficult or frequently impossible to easily switch control of the computer back and forth between participants, an activity that we see in face-to-face help giving, particularly during mutual problem solving. Even conversational turn-taking, so much a feature of face-to-face help giving, is somewhat more clumsy over an audio channel in the absence of nonverbal clues of expression, gesture, and pointing.

The LEEP Approach to Technical Problem Solving

Given all these difficulties, remote problem-solving interactions are likely to take longer and so are more costly than face-to-face ones. Therefore there may be a temptation to minimize the amount of technical help provided, and instead require students to draw on their own resources. And yet it seems that LEEP students are very happy with the amount and kind of help they receive from the Instructional Technology Office (ITO) and from their peers. How is this achieved? We see that a complex supportive ecosystem has evolved. We note some of the aspects below as they relate to our findings in other domains. Clearly this is just one part of the contributing success factors (see Gengler, this volume, for more details on ITO's user-centered focus as a critical component). A major managerial factor is the valuing of and resources allocated to the ITO. It is the way that all the elements interrelate with each other, and also interrelate with other aspects of the LEEP experience as described throughout this book, that enable the great challenge of technical problem solving to be addressed successfully.

We know that students hold the ITO in very high regard (Kazmer, 2000). When talking about their experiences with ITO, LEEP students mention not merely the technical expertise of ITO, but their empathy and reassurance. This would seem to be important to students, and is understandable given the combination of isolation and frustration that can arise when a distance learner encounters a technical problem. As well as this very careful demeanor while giving technical help, the ITO has a deep understanding of the higher-level goals of the LEEP students. This is because most ITO staff members are themselves library and information science graduates, or on-campus students working as graduate assistants. As a result, if a problem is encountered with creating one aspect of a Web page for an assignment for a particular class, it becomes easier to discuss the acceptability of perhaps a completely different way of achieving the desired effect that still fulfills the requirements of the assignment. Although we have noted the value of physical proximity of colleagues in the workplace help-giving studies, it seems that the ITO manages to maintain context and a form of social proximity via a shared understanding of the LEEP program and considerable effort in community building.

An important part of the success of LEEP overall is its creation and nurturing of a supportive online community, which in turn becomes a learning community (Hearne & Nielsen, this volume). This mutual support between students involves not just emotional support, practical advice in juggling competing demands (Kazmer & Haythornthwaite, 2001), and strategic advice on studying and how to become a distance education student, but also technical help giving and problem solving.

The whole domain of library and information science is imbued with an ethos of service, and so help giving is validated and supported. In many ways help giving is very similar to the traditional library reference interview (Bopp & Smith, 2001). The skills of good reference work have been analyzed and are taught in LIS schools, and there is a growing interest in remote reference (Sloan, 1998). An important reference skill is to understand the real information need of the patron, and how that may be different from the initial articulation of the request. Another skill is satisficing—agreeing on what kind of result will be good enough for the needs of the patron, given the available time and resources of both patron and librarian. This closely parallels the help-giving interactions we have observed. Consequently help giving becomes a part of normal activity in the LEEP learning environment, and the specialist help giving and problem solving of the ITO becomes more than an infrastructural element, no longer separate from the main content of teaching and learning.

Supporting Technical Problem Solving in Distance Education

We end with a section exploring the implications of our analysis of various workplaces and of LEEP, and the recurrent themes that emerged. For simplicity we group our suggestions into technological, managerial, and pedagogical solutions. However, as in our analysis of LEEP, we emphasize that to be effective, all three have to interact with each other and the overall sociotechnical infrastructure. Otherwise the whole point of the importance of context is lost.

Technological Solutions

Technological solutions used for the problem-solving episodes can vary in technological sophistication and hence in cost and current practicality. Some technologies are immediately usable and indeed have been used in LEEP. For example, the ITO uses Virtual Network Computing as a means to provide remote technical support. This software allows remote access to view and control another machine. Also, in teaching online searching using Dialog (by exploiting a simple Unix script), students are able to see the instructor doing a telnet-based search—a kind of virtual over-the-shoulder view (see leep.lis.uiuc.edu/support.html for details and examples of excellent online guides). Other relatively simple options to support remote problem solving include the taking of screenshots and e-mailing them back and forth as a way of establishing context, and similarly exchanging a quick sketch created in a drawing package. To be effective, such techniques need to be simple and fast enough to use that they do not get in the way of the problem solving they are intended to support.

The field of Computer Supported Cooperative Work (CSCW) involves the development of technologies to support interaction between people at a distance (see Twidale & Nichols, 1999, for an overview). Remote help giving certainly fits within this remit, and a variety of technologies have been developed and are available. These include video links to support nonverbal communication, and shared screens and telepointers so that two people can cooperate around an application at the same time knowing that they are seeing the same thing. One CSCW application that can readily be downloaded and investigated for this kind of use is Microsoft's NetMeeting.

It should be noted that considerable evaluation work of CSCW applications has been done, and it has been found that they do not always succeed, particularly if they do not fit well into the wider context of the use environment (Grudin, 1989). Thus, a two-way video link may be very helpful to problem solving in theory, but in a particular context it may require too much set-up time to be worthwhile or require too much bandwidth to be usable. CSCW technologies attempt to make the interaction as close as possible to the situation where the people are actually together in the same room, or the help-giver is leaning over the shoulder of the help-seeker. To the extent that this is currently possible, it addresses the additional problems of remote technical problem solving outlined above. However, remember that in the first part of this chapter we showed how even face-to-face help giving has its problems.

We are currently investigating the development of new interfaces and functionalities to address gaps between help-givers and remote users (Twidale & Brady, 2004; see also Prince, et al., 1999). Modern graphical user interfaces are very good at supporting efficient use by people who don't encounter problems, and can be relatively easy to learn the basics, given a little help. If the user is confused and the solution is just one or a few clicks away, well-designed interfaces can make it easy to guess the right thing to do, and good help can indeed be helpful. But for more complex tasks, or when an attempt fails, there is relatively little provision for supporting diagnosis of what has gone wrong and why, and for supporting trying out solutions.

What would a specialist computer interface designed to support problem solving look like? How would it be different from current interfaces designed to support smooth use and guessing of the next step? We are looking at techniques for capturing sequences of actions and then providing an easy-to-review visualization of what has been tried. The same record of actions can then be used in sharing a solution, both with the person asking for help and with others who might want to know, such as via an updatable FAQ (frequently asked questions) list. Our approach is analogous to existing screen capture programs such as Camtasia, but aims to allow greater tailoring and customization of explanations. We are also exploring whether a more maplike interface would help during problem solving when the help-giver and seeker are lost and looking for inspiration. Such a map would explicitly represent all available options and be updatable and annotatable based on what had been tried so far, and even what others had tried and found useful in the past. Another option is to provide ways to quickly compare the settings of two applications on different computers to see how they differ in order to address a common problem of a help giver complaining "but that works on my computer!"

Managerial Solutions

The main point to acknowledge is that students will have problems with technology (Ehrmann, 1999), and that a multithreaded solution is needed for the overall problem of technical support. Despite the best efforts of setting minimum technical competencies for incoming students, and providing excellent training and online information resources, technical problems will inevitably arise. Consequently it is important to provide resources to facilitate different kinds of help giving and problem solving. We are concerned that at times this provision may be overlooked or skimped because of limited budgets. Yet comfort with technology, and an infrastructure to facilitate problem solving, can be a significant contributor to students' satisfaction and persistence in the learning environment. In the absence of a rich-enough problem-solving infrastructure, faculty may worry that students will rely on them for technical help (Levy, 2003), not only adding to the burden of teaching online, but also having an impact in students' evaluations of their courses (Lackey, 2001).

As well as providing appropriate resources for technical support, it should be a managerial responsibility to help sustain an online learning community. There will never be the resources available for designated technical support people to solve every problem at the moment of need. Students ought to be encouraged (and helped) to try and solve as many problems themselves as possible, and to share their knowledge and help-giving skills with their peers. We concede that in teaching library and information science, the LEEP program has a distinct advantage here, since help giving is both part of the culture and part of the content of the domain. Nevertheless, help giving should be validated and encouraged regardless of the subject learned; it is a crucial skill in modern organizations that aspire to be learning organizations or to put the promise of knowledge management into effect. Simple kinds of encouragement might include extra validation or credit for help giving, support for shared problem solving, as well as moving away from paradigms of single student work to acceptance and encouragement of collaborative work.

Pedagogical Solutions

We do not believe it is feasible to rely solely on technical support personnel to help with all problems at all times. Each student who enrolls in a program brings different technical competencies and confidence. We doubt that it is possible, economically feasible, or even advisable to directly teach them all the technological skills that they will need. We are investigating how students may be taught how to investigate more kinds of problems themselves so that they only need to resort to technical support for the more obscure problems.

One possibility is an updating of Carroll's minimal manual approach (Carroll, 1990) to apply to modern computer applications. In brief, this involves teaching people a minimal subset of the features of an application, sufficient to be able to do something meaningful, and then encouraging them to explore other features on their own. Just suggesting that they might like to explore and to share what they find with their peers is unlikely to be enough. We believe that the skills of how to explore can be taught, even to those who are unused to learning about applications in this way and are somewhat afraid of the process. These meta-learning skills need not be anything exotic and could include tips such as: create a really simple file and investigate the feature by changing one thing at a time; or try to replicate the problem, but with the simplest case you can find so that the problem still remains. These are skills that people comfortable with learning technology through exploration have often developed over time, but which are rarely explicitly taught or even articulated to those with less experience.

In some cases (many, we hope) this exploratory approach will enable students to solve a problem or uncover a new useful feature themselves, and they should also be encouraged to share this knowledge with their peers. This, in turn, requires managerial and technological encouragement, so that it is both valued and easy to do. However, some problems will always be too tricky for students to solve themselves, and a student will need to draw on a fellow student or on technical support. These interactions, although very valuable and capable of solving complex problems (as we have described) are still somewhat time consuming. If we are to encourage them, we need to consider how to maximize their efficiency. One way is to teach the skills of asking for and giving help (Agre, 1994a, 1994b), and even to teach particular skills of remote help-asking and giving. Another way is to explicitly acknowledge why problem solving can be so fiddly (because of the difficulties involved in locating the problem, which we have illustrated). A discussion between the problem-solving participants about where the problem is and the different parts of the substrate and superstructure in which it might be hidden may also help in clarifying the discussion and arriving at a solution faster.

In summary, we believe that with appropriate managerial support, by teaching of the higher level skills of learning how to learn about technology and how to effectively discuss and resolve technology problems, coupled with suitable technologies to assist these discussions, it is possible to contribute to the rich technology problem-solving infrastructure that a distance education program needs. These suggestions complement the excellent technical support infrastructure already provided for LEEP by the ITO (Gengler, this volume), and suggest ways for other distance environments to approach and/or expand their own help-giving practices.

Conclusion

The technologies used in distance education offer great potential for innovative pedagogy and the creation of a vibrant learning community. This requires careful decisions about technology selection and ongoing revision. In this chapter we have stressed that technology problems will arise, and careful thought needs to be given to how to address them. We do not believe that all problems can be sidestepped by huge amounts of application training or off-loading responsibility to students. By studying a number of very different environments and identifying commonalities, we have shown how the resolution of technical problems has a very important social component. Collaborative problem solving between peers and with technology experts, drawing on a thorough understanding of the context of use of the technologies concerned, allows people to cope and to come up with solutions. We have looked at the particular challenges of distance education and considered how collaborative problem solving can be supported through a rich mix of self-help, peer support, and the help of technology experts. In order to succeed, this mechanism needs to be thoroughly integrated into the wider context of establishing and nurturing an online learning community.

Acknowledgments

We wish to thank Vince Patone for his help in describing the work of the LEEP Instructional Technology Office. This research was supported by the National Science Foundation under Grant No. 0081112.

Notes

1. To the best of our knowledge, we have no recorded incidents in which conflicts between LEEP staff advice and advice from other sources led to greater conflicts in work or home environments.
2. The examples used in this chapter are derived from real episodes. The actual examples are too complex in terms of the interactions and the contextual explanations required to make sense of them. We have tried to preserve the character of the interactions, however. This particular type of help-giving episode in which people start to cluster and related topics arise, is common to all of the sites we observed.
3. We are indebted to the Champaign Public Library for providing us with the names of Atlantic hurricanes during the 2002 season to use in our examples in this paper.
4. We also have some data from sites that did not work out for one reason or another (e.g., not enough sustained activity, difficulty in negotiating times for observations). These include a small local newspaper, a campus newspaper, a public library cataloguing department, and a three-person technology team supporting a medical clinic. We also collected data serendipitously from interactions observed in our own work environment. We do not consider these as primary sites because of the lack of continuity of our observations, but they still inform our work.
5. Listed alphabetically: Varinia Godoy, Karen Medina, Alicia Oryhon, Vandana Singh, Dinesh Rathi.

6. Although we have tried to avoid identifying the names of specific applications, this example best makes sense in the context of the application.
7. If the reader of this chapter has access to Microsoft Word, we encourage that reader to access the help function, select Contents and Index, and enter *header* as the search term.

References

Agre, P. (1994a). The art of getting help. *The Network Observer, 1*(2). Retrieved from http://polaris.gseis.ucla.edu/pagre/tno/february-1994.html.

Agre, P. (1994b). How to help someone use a computer. *The Network Observer, 1*(5). Retrieved from http://polaris.gseis.ucla.edu/pagre/tno/may-1994.html.

Bopp, R., & Smith, L. (2001). *Reference and information services: An introduction* (3rd edition). Englewood, CO: Libraries Unlimited.

Carroll, J. M. (1990). *The Nurnberg funnel: Designing minimalist instruction for practical computer skill.* Cambridge, MA: MIT Press.

Eales, R. T. J., & Welsh, J. (1995). *Design for collaborative learnability.* Proceedings of the First International Conference on Computer Support for Collaborative Learning, Bloomington, IN (pp. 99–106). Mahwah, NJ: Lawrence Erlbaum.

Ehrmann, S. C. (1999). Asking the hard questions about technology use and education. *Change, 31*(2), 25–29.

Gasser, L. (1986). The integration of computing and routine work. *ACM Transactions on Information Systems, 4*(3), 205–225.

Gengler, J. (this volume). User-centered support and technology in LEEP.

Grudin, Jonathan T. (1989). Why groupware applications fail: Problems in design and evaluation. *Office Technology and People, 4*(3), 245–264.

Hearne, B., & Nielsen, A. (this volume). Catch a cyber by the tale: Online orality and the lore of a distributed learning community.

Kazmer, M. M. (2000). Coping in a distance environment: Sitcoms, chocolate cake, and dinner with a friend. *First Monday, 5*(9). Retrieved from http://www.firstmonday.dk/issues/issue5_9/index.html.

Kazmer, M. M., & Haythornthwaite, C. (2001). Juggling multiple social worlds: Distance students online and offline. *American Behavioral Scientist, 45*(3), 510–529. (Reprinted in this volume)

Lackey, J. R. (2001) Who is really responsible for online students' technical support? Presented at Southeast EDUCAUSE Annual Meeting, Orlando, FL. ID No SER0108. Retrieved November 2, 2002 from http://www.educause.edu/asp/doclib/abstract.asp?ID=SER0108.

Levy, S (2003). Six factors to consider when planning online distance learning programs in higher education. *Online Journal of Distance Learning Administration, 6*(1). Retrieved from http://www.westga.edu/~distance/ojdla/spring61/levy61.htm.

Prince, R., Su, J., Tang, H., & Zhao, Y. (1999). *The design of an interactive online help desk in the Alexandria Digital Library.* Proceedings of the International Joint Conference on Work Activities and Collaboration, San Francisco, CA. (pp. 217–226). New York: ACM Press.

Sloan, B. (1998). Service perspectives for the digital library: Remote reference services, *Library Trends, 47*(1), 117–143.

Smith, L.C. (this volume). Faculty perspectives.

Twidale, M. B. (1999). *Over the shoulder learning: Supporting brief informal learning embedded in the work context.* Technical Report ISRN UIUCLIS?1999/2+CSCW. Retrieved November 2, 2003 from http://www.lis.uiuc.edu/~twidale/pubs/otsl1.html.

Twidale, M. B., & Brady, A. (2004). Wayfinding in an interface: Would a map help? GSLIS Technical Report.

Twidale, M. B., & Nichols, D. M. (1999). Computer supported cooperative work in the information search and retrieval process. *Annual Review of Information Science and Technology, 33,* 259–319. Medford: Information Today.

Teaching and Learning Online

CHAPTER 11

Pat Lawton
Rae-Anne Montague

Teaching and Learning Online: LEEP's Tribal Gleanings

Finding one's way through the maze of grand possibilities, only loosely related, and some in even fairly serious tension with one another, was, however exciting (and it was enormously exciting), a perilous business. With so many ways to turn, so few tracks laid down, and so little experience of one's own to go by, even small decisions . . . seemed enormously consequential—a reverseless commitment to something immense, portentous, splendid, and unclear.

GEERTZ, 1995, P. 101

Introduction

Maurice Merleau-Ponty (1981) suggests that our biology and our ontology are inextricably linked. A move to a new job or a new house, for example, renders our everyday world as different. Old habits may drop off and new ones form. New educational environments too bring with them a novel sense of time and space, and online education in particular offers unique opportunities for transformation. Technology has and will continue to change forms of teaching and learning (Laurillard 1993; Bates 1995; Harasim 1995). How might the teaching and learning in these new spaces differ from what was previously known about teaching and learning? How have ideas of teaching and learning evolved over the last decade within this new setting? What are effective practices for teaching and learning that have evolved in the online environment, and can they be articulated?

This chapter describes what is known about teaching and learning in LEEP (Library Education Experimental Program), the online master's program offered through the Graduate School of Library and Information Science (GSLIS) at the University of Illinois at Urbana-Champaign (UIUC). Launched in 1996, the LEEP program is one of the oldest continuing online educational offerings to utilize the Internet as its primary delivery tool and therefore offers an especially attractive case for exploring online education.

Since its inception, a number of methods have been employed to determine the factors that constitute good teaching and learning practices in this environment. This paper reviews and synthesizes what has been discovered about teaching and learning online over LEEP's eight-year history. Data sources include input from annual conference calls with faculty, discussing teaching in LEEP; research targeting many facets of LEEP, from communication patterns to the formation of virtual community; and an August 2002 retreat organized to explore best practices in LEEP. Data from this retreat, plus data from the aforementioned studies, form the basis for this review of the LEEP community's discoveries about teaching and learning online.

Program Description

The LEEP program began in 1996 as an experimental program option for students seeking an accredited master's degree in library and information science (LIS) online. In the eight years since its inception, LEEP has evolved into a dynamic community of learners with 223 students currently enrolled, and a total of 320 graduated (as of fall 2003).

LEEP classes include synchronous, asynchronous, and independent components as well as brief periods of face-to-face contact. Synchronous sessions with chat, audio, and graphics are typically scheduled once per week, and activities include discussions, group tasks, lecture, and oral presentations. Asynchronous activities involve electronic bulletin board postings, small group work, review of class archives, and e-mail. Independent learning activities provide opportunities for specialized learning, and include independent study, practica, community-based tasks, and theses.

LEEP students have face-to-face contact for 10 days at the beginning of their studies and return to campus each semester for 2 to 5 days thereafter. Face-to-face sessions include advising, mentoring, videos, tours, small group work, seminars, demonstrations, oral presentations, hands-on workshops, community meals, and opportunities for socializing. The on-campus component of the program is integral to developing connections and a sense of community among students and within the greater GSLIS/UIUC community. As Smith, Lastra, and Robins (2001) describe, participating in LEEP "is more than gaining knowledge as an individual; it also involves learning from others, developing skills in collaboration, and creating a strong professional identity and sense of community" (p. 349).

Model of Research and Practice

Faculty members have played and continue to play a key role in the design and development of the LEEP program. Interdisciplinary approaches to research are often employed in LIS and in the case of LEEP, faculty and doctoral student research interests in computer-mediated communication, interface design, collaborative learning, and online pedagogy have led to a variety of investigations. The LEEP Bibliography (http://www.lis.uiuc.edu/gslis/degrees/leep_bib.html) includes details of over sixty such studies and reports, which contribute to new knowledge and inform improvements in LEEP courses and program design.

The success of the LEEP model is well documented. In 2001, LEEP received the Sloan-C Award for Most Outstanding Asynchronous Learning Program. Much of the program's success can be attributed to the variety of formal (internal and external) evaluation processes that have guided program development. They include review by an independent consultant, semiannual faculty conference call discussions on teaching in LEEP, a comprehensive five-year program review, and standard university course evaluations (used in all classes). These processes have provided insights into specific aspects of the program and have also been used to demonstrate quality to prospective students, employers, university administrators, and others. However, these evaluative processes and research projects do not capture several other features that we find important for exploring best practices, including the articulation of implicit features, approaches, and/or strategies; and multidimensional cycles of change that contribute to continuous improvement. Moreover, these formal evaluations do not focus on tapping the insights and expertise of LEEP faculty, adjunct instructors, and students who have firsthand knowledge of effective teaching and learning online. The LEEP retreat and related activities were designed to address these gaps.

The LEEP Retreat

We initiated the LEEP retreat to explore the LEEP model by drawing on the experiences of actual participants. Following Freire (1993), we decided to promote self-directed dialogue with and among LEEP participants: students, alumni, faculty, staff, and administrators. As Freire notes, "Only dialogue, which requires critical thinking, is also capable of generating critical thinking. Without dialogue there is no communication, and without communication there can be no true education" (Freire, pp. 73–74).

The LEEP retreat provided the opportunity for all members of the community to identify and share teaching strategies, methods, and supporting technologies they have found most advantageous to their teaching and learning; in short, to identify and describe a model of best practices. The retreat was organized by the authors,

LEEP graduate and coordinator Rae-Anne Montague, and LEEP instructor Pat Lawton, and was funded by grants from the UIUC's Provost's Initiative for Teaching Advancement and the University of Illinois Alumni Association.

Three questions motivated the retreat and guide the discussion in this paper:

1. What are best practices in LEEP?
2. What have we learned about teaching and learning in LEEP?
3. How has our participation in this culture changed us as students, teachers, people?

The overall retreat project had four distinct phases:

- Phase One. In the six months before the retreat, electronic bulletin boards were made available for the broader LEEP community to meet virtually and begin discussing effective practices. From these discussions, early categories of best practices emerged that were used in phase two.
- Phase Two. A retreat Web site was created, linking information from the electronic bulletin boards, faculty conference call discussions of teaching strategies, and other resources about the LEEP experience. Information was grouped according to emergent themes and used by retreat participants as preliminary reading.
- Phase Three. A weekend-long, face-to-face retreat was held, which focused on best practices in online education. All faculty, students, alumni, administrators, and staff who had been involved in LEEP were invited to join the retreat. Thirty-nine people participated: 19 faculty, 11 students/graduates, and 9 staff. Retreat participants engaged in a variety of activities including presentations, focus groups, informal discussions, and large-group meetings.
- Phase Four. Data from the LEEP retreat was shared with the LEEP community and others interested in teaching and learning online via presentations and the Web site. Retreat organizers initiated and invited discussion via the electronic bulletin boards for sharing post-retreat reflections among participants and members of the community at large.

We employed two means to gather tacit knowledge through intergroup dialogue: asynchronous electronic bulletin boards and face-to-face focus groups. The asynchronous electronic bulletin boards discussion (phase one) enabled the retreat coordinators to identify themes that were important to the LEEP community, and these discussions determined the formation of focus group (phase three) categories. During the six-month pre-retreat period, there were 157 posts by 62 individuals. Based on these posts and feedback from faculty, staff, students, and administrators, fourteen focus group topics in three general categories emerged for the retreat as shown in Table 11.1.

TABLE 11.1. **LEEP Retreat Focus Group Topics in Three Broad Categories: Research, Services, and Teaching/Learning**

Research	Service	Teaching/Learning
Learning Styles Online	Administrative Support	Orientation /On-Campus Sessions
Research in LIS	Alumni Services/Life after LEEP	Group Work
Theory and Practice	Library Services	Faculty/Staff
Diversity in LIS	Technology Support	MS Curriculum
		Students/Grads
		Synchronous Live Sessions

Bulletin board participants' concerns logically grouped into three main categories that express various aspects of LEEP: theoretical concerns (research); administrative and support services (service); and components of LEEP related to pedagogy (teaching/learning). These categories offer a lens for understanding and exploring those aspects of the LEEP online learning experience considered important by participants.

Detailed notes from the focus group discussions constitute the primary data from the retreat. The evening before the focus groups, an experienced faculty member volunteered to brief note-takers on the art of taking notes. (Although focus group discussions were also tape recorded, the tapes' sound quality proved inadequate for use.)

Eliciting Tacit Knowledge

To facilitate the articulation of best practices for LEEP, we wanted to engage LEEP participants in dialogue that would result in a critical analysis of teaching and learning online, and would elicit participants' tacit knowledge of their online teaching and learning practices. Tacit knowledge is defined as "knowledge that enters into the production of behaviors and/or the constitution of mental states but is not ordinarily accessible to consciousness" (Barbiero, 2003, online). Tacit knowledge contrasts with explicit knowledge (i.e., knowledge that we are aware of knowing). Daniel A. Schon, in *The Reflective Practitioner* (1983), provides this example of tacit knowledge in action:

> A big-league pitcher's know-how is in his way of pitching to a batter's weakness, changing his pace, or distributing his energies over the course of a game. There is nothing in common sense to make us say that know-how consists in rules or plans, which we entertain in the mind prior to action. Although we sometimes think before acting, it is also true that in much of the spontaneous behavior of skillful practice we reveal a kind of knowing which does not stem from a prior intellectual operation. (Schon, 1983, pp. 50–51)

This "knowing-how or embodied knowledge is characteristic of the expert, who acts, makes judgments, and so forth without explicitly reflecting on the principles or rules involved. The expert works without having a theory of his or her work; he or she just performs skillfully without deliberation or focused attention" (Barbiero, on-line, 2003).

Teachers and learners in LEEP are experts in the online environment, developing better practices, often unconsciously. They have embodied and manifest a number of best practices, yet these may be unarticulated or tacit. The focus groups were designed to determine best practices in LEEP by facilitating dialogue that would prompt reflection on practice, and eventually the articulation of embodied best practices. (For more on eliciting tacit knowledge through dialogue and focus groups, see Crowley, 1999; Gibbs, 1997).

Best Practices in LEEP

Data from all phases of the LEEP retreat form the basis of our discussion of best practices. Not surprisingly, several of the categories of best practices that emerged from the LEEP retreat project are practices that were identified from these other data-gathering efforts throughout LEEP's history, and act as external confirmation of their results and ours. This chapter brings together the knowledge of effective teaching and learning practices in LEEP to date.

We use the term *best practices* to describe what is known about methods, strategies, and techniques that enhance teaching and learning online, as described by LEEP participants. Practices change and will continue to change over time. Change in practice is influenced by new developments in disciplinary theory and practice, expectations and capabilities of media and its uses, and social and cultural relationships among humans, technology, and the world. Implicit in this understanding of "best" practices is that they are not fixed, but rather are dynamic representations or interpretations, and thus may also be described as "better practices" (see also Burbules, this volume). For simplicity, we use the term best practices.

When GSLIS began this experiment in Internet-based distance learning, there was little available to prepare student and faculty pioneers. However, over time, knowledge about this venue has been discovered, created, shared, and passed on to and from instructors and students. Much of it is a "tribal knowledge," passed on within the culture. Knowledge has emerged by everyday participation in a culture that is caring and concerned with the success of its members, and communicates practical knowledge as a matter of course. Talking about what works and what doesn't work, the tried and the true, has become part of LEEP culture. In the sections that follow, we explore what the LEEP culture knows about its practices, orienting our discussion around the retreat's three guiding questions.

Q1: What Are Best Practices in LEEP?

Five responses dominate in answer to this question: (1) *orientation,* also known as *boot camp,* (2) *on-campus sessions* (face-to-face), (3) *group work,* (4) *synchronous sessions* (live sessions), (5) *order and organization.* The first four responses were suggested by bulletin board participants as they discussed LEEP best practices in phase one of the retreat, and these were used to form the basis of four focus groups. All four constitute highly interactive aspects of the program. The last response—order and organization—emerged from the final analysis of the retreat data, conference calls, and research papers. This concept appeared frequently enough in the data to warrant its own place as a category of best practice.

It is notable that two out of the five categories emphasize offline components of the hybrid program (orientation and on-campus sessions). These components are designed to supplement and support the core Internet-based program. Hybrid education models, also known as blended models, combine traditional and distance components. As Jeffrey R. Young (2002, online) notes, this robust alternative "offers the best of both worlds" for teaching and learning.

Boot Camp

Boot camp is the term that has emerged from the LEEP community to describe the initial face-to-face session that is required of all LEEP students. While some faculty members were initially reluctant to adopt the use of the term, it has nonetheless persisted as the result of self-naming by the student culture. The session is an intense period of study and technology training, and there are a number of stories concerning boot camp in the folklore that has arisen around LEEP, or *LEEPlore* (see Hearne & Nielsen, this volume). The boot camp name reflects not only the intensity and the sense of preparation for the future in a new role as student, but also the arduous, and at times disheartening, shared experience that serves (in the long term) to form deep and lasting bonds among LEEP participants. As the LEEPlore tells it, many friendships are created and carved in stone at boot camps, which are held for 10 days in July of each year. It is a significant factor in the bonds of the LEEP community and has also been the focus for much discussion and critique over the years. While somewhat controversial, it is still considered one of the features of LEEP that results in an approximately 95 percent retention rate. As one retreat participant shared, "I never went to *real* boot camp, but from what my hubby, dad and brothers tell me, it's not so much about torture as it is about a shared experience."

Boot camp is important because it immerses students in LIS and provides opportunities for forming friendships. Relationships that are important to participants include those with other students, faculty, staff, and administrators. Students at the LEEP retreat particularly appreciate the way others are accessible to all involved, and they repeatedly emphasize people and the atmosphere of welcome.

This atmosphere of welcome may be a result of a learner-centered approach to education and/or the culture of collaboration and caring pervasive in LEEP. The literature on *caring* from the field of nursing suggests that this attribute factors heavily into a patient's assessment of overall satisfaction with the nurses' performance. While one nurse may do all the same things as another—take your temperature, roll you over, ask how you are—a nurse may be more favorably evaluated simply by the presence or perception of an attitude of caring (Noddings, 1984). Similarly, there seems to be an atmosphere of caring in LEEP that is pervasive and palpable, and goes a long way toward its success. As one retreat participant noted about boot camp in particular, it is "a culture where everyone wanted everyone to succeed."

On-Campus Sessions
The LEEP on-campus sessions are required, face-to-face class meetings. Sessions are generally held for five days over an extended weekend. On-campus class meetings can, and in the eyes of students, should be a highlight of the semester, similar to homecoming. They provide faculty and students with the opportunity to meet and explore aspects of the class that do not easily transfer through computer-mediated communication. In a LEEP conference call, one faculty member described how, "on-campus sessions should emphasize activities that cannot easily be accomplished otherwise, face-to-face group work, access to local resources or local experts, content with a major visual and/or interactive components." For example, in a cataloging class, students were much relieved to have the opportunity for face-to-face problem solving with their peers and their monographs. The on-campus session can be a boost to the novice cataloger's sense of place and performance in the class. In general, on-campus sessions help students overcome frustration, lack of confidence, and any feelings of isolation they may experience.

The on-campus sessions also provide opportunities for students to improve their technical skills via workshops, develop their résumés with résumé-writing workshops, and engage in social opportunities from small group meetings to all-community gatherings.

Group Work
Group work is the practice that everyone loves to hate. Faculty and students alike endorse this as a best practice, even though it requires a great deal of hard work for all involved, and can bring frustration. As one student noted:

> I've had great LEEP group project experiences and not so great ones. One suggestion I wish faculty would take seriously is to consider all aspects of the project they are requiring and to provide some guidance (in the form of suggestions) on how to divide the work fairly and also perhaps a bit on how to proceed for complex projects.

Faculty members have used a variety of bases for forming groups—random selection, assignment based on knowledge of student interests and background, or self-selected groups formed around topics of interest. As in real life, it is not possible to completely avoid conflicts among group members. It is sometimes necessary to provide mechanisms such as majority and minority reports if a group cannot reach consensus. If bulletin boards are set up for each group to work in over time, the faculty member can monitor the ongoing discussion and serve as facilitator for the group as needed.

Group work may be conducted asynchronously or synchronously. Depending on the task(s), group work activities may take place during one session or last throughout the semester. Examples of different aspects of small group work are presented in Figure 11.1.

Clear and comprehensive instructions, provided in advance by instructors, are reported as most critical to the success of groups. Students want guidance on how to function within the groups, what to do and what is expected of them, and when and how they will be evaluated. Students are strongly opposed to evaluating one another and adamantly in favor of regular and thoughtful feedback from faculty. In the words of a student at the retreat:

> Expectations must be defined in advance—guidelines, contracts, plans. [The instructor needs to] make clear from the beginning how much of your grade is the group project, how much is group process, and how much is content. How do you assess group process?

Group work is arguably the most challenging aspect of teaching and learning in LEEP and one of the most beneficial. As one student noted in a retreat bulletin board post:

> When you are doing them [group projects], immersed in them, working through them, one of the most important features for the participants is the ethical dimension of "are you doing your bit?" I know that for many, conflicts about direction or the "right answer"

FIGURE 11.1. **Examples of Online Group Activities**

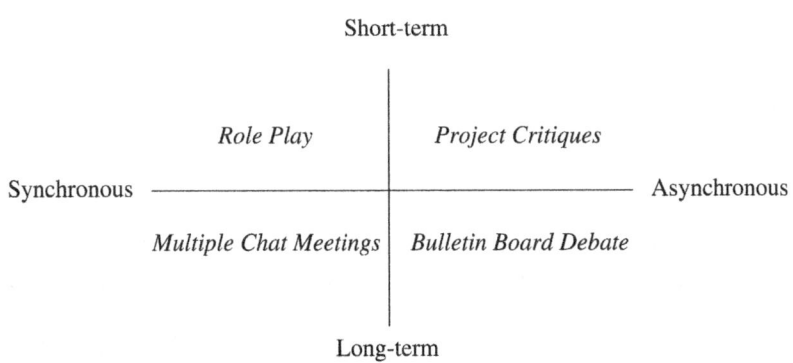

may be paramount. But in the group projects in which I have taken part, most of the aggravation/ill-feeling has been over disproportionate amounts of work. This goes beyond (far beyond, and prior to) mere grading. Even before the grading question rears its head, there is always the feeling that work ought to be shared equally, or at least equitably (meaning that everyone does what they are good at to the best of their ability).

Achieving this requires significant planning and oversight by faculty. At the retreat it was suggested that faculty have the opportunity to discuss these issues during a sort of boot camp for faculty, to further expose them to different technologies and techniques for managing group work.

Synchronous Sessions
Synchronous sessions are real-time, online sessions between instructor and students that use a combination of RealAudio delivery, class slides, and chat room discussion. The structure and frequency of these sessions varies from class to class and instructor to instructor, but most involve a two-hour session once per week. According to notes from a LEEP conference call, "In live sessions the faculty member must find ways to: (1) make effective use of the ability to interweave navigation of slides and other Web sites with audio narration; (2) monitor text-chat to respond to student questions; (3) use small group discussions; (4) involve guest speakers; and (5) integrate student presentations." One faculty member explains, "live sessions are engaging to the students when a variety of activities are planned. [Instructors must] be sure to allow time to respond to students' questions and explain how you want to integrate that activity into the overall structure of the live session time slot. Classes do need to be scripted to take best advantage of the time available."

Practices that have been identified as generally effective in live sessions include the use of visuals (including Web pages, images, charts, etc.) and music. One faculty member sings to students to call them into the classroom when small group activity time is finished.

Veteran online faculty members have noted that "less is more" in terms of content during live sessions. Student participation can be so great that the instructors must be flexible in allowing new areas of discussion to emerge. There is little pressure to stop discussions in an online class because electronic bulletin boards keep discussions alive. As one student at the retreat noted, "I love being in class, everything can get asked and be answered afterwards, better than on campus." Faculty noted they find the need to reduce the number of points addressed in a live session and are concerned that lectures may become overly simplistic. However, they also find that more content emerges asynchronously as a result of the intense synchronous sessions. As one retreat participant put it, there is a "need to plan and organize, provide a focus for the class, but [subsequently] there is a need to let it go and be a part of it as it unfolds."

Ruhleder (this volume) describes live session technology as enabling interaction that is immediate and inclusive, one that improves on face-to-face settings. Imagine that you are sitting in a face-to-face lecture and want to ask a question. If the speaker does not immediately see you raise your hand, by the time they do look up, it may be well past the moment to ask your question. Similarly, a student may have some experience or expertise to relate to the topic at hand. Again, in a face-to-face setting the moment to comment may pass, or the comment may interrupt the flow of the class. In LEEP, with live audio and chat, it is possible to make these comments without disturbing the flow of the session. Here, disturbance of the flow is de rigueur, and thus the continuous "interruption" constitutes the flow. Of course, some instructors and students do find interruption via chat disruptive. While students may choose to ignore the text, others are still reading and may begin their own conversation, straying from the task the lecturer deems important. Thus, changes in communication flow and authority are salient features of the synchronous online class.

Perhaps the most blatant yet subtle example of this is the whisper function available in chat sessions. By clicking on a name or names of others in the class, chat room participants can send private messages to others in the chat room. Similar to passing notes across the aisle in a face-to-face classroom, this behavior may seem problematic or even disrespectful. However, students reassured concerned faculty at the retreat by explaining they use this function principally to clarify issues, and that this action reflected a conscientious sense of self- and peer monitoring.

Order and Organization

Order and organization is a recurring theme from the retreat and conference calls. It is also seen in the research on LEEP (see, for example, Kazmer, 2000; Smith, Lastra, & Robbins, 2001). As Kazmer and Haythornthwaite (2001) note, "Students actively manage [online and offline] time, activities and relationships" (p. 527). Since content and tasks for online learning are interpreted remotely, it is imperative for course materials to be clear and organized. One wrong date or incorrect URL can throw off a busy student's day and, for adult learners, wasting time is a major offense. In the words of a retreat participant, "Instructors are rated by organization, students don't have time to waste."

The GSLIS curriculum is designed to be learner-centered and flexible. Flexibility in curriculum is often a new experience for students. As they move through the program, they are often surprised to encounter differences in class organization. These differences are a reflection of varied content, instructor autonomy and the wide range of instructional tools available to design the syllabi and class activities.

Students are quick to point out their personal favorites and are articulate about what works and what doesn't. For example, one retreat participant remarked, "My favorite syllabi are in table form, with readings, assignments, and due dates clearly and graphically delineated, and with helpful links to appropriate resources and readings."

Another participant favored variety by stating, "My favorite syllabi have been organized differently depending on the content." A third listed specific criteria for best syllabi. In her words:

What they have in common is:

1. Materials are scrupulously up-to-date WITH immediate e-mail and/or bulletin board notification when changes are made.
2. Readings are consistently available in ONE place.
3. Bulletin boards that include feedback sections and samples of previous work that has earned an "A" grade.
4. There is a site map for large syllabi.
5. Clear policies, due dates and requirements for assignments are provided in ONE place.

Q2: What Have We Learned about Teaching and Learning in LEEP?

Adjustments—Content, Process, and Technology
For students, the learning curve in LEEP is steepest early in the program. The initial stages of transition to LEEP seem to bubble over with content and processes—multitasking, communicating in a text-based environment, whisper function, bulletin board management, academic writing, integrating school and home/work life, and engaging in remote dialogue and reflection. Discovering the possibilities and sometimes the corresponding anxiety can be overwhelming. One experienced faculty member, who regularly teaches the required introductory class, is acutely aware of this. He offers students encouragement and strategies to overcome stress. For example, he promotes the general understanding that it's okay not to "get everything" in the first semester. Making this explicit helps students press ahead with the task(s) at hand. Perhaps more importantly, it aids them in developing a clearer realization of what they're embarking upon—understanding new and complex ideas and developing professional skills in an unfamiliar technology-rich environment requiring extensive engagement in terms of thought, practice, and reflection.

More Options and Opportunities
Teaching and learning never stop in LEEP. As one faculty member commented, "There is a lot of opportunity for learning in LEEP; the [electronic bulletin] boards are always there; it is a bottomless pit!" This leads to more and more teaching and learning. For example, if someone is reading something interesting that relates to class, it can easily be posted on an electronic bulletin board. Content is built based on the interests of students and instructors. As Smith, Lastra, and Robins (2001) note, "Students are less likely to look to the instructor as the only person with the answers,

and to see other students as having good information and experiences to contribute" (p. 356). In LEEP, dialogue abounds. Experts and novices from around the world discuss issues of special interest. Debates are carried out across time zones. Students whisper across oceans. Teaching and learning are no longer restricted to specific times and places. Teachers are learners and learners are teachers. Many traditional educational boundaries are broken. As one LEEP retreat participant remarked, "I no longer think of teaching as being just something I do at a certain time. I've been LEEPified."

Being *LEEPified* involves becoming a member of this particular learning community where complacency is rejected, growth abounds, and critical thought and collaboration are viewed as integral in the learning process.

Andragogy
The teaching and learning practices found to be most effective in LEEP are those that address and support what is known about the adult learner and how she or he learns. The theory of adult learning, formulated by Malcolm Knowles and termed *andragogy*, posits that the way adults learn differs from the way children learn, and in fact, much of what we know about pedagogy differs from andragogy. Due to years of lived experience and an awareness of time left in life, adult learners' approach to learning differs from a child's. Adult learners are distinguished by the following characteristics: they seek autonomy and self-direction; they are goal-oriented; they are centered on the problem at hand; and they need to know why they are learning something (Knowles, 1980).

The autonomous aspect of LEEP, characterized by asynchronous sessions and the highly participatory and collaborative aspects of LEEP discussion, serve the adult learner's needs for autonomy and self-direction. Debates and project presentations support the adult learner's desire to pursue her/his own goals and to focus on practical problems in the world. A sense of real-world applicability is heightened by guest speakers and panel discussions involving practitioners and researchers from around the world.

For LEEP instructors, the realization that the delivery of content must take a backseat to the learning process rather rocked their worlds; it is this that is at the heart of online learning as "different learning." Instructors realize that content in live sessions has to be reduced in favor of going with the flow and allowing class and the learning and teaching from many to just happen. This desire for process is characteristic of the adult learner: "Andragogy means that instruction for adults needs to focus more on the process and less on the content being taught. Strategies such as case studies, role playing, simulations, and self-evaluations are most useful. Instructors adopt a role of facilitator or resource rather than lecturer or grader" (Kearsley, 2003, online). Does online education then provide an ideal environment for the adult learner? Most LEEP instructors have been teaching adult learners for years, but it was the move to this new environment that sparked the discovery that letting go of content was the best strategy. The change of venue has enabled teachers to peer through the cracks in traditional teaching methods to serve the adult learner's need for process rather than content. If further research were to confirm that in fact online education has brought about a shift from content to process, this could indicate a profoundly beneficial outcome for adult learners in an online environment.

> Q3: How Has Our Participation in This Culture Changed Us as Students, Teachers, People?

Reflection and Growth
According to one retreat participant, "LEEP doesn't change you but it intensifies you." In addition to acquiring content knowledge and technology skills, participating in the LEEP environment seems to promote reflection and enhance intrapersonal awareness. One faculty member explained that the "primary motivator [to teach in LEEP] is the renewal aspect. It offers a chance to look at everything you do differently and to move to a more constructivist and dialogic mode."

It is not easy to recognize and/or articulate this sort of transformation. It happens tacitly. As one participant shared:

> When I think about what LEEP can and might do in terms of changing people is in the learning and thinking about learning and how you learn. You go into this new mode of learning . . . having the opportunity to learn differently and reflect on that . . . I've noticed that it is hard to explain what LEEP is.

Discovering new options and opportunities for teaching and learning is the norm in LEEP. As previously discussed, it is an invigorating environment and the often-unanticipated stimulation may lead to stress. Each participant must learn to manage it. At a recent panel discussion, one graduate shared his strategies with new LEEP students—make a plan and learn to take breaks. He also recommends being conscious about stepping away and finding a diversion. His preference: *Harry Potter*. Each night during the semester, he pulled away to read a chapter from the series.

The LEEP environment promotes and supports individual and communal growth. The robust nature of the hybrid program and the learner-centered approach to education permit individual strengths and weaknesses to be considered and accommodated. Students learn by constructing knowledge in a supportive environment. As one participant explained:

> It relates to that idea of being a communal person. That shared success. What is the culture of LEEP—community, shared success. If you are an independent person who doesn't feel comfortable working in teams, this would be difficult. You need to participate, that might be a challenge or easy for you—you need to be forgiving. If that doesn't work for you, LEEP will be hard.

LEEP forces individuals to consider norms and confront prejudices of traditional models of education. This challenge of perspective happens slowly. For example, according to one participant:

> The program has forced me to rely on collaborative work. I don't like to call and say 'I need help,' but the program and the openness, you are forced to look and share and be collaborative. It has taught me patience. It may be frustrating, but in the end, I have a lot more patience for the way people work and the way technology works and I'm hooked.

The effects of LEEP go beyond the virtual classroom. According to one faculty member, "Teaching in LEEP changes the way I teach face-to-face—Now if I don't have the back channel [side comments and conversations] I find I know less about what is going on. Real life is looking more like LEEP."

To grasp the possible significance of online education, we invite you to recall the classic story, "The Emperor's New Clothes," where a simple tailor uses his ingenuity to trick the vain emperor into wearing nothing by reassuring him that his new (nonexistent) vestments were absolutely elegant. This radical approach was necessary for the emperor to finally see the essence of himself as a human being. Consider that a parallel may indeed exist between the emperor/tailor relationship and that of traditional/online education, where online education affords ample opportunities to explore and reconsider the essence of teaching and learning. Smith, Lastra, and Robins describe this powerful transformation, noting:

> Faculty who teach in LEEP become much more self-reflective, not only about their teaching in the online environment, but also about what they do (almost intuitively) in the face-to-face classroom. The extent to which this contributes to increased quality in teaching, in whatever setting, deserves further investigation. (p. 358)

Conclusions and Future Research

What has been achieved and what is known about teaching and learning in LEEP vis-à-vis personal and communal reflection and transformation is noteworthy and has been corroborated by a number of studies by a number of researchers. Observation, interviews with students, faculty and staff, focus groups, and surveys have been used to approach the question of best practices for teaching and learning. Particularly important is that instructors and students alike have been consulted for their perceptions of what works and what doesn't. It is simple and can be very productive to ask instructors what is effective about their teaching, but to truly know this it is essential that students also be asked what constitutes effective teaching. A teacher may think that a particular technique or delivery is working very well, but in fact it may be received in a very different way. In the words of Michel de Certeau:

> The presence and circulation of a representation [teaching] . . . tells us nothing about what it is for its users. We must first analyze its manipulation by users who are not its makers. Only then can we gauge the difference or similarity between the production of the image and the secondary production hidden in the process of utilization. . . . (de Certeau, 1984, p. xiii–xiv)

This research, then, is on the right track. Action research may further the agenda, with the teachers engaging with the researcher in a cycle of practice and reflection. Such an engagement may result in new insights about teaching practices while creating change in approach and technique. Basically, such studies would entail observations of teaching in progress (easy to do with LEEP since researcher and teacher need not be collocated), interviews with the teacher about his/her experiences, and finally reflection on data generated through the observations and interviews (Schon, 1995). To take this action research agenda yet a step further in order to satisfy de Certeau's critique, one could add the element of student participation and include students in the interviewing process.

The LEEP retreat provided a unique opportunity to explore faculty, staff, and student knowledge of online education. The focus groups in particular served to promote intergroup dialogue, which enabled the transformation of a wealth of tacit knowledge into explicit understanding. The retreat results reveal participant perceptions of best practices in a successful online program. They are not intended to constitute a global framework of best practices and they aren't considered generalizable across programs. Notwithstanding the above, many ideas that emerged during the process are already being used to inform practice and to influence the ongoing cycle of improvement for GSLIS education and beyond. The tribal knowledge continues to grow, and we will continue to witness, capture, and record its progress for future participants in online education.

References

Barbiero, D. (2003). Tacit knowledge. In C. Eliasmith (Ed.), *Dictionary of philosophy of mind*. Retrieved October 27, 2003 from http://www.artsci.wustl.edu/~philos/MindDict/tacitknowledge.html.

Bates, A. W. (1995). *Technology, open learning and distance education*. London: Routledge.

Crowley, B. (1999). Building useful theory: Tacit knowledge, practitioner reports, and culture of LIS inquiry. *Journal of Education for Library and Information Science 40*(4), 282–295.

de Certeau, M. (1984). *The practice of everyday life*. Berkeley: University of California Press.

Freire, P. (1993). *Pedagogy of the oppressed*. New York: Continuum.

Geertz, C. (1995). *After the fact: Two countries, four decades, one anthropologist.* Cambridge, MA: Harvard University Press.

Gibbs, A. (1997). Focus groups. *Social Research Update 19.* Retrieved from http://www.soc.surrey.ac.uk/sru/SRU19.html.

Harasim, L. (1995). *Learning networks: A field guide to teaching and learning online.* Cambridge, MA: MIT Press.

Kazmer, M. M. (2000). Coping in a distance environment: Sitcoms, chocolate cake, and dinner with a friend. *First Monday 5* (9). Retrieved from http://www.firstmonday.dk/issues/issue5_9/kazmer/index.html.

Kazmer, M. M., & Haythornthwaite, C. (2001). Juggling multiple social worlds: Distance students online and offline. *American Behavioral Scientist, 45*(3), 510–529. (Reprinted in this volume)

Kearsley, G. (2003). Sequencing of instruction. In G. Kearsley, *Explorations in learning & instruction: The theory into practice database.* Retrieved October 27, 2003 from http://tip.psychology.org/sequence.html.

Knowles, M. S. (1980). *The modern practice of adult education: From pedagogy to andragogy.* New York: Cambridge, The Adult Education Co.

Laurillard, D. (1993). *Rethinking university teaching.* London: Routledge.

Merleau-Ponty, M. (1981). *Phenomenology of perception.* London: Routledge.

Noddings, N. (1984). *Caring: A feminine approach to ethics and moral education.* Berkeley: University of California Press.

Ruhleder, K. (this volume). Changing patterns of participation: Interactions in a synchronous audio+chat classroom.

Schon, D. A. (1983). *The reflective practitioner: How professionals think in action.* New York: Basic Books.

Schon, D. A. (1995). Knowing-in-action: The new scholarship requires a new epistemology. *Change,* November/December, 27–34.

Smith, L. C., Lastra, S., & Robins, J. (2001). Teaching online: Changing models of teaching and learning in LEEP. *Journal of Education for Library and Information Science, 42*(4), 348–363.

Young, J. R. (2002, March 22). 'Hybrid' teaching seeks to end the divide between traditional and online instruction. *The Chronicle of Higher Education.* Retrieved from http://chronicle.com/free/v48/i28/28a03301.htm.

CHAPTER 12

Rae-Anne Montague
Linda C. Smith

Faculty Perspectives

Since LEEP's (Library Education Experimental Program) inception in 1996, the Graduate School of Library and Information Science (GSLIS) at the University of Illinois at Urbana-Champaign (UIUC) has been able to reach out to nearly 600 students at a distance. Of these, 370 have already graduated with a master's degree in library and information science (LIS). Each student enrolls in at least 10 courses while completing the degree and thus works with several different faculty members. This chapter explores the challenges and opportunities online education has brought to GSLIS from a faculty perspective.

Almost everyone teaching in LEEP for the first time is new to teaching online. Those teaching in the early years were truly pioneers, trying out new technology and determining how to adapt face-to-face instruction to a mixture of online synchronous sessions, asynchronous discussions, and brief face-to-face periods with students. After eight years of LEEP, faculty members have accumulated considerable knowledge and experience regarding online course design and delivery. In addition, program administrators and instructional technology staff have a better understanding of ways to enhance faculty success and satisfaction in this new mode of teaching.

Online Opportunities for Faculty

According to Smith (2001), at GSLIS, "the motivation for developing an online degree option was twofold: to reach qualified students who wanted to pursue the degree but were place-bound, and to experiment with a new medium for teaching and learning" (p. 89). Online education has enabled the faculty to move beyond the limitations (in terms of time, place, and media) of the traditional classroom. As Ko and Rossen (2001) explain, "each time you teach online, you have the chance to acquire insights and experience that can be used as the basis for further exploration" (p. 276). Online education can provide a heightened awareness of one's teaching:

> This heightened awareness can be both illuminating and humbling. We find that the instructional design process becomes less implicit and more of a deliberate enterprise. Sometimes this leads us to make changes in the way we do things or to try out new approaches, not only in our online courses but in our on-campus classrooms as well. (Ko & Rossen, 2001, p. 277)

Thus, the pedagogical stimulation associated with online education provides faculty members with opportunities to (re-)discover the joy of teaching.

Online teaching also enables new connections with the wider world—with students, information, resources, and colleagues at a distance. Of particular interest in a graduate professional program for information specialists are the possibilities for involving practitioners in instruction in creative ways. Practitioners become involved in answering students' assignment-related questions, giving guest lectures, or teaching entire courses. Because instruction is no longer dependent solely on being in the same place at the same time, practitioners in any location can have an increasing role in preparing the next generation of information professionals.

Who Teaches in LEEP?

In keeping with the university's mission to continually improve the quality of programs, all GSLIS faculty have been involved with the development of LEEP. All GSLIS faculty have had some contact with LEEP students in their roles as academic advisors and supervisors of practica, independent studies, or theses. As well, all full-time faculty members are expected to teach LEEP courses as part of their regular teaching load, although the actual frequency balances the needs of LEEP students with other demands on faculty time (e.g., teaching on-campus students in the M.S., Certificate of Advanced Study, and Ph.D. programs, as well as the GSLIS undergraduate minor in information technology studies).

The success and growth of LEEP has meant that demand for LEEP courses has exceeded available faculty resources. To meet this demand, adjunct faculty members have been recruited to offer courses beyond the number and subject range that can be taught by full-time GSLIS faculty. For summer courses, adjuncts are often drawn from LIS faculty at other universities; in the fall and spring, adjuncts are drawn from practitioners who have prior classroom teaching experience. All are interested in the opportunity to teach capable students using a new medium. Just as the students can enroll from any location that has an Internet connection, adjunct faculty can reside anywhere. Like the students, they make the trip to campus each semester for the required on-campus session, giving them an opportunity to interact with full-time GSLIS faculty and staff as well as their students.

As is true in other graduate professional library and information science programs, GSLIS already makes use of some adjunct faculty for on-campus instruction. For online instruction, the potential pool of adjunct faculty is national in scope and offers new opportunities for enhancing instruction and course offerings. Given the critical role of LEEP adjunct faculty, program administrators and instructional technology staff have made increasing efforts to involve *e-adjuncts* in faculty development activities to promote a consistent standard of online instructional quality as well as a high level of faculty commitment to the program. Integrating adjunct faculty as valued members of the LEEP teaching and learning community increases their satisfaction with the teaching experience.

From fall 1996 to spring 2004, 78 individuals have taught one or more courses in LEEP: 33 are affiliated with UIUC (23 full-time GSLIS faculty; 2 faculty members from other campus units; 1 library faculty member; 2 doctoral students; 5 GSLIS professional staff members); and 45 are adjuncts from outside UIUC, only four of whom reside in Illinois (13 faculty affiliated with other LIS or IS schools; 16 librarians employed in academic libraries across the United States; 4 librarians, one each from a corporate, historical society, hospital, and public library; 11 LIS consultants; and 1 working in computing services for a professional society). All adjuncts hold at least an M.S. in library and information science and many hold Ph.Ds. Many are GSLIS alumni who appreciate the opportunity to share their expertise with new generations of students.

Course enrollments are generally capped at between 20 and 30 students, with faculty determining the class size. Few LEEP courses are large enough to warrant a teaching assistant. In the infrequent instances where teaching assistants are involved, they may help with technology-related tasks, as well as course management tasks such as fielding student questions, logging receipt of assignments, and assisting in grading, depending on the skills of the assistant and the needs of the faculty. Teaching assistants may also participate directly in teaching (e.g., during the on-campus session, collaboratively during live sessions, or as a guest lecturer with sole responsibility for a live session). Several LEEP courses have also involved team-teaching by faculty who may or may not be co-located (a model that provides one more example of the flexibility online education affords).

The LEEP Teaching Experience

To date, 47 different courses have been offered in LEEP, and students have also participated in practica (with libraries and practitioners near to the student's home location), independent studies, and thesis research. Although the range of courses is not as extensive as for the on-campus master's students, the offerings provide a strong foundation for work in a number of areas both in and outside libraries, including youth services, reference, cataloging, administration, and information technology applications. As Tyler (2001) notes, "LIS is a suitable subject for Internet education: learning is reinforced because the medium for delivery is the same as the subject, utilising the very IT systems that will be used by the student in the LIS workplace and in businesses" (p. 47). Although this interpretation is based on a somewhat narrow perspective on the LIS curriculum, a number of GSLIS courses involve study of information systems. In other courses LEEP students use information technology to seek, organize, and present information. There is, therefore, considerable overlap of content and process in an online LIS program.

The online courses are designed to be comparable in quality to those taught on campus, with students having the opportunity to gain the same knowledge, skills, and sense of professionalism. However, while there is a common set of tools available for course design, there is no single model that LEEP faculty must follow. Faculty are free to make their own determination of how to combine Web-based distribution of course materials, live synchronous sessions, and asynchronous bulletin board discussions in ways that help students meet the learning objectives of their particular course. With limited time for face-to-face (one day for a course per semester) and live sessions (up to two hours per week in a regularly scheduled slot), lectures can no longer serve as the sole means of presenting content. Course design includes the syllabus (sequencing of topics and readings), assignments (individual, group), and allocation of content delivery and learning activities (synchronous, asynchronous, face-to-face, or independent learning). For asynchronous communication, the faculty member must define conferences within the electronic bulletin board area and explain the function of each for communication and discussion. Faculty must find ways to foster participation and involvement, monitor nonparticipation, and reach out to students not fully engaged in the course.

Faculty and instructors in LEEP, like others providing online education, have found that some methods and techniques that work well in a conventional classroom do not transfer directly to an equally effective distance learning experience. However, possibilities arise for new ways of teaching and ways of applying traditional methods in novel contexts. A survey of LEEP faculty conducted in summer 2000 revealed the varied ways in which they use synchronous, asynchronous, and face-to-face means to reach their students and meet the needs of their courses.

Faculty have adopted and adapted the use of the "live lecture" synchronous session time in a variety of ways. They vary the frequency in which they offer lectures in this normally weekly session. Some use this time instead to hold synchronous "live office hours." Others have made wider use of this session, adding activities such as illustrated lectures, guest lectures and interviews, demonstrations of online search techniques, visits to and assessment of relevant Web sites, discussion with the entire class, responses to student questions, small group discussions, group work, exercises, role playing, reading picture books aloud, student presentations, and storytelling by students (in the Storytelling course).

The bulletin board system is a second major means of conducting courses. The system allows faculty to set up multiple boards, to characterize the purpose of each board, and to authorize either the whole class or smaller groups of students to make use of a given board. Functions served by bulletin boards include class discussions, group discussions, posting of information or announcements, technology support, introductions of class members, group projects, posting of individual assignments, and feedback on assignments.

Activities in the mandatory, face-to-face session on campus are quite varied, depending on the subject matter of the course. Faculty members plan activities that would be difficult or impossible to accomplish in a virtual classroom, given current LEEP technology. In fall and spring, the face-to-face session takes place about one-third of the way through the 16-week course; for summer, face-to-face sessions are held at the beginning of the 8-week course. Examples of on-campus activities include: telling stories and listening to experienced tellers (Storytelling course); a miniconference on the subject of the course with paper presentations and a panel discussion (History of Libraries); technical demonstrations, design activities, technical group work, and discussion (Interfaces to Information Systems); viewing and discussing videotapes illustrating communication techniques in the reference interview (Reference); teaching book discussion techniques and watching a video (Youth Services Librarianship); and talks by local specialists, computer clinics, and working groups (Systems Analysis and Management). Many faculty members also encourage students to allow time for on-site use of the rich library resources available at UIUC.

Independent learning opportunities are also frequently incorporated in LEEP. They may be carried out within the context of an individual course. For example, some faculty members have students take field trips to local libraries or archives to research services as part of their course requirements. The information they gather is then shared in the class environment. Faculty members also supervise entire courses based on independent learning through practica, independent studies, and theses.

Assessment of student performance is generally based on such factors as contributions to class discussion, presentations, and individual and group written assignments. Few courses, whether on-campus or LEEP, make use of examinations as an evaluation tool. Students are taught to post their assignments as Web pages and to send the instructor a URL, but they can also e-mail assignments as attachments. Faculty members have devised various means for providing feedback, including using electronic tools (e-mail or private bulletin boards for each student) and printing out papers, marking them up, and mailing them back. Some classes also take advantage of the Web as a publishing medium: drafts of student work can be posted giving an opportunity for other students to offer comments and suggestions. Some courses, like the Government Publications course, also showcase final student projects by publicizing URLs via relevant listservs. Once these publications are online, students can assemble their work into e-portfolios that they use in their job-seeking process.

Rewards and Challenges of Teaching Online

Overall, LEEP faculty members have found their online teaching experiences very rewarding. They value their involvement in program planning, research opportunities, and interactions with new students. Faculty satisfaction and student satisfaction go hand in hand. LEEP students are adult learners and most are keenly interested in pursuing their degree through GSLIS. Using a hybrid model that combines some face-to-face and synchronous time with asynchronous communication, faculty members are able to employ a wide range of tools and techniques to reach out to students. In particular, courses can be shaped to promote highly interactive, engaged learning environments. For example, faculty observe that the face-to-face session provides benefits to both faculty and students: students learn that they are not alone in finding some of the material challenging; they develop greater rapport with the instructor and with each other; and they can accomplish some tasks more efficiently and effectively than working from home. The robustness of the hybrid model results in positive outcomes for both students and faculty. Students become active learners and "faculty members feel deeply rewarded if they sense that they have made a difference in the lives of their students" (Kennedy, 1997, p. 60).

For many faculty members, online teaching may provide the first opportunity they have to consider and learn about teaching. As Sener (2002) explains, "one of the peculiarities of American higher education is that very few of its teachers have ever been exposed to any formal training on how to teach effectively. The implicit operating assumption is that being an expert on the subject matter is enough." Online education creates new opportunities for learning to teach. As noted earlier, this includes proactive approaches to creating a teaching community with opportunities for interaction and professional exchange. Now that LEEP has been in operation for a number of years, new faculty, before they begin teaching in LEEP, have the opportunity to learn from others. They can review materials and observe experienced peers in live sessions, and join a conference call held each semester where new instructors can ask questions and others can share experiences. Some of the questions asked have been: How do you mark-up online work to provide feedback? How do you incorporate grading for participation? What do faculty use in lieu of final papers? How do others set up groups and foster effective group work? How do you manage chat overload? How are guest speakers incorporated effectively into live sessions? Notes from conference calls are compiled and distributed to all LEEP faculty members. These notes are also being used to develop a handbook of online instruction for faculty.

The promotion of collaboration and dialog among faculty was also part of the rationale for the first LEEP retreat (see Lawton & Montague, this volume). At the retreat, faculty described a variety of rewards they found in online teaching, including:

- It is really liberating to not feel as though I'm filling the hours. There is a lot more decision making. That is burdensome, but it is also liberating. Let's me re-think my role as a teacher. I feel as if I'm not having to conform to some model that the students expect.
- I spend more time up front making decisions, but then enjoying the class and being a part of it as it unfolds.
- The space aspect is fabulous because it is not an issue—to be able to have guests from anywhere. I'm in the middle of the cornfields and yet it is not an issue.
- Sometimes I'm reading something that is interesting and relates to my class so I can post it and I don't have to think about it any more.
- I had to think about what I was trying to accomplish—what this is all about. Made me much more reflective.
- It provides new opportunities to contribute to the profession. It's wonderful to go back to the roots of how I learned and then to keep myself up to date. Terrifying sometimes, but exhilarating.

Faculty also shared some of the challenges they face, such as keeping up with technology, dealing with varied levels of student experience, or finding the right amount of content:

> When to stop! I give way too much content. I want to give them their money's worth, but have gotten feedback that less is better. How to get things to a more manageable level?

and providing feedback on assignments:

> On campus I can scribble notes in margins, but I can't do that electronically. I end up writing a couple of paragraphs at the end, which ends up being me writing an essay. How can I give specific feedback in a way that is not too time intensive?

The novelty and complexity of teaching in LEEP has provided faculty with a wide range of rewards—rewards that faculty consider to be significant, such as liberation from restrictive models of teaching, and the opportunity to reflect and contribute to the profession. These tend to compensate for the varied specific challenges they must work to overcome. On the whole, faculty speak enthusiastically about their experience with LEEP and project a sense of optimism for the continued development of online instruction as a successful approach to providing quality education.

Gauging Faculty Success and Satisfaction

Faculty and Program Success

There are a number of indicators of the success of GSLIS faculty in adapting to teaching online. Faculty members teaching in LEEP regularly appear on a campuswide list that recognizes teachers ranked highly by their students. These rankings are based on evaluations completed by students at the end of each semester. Seven full-time faculty members and four adjuncts have received this distinction for their LEEP courses, with several recognized multiple times. LEEP, as a program, was honored in 2001 with the Sloan Consortium (Sloan-C) award for the Most Outstanding Asynchronous Learning Network (ALN) Program (http://www.sloan-c.org). This international recognition is a clear reflection of the faculty's dedication and expertise. In 2003, Christine Jenkins, a GSLIS faculty member, was the first UIUC online instructor to be recognized with the Campus Award for Excellence in Off-campus Teaching. Jenkins describes her success online as a "combination of knowledge, dedication, imagination and communication." (A demonstration of her approach to teaching in LEEP is available at http://leep.lis.uiuc.edu/demos/jenkins).

Evaluation

Since the LEEP program began as an experiment, evaluation has been integral to gauging its success and guiding improvements. Various sources of evaluations provide a means of judging the success of the faculty and of the program. Two external program reviews have been conducted, one for the first year of the program (1996–1997), and one for the fifth year (2000–2001). Students contribute to electronic bulletin board forums specifically set up for "Feedback to GSLIS" and "LEEP Talk"; participate in open meetings held between students and administrators, conducted both online and during on-campus sessions; and complete course evaluations at the end of each semester (formerly paper based, the university has recently developed and made available online course evaluations). LEEP administrators also monitor the willingness of faculty and adjuncts to teach again in LEEP as a measure of their satisfaction; and examine results of formal research carried out by GSLIS faculty and doctoral students for feedback on the program. Most recently, a retreat on LEEP teaching and learning was held to specifically gather information on best practices (see Montague & Lawton, this volume). The list of best practices developed by faculty affirms the faculty's own sense of success and accomplishment. It included setting priorities and establishing time management schemes, Socratic dialog, opportunities for spontaneous teachable moments, convenience of incorporating specialist guest speakers, increased reflection on teaching objectives and methods, and new professional contributions (Montague, 2003).

These various forms of assessment have helped to identify ways to improve both individual courses and aspects of the program overall. In general, they have affirmed the soundness of the original design and the success that has been achieved in maintaining the high quality of the GSLIS master's program in this new medium.

Faculty Satisfaction

Faculty satisfaction is one of the five pillars of quality online education. It is defined as follows by Sloan-C:

> Faculty satisfaction means that instructors find the online teaching experience personally rewarding and professionally beneficial. Personal factors contributing to faculty satisfaction with the online experience include opportunities to extend interactive learning communities to new populations of students and to conduct and publish research related to online teaching and learning. Institutional factors related to faculty satisfaction include three categories: support, rewards, and institutional study/research. Faculty satisfaction is enhanced when the institution supports training in online instructional skills, and ongoing technical and administrative assistance. Faculty members also expect to be included in the governance and quality assurance of online programs, especially as these relate to curricular decisions and development of policies of particular importance to the online environment (such as intellectual property, copyright, royalties, collaborative design, and delivery). (Moore, 2002, p. 58)

The following summarizes 11 factors in LEEP program design identified by Smith (2001) that have contributed to faculty satisfaction.

1. Involvement of faculty in program planning

From the beginning, the GSLIS faculty felt that they had "ownership" of the LEEP program. Their views contributed to the design of the program, all faculty were expected to teach in the program, courses offered in the program had already been approved by faculty as M.S. degree course offerings, and a senior faculty member had responsibility for administrative oversight of the program. Subsequent recognition of the program as a successful innovation by others at UIUC and in the profession has been a source of pride to the faculty.

2. Close alignment with research interests

The GSLIS faculty is quite interdisciplinary, and a number of faculty have research interests relevant to the LEEP program in such areas as computer-mediated communication, computer-supported cooperative work, interface design, collaborative learning, online pedagogy, and design of digital library services. Investigations of research questions in the LEEP environment by a number of faculty and doctoral students have led to several original research publications and conference presentations.

Such studies contribute new knowledge, but also provide findings that can lead to improvements in LEEP course and program design. (See the research presented in other chapters in this volume, as well as the listing in the LEEP bibliography at the end of this volume, and online at http://www.lis.uiuc.edu/gslis/degrees/leep_bib.html.)

3. Extending the reach of the M.S. degree program
On-campus students in the M.S. program come from all parts of the United States and many other countries, but access is still limited to those who can relocate or live within commuting distance. Because the faculty feel that many other prospective students could benefit from the program, it has been very satisfying to reach a larger pool of talented students through LEEP.

4. Strong technology support for faculty and students
Many faculty and students are not expert users of technology and some could be characterized as novices. The LEEP technology support staff works closely with faculty, providing whatever support is required as courses are developed and delivered. Equally important, they train and consult with all students, relieving faculty of the burden of assisting students in answering technical support questions (including during live synchronous sessions in a technology support chat room). In addition the technology staff support a very reliable infrastructure, so that technology problems occur infrequently and thus do not interfere with teaching and learning. (See Gengler, this volume, for a chapter on the technology group's philosophy of support.)

5. LEEP program structure fosters a learning community
The initial on-campus session fosters close ties among LEEP students that are reinforced each time the students return to campus (one student has characterized this as the "reunion atmosphere" of the on-campus sessions). This provides a strong basis for continuing student-to-student communication (including *whispering* during live sessions, i.e., directing text chat to one or more selected individuals rather than to the class as a whole), collaboration on group projects, and openness to contributing in class and to the program as a whole. The faculty member does not have to work as hard to foster this collaborative environment as would likely be the case without these face-to-face encounters. In addition, students can help support each other, so there is less of a burden on the faculty member who is not the sole point of contact for students in the course. (See Ruhleder, this volume, for examples of student in-class help giving.)

6. Face-to-face and synchronous time in each course
Because the courses include some face-to-face and synchronous time, faculty do not have to eliminate activities that they feel contribute to the quality of the course but that would

be impossible to accomplish completely asynchronously. While it is essential that faculty consider how best to distribute content delivery over the three modes (synchronous, asynchronous, and face-to-face) and not simply try to replicate a face-to-face course online, this range of alternatives means there are fewer constraints on course design.

7. Administrative recognition of the demands of teaching online
Full-time GSLIS faculty members are not expected to design and implement LEEP courses in addition to all of their other responsibilities. They are granted some release time to prepare for LEEP courses and a reduced load the first time the course is offered.

8. Characteristics of the student body and quality of student performance
LEEP students are adult learners with backgrounds and work settings that allow them to make many substantive contributions to the class. They are highly motivated and eager to learn. They often can apply what they are learning in class immediately in the workplace. As a faculty member, one learns from the students at the same time that one often has very tangible evidence (in the form of student comments) that they understand the value of what they are learning in class both from the faculty member and their peers.

9. Availability of a range of tools with freedom to decide how to use them
Faculty do have certain constraints on course design: they are expected to schedule some live synchronous sessions, plan face-to-face activities for the scheduled on-campus session, make use of electronic bulletin boards for asynchronous communication, and use the LEEP virtual classroom environment rather than some alternative. But they have a great deal of freedom in making decisions about how best to use each of these modes of communication and in designing individual and/or group assignments. This allows faculty to be creative rather than conforming to some preestablished course template.

10. Control of class size
Enrollment management in LEEP courses takes into account, whenever possible, expressed faculty preferences on class size. Class size is generally between 20 and 30. Faculty express a preference for LEEP classes in this range because of the high amount of feedback required; difficulty of handling discussion during live sessions if the group is larger and of giving individualized help to a larger group; and overwhelming numbers of bulletin board posts that can result when a large group engages in asynchronous class discussions.

11. Quality of communication with students
Many discussions of asynchronous communication note the potential for increased quality of class discussion compared to face-to-face classes, and many LEEP faculty

members concur with this observation. Some faculty also feel they come to know their students better as individuals because of the ongoing communication throughout the semester across multiple modes.

Future Directions

Throughout the eight years that have passed since LEEP was launched, faculty have played a key role in the program's success. Faculty members have shaped program development, and have themselves been transformed from online pioneers into experienced online course designers and teachers. As described above, challenges to effective teaching still exist in the online classroom. Understanding gained through practice and research will help overcome difficult issues confronting faculty. Online options like LEEP will also provide opportunities to reach otherwise underserved populations and to develop new models of education, both intrainstitutional (e.g., hybrid formats for courses) and interinstitutional (e.g., consortial arrangements).

The full potential of online education has yet to be realized. As Anderson (2003) describes:

> We are developing a growing mosaic of distance education technologies and practices, with no single "best way" to user interaction. Each institution, discipline, region, and user group will develop unique cultural practices and expectations related to their need for and use of interaction. This is not to say that all applications are equally effective or efficient. Too much of our practice in distance education is not "evidence based," and our actions and instructional designs are often grounded on untested assumptions about the value of modes of interaction (or lack thereof). Thus, the research opportunities that focus on interaction in all its forms are boundless, yet critically important. (Anderson, 2003, p. 141)

Multiple modes of interaction—with students and with each other—remain key to the success and satisfaction of LEEP faculty. Ongoing research and self-reflective practice will continue to enable advancements in online instruction by LEEP faculty and development of best practices that can be shared more widely.

References

Anderson, T. (2003). Modes of interaction in distance education: Recent developments and research questions. In M. G. Moore & W. G. Anderson (Eds.) *Handbook of distance education* (pp. 129–144). Mahwah, NJ: Lawrence Erlbaum Associates.

Kennedy, D. (1997). *Academic duty*. Cambridge MA: Harvard University Press.

Ko, S., & Rossen, S. (2001). *Teaching online: A practical guide*. Boston: Houghton Mifflin.

Montague, R. (2003). LEEP Retreat: Exploring best practices in online education. In *Distance learning administration annual conference proceedings 2003* (pp. 101–104). Carrollton, GA: State University of West Georgia.

Moore, J. C. (2002). *Elements of quality: The Sloan-C framework.* Needham, MA: Sloan Center for OnLine Education.

Sener, J. (2002). Online learning: Myths, realities and pathways to reform. Retrieved January 4, 2004 from: http://www.online.uillinois.edu/oakley/Sener_16Aug02.doc.

Smith, L. C. (2001). Faculty satisfaction in LEEP: A Web-based graduate degree program in library and information science. In *Online education volume 2: Proceedings of the 2000 Sloan summer workshop on asynchronous learning networks* (pp. 87–108). Needham, MA: Sloan Center for On-Line Education.

Tyler, A. (2001). A survey of distance learning library and information science courses delivered via the Internet. *Education for Information, 19*(1), 47–59.

CHAPTER 13   *Christine A. Jenkins*

The Virtual Classroom as Ludic Space

> *I don't mind the virtual classroom, but I don't like it. Instead of hearing voices I read words, so I don't get verbal clues. It's like being near-sighted and being in a crowd without my glasses on, or talking to people in a dense fog.*
> (LEEP GUEST LECTURER)

> *In the virtual classroom, I have more tricks up my sleeve. I feel more genuine and real. I have more immediate contact with students. I feel like a plate spinner, a juggler, paying absolute attention to the moment.*
> (LEEP INSTRUCTOR)

Teachers hold varied views of online teaching. Some view the virtual classroom as a space that is inferior to the face-to-face classroom, similar to—but less than—the traditional classroom setting. Students can *type* in the chat room environment but they cannot actually *talk*. Students can *read* what their classmates have to say, but they cannot actually *hear* them. Characterized by what it is not, the virtual classroom is seen by some as a shadow realm. Like Gertrude Stein's famous portrayal of her Oakland, California birthplace, "There is no there there."

Certainly some instructors who teach in the virtual classroom would agree with Stein's description. Other instructors see little difference between the virtual and the face-to-face classroom; the two environments may seem different initially, but once the technology is mastered, there is really no substantial difference between the two. Still others describe the virtual classroom as a unique space with attributes independent of the capabilities of the face-to-face environment. This chapter focuses on the

LEEP (Library Education Experimental Program) virtual classroom at the Graduate School of Library and Information Science (GSLIS) as an educational setting whose affordances are only beginning to be explored and utilized.

Like their on-campus counterparts, online distance education classes include both synchronous and asynchronous elements. Many of these elements are functionally identical: students prepare for class meetings by reading texts, whether those texts come to them electronically or via a book from a campus library; written assignments are the same, regardless of how they are delivered to the instructor; and so on. However, other comparisons between the two modes of instruction yield more substantive differences.

The components of the LEEP virtual classroom include (1) a chat room environment, capable of hosting a single large class or simultaneous small groups, (2) a visual display that includes texts, slides, and/or Web sites, and (3) real-time audio for broadcasting live lectures by the instructor or guests (who may be physically present in the studio or participating via telephone), and music. All LEEP classes meet on a regular basis in the real-time virtual classroom. Most have two-hour weekly meetings. Some alternate between regular and as-needed class sessions, with weekly meetings during the early part of the semester and less frequent meetings as students work on term projects. Due to initial limitations in distance education technology, some instructors for the earliest offerings of LEEP classes kept synchronous class meetings to a minimum, but many of those pioneers felt their instruction was hindered by the lack of real-time group meetings, and regular weekly or semiweekly synchronous meetings have become the norm.

This chapter explores LEEP instructors' experiences of the real-time virtual classroom and the potential and actual uses of the virtual classroom as an engaging educational setting that provides *ludic space* (a place for play) for at least some of the participants. Ludic space is a term credited to anthropologist Victor Turner, who used it to describe spaces designated for play (Turner, 1982). This concept, however, has been expanded to describe a variety of spaces, including virtual spaces, designed for playful activity and designed to facilitate interaction across barriers between diverse participants. For example, in a recent paper on working with children with visual limitations, ludic space describes the ideal playground in which all children can gather in "a space of inclusion" (Vieira Machado & Garcia, 2002).

Observations are based on my own experience as a LEEP instructor, plus selective interviews with other LEEP faculty and guest speakers (four faculty members who teach in the LEEP format on a regular basis, three guest speakers who have made presentations to LEEP classes on a regular basis, and one LEEP program administrator who is a former LEEP student). I asked interviewees to describe their experience of the virtual classroom. Some responses were highly visual and sensory, while others were almost devoid of sensory details. Overall, their perceptions of the virtual classroom were highly individualistic, but fell into three general groups: (1) Instructors who describe the virtual classroom in terms of what it is *not* (e.g., it is *not* a face-to-face classroom); (2) Instructors who see the virtual and face-to-face classrooms as outwardly different but fundamentally identical; (3) Instructors who see the virtual classroom as a space that is similar in function to the face-to-face classroom, but whose attributes and characteristics combine to create a setting that is profoundly different from the on-campus classroom.

Computer technology provides the connection between students and instructors, and for some instructors that link is the primary—and perhaps only—useful quality of the technology. One of the paradoxical goals of communication technology is to make that connection invisible, in the same way that a pencil is an essential work-enabling tool that is not generally considered on a conscious level. This is an example of successful technology—an instrument that enables or helps with a task and is most successful when it is least noticed. It is only when it malfunctions—the pencil lead breaks or the eraser has hardened—that we become acutely aware of the instrument. Therefore, we might experience the success of a communication technology in inverse ratio to our conscious awareness of it during use.

Instructors in the first group were intensely aware of the technology's presence and its shortcomings in comparison to the face-to-face classroom. For example, the lack of visual information about the students in the virtual classroom's text chat environment prevents the instructor from reading facial expressions or body language as he or she would in a face-to-face environment. The slower pace of conversation between teacher and student via RealAudio and text chat in the virtual classroom is compared unfavorably to the near-instantaneous voice communication of the face-to-face classroom, and the delays in sound transmission in the electronic environment are seen as an impediment to classroom communication. These instructors' view of the virtual classroom might be termed the *deficit model*.

Instructors in the second group are able to overlook the differences between the traditional and the virtual classroom. The course material is the same, the issues raised and the questions asked or answered by students are the same, and the content of the communication in the virtual classroom is similar to that in the face-to-face classroom. The absence of visual cues and the slower response time are not significant to these teachers, who subscribe to a *no difference model* for the virtual classroom.

Instructors in the third *ludic model* group seem to view the technology as *both* visible and invisible. The technology enables communication between and among students and the instructor and creates a shared space in which these physically dispersed individuals can meet and communicate. While the technology's current limitations prevent or hinder some forms of communication, other forms are enabled and/or enhanced. In comparing a lead pencil to a felt-tip pen, for example, it is clear that while they are functionally similar, they also have differences that may favor one over the other, depending on the needs of the user. A pencil can remain functional for years and pencil marks can be deleted with relative ease, while the pen will dry up over time and its marks are often difficult to erase. However, lettering created with a felt-tip pen is visible from greater distances than pencil lettering, and a felt-tip pen can be used to write a message on non-pencil-friendly surfaces, such as the back of one's hand. Different communication modes generate different functionalities.

Diverse Perceptions of the Virtual Classroom

In a face-to-face classroom, the instructor and the students are in a single room together. They can see and hear each other more or less instantaneously. They communicate via words, gestures, and body language. The virtual classroom is actually comprised of a number of rooms: the room where the instructor and his/her computer are located (this can be the LEEP technical studio or the instructor's office or home), and the homes, offices, or computer labs where each student is located during an online class session. Between these synchronous class meetings, the classroom expands to encompass other physical spaces where discussion carries over during the week via electronic bulletin boards and e-mail: offices, homes, and even hotel rooms for faculty; homes, offices, labs, and other dispersed locations for students. Indeed, as wireless communication develops and computers become more portable, the classroom can be almost anywhere. If this room configuration were transposed to an on-campus setting, the instructor and each student would occupy separate rooms, with the communication technology providing a connecting passage—perhaps a tunnel or hallway—between the two locations. *Deficit model* instructors experience the metaphorical passageway between rooms as a large and featureless space—as a distance to be bridged, or a gap or chasm that must be leaped or otherwise overcome. Not surprisingly, instructors in this group consistently describe the virtual classroom in terms of its inferiority to the on-campus classroom.

I interviewed an academic staff member who gives online guest lectures and Q&A sessions with LEEP students on a regular basis. He described his frustration with the virtual classroom environment in contrast to the face-to-face classroom setting.

> I don't *mind* the virtual classroom but don't like it. Instead of hearing voices I read words, so I don't get verbal clues. It's like being near-sighted and being in a crowd without my glasses on, or talking to people in a dense fog. I can tell students are there but not clearly. I don't feel isolated exactly, but because I can't see them, I'm missing all the cues that I need to decide what I'm going to say. Because I'm a visitor, I feel like I have to be more formal, like I'm in a jacket and tie and the students are more casual and definitely more comfortable. They already know each other, but I'm separate from them. I'm the outsider.

Some experienced LEEP instructor "insiders" experience similar frustration at the lack of visual student contact. One such instructor likened her computer screen to a closed window. During an online session, she knows her students are out there, but she can't see, hear, or feel their presence.

> The students really are *very* far away. When I lecture I'm not literally shouting, but it feels like it sometimes. I'm straining to make myself heard, to reach my students. In on-campus classes, I can tell from students' faces what they understand and what they have questions about. In LEEP classes, this just isn't possible.

Other instructors view the deficit modelers' vast distance between the students' rooms and the teacher's room as no space at all. To them, the virtual and online classrooms appear interchangeable, technological dissimilitude notwithstanding. These *no difference model* online teachers acknowledge that there are indeed some differences between the two, but the differences are not significant ones. For example, although the time that elapses between an instructor's question and a student's response is longer in the virtual classroom than in the on-campus classroom, this disparity does not really alter the interaction or the result. Likewise, teaching the same content to students in the same program means that the similarities far outweigh the differences. According to one such instructor, his longtime familiarity with and use of computer technology—"I've had e-mail for 25 years"—enables him to integrate technology into his face-to-face classes to such an extent that putting the class online simply adds one more form of technology to the preexisting mix. As a result, he reported experiencing very little difference between face-to-face and online class meetings.

And finally, there is the *ludic model* group of LEEP instructors who, like the deficit model group, picture the online environment as comprised of several spaces: the teacher's room, the students' rooms, and a distinct connective space between them. The difference between the two groups lies in their visualization of that connective space. Members of the deficit model group see it as a lengthy passage through which teachers and pupils must shout to be heard. In contrast, members of the ludic model group view the passageway itself as the central virtual classroom. Although students and teachers are sitting in front of computer screens separated by great distances and multiple time zones, these instructors experience the LEEP classroom as the common connective space that they can all inhabit together. The virtual classroom becomes a gathering place in which all may participate using a panoply of communication channels to collaborate in creating a playful and participatory ludic space that verges on what philosopher and theorist Mikhail Bakhtin would describe as carnivalesque (Turner 1982; Bakhtin, 1984).

To the instructors in this group, the limitations of the communication technology paradoxically enhance communication by allowing students a richer range of opportunities to contribute to synchronous online discussions. The combination of audio delays (up to 10 seconds between an instructor's question and when the student hears the question on RealAudio) and rapidly transmitted text chat messages and responses results in a mélange of interactions that proceed at different speeds, as threads that combine text and audio overlap with text-only threads. No single voice—including the voice of the instructor—can entirely dominate the meta-narrative of intertwined threads in the mix of visual and auditory texts.

Participation in an online conversation requires conversants to actively signal their presence in the text stream, and this cannot occur until the writer submits his/her message by hitting the computer's Enter key. LEEP conversational conventions have evolved through practice, as participants have found that a multisentence message is more readily communicated in single-sentence, or even half-sentence, utterances. A writer's message cannot be received and read by others until he/she intentionally interrupts the flow of thought and text. Anything longer than the briefest message is broken by the writers themselves, who *must* pause, *must* break their own message *in order to* transmit their message to others. Thus, each time a message is sent, a space opens in the metanarrative that may be filled by someone responding to an earlier message. What might initially appear to be chaos is in actuality a complex dance of *braided conversations* between and among the students on the screen (via chat) and the instructor (via both speech and chat).

Table 13.1 gives an example of braided conversations. It is an edited transcript of a text chat that took place during a young adult literature class discussion about the book *Monster,* by Walter Dean Myers (HarperCollins, 1999). Names are pseudonyms, with upper/lower case preserved from the original. The novel is told from the perspective of Steve, a young man accused of participating in a fatal robbery. The book is the account of Steve's trial.

One ludic model instructor described the virtual classroom as chaotic, but "a good chaotic." Her average class enrollment is approximately 35 students per section. As a result, there are too many student voices on the screen to catch everyone's words, but "the archives [of each live session] allow me to catch all the pearls cast to the floor." She likened her planning process for each two-hour class meeting to writing a sonnet, with its strict format and rhyme sequences. The limits of time and space force her to think creatively in order to present content in ways that would encourage student engagement and create an online learning community.

She likened entering the virtual classroom to "diving into a well." In the LEEP classroom, she offers:

we all have our heads in the well . . . I'm more in my head and more myself than any other time of day. I'm really within inner space, broadcasting from my very own space. In the virtual classroom, I have more tricks up my sleeve. I feel more genuine and real, I have more immediate contact with students. When I've taught from my home computer [rather than the LEEP studio], I've felt even more intimate—on my own in my own private space.

TABLE 13.1. **Example of a Braided Conversation**

Text Chat Transcript	Explanation
[ProfCAJ] What did you think of the style? Was the combination of script and hand-written text effective?	
[sal] Really unique–makes it very readable.	*Responding to ProfCAJ*
[Melanie] I liked the style. I like books written in different ways–poetry, screenplays, etc.	*Responding to ProfCAJ—starting a thread re book's mixed-media format*
[Jane] BOTHERSOME! handwriting of someone from the wrong decade.	*Responding to ProfCAJ—starting a thread re font used in Steve's diary*
[Ira] I very much like the way it flowed–I imagined it differently than if it were written in a normal format	*Responding to ProfCAJ—continuing a thread re book's mixed-media format*
[Nell] I thought it would be hard . . . but i thought it read very quickly, very vivid	*Responding to ProfCAJ—starting a thread re author's writing style*
[jackie] The style is easier to "see" as the character sees, so several ways of getting into the story.	*Responding to ProfCAJ—continuing a thread re book's mixed-media format*
[Sara] Right, Nell, VERY vivid. Such a visual book.	*Responding to Nell—continuing thread re author's writing style*
[ProfCAJ] Do you mean the handwriting was bothersome, or the whole construction, Jane?	*Responding to Jane—continuing thread re font used in Steve's diary*
[Anna] My students love the book and ask for it by saying, the book written as a play.	*Responding to ProfCAJ—continuing a thread re book's mixed-media format*
[Hal] I liked how it pointed to social issues without seeming heavy-handed.	*Responding to ProfCAJ—starting thread about book's themes*
[Jane] The choice of handwriting to use for the custom font was bothersome for me—I'm very type/font focussed in my job	*Responding to ProfCAJ—continuing thread re fonts used in Steve's diary*
[Kari] right Hal. we saw it as it happened. not him only telling his side of the story	*Responding to Hal—continuing thread re book's themes*
[ProfCAJ] Jane, It would be interesting to see what would have worked better with regard to the font of the hand-written parts	*Responding to Jane—continuing thread re font used in Steve's diary*
[Paul] format somehow appropriate for the content—"visual" approach mirrors the impact that appearance has on the characters (skin-color, etc.)	*Responding to ProfCAJ—continuing thread re book's mixed-media format*
[ProfCAJ] So, do we see "the truth" about Steve's role in the holdup? What do *you* think happened?	
[Jane] I immediately thought Not Guilty based on the handwriting style—keep wondering if the author intended that	*Responding to ProfCAJ—continuing thread re font used in Steve's diary*

continued on next page

TABLE 13.1. *continued*

Text Chat Transcript	Explanation
[Anna] I could not decide if he was guilty. At first I thought definitely yes and later maybe not	*Responding to ProfCAJ—starting thread re uncertainty re Steve's guilt*
[Sara] I think the beauty if Steve WAS the lookout but managed to convince himself he wasn't.	*Responding to ProfCAJ—starting thread re Steve's moral uncertainty*
[paul] legally, perhaps, not guilty, but definitely guilty in a moral sense . . .	*Responding to ProfCAJ—continuing thread re Steve's moral uncertainty*
[Pat] Sara, I think he convinced himself that since he got no money and did not pull the trigger he was innocent	*Responding to Sara—continuing thread re Steve's moral uncertainty*
[Melanie] Yes I thought he was the lookout but got a lucky break	*Responding to ProfCAJ—starting thread re Steve's "lucky break"*
[Lana] Yes, Anna, it seemed to me that Steve wasn't even sure whether he was guilty or not	*Responding to Anna—continuing thread re uncertainty re Steve's guilt*
[Ally] though I think that Steve's guilt was never conclusively stated in the novel. Like it was secondary, or irrelevant to the point of the story. I loved that element of Monster.	*Responding to ProfCAJ—starting a thread re plot ambiguity*
[Sara] Melanie, everyone, I found myself WANTING him to get a lucky break although in real life I probably wouldn't!	*Responding to Melanie—continuing thread re Steve's "lucky break"*
[hal] The point is not so much whether he is innocent or guilty, but that the punishment MAKES him guilty, even in his own mind, even if he is ultimately not.	*Responding to ProfCAJ*
[Jen] Sara, I thought that too. I became involved with him as a person	*Responding to Sara—continuing thread re Steve's "lucky break"*
[paul] me too, Ally . . . i thought it was all about the label MONSTER instead of "whodunnit"	*Responding to Ally—continuing thread re plot ambiguity*
[ari] the play format allowed us to see his actions as well as to hear his inner thoughts	*Responding to ProfCAJ—picking up thread re book's mixed-media format*
[Jane] Who can be a monster with that handwriting??—yes, I'm obsessed.	*Responding to ProfCAJ—continuing thread re font used in Steve's diary*
[Ally] yes paul. the idea of who are you, who do others think you are, and what is the truth?	*Responding to Paul—continuing thread re plot ambiguity*

This instructor felt that her role was a combination of host and leader in, first, establishing a time and a place for her virtual classroom, and second, planning and directing the sequence of activities during the synchronous class session: "I feel like a plate spinner, a juggler, paying absolute attention to the moment" (see also Kazmer & Haythornthwaite, 2001, for other cases where the concept of juggling comes into LEEP life).

Another interviewee, a former classroom teacher and graduate of the LEEP program, currently serves as one of the program's on-campus administrators. In describing her experience on both sides of the instructor/student equation, she stressed the humor that she found in classroom interactions that continually interwove course content and students' multiple connections through shared hardship and personal stories. "Each class establishes its own in-jokes that become touchstones for the class." Her best advice for incoming students and new instructors was to "embrace the chaos." For her, the virtual classroom was decidedly different from the face-to-face classroom, but in ways that she found pleasurable. In an environment without actual faces, a student's name becomes his/her face, as each utterance in text chat is preceded on the screen by the speaker's name in brackets. But students can change their nicknames—and thus their visible faces—at will. And when that collection of letters is the sole indication of a speaker's identify, how long will it take before the classmates of a self-christened "HarryPotter" begin asking him/her questions about Hogwarts? (See Table 13.2 for an example of the use of nicknames.)

Table 13.2 gives an excerpt from text chat during a role-playing exercise using the scenario of a community meeting charged with addressing gender inequity in sports and extracurricular funding at the local high school.

In her earlier classroom teaching career, the interviewee recalled veteran teachers who advised her to "never let them see you smile" because a teacher's laughter would disrupt classroom discipline. In the case of the LEEP classroom, however, a free-spirited approach can work to offset and defuse student frustration and bring the class together. The "who's on first?" confusion over scrambled communication caused by the vagaries of distance education technology can often be eased by laughter.

> In LEEP, the instructor's laughter does *not* mean losing control. Instead, a sense of humor is integral to class. It eases communication. Things *will* screw up and get confusing. If the instructor can accommodate this, they remain in control, which is what is needed in this space. Humor—an acceptance and wry acknowledgment of glitches, chaos, misstatements, misspellings—allows the instructor to accommodate mistakes, things *not* as they should be. To relieve tension, there must be humor.

Another like-minded interviewee described her experience of the virtual classroom as a frequent guest lecturer in both on-campus and online classes:

TABLE 13.2. **Example of Text Chat Using Nicknames**

*** Mary is now known as MaryCuree
<MaryCuree> Hi, I'm a physicist with a young daughter. So, what do you all do?
<Pat> How about advisor of school paper
<Julie> I want to be the debate coach and english teacher!
<brenda> i'll be Ms. Bookworm
<brenda> the high school librarina
<MaryCuree> Change your nicks, everyone!
<brenda> who can't spell
*** brenda is now known as bookworm
<bookworm> so what do we propose for our plan with the $$ that the business in the community will provide
*** Julie is now known as Contentious
*** Pat is now known as MsEditor
<MaryCuree> I think that we need to improve the atmosphere in the science and math classes for young women.
<Contentious> I hear there is a problem—let's have a debate!
<bookworm> ms. book worm trying to stay on task here
<MaryCuree> As far as I'm concerned, we can scrap the entire athletics budget, and devote the funds to academics.

> As I'm lecturing via RealAudio, students are responding and commenting via text chat. Logically it seems like having students comment and talk during a presentation would seem rude, but instead it assures me that they are listening. It's so counterintuitive—it actually feels *more* interactive than an on-campus class—there's so much going on.
>
> You can't see the students, but it's very visual. The screen with its particular arrangement, with slides and text, plus the names of the students who are there listed along the side. Their geographic location doesn't feel important because where they *really* are is in that classroom on the screen. And *they* know they are all there together with you in that virtual classroom—when they enter they say 'hi' to each other, and when they leave at the end of class, they say 'goodnight.'

She characterized the virtual classroom as "a secret place for a group that only exists in this time/place continuum. The space appears, and at the end of two hours, it disappears. Being there feels like being part of a secret club. There are rituals and routines and passwords that go with being a member—when you're there, you're 'in with the in crowd.'"

Another adjunct faculty member who had taught both on-campus and online courses described her experience of the virtual classroom as follows:

> It's a 3-D spider web with me in the middle [and] things—students and texts—popping up in all directions on the screen. Students are like points of light, like dots in space. When they speak in text chat, they become more visual, they appear with faces. [As an

instructor of young adult literature] I'm the trail guide through a wilderness of books. The points of light spiral out and then converge in the place where I'm leading them.

During the interview, this instructor described the somewhat chaotic humor she saw as integral to the virtual classroom.

> In these braided text chat conversations, there's so many things going on—and more opportunities for double or triple meanings. With so many of us typing all at once, it's much faster than face-to-face. It's an intense environment. It's like a sleigh ride down a steep hill with so many people talking at once, and yet everyone who types gets their words on the screen. No one is drowned out, because on the screen you can see all of the voices. No one disappears. No one is invisible, unlike the person at the back of the row [in a face-to-face class]. People can be silent, but their name is right there on the list, so they are also *right there* in the classroom. My role as instructor is to direct the braid and keep things flowing together. It's a group effort—working together in this very funny way, in an odd environment, but still, everybody's working together. . . . You're creating a text together that you see right before your eyes. It's creative, like 'Hey, I know. Let's put on a show! Let's try doing this—or that—and see what happens!'

Like the LEEP administrator above, this instructor singled out humor as a key element of the LEEP virtual classroom.

> There's a lot of humor during [synchronous] classes. There's something ultimately sort of silly in the ten-second delay—I ask a question and wait (one-one thousand, two-one thousand . . .). Students type in a question and wait. We're all in awkwardsville together, and it makes you laugh together. And while we're waiting we read the words of other students who wrote something, say, five seconds ago, so there's more opportunities for non sequiturs, which are often funny. When you're trying to somehow make connections and you're not face-to-face, humor is a humanizing force in that environment.

Each ludic model instructor described the virtual classroom as a space that is essentially separate from real life, but whose attributes enable instructors and students to collaboratively transform the space into a range of fantastic or realistic environments. The face-to-face classroom is peopled by teachers and students who resemble—and who, in fact, *are*—the same people that one may meet in the grocery store or on the street. The walls, windows, and stairs of the classroom building create a space that is separate from the apartments and offices where students live and work, but are undeniably similar in material and construction. A window may be double-hung or sealed, glass or plexiglass, but there is common agreement that the (usually) rectangular structure that allows light to pass through a wall and enables one to see the outside world from inside a room is a window. In contrast, the virtual classroom is a malleable shared mental construct created and delineated by the instructor and the students; the sensory details are left to the individual participant. It is the group's discussion and activities during the two hours of synchronous class that define that virtual classroom as a space that belongs exclusively to that instructor and those students for that weekly block of time.

The Virtual Classroom as a Space for Play

How might we explain the responses of the ludic group of LEEP instructors to the virtual classroom? What framework might be used to understand their experiences? During these interviews, I was struck by the frequency of terms that connote *play*. The classroom is a space in which there is humor and laughter, a place of friendly chaos and non sequiturs, where instructors and students are juggling and spinning and "paying absolute attention to the moment." Time spent in the virtual classroom is intense, high energy, exhilarating, playful.

In *Homo Ludens,* historian Johan Huizinga examines the essential nature of play in human culture (Huizinga, 1950). His title suggests that *homo sapiens* (the being that thinks) can perhaps be more aptly described as *homo ludens*—the being that plays. Huizinga defines play as "voluntary activity or occupation executed within certain fixed limits of time and place, according to rules freely accepted but absolutely binding, having its aim in itself and accompanied by a feeling of tension, joy, and the consciousness that it is 'different' from 'ordinary life'" (p. 28). He describes the attributes of play:

> Play begins, and then at a certain moment it is 'over.' . . . While it is in progress, all is movement, change, alternation, succession, association, separation. . . . More striking even than the limitation as to time is the limitation as to space. All play moves and has its being within a playground marked off beforehand . . . within which special rules obtain. All are temporary worlds within the ordinary world, dedicated to the performance of an act apart. Inside the playground an absolute and peculiar order reigns. (pp. 9–10)

Huizinga also characterizes the group of individuals engaged in play:

> A play-community generally tends to become permanent even after the game is over. . . . the feeling of being 'apart together' in an exceptional situation, of sharing something important, of mutually withdrawing from the rest of the world and rejecting the usual norms, retains its magic beyond the duration of the individual game . . . it loves to surround itself with an air of secrecy. Even in early childhood, the charm of play is enhanced by making a secret out of it. (p. 12)

It is striking how many of Huizinga's characteristics of play are found in the virtual classroom. The attributes that do not match, such as in the voluntary nature of play versus the quasi-voluntary nature of selecting a course to fulfill degree requirements, are outnumbered by those that do. Perhaps the "rules" of the virtual classroom, which are dictated by the features and the limitations of computer technology, plus its password-protected privacy and its general invisibility as an identifiable space, all contribute to the playfulness some instructors find in the virtual classroom. Viewed through the lens of Huizinga's theory, the deficit model of the virtual classroom is turned on its head. Instead of focusing on elements of face-to-face teaching that are absent in virtual space, we find ourselves asking: What aspects of the virtual class are missing from the face-to-face class, which must meet in the quasi-public space of a campus classroom that does not appear and disappear with the students?

The Virtual Classroom as Carnival Space

Another theorist whose work can inform our understanding of the playful virtual classroom is Mikhail Bakhtin, who described the concept of carnival in *Rabelais and His World* (Bakhtin, 1984). Bakhtin noted the strong element of play in the medieval carnival and extrapolated that model to the modern world: "Carnival is not a spectacle seen by the people; they live in it, and everyone participates because its very idea embraces all people. While carnival lasts, there is no other life outside it. During carnival time life is subject only to its own laws, that is, the laws of its own freedom" (p. 7). So, too, the online classroom is not a screen you watch, but a space you join and a multivocal narrative that invites you to add your own voice. Like the carnival, the virtual classroom is a space outside of space, and a "time out of time" separate from the strictures of mundane life. Experiences within that space may be—at least potentially—"more genuine and real" with participants "paying absolute attention to the moment." Indeed, the multivocal narrative is one of the central elements of the virtual classroom in providing an environment where no utterance is obscured or overshadowed by other voices. In this setting, every student contributes to a common online text chat, as every student who writes and hits Return button has his/her words added to the text narrative that is being collaboratively created by instructor and students during the two hours of the LEEP synchronous class meeting.

The Future of the Ludic Classroom

Some teachers will no doubt continue to view the virtual classroom as an inferior version of the face-to-face classroom. As technology improves, the virtual classroom may come to resemble real life so closely that the no difference model will predominate among online educators. By the same token, however, it seems likely that there will continue to be instructors who experience the virtual classroom as ludic or carnivalesque space. And as teachers become more comfortable with this playful environment, new questions and modes of instruction will develop and emerge.

Several questions arise in considering the future of the virtual classroom. If the virtual classroom is viewed as play space, what opportunities for creativity open up for new and multiple channels of teaching? Music, for example, is broadcast prior to each online session so that students may check and adjust their audio connection before class begins. The music creates a festive atmosphere in the classroom, but it can also be used to convey information. When I select music to play immediately before classes "going live," I select songs or genres for my classes that will reflect the course content. For example, during the classtime in my youth services librarianship classes in which we identify and discuss opportunities for collaboration between school and public libraries and other agencies serving youth, I play selections from Broadway musicals, which are themselves the result of collaboration between dramatists, composers, and lyricists; musicians, actors, and dancers; set designers, stage crews, and so on. How else might the technological features of an online environment contribute to students' education? The synchronous virtual classroom, as experienced by LEEP instructors and students, is a key element in the success of the LEEP program. The implications and possible uses of the virtual classroom as educationally effective ludic space have only begun to be explored.

References

Bakhtin, M. (1984) *Rabelais and his world.* (Helen Iswolsky, Trans.). Bloomington, IN: Indiana University Press.
Huizinga, J. (1950) *Homo ludens: A study of the play element in culture.* Boston, MA: Beacon Press.
Kazmer, M. M., & Haythornthwaite, C. (2001). Juggling multiple social worlds: Distance students online and offline. *American Behavioral Scientist, 45*(3), 510–529. (Reprinted in this volume).
Turner, V. (1982) *From ritual to theatre: The human seriousness of play.* New York: PAJ Publications.
Vieira Machado, E., & Garcia, N. (2002). *Ludic Space: A space of inclusion.* Proceedings of the 11th ICEVI (International Council for Education of People with Visual Impairment) World Conference. Noordwijkerhout, The Netherlands. Retrieved October 23, 2003, from http://www.icevi.org/publications/ICEVI-WC2002/papers/01-topic/01-garcia.htm.

Management and Administration

CHAPTER 14   Leigh S. Estabrook

The Distance Education Program from the Management Perspective

The management of the University of Illinois at Urbana-Champaign (UIUC) LEEP program has been shaped by three sometimes conflicting forces: (1) the desires and ambitions of the Graduate School of Library and Information Science faculty (GSLIS); (2) the human and financial resources of the school; and (3) campus and statewide policies and practice toward distance education students. This chapter describes how LEEP (Library Education Experimental Program) was designed and managed from an administrative perspective, addressing the question: How was the program designed to reconcile these elements, many of which are similar to those faced by other distance education programs, to create a strong, stable, and well-regarded Master of Science offering?

Program Beginnings

In October 1995, the Illinois Board of Higher Education (IBHE) formally refused to consider a request from UIUC to offer its Master of Science degree in library and information science in Chicago. The decision was a political one, driven by strong connections between Rosary College (now Dominican University), which has a program in library and information science, and the Illinois state legislature. The decision marked the end of the University of Illinois's ten-year struggle to respond to employer and alumni demand to offer the state-supported program in other parts of the state (a more detailed discussion of the University of Illinois's efforts to develop a program in Chicago is given in Estabrook, 2003).

In response, as dean of GSLIS (1986–2001), I hastily drafted a proposal entitled "Using New Information Technologies to Support Delivery of the UIUC Master's Degree in Library and Information Science," which outlined a way to offer the University of Illinois's master's program independent of location. While IBHE refused to permit the program to be offered in another place, it did not challenge the existing campus-based program. As long as classes met using Internet delivery of education, and face-to-face instruction outside our community-college district comprises less than 20 percent of program, the school only needed campus-level approval not "site approval" from IBHE.

Faculty received this draft plan with an unexpected openness to thinking about possibilities. Although Web-based instruction was relatively new, the school had already used the technology to teach collaboratively with faculty at the University of Michigan and at Indiana University. At that time (in 1995), no other LIS school taught its entire program using Internet technologies. The most common technology used was video broadcasts to sites around a state where students and a teaching assistant would gather.

In a month-long conversation, much of it over e-mail, the GSLIS faculty refined the proposal. The proposal formed the basis for negotiations between GSLIS and the UIUC campus, and by January 1996 the school completed a business plan for University of Illinois provost Larry Faulkner. The school requested $720,000 from the university to subsidize the first three years of a Library Education Experimental Program (LEEP). Because the LIS master's program was to be reaccredited in fall 1997, we asked to begin LEEP with 25 students in the summer semester of 1996. This would provide the opportunity to have LEEP evaluated by the accreditation team and offer reassurance to students who might be concerned about quality or acceptance of a program taught primarily over the Internet. In response to the request, the provost's office agreed to provide $587,000 for LEEP, with the expectation that GSLIS efforts would provide a learning opportunity for the campus on how to use the Internet to deliver a full educational program.

In February 1996, GSLIS announced the program. Four months later in July of 1996, LEEP began with 31 students—almost all from Illinois, but six were from out of state, one of whom came from Alaska.[1] The students started with a two-week, on-campus session (later known as *boot camp*). This session included instruction in using distance technologies, introductions to the UIUC library and GSLIS faculty and staff, a two-semester, one-hour core course entitled "Libraries, Information and Society," and various opportunities for students to socialize and build community. This was the only extended period of time during the degree program that students were required to be in Champaign-Urbana. In the fall, students began taking LEEP courses using a combination of chat rooms for synchronous and bulletin boards for asynchronous sessions, and e-mail. (Audio streaming for transmitting and/or recording sessions began in year two of the program. This allowed the technology staff to archive sessions and make them available for review at a later time.) Students—then and now—come to campus once each semester for a face-to-face session with the instructor and other students.

LEEP's Design

As faculty in GSLIS discussed the viability and desirability of beginning LEEP, they reasonably insisted that it be as good as the school's on-campus Master of Science degree. The professional program in library and information science had been (and continues to be) ranked among the top three in the United States and Canada. In 1995, when LEEP was first conceived, distance education using computer technology was in its infancy. The public and many academics then had reservations about the quality of distance education.[2] Faculty decided the program must provide: (1) social and professional interaction among students and faculty, (2) teaching equivalent to that received by on-campus students, and (3) sufficient library resources. Providing access to library materials was more challenging in 1996 than it is now. Electronic reserve material, developed for LEEP students, was relatively new and few standard resources beyond the library catalog were online. Students did not have the comparative wealth of online journals they have now and Internet-based bookstores were only beginning.

An equally compelling goal in design was that LEEP not weaken on-campus teaching and faculty research. For thirty years, a small number of GSLIS faculty members had taught face-to-face in other parts of Illinois as an overload to their regular teaching assignment. This meant faculty traveled at night or on weekends by car, bus, and university planes to deliver professional education to individuals who could not travel to Champaign-Urbana. As the university's expectations for teaching, research, and outreach increased during the 1980s, and as many LIS schools closed, it was imperative that surviving schools fully meet the standards of their universities. In my role as dean, I was particularly concerned that this kind of travel and overload teaching took time away from research and weakened the school.

GSLIS faculty and administrative staff in fall 1995 designed LEEP to address these various concerns, before faculty members were asked to vote on a proposal to implement it. The design presented to the faculty involved six main points. First, LEEP would be taught using the Internet with some synchronous teaching sessions augmenting asynchronous instruction. Second, students would come to campus for one face-to-face meeting per semester in Champaign-Urbana. Faculty would then not need to travel, but would have ways to engage directly with their students. The on-campus visit would also provide a way for students to use those library resources that were not Web-based or could not be made available through electronic reserve. Third, all faculty would be involved. There was to be no differential treatment based on rank, age, or other factor. Fourth, LEEP teaching would be on-load, part of the regular assignment of faculty with the expectation that each faculty member would

TABLE 14.1. **Financial Model for LEEP Start-up (April 1, 1996)**

	Financial Year	
	1997	1998
Expense Items		
New/adjunct faculty	$ 100,000	$ 200,000
Summer money for faculty		35,000
Assistant Dean		25,000
Technology support staff	35,000	60,000
Graduate and research assistants	20,000	60,000
Mentors and evaluation	5,000	10,000
Equipment and software	30,000	55,000
Telecommunications	5,000	5,000
Travel	1,500	10,000
Supplies, mail, office	5,000	20,000
Clerical (1/2 time)	12,000	13,000
Admissions clerk (1/2 time)	6,200	13,500
Promotion and advertising	5,000	10,000
Outreach coordinator	17,500	0
Special activities	1,000	3,000
Extramural		10,000
Contingency	10,000	10,000
Total Expenses	$ 253,200	$ 539,500
Tuition Income		
Resident (25)		120,520
Nonresident (25)		171,626
Subsidy	250,000	250,000
Total LEEP budget	250,000	542,146

teach in LEEP every other year. Fifth, as faculty were learning how to teach using distance technologies, they would receive either summer money or release from one course in the semester prior to teaching a LEEP course for the first time; and during the first semester a faculty member taught a LEEP course, that course would be his or her only teaching assignment. Finally, the school was to provide strong technological support for both students and faculty. Faculty members were not to spend their time fussing with technology or trying to help students learn how to use it. Their task was to teach substantive content. This was the way LEEP was implemented and this is the way it is currently operating with minor changes.

Among the expense items in the business plan (see Table 14.1) presented to the University of Illinois provost were funds for (1) adjunct faculty to support classes from which tenure and tenure-track faculty were released; (2) technology staff to develop infrastructure and support student and faculty learning; (3) administrative support to manage admissions, advising, and mentoring; (4) up to five additional faculty lines to support the larger enrollment; and (5) technology, including upgrades to faculty equipment every two years.

Choices in Financial and Resources Management

The design of LEEP was obviously costly. To achieve a balanced budget requires 40 percent or more of the students to be out-of-state (paying out-of-state tuition at a rate approximately twice that of in-state tuition). An alternative strategy would have been to create LEEP as a separate program supported by a higher tuition paid by all LEEP students regardless of residence status. But to design LEEP as a separate cost center would have required that the LEEP and on-campus programs also be separate and probably have separate classes. We foresaw a situation in which LEEP would be rich in technology and resources, while the on-campus master's degree would be poor, thus failing to enrich the school as a whole. Also, it was likely that significant parts of the differential tuition would be taken up with additional administrative costs, thus not providing a better financial alternative. (A more detailed discussion of the reasons for our decision not to create LEEP as a separate program may be found in Estabrook, 2001.)

Ultimately, the goals of the faculty drove a decision to treat LEEP as a scheduling option, rather than a separate program. By the fourth year of operation (2000–2001), tuition from 115 LEEP students was sufficient to cover the added costs. By the seventh year (2002–2003), the school had 174 LEEP students. Their tuition, which is allocated directly back to the school in the year it is generated, proved to be an important cushion when state-mandated cuts to the university in 2003 led to an 8 percent rescission for the school.

Staffing LEEP

LEEP is an integral part of the school, and thus staff members at all levels are involved in supporting it. For example, one longtime support staff member knows everything about housing arrangements for the required summer session and semester on-campus visits, and colleagues of hers arrange food and space for social events. The admissions officer handles both LEEP and on-campus admissions folders. As a consequence, we have found it important to include all staff in the school in any decision making about LEEP. When administrators originally decided to change the summer on-campus session from 14 to 10 days and add a second session, they initially neglected to consult with the person who knows most about housing—a serious error.

Implementing LEEP has required the school to create several key staff roles: an associate dean with primary responsibility for LEEP was appointed immediately, as was a director of instructional technology. The individual initially appointed as associate dean was a faculty member who had great enthusiasm for using new technologies. Within a short time it became apparent that the position required someone with quite different skills—someone who could attend to the details and logistics underpinning the program: someone who could make sure everything worked. Linda Smith's willingness to take on that role early in LEEP's development has made all the difference in its success. Associate Dean Smith has had full oversight for all elements of LEEP. This includes recruiting adjunct faculty, scheduling, working with student problems and needs, and managing the boundaries between the school and various university administrative units. Beginning in 2000, she hired a doctoral student for fifty percent time to act as LEEP coordinator, as a way to handle communications and logistics as LEEP enrollment grew.

When LEEP began, Vince Patone, with a background in psychology and interest in uses of technology, headed the Instructional Technology Office. At the time it began, Patone was a graduate assistant in GSLIS. He became full-time when he graduated. He and a small staff created the software platform for LEEP, which was then integrated into the school's overall technology structure.

The decision to create a new platform was an expensive one, but at that time commercial software to support Internet-based learning was primitive and expensive. Moreover, it was not possible to respond to the GSLIS faculty ideals for the program without designing our own system. Patone's office managed software development, the implementation and management of Web-based bulletin boards ("Web boards"), live online sessions, technology instruction and support for students and faculty, and the LEEP Web site and server. As that office has grown, LEEP graduates have been hired as assistants, and a cadre of student assistants now support students both off- and on-campus, on all aspects of instructional technology for the school.

Supporting Faculty

As noted above, all GSLIS faculty are involved in LEEP teaching. The school also hires adjunct faculty to teach in specialized areas and to fill in for faculty on leave or committed to other teaching assignments. When adjunct faculty members have enjoyed LEEP teaching and been successful, the school has worked to appoint them regularly. As a result, a dozen or more adjunct faculty—most of whom do not reside in Champaign-Urbana—are frequent and regular teachers.

Faculty members both on and off campus have needed help in becoming successful LEEP teachers. Some problems are simple, such as making sure faculty make early decisions on syllabi and course readings. Some are more complex, such as making sure faculty don't change syllabi and meeting times without advance notice. As distance students juggle multiple roles they often work and plan ahead, and it seems difficult for them to change once a course has begun. In response, the program also plans ahead (e.g., setting dates for on-campus sessions one year in advance). Faculty members have needed to adjust to a different pace of work. Distance students tend to engage in their work through Web boards and e-mail on an almost daily basis, changing the notion of set hours for being in class and for office hours. The decision not to rehire an adjunct faculty member has, most often, involved a concern that she or he is not sufficiently responsive to students.

With few exceptions, the most successful on-campus teachers have become the most successful LEEP teachers. Faculty who enjoy interactions with students and the opportunity to adapt teaching to the needs of individual students have more direct contact with LEEP students than they might in a face-to-face course with a group of students in the classroom. But faculty who want to be responsive also need to learn how to set boundaries. When a student writes e-mail to a faculty member at 9 P.M. on a Saturday night with a follow up Sunday morning asking why she hasn't been answered, a faculty member cannot feel guilty (as has happened), but needs to use the occasion as a reminder to be clearer to students about what they can expect as responses.

Evaluation

During the first year of LEEP, the school hired an external evaluator to assess the program and provide feedback for redesign. The American Library Association accrediting team visited in fall 1997 and evaluated LEEP as part of an overall evaluation. The program received a highly favorable evaluation in its five-year review by UIUC's Graduate College. Teaching in each course is evaluated with standardized university instruments, and meetings with faculty and staff have provided opportunities to assess LEEP. LEEP's receipt of the 2001 Sloan-C Award for the Most Outstanding Online Teaching & Learning Program provided external validation of the quality of the program. The school's upcoming (fall 2004) American Library Association accreditation visit is intended to have, as its special emphasis, evaluation of LEEP.

As well as the routine class and instructor evaluations, the dean and associate dean hold a meeting with LEEP students each semester via one way audio, and two-way text chat. These meetings provide an opportunity to hear concerns, provide reassurance, and consider mid-semester changes. For many years, while I was dean, I taught the initial on-campus summer session. This meant that students knew me personally, not just in my administrative role. It seems to have made it easier for students to provide feedback and evaluation over the course of their degree program.

Other Administrative Issues

Recruitment

To recruit students for the first LEEP session, the school sent out a press release on February 15, 1996. Five days later I sent the following e-mail to GSLIS faculty:

> Well we are showing strong Chicago area interest. Almost 50 inquiries since Thursday afternoon when press release when out. 24 are from Chicago and immediate environs. 6 others from downstate. 5 from California. Rest are scattered. Almost none from immediate surrounding states, but Iowa, Wisconsin and Indiana have LIS schools. I talked to Hinsdale paper yesterday.

The school also sent print information to Illinois libraries and placed advertised in professional journals prior to the beginning of the program. While this continued for the next year, since then the primary way of recruiting has been through listservs, presentations at conferences, and word-of-mouth, particularly from our graduates.

Admissions

Success in recruitment and of the program is reflected in the increased number of people applying for the program. During the early years, 75 to 85 percent of applicants were admitted—all meeting the school's admission's requirements. Those students were unusual in their risking enrollment in an untested program and using untried technology. In the 2003–2004 academic year, applications have reached a point where 56 percent were admitted from in-state applicants and out-of-state enrollments are approximately even. Of those who begin the program, close to 95 percent complete it.

Advising

Consistent with LEEP's status as a "scheduling option" all students are assigned faculty advisors from the entire GSLIS faculty. During the first two years, the school also created a group of professional mentors who were available to LEEP students, but students made few connections to them so the mentor program was dropped. The one difficulty with the advising system is that many faculty members are not on campus during the summer session the LEEP students first attend. In response, we have brought in others—both faculty and administrators—to fill in over this period, but students often are still eager to meet their *real* advisor.

Placement

Placement is also fully integrated across student groups. Last year the school began to use an online placement system. Job ads received by the school are placed on an electronic bulletin board. We have found that a number of the students stay at the place at which they were employed while students, but in a professional position.

Integrating LEEP into the University and the State

The greatest administrative challenge in developing LEEP has been integrating the students into the university administrative systems. From the university's and state's perspectives, LEEP students are *extramural* students who must register separately through the Academic Outreach office. University administrative systems that were developed to assist small continuing education efforts were not easily adapted to LEEP. We have been challenged to make sure transcripts did not differentiate between LEEP and on-campus students, to find ways students could get their identification card without having to have their picture taken *in person* at an office on campus, and to allow students to use the university's online registration system.

Current Profile
There are currently 223 LEEP students, 117 from Illinois and 106 from outside the state. LEEP students have lived in 46 of the 50 states (all but Arkansas, Mississippi, Rhode Island, and South Carolina), Argentina, Bahamas, Belgium, Canada, China, France, Germany, Italy, Japan, Netherlands, Mexico, Saudi Arabia, Thailand, and the Virgin Islands. In six years (1997 through 2003), 320 individuals have graduated from LEEP.

Current LEEP tuition and fees (per unit/4 credit hours) are $1,264 for in-state students and $2,784 for out-of-state students. The entire program requires 10 units (40 credit hours) of academic work.

Unanticipated Consequences

The decision to integrate LEEP into the school rather than add it as an ancillary program had significant organizational consequences, some of which we had not anticipated. We knew that it would be important to involve all faculty members in teaching with LEEP technologies. We did not anticipate how quickly Web boards and other tools in LEEP would become integrated into on-campus courses, nor how quickly faculty would adopt new technologies as an integral part of their on-campus teaching. We realized that allowing on-campus students to take LEEP courses would enhance the elective offerings to all students, but we did not realize how many outstanding faculty from around the United States would be willing to teach in LEEP.

Today LEEP is integrated into all aspects of the school. The Instructional Technology Office staff, originally hired to support LEEP, is part of a reconfigured technology services unit that serves the entire school. The student professional organizations have devised a variety of methods to reach out to LEEP students and schedule meetings during students' on-campus sessions. Outside lectures and the graduation ceremony are routinely Webcast and archived for students who cannot be physically present. At least half of the student awards presented at graduation now go to LEEP graduates. And LEEP students represent about 40 percent of the number of master's degree students currently enrolled in GSLIS.

Notes

1. The Alaska student was a major reason the NOVA television program titled *Net Learning* included LEEP. The log cabin home of the student added a special touch.
2. Maureen Wynkoop's study of "Hiring Preferences for Libraries" demonstrates that these reservations still exist in 2003. See http://www.camden.lib.nj.us/survey resultstables.htm#table3.

References

Estabrook, L. S. (2001). Rethinking cost-benefit models of distance learning. In *Elements of quality in online education* (Volume 3 in the Sloan-C Series). Sloan Foundation.

Estabrook, L. S. (2003). Distance education at the University of Illinois. In D. Barron (Ed.), *Benchmarks in distance education: The LIS experience*. Westport, CT: Libraries Unlimited.

CHAPTER 15

Jill Gengler

User-Centered Support and Technology in LEEP

Our Mission Statement

The Instructional Technology Office endeavors to prevent technology from being a barrier to the educational process. We take a user-centered approach to help people use technology in instruction and learning in order to make the educational process as beneficial as possible.

A User-Centered Approach

Because LEEP (Library Education Experimental Program) is a computer-based distance-learning program, people assume that it's built with the latest cutting-edge technologies, and that our students are incredibly savvy computer users. They assume that our instructors are computer geniuses, and that the people providing technical support are antisocial geeks who care more about their computers than about their users. After all, isn't all technology support like that?

While it is safe to say that some of our students *are* skilled computer users and some of our instructors actually *are* computer scientists, the majority of people in both groups don't fit either description. And most of the LEEP program's technical support staff members (the Instructional Technology Office or ITO) have no formal background in computing or programming. What the ITO has is a strong commitment to service that is grounded in our roots as librarians, and that commitment drives us to tailor the technological aspects of the LEEP program to the needs of our users.

LEEP students come to the program to learn about librarianship and information science. Most are not in school to learn how to program, how a computer works, or what an Internet protocol is. Of course, if they *do* want to learn these things, classes in those subjects are available within our department. It is our goal, however, to take on the burdens associated with technology so that technology becomes transparent to the user, and instructors and students can focus solely on content and the learning experience.

A user-centered approach means that our students and instructors drive what the ITO does and what technologies are used in the LEEP program. For example, while 90 percent of our user population uses some version of Microsoft Windows, roughly 9 percent of our users prefer the Apple Macintosh operating system. Rather than telling those users (and others who use Linux) to switch to Windows or find another graduate studies program, the ITO works hard to assure that our systems are compatible with all of these platforms. Striving for platform independence results in extra work for the ITO. The struggle to find a cross-platform, browser-based chat room has taken a tremendous amount of development time. In the same vein, we do not require our users to have any specific Internet browsers, word processing programs, or Internet service providers. The ITO takes on this work so that our users do not have to conform to an artificial standard that might prevent some from furthering their education. As Grudin (1989) points out, oftentimes decision makers will choose to implement tools that benefit them, but at the cost of extra work on the part of other group members. Such tools will fail as the group refuses to use and adapt the new technology. The ITO, in its role as decision makers for what technology tools will be used in the LEEP program, has made every effort to implement packages that benefit the users without requiring extra effort in the form of a steep learning curve or purchases of extra hardware or software.

Our Technology

One of our favorite stories in the ITO relates to the time representatives from another university came to observe our office during a live session. While we wanted to talk about our commitment to user support and outreach, the visitors could hardly be bothered to listen. Instead, they were frantically writing down the makes and models of the computers in our office and listing the software packages we were using. We could have set up a Radio Shack TRS-80 (circa 1983) to randomly flash fake alert messages and binary numbers, and the visitors would have believed it to be the key to our success!

So what are the key LEEP technologies? It's easier to list what they're not. The ITO does not require that users have the latest equipment, the greatest software, or the fastest available Internet connection. In keeping with our belief that technology should never be a barrier to participation in LEEP, we have kept the technological requirements as low as possible. Prospective students often ask if they need broadband Internet access to participate in the program. No, they don't. We support students who have Windows 95, 100 MHz processors, and 28.8 kbps–modems. Compared to a new computer, such a machine is almost unbearably slow, but it does the job. Since buying a new computer can be a major financial burden (and thus a barrier to education), we do not exclude students with older systems.

The result of this willingness to support user diversity is that the underlying LEEP technology isn't cutting edge. Students and instructors need only to have a reliable Internet connection, a Web browser, and RealAudio player (free software that provides access to both live and archived sound files). No specialized expensive software, no plug-ins, no high bandwidth needs. In fact, other than the Internet connection (which costs $10 to $30 per month), none of our requirements cost the user anything. Occasionally the ITO is asked why we don't use streaming video instead of just audio for our synchronous live sessions. With our student population, we have enough of a challenge providing a consistent, high-quality audio feed. Incorporating *talking head* video would not significantly increase instructional effectiveness, and would make class participation all-but-impossible for modem users.

Behind the scenes, the technology becomes more complex, but is still not out of the ordinary. As of early 2003, the primary LEEP server is a Dell PowerEdge 6400 with dual Pentium III Xeon processors and 512 MB of RAM. The server was purchased in August of 2001 and originally ran Windows NT 4.0, but it has since been upgraded to Windows 2000 in the interest of stability. Since our users expect the LEEP server to be up and running all the time, we have taken steps to maximize uptime. The LEEP server has a RAID 5 SCSI disk controller so that we can lose one hard drive and keep the server running, power redundancy in case one of the server's power supplies fails, and a smart uninterruptible power supply that adjusts for power fluctuations and can gracefully shut down the server in case of a major power outage. The server is backed up each night to 40/80 GB DLT tape using Arcserve 2000.

Although the LEEP server is running on the Microsoft Windows 2000 operating system, we've worked to keep it free of other Microsoft software, such as their Web server (Internet Information Server or IIS) and programming languages (VisualBasic, VBScript, Active Server Pages [ASP], .NET, and so forth). We have made this decision, in part, to keep open the option of moving our systems to the Linux operating system and toward open source software in general. We believe it is important for an independent-thinking university to avoid committing to one vendor's commercial software. In addition, we have intentionally avoided all-in-one software in favor of smaller specialized tools that work together to create a more complex system. The key software packages running on the LEEP server are:

- Web server—O'Reilly Web Site
- IRC (Internet Relay Chat) server—ConferenceRoom
- FTP (File Transfer Protocol) server—Texas Imperial Software WFTPD Pro
- Audio server—Real Server 8.0

- NNTP (Network News Transfer Protocol) server—NetWinSite Dnews
- Web e-mail gateway—WebMail

The LEEP server also runs BlackIce Defender and Norton AntiVirus to protect the server from malicious attacks such as hacker attacks, viruses, trojan horses, and the like.

Over the years, our staff software developers have organically built up a custom codebase of front-end software that our users experience as "the LEEP instructional system." We've followed a strategy of building modular components that rely on simple, proven, back-end technologies. For example, our Web-based bulletin board system is programmed in Perl as a front-end to the Dnews NNTP server. We focus on crafting the user experience, and let the software developers at NetWinSite focus on the NNTP news server. By building our Web bulletin boards on top of a standard Internet protocol, we can always change NNTP servers in the future for cost, compatibility, or performance concerns, without our users being affected.

Our approach is in direct contrast to that taken by other distance learning programs and commercial software providers, who continually try (and fail) to build comprehensive software systems for distance learning. By unifying all of their distance learning tools together into one software package, they sacrifice the ability to change feature sets quickly and to adapt to student and instructor needs. And if one tool underperforms, the whole system can fail.

Our approach allows us to provide a wide feature set to our users without having to train them on the details of each underlying system, by building consistent Web-based interfaces that hide the complexity of back-end systems such as our FTP server, NNTP server, and Real Server.

The People of ITO

The ITO user-centered approach reflects the background of the ITO employees, most of whom either hold or are working toward degrees in library and information science. The current staff consists of two full-time staff members, one three-quarters-time staff member, and one half-time developer (whose time is shared with another unit within the school). In addition, the ITO has three graduate assistants who work 20 hours per week and three graduate assistants who work 10 hours per week. Our staff is first-rate, including the graduate assistants. It isn't a stretch to say that if all of our hardware and software failed, so long as we have a good staff, we could keep the LEEP program running.

When hiring, we look for people who demonstrate patience, empathy, intellectual curiosity, and a sense of humor. If you aren't able to laugh at yourself and at computers, the stress of working in the ITO will wear you down quickly! We don't emphasize technology skills as strongly because those can be acquired if you're interested; patience and kindness are much more rare. We have also discovered over the years that it is better to be short a staff member than to hire someone just for the sake of having an extra pair of hands. If someone joins our group, but does not share our vision and work ethic, tensions can develop that damage the "can do" spirit of the ITO and lower morale.

The ITO staff works hard to reduce user anxiety and to take the sting out of working with technologies that often are counterintuitive and unreliable. We have all been in situations where we've turned to technical support for help with some problem or to ask a question, only to be treated rudely or ridiculed for our lack of knowledge. That's a very unpleasant situation, and is one that we feel no one should have to endure. The strong commitment of our profession to service is the root of the ITO approach to training and supporting users.

Whenever our users have a technical problem, we try not only to fix the problem, but also to educate the user. Our users are empowered to take that knowledge and fix similar problems on their own in the future. This is beneficial for ITO in terms of workload, helps our users become more confident in their abilities, and builds trust. We have also seen students who entered the program as technology novices go on to become Web masters and the "go to" technical people in their organizations, thanks to the increased confidence they gained working with technology in such a supportive environment.

Working with New Students

Overcoming students' fears of technology, distrust of technical support people, and anxiety are the primary goals of the ITO during the two-week on-campus session that begins the LEEP experience (commonly referred to as *boot camp*). This is a very stressful time for new students. Not only are they beginning graduate school, possibly changing careers, leaving home and family for two weeks, they also must meet new people, live in dormitories, and complete an intense introductory course. For many people, these anxieties are heightened by a fear of technology. In the first few days of the on-campus experience, we work to reduce students' fears through our technology workshops. We also strive to make sure that they are ready to fly on their own when they return home.

LEEP students come from a wide range of technical expertise, from complete computer novices to people who could teach the ITO staff members a thing or two about technology. In the first three years, we assumed that this experience gap would narrow as more people used computers and the Internet. The gap, however, continues to exist. The novices (defined as people who need instruction on basic Windows concepts such as copy/paste and on tools such as e-mail and electronic bulletin boards) seem to stand out more, as most of their classmates are already very familiar with the basic tools.

Why do complete novices choose to join the computer-intensive LEEP program? In informal discussions with some of these students, they indicated that either they had used computers in a library setting (such as a catalog system or an online database) or had friends or family they considered experts capable of helping with the technology. Their lack of understanding about what would be expected of them, coupled with an intense desire to earn a degree, seem to have allowed them to join the program without worrying about the details of technology.

Optional, Entry-Level Workshops
We begin by covering basics such as how to access and use Web-based e-mail and electronic bulletin boards. In the earliest years of the LEEP program, we required all students to attend every technology workshop. We soon found this approach problematic, however. Our more advanced users (some of whom work as Web masters, system administrators, and computer scientists) were bored by these topics. In turn, their obvious boredom and frustration poisoned the classroom dynamic, leading our less-experienced users (some of whom have never used a computer) to feel too embarrassed to ask for help or to admit they weren't familiar with a topic. As a result, the first workshops are now optional. To help students determine if they should attend the optional workshops, the ITO sends a self-assessment questionnaire to students along with a welcome letter from our office.

Since these optional workshops are small and informal, we can begin to build relationships with students who are less technically experienced. We remind the students that no one is born knowing how to use a computer, and that it takes instruction and practice to gain confidence. This is one place where a sense of humor is invaluable, and we use personal anecdotes and laughter to connect with the new students. Our lack of formal computer science backgrounds is also very helpful. Since many of us in the ITO are self-taught in technology skills, we can relate well to students who are nervous about having to deal with "computer people."

During the workshops, one person presents material at the front of the computer lab, while three or four other ITO staff members circulate through the lab, answering questions and looking for students who seem to be struggling. When it seems someone is lost, an ITO staff member will sit down with that student and work through the problems that they are having; we then make a concerted effort to repeatedly look in on that student and check for understanding.

Many people tell us later how much they appreciated the early one-on-one attention and personalized coaching. As Haythornthwaite points out, "the tight formation of community that begins during boot camp sustains students through the early portions of their program" and "LEEP students include in their wider definition of the community the technical staff who provide essential start-up information, and who help them whenever they are having difficulties" (Haythornthwaite, Kazmer, Robins, & Shoemaker, 2000). Some students even claim that our support kept them in the program. Once, during a workshop, a student suddenly started crying in frustration; she had never used a computer before and was too embarrassed to ask for help. This student had been making it through the workshop by mimicking the actions of the students around her, but when asked to put a floppy disk in the computer, she hadn't seen what her neighbors had done and her inability to perform this basic task had completely unnerved her. We rushed to help her and worked to give this student extra help during boot camp and her first few semesters as a LEEP student. This student gradually built up confidence, but knew that she could always turn to the ITO if she encountered a problem she couldn't solve. When this student finished her degree, she came back to our office on graduation day. She cried again, but this time they were joyful tears, the result of working so hard and achieving something she had dreamed of for many years. If this student had faced uncaring technical support on that first day, she probably would not have stuck it out and earned her degree or her computer skills. Instead, she writes, "Just wanted you to know how much I have enjoyed this experience that I shall remember for a lifetime. Yes, there were many tears, but through it all, I feel so blessed to have such super mentors as you. . . . When I think back to those first few days of boot camp when I cried buckets, I shall always remember your encouragement and your kindness. Thanks so much. You kept telling me that I would be just fine, and I am not sure when I finally started to believe it, but here I am, an alum!"

Required Workshops
The required workshops are similar in feel to the optional workshops, but they are larger and cover more challenging material. The required workshops teach students how to attend a LEEP synchronous session (otherwise known as a live session), and how to create and post Web pages on the LEEP server. Since we already know the students who have identified themselves as novices, we are able to watch them closely for signs that they may be lost or struggling to keep up. We can treat these students as "old friends" since we know their names and a little bit about them.

Here and elsewhere in LEEP, we strive to create a community. We begin here by using first names for all students, making jokes, and connecting with people as individuals. We also try to build a sense of belonging by inviting current students and graduates to log into the live session chat room to greet the new LEEP students. Our new students get a chance to practice interacting in the chat room and are reassured by the veterans that they will be able to make it through the program. In these sessions, the new students also learn that the ITO staff tends to reuse the same silly jokes and gags over and over. If it works, we don't fix it.

We emphasize in these workshops that we don't expect students to remember everything we are presenting in the short amount of time we have. The goals of the workshops, instead, are to familiarize students with LEEP systems and to encourage students to feel comfortable using us as a technology resource. Rather than struggling with a technical problem for hours on end, feeling angry and frustrated, we want them to contact us as soon as they feel a problem is out of their control. Two things that we do expect our students to remember are the ITO toll-free phone number and the ITO e-mail address. We actually have students chant the phone number and e-mail address out loud during the workshops!

Optional Review Workshop
Students are also encouraged to attend an optional review workshop at the end of boot camp. By the end of the intense two-week period, most students are too tired to absorb or recall anything, so this session is primarily a chance to remind students again to contact the ITO for help and to let them know that we are proud of their accomplishments in beginning their graduate study.

As we teach these workshops, the ITO staff members make a conscientious effort to use clear language and simple examples to take the sting out of raw technical language. For example, instead of asking students to connect to the LEEP IRC server running on leep.lis.uiuc.edu at port 6667 via our Java client (after first explaining what an IRC server is, what a hostname is, and what a port is), we simply show them how to log in to the LEEP chat room in a Web browser. There are pros and cons to shielding students from technical details: while this lowers technology-related anxiety, it also prevents the students from learning useful information. We believe, however, that lowering the level of student anxiety during the initial workshops is worth the trade-off. Students can always gain experience with more obscure aspects of technology later. Despite our best efforts, most people do encounter technical glitches that require in-depth work and some acquisition of technical skills. We use these and encourage the students also to use these as opportunities for learning, using LEEP as the real-life example.

Our interactions with new LEEP students are not limited to the technology workshops. ITO staff members go out of their way to greet new students in the hallways and to invite students into our office for help. We are also willing to be a shoulder to lean on (or to cry on) when the pressure of boot camp becomes too great. We provide recommendations for restaurants and quiet spots so students can get away from the stress of GSLIS. One ITO staff member even leads new students on a fun, unofficial walking tour of the University of Illinois campus!

Students respond well to such a supportive atmosphere. The feelings of technology-related fear and distrust may never fully leave some people, but most of our students eventually become comfortable with turning to the ITO for help. In fact, some of our alumni continue to call on the ITO for help. We encourage students to think of the Instructional Technology Office as the reference desk at a great library: a place you can go when you have questions or need information. That model tends to be familiar and reassuring for most library and information science students. Indeed, this supportive approach has worked so well that it has been extended to the traditional on-campus students in an effort to reduce their concerns about emerging technologies in the library and information science field.

Working with Instructors

While our students are very important to our program, they are only part of the larger picture. Our instructors also need support, and while their experiences and expectations differ from those of the students, the ITO employs the same user-centered approach. Since there are far fewer instructors than there are students, we are able to tailor our instruction and support to the individual.

One of the great advantages of LEEP is that we are able to draw on experts from all over the nation; our students and our program benefit from the depth of perspectives our adjunct instructors bring to LEEP. A difficult challenge, however, is training instructors we have never met and who will not be visiting the Urbana-Champaign campus until halfway through the semester. Training a small number of instructors at a distance can be just as difficult as training large numbers of LEEP students in person!

New adjunct instructors hear from the ITO by e-mail and by phone as soon as we learn that they will be teaching a LEEP class, sometimes a semester in advance. We work with them to assess how much experience they have with using e-mail, a Web browser, making Web pages, and using electronic bulletin boards. If they feel uncomfortable with technology, we schedule a series of one-on-one sessions to talk through how to use the tools, and we encourage them to consider carefully how they might incorporate these tools into their teaching. We're always willing to work with instructors to incorporate new ideas and new technologies. If the instructor is interested, we will pair her up with a veteran teacher so the new instructor can observe a LEEP class in action and ask questions that the ITO isn't able to answer.

As we do with our students, the ITO shoulders a lot of the technology work in order to keep the instructors' focus on their class content. Two of the ITO staff members attended a presentation on teaching in LEEP given by Professor Christine Jenkins. During the question and answer portion of the presentation, Professor Jenkins was asked a detailed question about the technology used in her class. After looking around to find the ITO staff members, Professor Jenkins replied that she couldn't answer the question; that's what the ITO was always there for, and she invited the questioner to approach us after her session. We were happy to answer the question and delighted with Professor Jenkins's response.

In the eight-year history of the LEEP program, the ITO has developed strong ties with our faculty. While we thoroughly enjoy working with new people every semester, we admit to being relieved when we see familiar names on the upcoming semester's course schedule. In the past year, we have met with many of our repeat instructors to find out what techniques they would like to try in their LEEP classes, but have avoided because of real or perceived technology limitations. As a result of these meetings, the ITO is beginning to investigate appropriate uses of streaming video and software that allows instructors to mark up assignments online.

ITO Challenges

While we have enjoyed the growth and achievements of the LEEP program, we are well aware that we must always look forward and adapt to new techniques and technologies to continue our success. The software and technical infrastructure of the LEEP program have grown organically over the last eight years, and the age and the limits of the system are beginning to show. In looking at redesigning the LEEP systems, we are considering moving away from Windows to a Linux system, switching to open source software (such as the Apache Web server), redesigning our user databases, and rebuilding our custom software. This will not be an easy process and will certainly be time-consuming. Since we can't simply tell our users to go away and stop asking us questions, that time to reflect and analyze is scarce. It's the classic "building the airplane while trying to fly it" problem.

For example, we haven't even been able to move to a new chat client that we've desperately needed for years. We have been using the same browser-based Java chat client since 1997. We believe we can move to an updated version that would not contain the bugs and unpredictability we have had to work around for the past six years (though it's likely to have new issues), but we cannot ask the users to move to a new client in the middle of a semester, which would be far too disruptive. The ITO also has not had time to test the new client during the regular semester: we are busy running classes and providing technical support. We attempted to implement and test the new client over a recent month-long class break, but ran out of time. Again, we were too busy training new instructors and helping people prepare for the new semester to be able to devote ourselves to this long-term goal. We are hopeful that we'll have time to test the client and provide user education before the beginning of the next semester.

We also lack time to fully keep up with new and emerging technologies. The field of instructional technology changes rapidly, but the LEEP systems haven't always kept pace with these changes. While it is beneficial to have simple, stable systems, we cannot overlook new tools just because they might not fit the manner in which we have always approached problems. Again, however, such research can be time-consuming, and time is a precious commodity. Even the simple act of trying to read a magazine or a technology news site can be hard; reading isn't always seen as working, and people will usually interrupt your research in order to present pressing concerns.

However, as with so many other aspects of LEEP and the ITO, the biggest challenge involves the people. It can be very stressful working in ITO: we are constantly expected to perform miracles (often at the last minute) for users who may not always understand or appreciate how hard we work or how challenging our jobs are. On top of that, we have to respond in a cheerful, supportive way, which can be difficult at times. Every summer, we work with approximately 80 new students, and have to be excited once again about people making their very first "Hello World!" Web page. After a few years, it can be very hard to find that energy. Keeping our staff from burning out or becoming bitter calls for some creative thought. We work hard, so we try to reward ourselves with toys and candy in the office, outings to movies or pubs after work, and lots of practical jokes. In fact, April Fools' Day is considered the greatest of all holidays in the Instructional Technology Office. Recharging our batteries is very important if we're to be upbeat and helpful day in and day out.

A related problem is that it is difficult to continually hire new graduate student workers, train them, and see them graduate within a year or two. Talented and gifted people work in our office, and it is hard to let them go when it is time for them to graduate. We are thrilled to populate the library and information science world with so many strong graduates, but many are sorely missed when they leave to begin their professional careers.

Conclusion, or "It's the People, Stupid!"

Despite the never-ending challenges of working with technology and supporting users who are diverse in experience, expectations, and computer systems, the LEEP program continues to be a wonderful professional experience. Time is pressing and users can be demanding, but the opportunity to design, build, and support systems for such a successful and supportive community is rewarding. Many of our students and instructors are vociferous in their praise of the Instructional Technology Office and their kind words (and shipments of cinnamon fudge) can keep our staff upbeat through almost anything.

Our user-centered approach drives the work done in the ITO and we take a number of steps to meet the needs of our faculty and students. We choose tools that allow our users to get their work done without requiring a sharp learning curve. As the decision makers, we could have chosen software and hardware packages that were easy for us to support, but difficult for the students and faculty to learn or costly for them to purchase. As Grudin (1989) discusses, however, this would have led to failure. Instead, we have taken on the challenge of locating and implementing tools that our users find easy to use and flexible. We also feel it is important to give users the informational tools to solve technology problems independently so that they can overcome challenges and gain the understanding and confidence they will need to go on to succeed in the library field. In order to build up self-assurance and trust in our users, we pay a lot of attention to their needs as we introduce them to the technology. We also work to reassure them that they are not alone and that they should always turn to our office when they need help or are feeling frustrated.

We never forget that our users are the whole reason the LEEP program exists and our primary job is keeping them happy and satisfied. While we can't reach everyone all of the time, we do aim to please the majority of people most of the time. What's the key to LEEP technology? As we've heard students say, "It's the people, stupid!"

References

Grudin, J. (1989). Why groupware applications fail: Problems in design and evaluation. *Office: Technology and People, 4*(3), 245–264.

Haythornthwaite, C., Kazmer, M. M., Robins, J., & Shoemaker, S. (2000). Community development among distance learners: Temporal and technological dimensions. *Journal of Computer-Mediated Communication, 6*(1). Retrieved from http://www.ascusc.org/jcmc/vol6/issue1/haythornthwaite.html. (Reprinted in this volume)

CHAPTER 16 *Susan E. Searing*

Reshaping Traditional Services for Nontraditional Learning: The LEEP Student in the Library

Academic libraries are increasingly called upon to meet the information needs of off-campus students and instructors. As Internet-based teaching evolves, librarians must deal with critical questions: How do the information needs and behaviors of online learners differ from those of students in traditional classrooms? How can the library respond promptly and efficiently to new service demands? Librarians working with distance education programs have discovered that the preexisting campus library structure, the expectations of online learners, the technologies employed, and the curriculum itself all shape the demand for and provision of library resources.

This chapter examines library support for online distance education, using examples from the LEEP (Library Education Experimental Program) option of the graduate program in Library and Information Science (LIS) at the University of Illinois, Urbana-Champaign (UIUC). It begins with a brief overview of the literature on library support for LIS distance education. (Basic sources on library support for distance education in general are described in the appendix.) Next, the library collections and services that are made available to distant UIUC LIS students and teachers are described. There is consensus in the field regarding the basic components of the library support for online distance education, and other university libraries offer similar services. Integral to the LEEP program, however, are several factors that significantly influence the demand for and provision of library services, and thus contribute to the program's unique "information ecology" (Nardi & O'Day, 1999). These factors are explored in this chapter: the information-intensive curriculum, the wide geographic distribution of students and teachers, the enduring importance of the physical library, and the active demonstration of librarianship's professional values. The concluding section describes several ways that LEEP has changed the UIUC library's operations, and the impact that librarians in turn strive to have on aspiring information professionals in the LEEP program. Throughout this chapter, the terms *remote student, distant student, LEEP student,* and *online learner* are used interchangeably.

Background: Academic Libraries and Online Education

Online learning, whether local or remote, noticeably impacts library operations. On many campuses, for instance, the librarians responsible for library orientation work closely with teaching faculty to incorporate information literacy training into student assignments and to provide links from course management software to library-based resources. Support for online *distance* education in particular has become an established component of academic library services. Libraries have created new positions devoted solely to the support of distance education or, more commonly, added such duties to traditional positions in reference and access services.

The professional literature of librarianship describes the difficulties inherent in satisfying distant learners' information needs and documents the policies and strategies that are coalescing as best practices. Complementing a growing body of research and evaluation, countless reports of innovations at individual libraries serve as case studies. The description of library support for the Florida State University School of Information Studies Web-based curriculum is an excellent example of this genre, providing a chronology of service development and clearly delineating the various players and the politics involved (Burnett & Painter, 2001). Such publications, along with other information resources such as e-mail discussion groups, are of critical importance because this specialty area is not well represented in the LIS curriculum (Kascus, 1994; Hoerman & Furniss, 2000; Latham & Smith, 2003).

While publications abound regarding library support for distance education in general, librarians have written very little about the specific challenges and rewards of supporting graduate-level LIS distance education. Nor have LIS educators focused attention on library support for remote learners, as evidenced by the scant mentions of the library in a recent compendium of program descriptions and histories (Barron, 2003). The dearth of research is puzzling, given that many LIS programs have a long history of offering courses at off-campus sites, via correspondence, or through audio- and videoconferencing, and thirty-eight accredited master's-level programs in the United States now include an online distance education option (American Library Association, 2004).

A handful of studies report empirical data on library services for LIS distance education, but none of them zero in on Internet-delivered programs (Kim & Rogers, 1983; Barron, 1987; Hoy & Hale, 1991; Stephens, 1998; Douglas, 2002; Latham & Smith, 2003). Experiences with the LIS program at Louisiana State University inform a rare view of distance education library services through the lens of systems theory

(Dawson & Watson, 1999). The authors argue that both libraries and distance education programs are complex systems, embedded in the larger systems of the university, higher education, and government. Librarians who understand these interacting systems can take advantage of new opportunities to form partnerships with teaching faculty, so that "the librarian is actively involved in the entire process [of course development and delivery] and his/her contributions are integral to the success of the course" (p. 20).

Firsthand accounts by LIS students are all too rare and seldom focus on library issues; Hooke (1999) argues from the student's perspective for more readily accessible scholarly literature online. Kazmer interviewed LEEP students and uncovered preferences for library services within the broader context of distant students' learning styles and the rigors of technology-mediated education. LEEP students want rich online collections, rapid delivery of printed materials, reference service and technical support during evenings and weekends, appropriate training options, and a single point of contact (Kazmer, 2002). Fortunately, these expressed needs match the components of successful distance education library services as defined by librarians (Goodson, 2001).

Library Support for LEEP: Collections and Services

Academic librarians conceptualize their work as two large, overlapping endeavors: building and managing *collections* of information in various formats (print, audiovisual, electronic, etc.), and providing *services* that connect library users to the information they seek (research consultations, bibliographic instruction, interlibrary loan, etc.). This section describes the means by which LEEP students access information collections and supportive services through the UIUC libraries. The following section outlines the distinct roles that various campus units play, individually and cooperatively, in the provision of library services for remote students.

Access to Information Collections

Remote students deserve and expect the same level of access to books, journals, and other media that on-campus students enjoy. Access from a distance involves two related processes—discovery and delivery. *Discovery* refers to the identification and location of needed information. *Delivery* means getting the information into the hands of the person who needs it. To aid in the discovery of relevant materials, the UIUC library provides:

- An online catalog of its print holdings, and increasingly electronic holdings, too (http://www.library.uiuc.edu/catalog).

- ILLINET Online, a combined catalog for a consortium of fifty-six academic libraries in the state (http://library.ilcso.illinois.edu/uc).
- A searchable database of thousands of full-text electronic journals and dozens of indexing and abstracting services, many of which also include full-text articles (http://www.library.uiuc.edu/orr).
- Alphabetic menus of subject-specific electronic journals (for example, the LIS list at http://www.library.uiuc.edu/lsx/ejournals.php).
- Numerous online reference tools linked from the UIUC library Web pages.

In short, the UIUC offers a substantial digital collection, plus useful online tools for mining its print collection.

The discovery tools listed above are freely available on the Web, but when it comes to delivering actual content, the library must make sure that only legitimate users are recipients. To facilitate off-campus use of licensed resources, the UIUC library maintains a proxy server—software that allows remote users to identify themselves by typing in their campus ID and to be authenticated for access to restricted online collections.

For the most part, the library's advances in electronic access were not undertaken to serve distance education students in particular, but rather reflect the inexorable move of academic libraries into the Web environment, to the benefit of all users. Some online services, however, were developed specifically for the LEEP program. These include:

- An electronic course reserves service that scans copies of required class readings (typically journal articles and chapters from books) and mounts them on a protected Web site (http://www.library.uiuc.edu/lsx/reserves.htm).
- A virtual new books shelf that spotlights new print acquisitions in library and information science (http://www.library.uiuc.edu/lsx/acquis.htm).
- A core collection of electronic books licensed from netLibrary (http://www.netlibrary.com).

Although these innovations in content delivery were initially targeted to the LEEP community, they have proven popular among on-campus users as well.

Despite the wealth of information online, delivery of printed materials from the UIUC library collections remains a critical service. After searching the online catalog and discovering useful printed works, distant UIUC students place requests for individual items through a Web form. Books are retrieved and sent via a commercial courier to the requester's home or office. Journal articles are retrieved, copied, and sent as either photocopies or password-protected computer files. Distant students are not limited to the UIUC's holdings; they may ask the library staff to obtain books and articles from other libraries on their behalf. The delivery of printed materials is free of charge except for the cost of return postage.

Access to Reference and Assistance Services

In the on-campus environment, library users have ready access to research assistance and instruction in the use of library resources. For off-campus students and faculty, the walk-up reference desk is replaced by:

- toll-free phone numbers to reference and help desks
- e-mail reference service, provided by both generalist librarians and subject specialists
- an Internet chat line

Using these interactive modes, students can ask factual questions, seek advice on literature search methods, or alert librarians to technical problems, such as interrupted access to electronic journals. UIUC campus libraries also provide various FAQs and search tips through their Web pages. More proactively, the LIS specialist librarian regularly scans the general-purpose Web boards maintained by the school for LEEP and on-campus students, looking for queries that she can answer using library resources.

The use of multiple media for student-librarian communication is key to the full integration of the library into distance learning. It is equally important to foster self-reliance by teaching students information-seeking skills. Library instruction is incorporated into the on-campus summer orientation for incoming LEEP students. They are introduced to the online catalog, core indexes and abstracts, and special features of the library's Web site. They are also taught how to access library resources remotely and how to request delivery of printed materials. In addition, new LEEP students tour the physical library. An optional online tutorial, created by students in an LIS course on reference and instruction systems, focuses on understanding the concepts of scholarly publishing and peer review and on identifying research articles (http://www.library.uiuc.edu/lsx/tutorial/tutorial.html). Throughout the year, when invited by instructors, librarians participate in online classes and mid-semester on-campus sessions and prepare class-specific resource guides.

Library Support for LEEP: Organizational Structures and Cooperation

Tension exists within the library profession around a basic question: Should distance education services be assigned to a designated librarian or department, or should such services be completely integrated into business as usual? In the separated model, a full-service library unit dedicated to the needs of distant students and faculty provides users with one-stop shopping. In the integrated model, the library's access services unit handles book delivery, the reference librarians field research questions, the library instruction experts design tutorials and lead workshops, and so on. Persuasive arguments can be made in favor of either model. However, organizational structures and cultures usually prevent a simple either/or resolution to this debate.

Except for a few brand-new online institutions, distance education programs in higher education have been layered over existing curricula and campus organizational structures. At a large university like the UIUC, the preexisting organization is extremely complex, and the library's organization mirrors that complexity. LEEP students and instructors are offered some elements of the separated model and other elements of the integrated model, as several units and numerous individuals must work together to meet their information needs. The four key players are:

- Academic Outreach Library (http://www.continuinged.uiuc.edu/outreach/library/library.cfm)
- Library and Information Science Library (http://www.library.uiuc.edu/lsx)
- Virtual reference service administered by the Reference Library and the Undergraduate Library (http://www.library.uiuc.edu/ugl/vr)
- Graduate School of Library and Information Science, especially its teaching faculty and instructional technology staff (http://www.lis.uiuc.edu/)

The Academic Outreach Library provides basic support for distance education in all disciplines by retrieving and delivering books and articles from the UIUC library collections and by maintaining a Web site that serves as a gateway to the campus libraries for distant students. The unit is funded and administered through the university's Division of Academic Outreach, which handles student enrollment for off-campus courses and thus certifies that students are eligible for these special no-cost library services. The librarian also ensures that students are properly registered to check out books and use restricted online resources.

The Academic Outreach Library was established in an earlier era of distance education, when satellite classes around the state of Illinois were the primary mode of off-campus instruction. Today, many classes are conducted online, students are located around the globe, and the Web is the primary medium for support services as well as instruction. If it were functioning by itself, the Academic Outreach Library would be a classic illustration of the separated model, but in actuality its work is synchronized with other units' work.

The second key player, the Library and Information Science Library, serves the faculty and students of the Graduate School of Library and Information Science. It offers a full range of traditional services and houses a core collection of books, journals, and nonprint media reflecting the range of the LIS curriculum, from information architecture and interface design to cataloging and storytelling. The LIS Library licenses core indexes, journals, and other reference materials for online access, and its Web site serves as a gateway to both local and global LIS information.

The LIS Library is one of more than forty departmental or branch libraries at the University of Illinois. Like other departmental libraries, it operates semiautonomously, controlling its own collection budget but depending on centralized cataloging, systems maintenance, and other functions. The discipline-based departmental libraries are fundamental to the library organization at the UIUC, and consequently the LIS Library has long been perceived as the legitimate provider of services to LIS faculty and students, whether on campus or at a distance. Despite the increasingly interdisciplinary nature of scholarship, many universities still follow the model of distributed subject libraries. At the UIUC, LIS students and faculty are welcome in all campus libraries, but the LIS Library is their "home" library.

The third player in the provision of library service to LEEP students emerged in the spring of 2001, when the Reference Library and the Undergraduate Library began collaborating to provide a real-time text chat reference service over the Web (Kibbee, Ward, & Ma, 2002). The virtual reference service was not designed to support distance education per se, but rather to serve the entire UIUC community. It has proven very popular with LEEP students.

The fourth and final player is the Graduate School of Library and Information Science, which collaborates with the LIS Library on many levels. The school's technology staff facilitated the setup of software and file transfer processes for the electronic reserves service and continues to provide technical advice and server space. The LEEP home page prominently displays links to library Web pages. Several LIS instructors strengthen connections between students and the library by inviting the LIS librarian to lecture in online class sessions or by scheduling library time during mid-semester on-campus sessions. When students experience difficulties accessing online information, staff members at GSLIS and the library often cooperate to resolve the problem. This strong, flexible relationship between the library and the instructional unit makes it easier to shape and maintain curriculum-related library services for remote learners.

Despite the best efforts of all concerned to explain clearly who does what, the spread of responsibilities over several units inevitably generates some confusion. LEEP students crave a single point of contact for posing questions and resolving problems (Kazmer, 2002), but the UIUC's departmental library structure provides multiple service points. Consequently, some distant students do not take full advantage of library resources and services because they find them bewilderingly complex.

Although imperfect, the UIUC library service configuration recognizes the strengths and weaknesses of the various cooperating units, and on the whole has been judged successful in meeting student needs.[1] The LIS Library staff, for example, is ideally suited, by virtue of its disciplinary expertise, to work closely with students on in-depth research questions and to introduce them to the literature and search strategies most useful in LIS. However, the LIS Library is not equipped to provide home delivery of materials. The Academic Outreach Library, on the other hand, despite its small staff and the growing demands placed on it, responds quickly to delivery requests. Neither the LIS Library nor the Academic Outreach Library can reply to user queries promptly outside normal office hours, but the virtual reference chat line is available on nights and weekends. The librarians and staff in each unit have forged solid working relationships, make frequent referrals to each other's services, team-teach workshops for new students, and collaborate to solve remote users' technical problems. Such collaboration is essential to the success of the integrated library service model.

Lessons from LEEP: Pressures and Opportunities

Over the eight years that library services for LEEP have been evolving, four factors have been especially influential in shaping decisions and inspiring new initiatives:

- the nature of the graduate LIS curriculum
- characteristics of LEEP students and faculty
- the physical library
- the ideals of the library profession

In varying degrees, similar factors may drive the development of library services for other disciplines or in other institutional contexts.

The Information-Intensive LIS Graduate Curriculum

Through graduate-level coursework, students become conversant with a field's literature and acculturated to its values. In professional fields such as LIS, students are expected to attain a high level of information literacy in the field, so that they can seek and find the information they will need to stay current throughout their careers. LIS students are frequently required to demonstrate their information skills by producing bibliographies, pathfinders, and Web sites, in addition to traditional term papers. The LIS curriculum is arguably among the most demanding in its emphasis on independent information seeking, since information retrieval and use lie at the heart of the discipline. In the spring 2002 semester, LEEP students represented only 18 percent of the total student population enrolled in distance courses at the UIUC, yet they accounted for 64 percent of the Academic Outreach Library's delivery requests.

The information-intensive curriculum is problematic in light of the relative scarcity of LIS collections (Wagner & Dalrymple, 2003, p. 21). Only 49 graduate LIS programs in the United States are accredited by the American Library Association; several states have no program within their borders. Paradoxically, while the scarcity of degree programs in LIS contributes to the popularity of distance education options, it complicates the students' task of finding information resources close to home to support their coursework. In other disciplines, such as business, students may turn to nearby colleges or even well-stocked public libraries for the information they need. But institutions that don't offer an LIS degree are unlikely to hold expensive core resources such as *Library and Information Science Abstracts*. Even if nearby libraries subscribe to a few practical journals or purchase how-to guides for their own staff, these in-house professional collections may not be accessible to the general public. The phenomenon of the *victim library* burdened by the demands of unaffiliated users has been noted in the literature (Dugan, 1997), but alas, distant learners in LIS have few libraries to victimize when seeking the specialized literature of the profession. To the degree that online distance education succeeds as a means for delivering highly specialized academic curricula—non-Western foreign languages are often cited as an example—the lack of adequate library collections located where students live will continue to put pressure on the host institution.

Characteristics of LEEP Students and Faculty

In many ways LEEP students are typical distance students. On average they are older than on-campus students and exhibit the behaviors and attitudes often associated with adult learners. Most work full-time, and many have family responsibilities. They are accustomed to multitasking, are focused on outcomes, and desire quick and efficient methods for finding information. They place a high value on institutional responsiveness, trustworthy personal contacts, effective training, robust technology, and readily available technology support (Kazmer, 2002).

In some respects, however, LEEP students differ from the traditional population of distant students who engage in learning at off-campus centers. As online learners, LEEP students are spread around the globe. This geographic dispersion means that students are relatively isolated. They cannot turn to a fellow student in the computer lab or library to get impromptu advice, and therefore probably rely more heavily on instructors and support staff. Most contacts between librarians and LEEP students are one-to-one interactions mediated by e-mail, Web forms, or toll-free telephone numbers. In addition, one-to-many and many-to-many communication is achieved through Web boards maintained by GSLIS. While it is technologically feasible for libraries to sponsor Web boards, students are more likely to monitor routinely the boards associated with their school and courses. LEEP Web boards are utilized to publicize new library resources, planned downtimes for electronic services, and changes in library policy.

Librarians who design and deliver services to distance education programs must nurture relationships with teachers as well as with students. Faculty members need library-based information to prepare their syllabi and reading lists. Furthermore, faculty members are important partners in instilling good library research habits in students. A professor's attitude toward the library will be communicated to students directly or subtly; messages about library use are implicit in expectations for student performance. Like the student body, the LEEP faculty is geographically dispersed; it includes both full-time resident professors and part-time adjunct instructors in Texas, Pennsylvania, North Carolina, California, and elsewhere. On-campus faculty must become adept at advising students regarding special library services that they themselves do not require (and indeed, are not eligible for), and distant faculty may fumble when guiding students' library use, simply because they themselves lack extensive experience with the UIUC libraries. A strong librarian-faculty relationship helps to surmount these difficulties.

Successful LEEP teachers are daring and creative in their use of information technology, and their willingness to experiment with new products and software is contagious. When the UIUC's Reference Library and Undergraduate Library launched their live chat reference service on the Web, LEEP students were among the first to try it, and they continue to use it heavily. In contrast to e-mail messages, Internet chat allows a more nuanced conversation between the librarian and the information-seeker—an advantage for difficult questions. At the same time, it is less personal than a face-to-face or telephone inquiry and therefore shields the questioner somewhat from the embarrassment of asking for help.

Compared to on-campus students, a larger portion of LEEP students' inquiries involve problems with accessing electronic resources. A Web-based curriculum naturally fosters dependence on Web-based information sources, but access to electronic library collections can be fraught with difficulties and interruptions. Resolving these problems may be as simple as furnishing the student with a better URL or as complex as renegotiating a contract with a database supplier. Reliable access to electronic scholarly information sources is essential for online graduate coursework.

Because LEEP is designed for individuals in a distributed online environment, UIUC librarians have not developed satellite print collections, nor have they partnered with other libraries to provide materials or services. These are tried-and-true methods to support more traditional distance education programs, where classes meet together at off-campus locations. However, clusters of LEEP students have emerged in certain parts of the country, notably Alaska, Nevada, Oregon, and the Chicago area. If this trend continues, or if GSLIS in the future contracts with other universities or employers to provide Web-enabled classes for groups of co-located students, satellite collections or partner libraries might be advisable.

The UIUC Libraries as Places

Do distant users need to understand how the physical collections are organized? As noted above, the UIUC library is decentralized. The departmental library system baffles on-campus students and faculty at first, but over time they discover which libraries in addition to their home library are necessary to their research. The LIS Library functions as a referral point to connect on-campus LIS students and faculty with other appropriate departmental libraries.

For off-campus students, the physical scatter of collections and expertise is both less and more problematic. On the one hand, they are spared trudging from library to library to retrieve books and articles; they can simply request any materials they need through the Academic Outreach Library. On the other hand, they struggle mightily to comprehend the University Library's organization, perhaps because they don't experience the kinetic learning that cements on-campus students' understanding of what's where.

LEEP students value a systematic introduction to the physical organization of library resources. When asked to evaluate their library orientation sessions, they consistently praise the short tour of the LIS Library and associated service points in the main library building. The tour presents the library in a friendly light and begins the process of building relationships between the LIS Library staff and individual students. It gives students a framework to think about the LIS Library and the wider University Library, which they may unconsciously draw upon as they navigate its Web pages, since large segments of the library's Web space mirror the departmental library organization. In an era when many librarians eschew tours in favor of asynchronous online tutorials, the reactions of LEEP students are a reminder that a sense of place still matters.

The Ideals of the Profession of Librarianship

The departmental library system at the UIUC puts pressure on each library to respond to new initiatives within the academic programs they serve. In the case of the LIS Library, the small staff added LEEP support to an already full set of responsibilities. At the same time, LEEP brought new energy and excitement to their work and allowed them greater scope to apply the ideals of the library profession.

The creation of an electronic reserves system for LEEP illustrates how the strong service ethic of librarianship overcame common barriers—lack of time, know-how, and money—to provide an innovative solution. As of 1997, no UIUC library had ventured into providing required course readings over the Web.[2] Leigh Estabrook, then dean of GSLIS, believed that the library could provide more consistent quality control and copyright compliance than if individual professors continued scanning and posting course readings on their own Web sites. Because the LIS Library had neither the technical expertise to design an e-reserves system nor funds to purchase a commercial system, a group of students in a LEEP course adopted e-reserves planning as their term project. After they developed a proposal and cost estimates for the start-up and ongoing operations, GSLIS personnel recommended software and created a directory for e-reserves on the LEEP server. Using a scanner borrowed from the University Library's Systems Office, the LIS Library became the first library on the UIUC campus to offer a full-fledged electronic reserves service.

Distance education projects frequently employ entrepreneurial or ad hoc tactics to mobilize resources and expertise and to fuse strategic short-term or long-term partnerships. Yet there are clearly limits to what an existing library department can provide without added resources and without compromising service to on-campus users. The greatest stress is felt when LEEP students are actually on campus and making intensive use of the library. The ten-day summer orientation includes a highly condensed course, "Libraries, Information and Society," which features several assignments that require students to seek information beyond the textbook. The mid-semester on-campus sessions are also extremely busy. Every fall, for example, the large "Information Organization and Access" class gathers for a half-day "research fest" in the LIS library.

The LIS Library staff members believe that students do not learn about LIS through reading and in-class experiences alone, but also through their interactions with information professionals. On-campus LIS students have many opportunities to form relationships with campus librarians as role models or mentors. The more isolated LEEP students, especially those not concurrently employed in libraries or information agencies, have fewer opportunities to observe professionals in action and to shape their own service ideals on the basis of the service they receive. Therefore, as the students study the ethics and values of librarianship, the staff strives to model them by adhering to high standards for service.

During on-campus sessions, the staff juggles work schedules to provide extra hours of reference assistance and workshops on evenings and weekends. The LEEP calendar now governs many areas of the LIS Library's operations, from when the staff sends journal volumes for binding to when they take vacations. Even routine interactions take on a distinctive tone. Responding to an e-mail reference question from a LEEP student, a librarian will embellish the answer with the details of how she found the information. The average library user is only interested in the answer, but students of LIS learn from the process as well.

Like the students, faculty, and staff of LEEP, the library staff finds energy and inspiration in the community of online learners and teachers to which they now belong. They feel privileged to have a role in preparing the new generation of librarians and information workers and in helping to shape new modes of teaching and learning. Within the larger library organization, the LIS Library is perceived as doing interesting and cutting-edge work.

Conclusion

Inevitably, library support for distance education will be built on the institution's existing framework of library services, and thus no two campuses will develop identical library support programs. Although distance education courses worldwide vary greatly in their curricula and delivery modes, the necessity of adequate library support, especially for graduate-level learning, is incontestable. Many years will pass before all knowledge is available online. In the meantime, librarians can help remote students to access both online and printed information. Although students desire a single contact person or office, distance education library services typically achieve success through cooperation and task sharing, both within and outside the library.

The University of Illinois, Urbana-Champaign, provides a model in its library support for an online master's degree in LIS. It has developed core services for the LEEP program, including electronic course reserves, a growing collection of online journals and books, an orientation program for new students, and prompt delivery of materials from the print collections. Even more importantly, principles of collaboration and cooperation shape the library's strategies. The library staff views its role in online learning as the natural outgrowth of the profession's mission and ideals.

Acknowledgments

Thank you to Pat Cardenas, Sandy Wolf, Linda Smith, and Christine Jenkins for providing facts and feedback on the initial draft of this chapter.

Notes

1. Informal comments posted to GSLIS Web boards indicate a high level of satisfaction with the services as currently provided. A survey of LEEP students and faculty conducted as part of the five-year review of the program also gave library services high marks.
2. Around this time, the Chemistry Library began scanning and posting unpublished materials such as problem sets, but they had not experimented yet with published readings such as journal articles and book chapters.

References

American Library Association (2004). 2004–2005 directory of institutions offering ALA-accredited master's programs in library and information studies. Retrieved March 16, 2004 from http://www.ala.org/ala/accreditation/lisdirb/lisdirectory.htm.

Barron, D. D. (1987). Perceived use of off-campus libraries by students in library and information science. In B. M. Lessin (Ed.), *The Off-Campus Library Services Conference Proceedings* (pp. 56–64). Mt. Pleasant, MI: Central Michigan University Press. Retrieved August 18, 2003 from http://ocls.cmich.edu/3rdOCLSCP.pdf.

Barron, D. D. (Ed.) (2003). *Benchmarks in distance education: The LIS experience.* Westport, CT: Libraries Unlimited.

Burnett, K., & Painter, M. (2001). Learning from experience: Strategies for assuring effective library and information services to Web-based distance learners. In H. A. Thompson (Ed.), *Crossing the Divide: Proceedings of the Tenth National Conference of the Association of College and Research Libraries* (pp. 131–136). Chicago: Association of College and Research Libraries.

Dawson, A., & Watson, D. (1999). A marriage made in heaven or a blind date: Successful library-faculty partnering in distance education. *Catholic Library World 70* (1), 14–22.

Douglas, G. (2002). Speaking out: Analysis of experiences and opinions reported by recent graduates of the University of South Carolina's MLIS program. *Journal of Education for Library and Information Science, 43*(1), 16–31.

Dugan, R. E. (1997). Distance education: Provider and victim libraries. *Journal of Academic Librarianship, 23*(4), 315–318.

Goodson, C. (2001). *Providing library services for distance education students: A how-to-do-it manual.* New York: Neal-Schuman.

Hoerman, H. L., & Furniss, K. A. (2000) Education for provision of library services to distance learners: The role of the LIS schools. *Journal of Library Administration, 32*(1/2), 247–257.

Hooke, J. (1999). The perils of the virtual student in cyberspace. *Journal of Electronic Publishing, 5*(1). Retrieved August 26, 2003 from http://www.press.umich.edu/jep/05–01/hooke.html.

Hoy, C., & Hale, M. L. (1991). A comparison of references cited by on-campus and off-campus graduate library science students. In C. J. Jacob (Comp.), *The Fifth Off-Campus Library Services Conference Proceeding* (pp. 123–127). Mount Pleasant, MI: Central Michigan University. Retrieved August 18, 2003 from http://ocls.cmich.edu/5thOCLSCP.pdf.

Kascus, M. A. (1994). What library schools teach about library support to distant students: A survey. *American Journal of Distance Education, 8* (1), 20–35.

Kazmer, M. M. (2002). Distance education students speak to the library: Here's how you can help even more. *The Electronic Library, 20* (5), 395–400.

Kibbee, J., Ward, D., & Ma, W. (2002). Virtual service, real data: Results of a pilot study. *Reference Services Review 30* (1), 25–36.

Kim, M. T., & Rogers, A. R. (1983). Libraries for librarians: Identifying and evaluating resources for off-campus graduate programs in library and information science. In B. M. Lessin (Ed.), *The Off-Campus Library Services Conference Proceedings* (pp. 191–200). Mt. Pleasant, MI: Central Michigan University Press.

Latham, D., & Smith, S. M. (2003). Practicing what we teach: A descriptive analysis of library services for distance learning students in ALA-accredited LIS schools. *Journal of Education for Library and Information Science, 44* (2), 120–133.

Nardi, B. A., & O'Day, V. L. (1999). *Information ecologies: Using technology with heart.* Cambridge, MA: MIT Press.

Stephens, K. (1998) The library experiences of postgraduate distance learning students or *Alice's Other Story*. In P. Brophy, S. Fisher, & Z. Clarke (Eds.), *Libraries Without Walls 2: The delivery of library services to distant users* (pp. 122–142). London: Library Association Publishing.

Wagner, M., & Dalrymple, P. (2003). Dominican University (River Forest, IL) and the College of St. Catherine (St. Paul, MN) distance learning experience. In D. D. Barron (Ed.), *Benchmarks in distance education: The LIS experience* (pp. 13–22). Westport, CT: Libraries Unlimited.

Appendix: Key Sources in Distance Education Librarianship

The bibliographies compiled by Latham, Slade, and Budnik (1991), Slade and Kascus (1996, 2000) and Slade (2002), along with Slade's (2000) in-depth review of international trends and issues, are excellent starting points. Sloan and Stoerger maintain a well-selected annotated set of Web links on library support for distance learning. Goodson's (2001) book-length manual (which treats all aspects of distance education librarianship and provides lengthy resource listings, sample policies, and more) constitutes a milestone in the documentation of best practices in distance education librarianship.

Dupuis and Thompson-Young have created a concise summary of the issues facing libraries, with links to recommended resources and models. Addressing of the growing audience for information on distance education library work are the short-lived online *Journal of Library Services for Distance Education* (http://www.westga.edu/~library/jlsde) and the new commercially published *Journal of Library and Information Services in Distance Learning* (Haworth Press). Both *Library Trends* (Haricombe, 1998) and *The Reference Librarian* (Iyer, 2002) have devoted issues to the theme of remote users.

The *Guidelines for Distance Learning Library Services* are frequently referenced in both formal and informal communications; they are arguably the most influential publication in the field. These guidelines cover all aspects of library support, from philosophy to finances, and serve as rough benchmarks against which evolving services can measure their progress (Association of College & Research Libraries, 2000).

Librarians who work with distance programs have been networking professionally since 1982 at the biennial Off-Campus Library Services conferences; the published proceedings of those events are a rich source for shared experiences, novel ideas, and moral support (Lessin, 1983, 1986, 1987, 1989, 1991; Jacob, 1991, 1993, 1995; Thomas & Jones, 1998; Thomas, 2000; Mahoney, 2002). Internationally, the Libraries Without Walls conferences serve a similar function (Irving & Butters, 1996; Brophy, Fisher, & Clarke, 1998, 2000, 2002). The Association of College and Research Libraries' Distance Learning Section regularly sponsors presentations and discussions during the semiannual American Library Association Conferences (http://caspian.switchinc.org/~distlearn/). In addition, librarians can turn to an active e-mail discussion group, OFFCAMP-L, for support and advice from experienced colleagues (http://ocls.cmich.edu/offcamplist.htm).

Sources

Association of College and Research Libraries. Distance Learning Section. (2000). ACRL Guidelines for Distance Learning Library Services. *College & Research Libraries News, 61*, 1023–1029.

Brophy, P., Fisher, S., & Clarke, Z. (Eds.). (1998). *Libraries without walls 2: The delivery of library services to distant users*. London: Library Association.

Brophy, P., Fisher, S., & Clarke, Z. (Eds.). (2000). *Libraries without walls 3: The delivery of library services to distant users*. London: Library Association.

Brophy, P., Fisher, S., & Clarke, Z. (Eds.). (2002). *Libraries without walls 4: The delivery of library services to remote users*. London: Library Association.

Dupuis, E., & Thompson-Young, A. *Beyond the administrative core: Creating Web-based student services for online learners: Resources: Library services*. Retrieved August 26, 2003 from http://www.wiche.edu/telecom/projects/laap/resources/library.htm.

Goodson, C. (2001). *Providing library services for distance education students: A how-to-do-it manual*. New York: Neal-Schuman.

Haricombe, L. (Ed.). (1998). Service to remote users. *Library Trends, 47*(1), whole issue.

Irving, A., & Butters, G. (Eds.). (1996) *Proceedings of the First "Libraries Without Walls" Conference.* Preston, England: Centre for Research in Library and Information Management.

Iyer, H. (Ed.). (2002). Distance learning: Information access and services for virtual users. *The Reference Librarian 77,* whole issue.

Jacob, C. J. (Comp.). (1991). *The Fifth Off-Campus Library Services Conference Proceedings.* Mount Pleasant, MI: Central Michigan University. Retrieved August 26, 2003 from http://ocls.cmich.edu/5thOCLSCP.pdf.

Jacob, C. J. (Comp.). (1993). *The Sixth Off-Campus Library Services Conference Proceedings.* Mount Pleasant, MI: Central Michigan University Press.

Jacob, C. J. (Comp.). (1995). *The Seventh Off-Campus Library Services Conference Proceedings.* Mount Pleasant, MI: Central Michigan University Press.

Latham, S., Slade, A. L., & Budnick, C. (1991). *Library services for off-campus and distance education: An annotated bibliography.* Ottawa: Canadian Library Association.

Lessin, B. M. (Ed.). (1983). *The Off-Campus Library Services Conference Proceedings.* Mt. Pleasant, MI: Central Michigan University Press. Retrieved August 26, 2003 from http://ocls.cmich.edu/1stOCLSCP.pdf.

Lessin, B. M. (Ed.). (1986). *The* [2nd] *Off-Campus Library Services Conference Proceedings.* Mt. Pleasant, MI: Central Michigan University Press. Retrieved August 26, 2003 from http://ocls.cmich.edu/2ndOCLSCP.pdf.

Lessin, B. M. (Ed.). (1987). *The* [3rd] *Off-Campus Library Services Conference Proceedings.* Mount Pleasant, MI: Central Michigan University Press. Retrieved August 26, 2003 from http://ocls.cmich.edu/3rdOCLSCP.pdf.

Lessin, B. M. (Ed.). (1989). *The* [4th] *Off-Campus Library Services Conference Proceedings.* Mt. Pleasant, MI: Central Michigan University. Retrieved August 26, 2003 from http://ocls.cmich.edu/4th OCLSCP.pdf.

Lessin, B. M. (Ed.). (1991) *Off-campus library services.* Metuchen, NJ: Scarecrow Press. [Selected papers from the first four Off-Campus Library Services Conferences.]

Mahoney, B. (Ed.). (2002) *The Tenth Off-Campus Library Services Conference Proceedings.* Mount Pleasant, MI: Central Michigan University.

Slade, A. L. (2000). Keynote address—International trends and issues in library service for distance learning: Present and future. In P. Brophy, S. Fisher, & Z. Clarke (Eds.), *Libraries without walls 3: The delivery of library services to distant users* (pp. 6–48). London: Library Association Publishing.

Slade, A. L. (2002). *Library services for distance learning: The fourth bibliography.* Retrieved August 26, 2003 from http://uviclib.uvic.ca/dls/bibliography4.html.

Slade, A. L., & Kascus, M. A. (1996). *Library services for off-campus and distance education: The second annotated bibliography.* Englewood, CO: Libraries Unlimited.

Slade, A. L., & Kascus, M. A. (2000). *Library services for open and distance learning: The third annotated bibliography.* Englewood, CO: Libraries Unlimited.

Sloan, B., & Stoerger, S. *Library support for distance learning.* Retrieved August 26, 2003 from http://www.lis.uiuc.edu/~b-sloan/libdist.htm.

Thomas, P. S. (Comp.). (2000) *The Ninth Off-Campus Library Services Conference Proceedings.* Mt. Pleasant, MI: Central Michigan University. Also published as: Casey, A.M. (Ed.). (2001) *Off-Campus Library Services.* Binghamton, New York: Haworth Press; and as Casey, A. M. (Ed.). Off-campus library services. *Journal of Library Administration, 31*(3/4)/*32*(1/2), whole issue.

Thomas, P. S., & Jones, M. (Comps.). (1998) *The* [8th] *Off-Campus Library Services Conference Proceedings.* Mount Pleasant, MI: Central Michigan University.

CHAPTER 17

Lanny Arvan

The View from Campus Administration

Introduction

It is a privilege to be given this opportunity to write on campus educational technology issues and relate those to the many and varied accomplishments of the LEEP (Library Education Experimental Program) program. Let's begin with the following organizing questions for the sake of comparison. After addressing those, we will attempt to make some conclusions about where this will lead us.

First, what lessons transfer? LEEP is a moderately sized graduate program populated with a few hundred adult learners who are mature working professionals with a substantial history of work. The campus as a whole at Illinois is huge with an undergraduate population in excess of 26,000; the vast majority are traditional residential students (traditional in the sense of age and work experience). Are the views of good technology and good pedagogy robust enough to work well with both audiences? If not, then what changes in approach must be made to accommodate the demographic differences?

Second, what is the role of the campus in terms of faculty development and support infrastructure? The Graduate School of Library and Information Science largely provides it own technology for online instruction. The technology was designed with LEEP courses in mind, to include a course Web site as a way to distribute readings and other course materials, a Web board for asynchronous interaction, and a combination of streaming audio, live text chat, and slides to accommodate the very important synchronous sessions. While there is some heterogeneity across the LEEP courses, relative to the situation at the campus level the LEEP courses appear uniform. Consequently, the instructor technology needs can be precisely targeted. LEEP courses have neither a need for sophisticated quiz and survey tools nor a need for complex online grade-book functionality, mainstay technologies for large multisection courses. Since LEEP staff work closely with faculty, especially first timers, the faculty development function is built into the course construction and teaching experiences. Such close collaboration is desirable and does happen at the campus level, but the ratio of the faculty being supported to support providers is much higher at the campus level and so on average the relationship is less intensive.

Third, how does cost fit in? LEEP is financed in part by the out-of-state students it enrolls. They pay a substantially higher tuition. The incremental revenues have been used to finance a variety of supportive investments. Particularly noteworthy is that LEEP provides course buyouts for faculty as they develop their LEEP courses, a practice that helps to encourage faculty to participate in the program. The LEEP support model can work well for other graduate professional programs that can charge a like or even higher tuition, and that have similar faculty salaries and student to faculty ratios. It is interesting to observe that LEEP has established a high-caliber program with little or no reliance on videoconferencing. Supporting low-bandwidth technologies is less expensive, particularly in terms of the human support costs. Moreover, once the students adjust to the online environment they will likely show greater satisfaction than their counterparts in a videoconferencing class because of the greater reliability of the low-bandwidth technologies. This is an important lesson. LEEP has done admirably in using the incremental tuition revenues to offset the disadvantages from not being able to convene face-to-face classes.

And what of support that must rely in essence on in-state tuition only? (The vast majority of undergraduates are from within the state of Illinois, though there has been a recent modest increase of international undergraduates.) Like LEEP, several other departments and colleges provide their own support for instruction. Faculty members have space for Web publishing that can be used for research and instruction. Some units have developed repositories of sharable materials and provide assistance for faculty to use those materials in research and instruction. But on the whole, teaching is viewed as teaching, whether technology assisted or otherwise, and absent additional revenue streams it is hard to see that changing. Rewards measured in terms of promotion and tenure and salary increase are based on a pre-Web view of the campus mission—teaching, research, and service—yet with the recognition that the emphasis is heavily tilted toward research. If teaching with technology takes added time and effort as compared to traditional teaching, and there is much to indicate that it does, then in most units that cost is borne by the instructor. The upshot is that there is a group of innovative faculty members who have done creative things teaching with technology yet wonder why the institution isn't more supportive of their efforts, and another group of faculty who have not become engaged with the technology at all and wonder why they should bother.

What Lessons Transfer?

The psychologist Jerome Bruner, among many others, believes there are universal motivators for learning. Good instruction taps into those motivators to engage the student. Bruner focuses on three main factors: (1) curiosity, (2) a desire to achieve competency, and (3) a desire to communicate with others (Bruner, 1974). Based on my limited direct encounters with LEEP students, it is evident that they possess these factors in abundance. They are effusive about the LEEP program itself and also about how the program complements their careers. The program is demanding and the students appreciate that. They also see the program as relevant, both in terms of the intellectual growth it engenders and the useful credential it provides. This image of the LEEP student, highly engaged and with a strong desire to learn in a social context, is consistent with the view of other adult learners in professional programs on campus, such as the Executive MBA. Colleagues have reported that it is fun to teach the "execs" because they are so lively and have so much to bring to the table, this in spite of general rustiness school-wise and the occasional severe technical academic deficiency.

Contrast this view of LEEP students with the picture of undergraduates that emerges from the National Survey of Student Engagement (NSSE, http://www.indiana.edu/~nsse). The NSSE results indicate an impatient student body that believes that learning is something to be consumed, not unlike fast food. While the NSSE indicates that most students are satisfied with their education, such quantitative metrics as time spent out of class studying indicate that typical students are not engaged with their schoolwork; mean hours of study time reported is in the single digits (for a student taking 15 credit hours a recommended norm is 25 hours per week of study time). One might characterize the situation as "benign alienation." NSSE results indicate the disengagement is exacerbated in public universities as compared with smaller liberal arts colleges as well as with juniors and seniors as compared with freshmen.

Russell Durst makes a compelling argument that the issue is not student shirking per se, but rather that there are serious conflicts in expectations between the students' extreme pragmatism on the one hand, and the faculty's theoretical orientation on the other (Durst, 1999). When students don't see the relevance of the theory, which is all too frequent, they become confused and frustrated and look for ways to get through and get by in a course without receiving a bad grade in the process. Faculty members frequently interpret this student response as shirking and become angry that they have to spend their scarce time on a bunch of slackers. Durst himself argues for a compromise approach midway between the student and faculty extremes. Whether this prescription is correct or not, it is apparent that the instructor has basically one of two distinct paths to follow—either teach the course the way the subject matter demands and inadvertently leave behind a significant fraction of the class, or pay close attention to student motivation and engagement and thereby likely omit a significant part of the traditional syllabus. An interesting aspect of teaching with technology is that because the technology makes it much easier for the instructor to see the student work and observe the depth of student understanding, the technology has encouraged some faculty to take the second path.

Yet it is misleading to envision that the technology dictates the pedagogic approach. Rather it seems that faculty have teaching requirements and attempt to match the available technologies to those needs. The same technology may be utilized in several different ways. Consider the most obvious example, the Web board. LEEP uses the threaded discussion as a primary way for students to comment on, argue, and debate course subject matter. When done well, the thoughtful student input and extensive dialog promotes a strong sense of community in the class. Individuals become recognized for what they write and develop an online persona based on that. Students tend to open up more than in a timed face-to-face setting, and that openness contributes to the sense of community in the class. The threaded discussion is at the heart of an ALN course. (ALN stands for asynchronous learning network, an expression coined by Frank Mayadas of the Alfred P. Sloan Foundation, which refers to class environments where students can participate in the online environment when and where it is convenient for them; http://www.aln.org.)

One might envision that in a course with face-to-face meetings the threaded discussion would amplify the in-class discussion, thereby allowing the discourse to conclude when the topic has been played out rather than to stop because the bell has signaled the end of class. Indeed, in many classes the threaded discussion is used for just this purpose. However, this use is far from universal. Some instructors have tried threaded discussion and abandoned it. They argue that in their class the student writing is forced instead of contributive. The student posts are clearly intended to satisfy an instructor-imposed requirement rather than to fill a need to express a view on the subject. This creates the impression that the Web Board is "make work" rather than an enhancement to learning.

Other instructors use the bulletin board functionality primarily as a help tool. Students who are stuck completing an assignment pose a query about the problem they are working on. A teaching assistant or other students in the class post comments or responses. Yet other students in the class (lurkers, who are also having difficulties with the assignment) can read these posts and learn from them. It is interesting to note that this particular use favors a large class environment. There needs to be a critical mass of students (or a teaching assistant assigned to monitor the Web board) so that students posting their queries have a reasonable expectation they will get a response in a timely fashion. Long lags between initial post and response undermine the utility of the process. Indeed, given the prevalence of instant messaging by the students, those with established peer communities may opt to instant message with a group of classmates rather than post to the class bulletin board, largely because the response will be immediate.

Still other instructors use the bulletin board to have students complete writing assignments that are sharable with their classmates. This particular use is quite popular in foreign language courses. Students are writing seriously, but for the instructor, not their classmates. The writing is made available to the class as a whole so students can benchmark their work to the work of their classmates. This is a powerful yet underappreciated use of the technology. Part of the conflict Durst identifies is that students regularly find they come up short on instructor-imposed norms and that this has the cumulative effect of beating them down. If as an alternative instructors made it clear that student work would be evaluated in terms of the work of their peers, the objective would seem more readily obtainable for the students.

These good uses notwithstanding, most instructors who use the course management systems that the campus supports do not use the bulletin board functionality. The likely explanation is a combination of instructor orientation and scarce faculty time. The instructor in a traditional class focuses on the live class session—preparing the lecture or other class activities, concentrating on points of emphasis, and making sure handouts and presentation materials are prepared—and likely doing all of this in a just-in-time fashion. If the technology is to make a significant impact on the way these instructors teach, it has to do that "where they live" rather than force them to "move to a different neighborhood" to take advantage of the tools the campus provides.

The live sessions that are part of LEEP courses offer an intriguing view of what a technology-enabled, face-to-face classroom might be like in the future. As wireless network technology becomes deployed around campus and as the expectation becomes that students will bring suitable devices to class to communicate over the network, the campus will establish a capability that is already available to LEEP students during the synchronous sessions. These sessions are full of side conversations, among the students and between student and teaching assistant, as the instructor delivers the main presentation. The friendly banter and lively interchanges keep the students actively engaged in the class. The instructors, who are challenged to keep up with this flow as they proceed through the session, seem to welcome the student interactions because they indicate that the students are wrestling with the material being presented.

Faculty members who, in the face-to-face classroom, have embraced active learning techniques to engage their students should be curious about whether the technology can further promote active learning. The LEEP examples suggest several questions that require answers for the approach to translate to the on-campus environment. How can the instructor un-tether from the computer presentation station to better interact with the class on the one hand, yet monitor teaching assistant and student comments to keep up with the class on the other? When or should the instructor cease the main presentation to allow the side discussions to proceed without distraction? If instructors try this approach will they lose their sense of control in the classroom, and are there methods for the instructor to cede control to the class for a period and then reassert control after that interval has concluded? While the campus is not yet ready to advocate this sort of teaching as standard practice, certainly it is an area to be watching and a place where further experimentation would be welcome.

What Is the Role of the Campus?

The campus must promote and transfer models of good teaching with technology. The LEEP model, which mixes the live synchronous sessions with the basic ALN model, provides a good view of how the technology may be utilized successfully. Several other interesting approaches have emerged on campus.

One such approach is termed Just-in-Time Teaching (http://webphysics.iupui.edu/jitt/jitt.html). On our campus it was first adopted in the Physics Department. It has since made in-roads into some psychology and educational psychology courses, and is gaining a small following elsewhere around campus. It offers instructors a holistic view of the online and in-class activities, allowing each to support the other. Another approach, particularly well suited for courses not in the major that meet distribution requirements (e.g., organic chemistry for pre-med students, differential equations for engineering students, and economics for business students), is to use the technology to enable a substantial amount of self-pacing via animated simulations and discipline-specific software as well as quizzes and online homework that mark student progress (Arvan, Ory, Bullock, Burnaska, & Hanson, 1998). Yet another approach is to focus the online part of the course on student projects. This tends to make the instruction more student-centric and encourages the students to think of their course work as research, as suggested by the 1998 Boyer Commission Report. Certainly making student research the course focus can be done in the traditional classroom. The value of the Web technology in this regard is to enable the sharing of the student work with peers and holding out the potential for publication to outsiders. Web publication and potential reuse of course work is a strong motivator for students, making the approach more powerful and more likely to be successful. Yet it does suggest an important issue. What should happen to the student work after the course has concluded? If it is to be archived, should that be done student by student on their own personal Web sites, course by course in an institutional repository of learning materials, or some other way?

The campus also has responsibility to support the software infrastructure. In the past the technology has imposed an either/or approach; either an instructor uses the software supplied by the unit or uses the software supplied by campus, but not both. The campus is moving to an enterprise learning management system that will have core basic functions: document sharing, bulletin board, live chat and whiteboard, calendar, grade book, and workflow management, particularly with student assignments. This software will have interfaces that unit software providers can write for and thereby integrate what they provide with what the campus supports. The goal is a hybrid support environment that appears seamless to the students.

In considering the software infrastructure, scaling and particularly reliability of performance have been and will continue to be critical drivers. We have already indicated there are about two orders of magnitude more students to support at the campus level than at the LEEP level. The support is to be done with about one order of magnitude more human and capital resource. These support needs and realities encourage a single massive software environment, and that some potential diversity in offerings will be strategically sacrificed for the sake of maintaining quality of service of existing offerings.

The campus also needs to provide requisite training and support for this software. Yet the goal is to develop self-sufficiency with the technology among the faculty. The hope is that technical literacy is acquired en passant as instructors teach with the technology, and that instructors will take in stride future software upgrades and possible changes in software offerings via modest adjustments in their own approach to instruction.

What about Cost?

Prior to spring 2000 many were making the argument that use of the Internet in instruction was the wave of the future and that it needed to be supported, in spite of the significant price tag, lest we fall behind our current more forward-thinking peers and the entrants into online higher education. A new paradigm had emerged and the university had to reorganize itself to function well in the ensuing era. As fallout from the burst of the dot-com bubble, a lot of this type of thinking has been cast aside as hyperbole and myth. There is still a core belief that technology is useful for instruction and advancing the teaching and learning mission, and that educational technology needs to be supported as such. But there is also now a sense of prudence—we need to live within our means and not mortgage the other successful activities on campus to finance educational technology investments. For reasons articulated in the introduction, this means that having every unit adopt the LEEP model will not become the approach on campus any time soon.

The critical issues are how to sustain utility support for teaching with technology while allowing for innovation both in the teaching practice and in the technology itself in this more cautious environment. While there is no roadmap for the campus to follow, it is clear that the historical approach where the innovation and the production activities were blended will no longer work. It is also clear that experiments that appear to succeed when done at small scale will nonetheless fail unless they produce a way to be sustaining at large scale.

Where Might We Be Heading?

Both the Boyer Commission report and the National Survey of Student Engagement suggest that we research universities are seriously underserving our undergraduate student populations. This is a very large liability on the institutional balance sheet. Yet these same students also need to be seen as assets, generally in terms of their intelligence and their energy, and specifically in their tech savvy and their comfort operating in a technology culture. In order to succeed in the current environment, we must bring these students in as collaborators: co-creators of online learning objects, primary movers in course redesign with technology, and critics of faculty-centric approaches that may not work for them as learners. They are the abundant resource on campus and we need to get smarter about utilizing this resource to promote teaching and learning. We also need to rethink our views of educational technology, from something that increases faculty workload to something that empowers students, as learners but also as creators.

References

Arvan, L., Ory, J. C., Bullock, C. D., Burnaska, K. K., & Hanson, M. (1998). The SCALE efficiency projects. *Journal of Asynchronous Learning Networks, 2*(2). Retrieved from http://www.aln.org/publications/jaln/v2n2/v2n2_arvan.asp.

Durst, R. K. (1999). *Collision course. Conflict, negotiation, and learning in college composition.* Urbana, IL: National Council of Teachers of English.

Boyer Commission on Educating Undergraduates in the Research University (1998). *Reinventing undergraduate education: A blueprint for America's research universities.* Retrieved October 28, 2003 from http://naples.cc.sunysb.edu/Pres/boyer.nsf/.

Bruner, J. S. (1974). *Toward a theory of instruction.* Cambridge, MA: Belknap Press.

Compiled by Rae-Anne Montague

LEEP Bibliography

This bibliography lists publications about LEEP (Library Education Experimental Program) written by LEEP students, faculty, researchers and alumni, and journalists reporting on LEEP (as of November 2003). The bibliography is maintained online by Rae-Anne Montague, and updated regularly at http://www.lis.uiuc.edu/gslis/degrees/leep_bib.html. See the site for links to related information available online about on-line education, and educational directories. URLs are given here for publications that are available at permanent sites. Online versions of some of the papers may be available from individuals' Web sites; see the LEEP bibliography site for links.

I. LEEP in the News

"The Award for Most Outstanding ALN Program Will Be Awarded to the LEEP Program . . ." Sloan-C Honors and Awards (November 16, 2001). Available: http://www.aln.org/aboutus/awards2001.asp.

Block, Marylaine. "How Well Does Distance Learning Work?" *ExLibris—An E-Zine for Librarians* 83 (January 12, 2001). Available: http://marylaine.com/exlibris/xlib83.html.

Carnevale, Dan. "Researchers Find Social Bonds to Be Important in Distance Education." *The Chronicle of Higher Education* (October 5, 2000). Available: http://www.chronicle.com/free/2000/10/2000100501u.htm.

Chepesuik, Ron. "Learning without Walls." *American Libraries* 29, no. 9 (October 1998): 62–65.

Focus 580 (radio talk show) featuring Dean Leigh Estabrook and Information Technology Manager Vince Patone (October 9, 1998). Available: http://leep.lis.uiuc.edu/rafiles/public/580_oct09_98.ram.

"Fresh Faces: The First Conversation In This Series Is with Mary Pergander, Director of the Lake Bluff Public Library." *The Illinois Library Association Reporter* 21, no. 1 (February 2003): 4–5. Available: http://www.ila.org/pub/reporter/vol21no1.pdf.

"Fresh Faces: The Third Conversation in This Series Is with Melissa Henderson, Children's Librarian, Ela Area Public Library District in Lake Zurich." *The Illinois Library Association Reporter* 21, no. 3 (June 2003): 4–5. Available: http://www.ila.org/pub/reporter/vol21no3.pdf.

Galligan, Mary. "Distance Learning Takes a Leep3 Forward," *Illinois Libraries* 80, no. 4 (fall 1998): 236–238.

Harmon, Amy. "Cyberclasses in Session." *New York Times* (November 11, 2001). Available (free registration required): http://www.nytimes.com/2001/11/11/education/11ED-OLIN.html.

Johnson, Jennifer. "A Dream Come True." *The Mount Prospect Journal* (April 25–30, 2001): 41. Available: http://www.lis.uiuc.edu/gslis/degrees/Rose-Journal1A.jpg and http://www.lis.uiuc.edu/gslis/degrees/Rose-Journal2A.jpg.

Kline, Greg. "Grads Seek Education Online." *News Gazette* (Champaign, IL) 150, no. 287 (May 12, 2002).

Moffitt, Casey. "New Program Offers Degrees with Online Classes." *Oak Leaves* (July 26, 2000).

Net.LEARNING: The PBS Documentary, first broadcast September 1998 on PBS.

Oder, Norman. "LIS Distance Ed Moves Ahead." *Library Journal* 126, no. 16 (October 1, 2001): 54–56. Available: http://libraryjournal.reviewsnews.com/index.asp—layout=articleArchive&article Id=CA163487.

Temkin, Jody. "A New Information Age," *Chicago Tribune* (October 1, 2000).

Thomas, Margaret. "Crossing over . . . to the Corporate Sector." *Library Journal* 126, no. 14 (September 1, 2001); 48–50. Available: http://libraryjournal.reviewsnews.com/index.asp?layout=article_Archive&articleid=CA152764.

II. Articles about the LEEP Experience from a Student Perspective

Arnold, Allison. "Third Semester, Sixth Course." *Informant, Bulletin of the Special Libraries Association, Illinois Chapter* 65, no. 2 (November 2000): 14–15.

Buxton, Karen A. "Library Education at a Distance: The University of Illinois LEEP3 Program." *Alki: The Washington Library Association Journal* 16, no. 3 (December 2000): 18–19. Available: http://www.wla.org/alki/dec00.pdf.

Claussen, Joanne. "Library School at the Turn of the New Millennium: One Student's Experience." *Law Librarians in the New Millennium* 1, no. 2 (fall 1999): 2–3, 7. Available: http://www.westgroup.com/pdf/llnm/nlfall99.pdf.

Hall, Katherine. "Distance Education: An Insider's View." *American Association of Law Libraries Spectrum* 4, no. 8 (May 2000): 30–31. Available: http://www.aallnet.org/products/pub_sp0005.pdf.

Oldoski, Lisa. "Building Personal Communities in the Virtual Realm." *Alki: The Washington Library Association Journal* 17, no. 1 (March 2001): 10–11. Available: http://www.wla.org/alki/mar01.pdf.

Ross, Larry. "Urbana-Champaign on the Potomac: The University of Illinois' LEEP Program." *Law Library Lights* 44, no. 5 (May/June 2001): 9–10. Available: http://www.llsdc.org/lights/.

Skhal, Kathryn. "Confessions of a Covert Library Student: Distance Education and the Working Paraprofessional." *Pacific Southwest Regional Medical Library Latitudes* 12, no. 4 (July/August 2003). Available: http://nnlm.gov/psr/lat/v12n4/confessions.html.

III. Informational Works by LEEP Faculty, Administrators, and Others

Bowker, Geoffrey C., Vincenzo Patone, and Susan Searing. "The University of Illinois Graduate Library School LEEPs into the Future." in *SPEC Kit 234 Transforming Libraries: Issues and Innovations in Distance Learning* (ARL, 1998): 23–27.

Estabrook, Leigh S. "LEEP3 at the University of Illinois." *Journal of Education for Library and Information Science* 38, no. 2 (spring 1997): 157–160.

Estabrook, Leigh S. "New Forms of Distance Education: Opportunities for Students, Threats to Institutions." Paper presented at the ACRL 9th National Conference (April 1999). Available: http://www.ala.org/Content/NavigationMenu/ACRL/Events_and_Conferences/estabrook99.pdf.

Estabrook, Leigh S. "Building Communities through Information Technologies." Paper presented at the University YMCA (Champaign, IL, April 16, 1999).

Estabrook, Leigh S. "Will Distance Education Destroy the University?" Lazerow Lecture, Florida State University, September 17, 1999. Available: http://alexia.lis.uiuc.edu/~leighe/willdistance.html.

Estabrook, Leigh S. "Distance Education at the University of Illinois." In *Benchmarks in Distance Education: The LIS Experience*, edited Daniel D. Barron. Westport CT: Libraries Unlimited, 2003, 63–73.

Hearne, Betsy. "Once There Was and Will Be: Storytelling the Future." *Horn Book Magazine* 76, no. 6 (November/December 2000): 712–719.

Jenkins, Christine. "Far Out Learning," *School Library Journal* 46, no. 2 (February 2000): 46–49.

Kazmer, Michelle M. "Distance education students speak to the library: Here's how you can help even more." *The Electronic Library* 20, no. 5 (2002): 395–400.

Maeroff, Gene I. "Delivering the Goods." In *A Classroom of One: How Online Learning Is Changing our Schools and Colleges*. New York: Palgrave Macmillan, 2003, pp. 20–33.

Montague, Rae-Anne. "LEEPing into Challenge and Opportunity." *Library Mosaics* 13, no. 4 (July/August 2002): 8–9.

Schneider, Karen G. "Internet Librarian: A Giant LEEP Forward." *American Libraries* 29, no. 2 (February 1998): 64. Available: http://www.ala.org/Content/NavigationMenu/Products_and_Publications/Periodicals/American_Libraries/Internet_Librarian/1998_columns/February_1998__A_Giant_LEEP_Forward.htm.

Searing, Susan E., and Yan Xu. "Supporting Distance Education with Technology: The Library's Role." *Informant, Bulletin of the Special Libraries Association, Illinois Chapter* 66, no. 1 (September 2001): 7, 10–12.

Smith, Linda C. "Pedagogy in Educating Information Specialists: Lessons Learned from Internet-Based Distance Education." Paper presented at the German-Dutch University Conference: Information Specialists in the 21st Century. Fachhochschule Hannover University of Applied Sciences Department of Information and Communication, October 14–15, 1999.

Strong, Robert W., and Glynn E. Harmon. "Online Graduate Degrees: A Review of Three Internet-based Master's Degree Offerings." *The American Journal of Distance Education* 11, no. 3 (1997): 58–70.

"Teaching at an Internet Distance: The Pedagogy of Online Teaching and Learning." Faculty Seminar on the Pedagogy of Online Learning. (December 1999, University of Illinois). Available: http://www.vpaa.uillinois.edu/reports_retreats/tid_final-12-5.doc.

Woodbury, Marsha. "LEEP3—Distance Education Tips." In *The Cyclone of Change: Natural Disaster or Carnival Ride?* New York: Association for Computing Machinery, 1997, pp. 151–152.

Woodbury, Marsha. " LEEPing into Distance Education." *The CPSR Newsletter* 15, no. 1 (winter 1997): 11–12.

Woodbury, Marsha. "A LEEP into Distance Education." *ALN Magazine* 1, no. 2 (August 1997). Available: http://www.aln.org/publications/magazine/v1n2/woodbury.asp.

IV. Research Papers and Presentations

Bregman, Alvan, and Caroline Haythornthwaite. "Radicals of Presentation: Visibility, Relation, and Co-presence in Persistent Conversation." *New Media and Society* 5, no. 1 (2003): 117–140.

Bregman, Alvan, and Caroline Haythornthwaite. "Radicals of Presentation in Persistent Conversation." In *Proceedings of the Hawai'i International Conference on System Sciences* (Maui, Hawaii, January 3–6, 2001).

Estabrook, Leigh S. "Rethinking Cost-Benefit Models of Distance Learning." In *Elements of Quality Online Education*, edited by John Bourne and Janet C. Moore. Needham, MA: Sloan Center for Online Education, 2002, pp. 71–80.

Haythornthwaite, Caroline. "A Social Network Study of the Growth of Community among Distance Learners." *Information Research* 4, no. 1 (1998). Available: http://www.shef.ac.uk/~is/publications/infres/paper49.html.

Haythornthwaite, Caroline. "Collaborative Work Networks among Distributed Learners." In *Proceedings of the 32nd Hawai'i International Conference on System Sciences* (Los Alamitos, CA: IEEE Computer Society Press, January 1999). Available on CD-ROM.

Haythornthwaite, Caroline. "Networks of Information Sharing among Computer-Supported Distance Learners." In *Proceedings of the Third Conference on Computer Support for Collaborative Learning*, edited by Christopher Hoadley and Jeremy Rochelle (Palo Alto, California, December 12–15, 1999, pp. 218–222).

Haythornthwaite, Caroline. "Online Personal Networks: Size, Composition and Media Use among Distance Learners." *New Media and Society* 2, no. 2 (2000): 195–226.

Haythornthwaite, Caroline. "Tie Strength and the Impact of New Media." In *Proceedings of the Hawai'i International Conference On System Sciences* (Maui, Hawaii, January 3–6, 2001).

Haythornthwaite, Caroline. "Exploring Multiplexity: Social Network Structures in a Computer-Supported Distance Learning Class." *Information Society* 17, no. 3 (July 2001): 211–226.

Haythornthwaite, Caroline. "Building Social Networks via Computer Networks: Creating and Sustaining Distributed Learning Communities." In *Building Virtual Communities: Learning and Change in Cyberspace*, edited by Ann Renninger and Wes Shumar. Cambridge: Cambridge University Press, 2002, 159–190.

Haythornthwaite, Caroline. "Strong, Weak and Latent Ties and the Impact of New Media." *Information Society* 18, no. 5 (October, 2002): 385–401.

Haythornthwaite, Caroline, and Michelle M. Kazmer, eds. *Learning, Culture, and Community in Online Education: Research and Practice*. New York: Peter Lang, 2004.

Haythornthwaite, Caroline. "Supporting Distributed Relationships: Social Networks of Relations and Media Use over Time." *Electronic Journal of Communication* 13, no. 1 (2003). Available: http://www.cios.org/getfile/haythorn_v13n1.

Haythornthwaite, Caroline, and Alvan Bregman. "Getting New Users Active in Shared Spaces, or, the Unintended Writing Consequences of Internet-Based Distance Learning." Paper presented at the Computers and Writing Conference, Muncie, IN, May 2001.

Haythornthwaite, Caroline, and Michelle M. Kazmer, "Bringing the Internet Home: Adult Distance Learners and Their Internet, Home, and Work Worlds." In *The Internet in Everyday Life*, edited by Barry Wellman and Caroline Haythornthwaite (Oxford, UK: Blackwell's Publishers, 2002): 431–463.

Haythornthwaite, Caroline, Michelle M. Kazmer, Jennifer Robins, and Susan Shoemaker. "Community Development among Distance Learners: Temporal and Technological Dimensions." *Journal of Computer-Mediated Communication* 6, no. 1 (September 2000). Available: http://www.ascusc.org/jcmc/vol6/issue1/haythornthwaite.html.

Kazmer, Michelle M. "Coping in a Distance Environment: Sitcoms, Chocolate Cake, and Dinner with a Friend." *First Monday* 5, no. 9 (September 2000). Available: http://www.firstmonday.dk/issues/issue5_9/kazmer/index.html.

Kazmer, Michelle M. "Disengaging from Intrinsically Transient Social Worlds: The Case of a Distance Learning Community." Ph.D. dissertation, University of Illinois at Urbana-Champaign Graduate School of Library and Information Science, 2002.

Kazmer, Michelle M. "Online Learning and Community Embeddedness: How Existing Ties Transform the Growth of Relationships between Educational and Community Settings." Paper presented at the Information, Communication, and Society / Oxford Internet Institute Symposium, Oxford, UK, September 17–20, 2003.

Kazmer, Michelle M., and Caroline Haythornthwaite. "Juggling Multiple Social Worlds: Distance Students Online and Offline." *American Behavioral Scientist* 45, no. 3 (November 2001): 510–529.

Lavagnino, Merri Beth, Geoffrey C. Bowker, Bryan Heidorn, and Mindy M. Basi. "Incorporating Social Informatics into the Curriculum for Library and Information Science Professionals," *Libri* 48 (1998): 13–25.

Lesht, Faye, and Najmuddin Shaik. "Best Practices in Helping Students Complete Online Graduate Degree Programs." Paper presented at the 19th Annual Conference on Distance Teaching and Learning, Madison, WI, August 4–6, 2003.

Montague, Rae-Anne, and Pat Lawton. "Articulating a Model for LIS Distance Education: Reflections on Research and Practice from the LEEP Retreat." Paper presented at the Association for Library and Information Science Education Annual Conference, Philadelphia, PA, January 23, 2003.

Montague, Rae-Anne. "LEEP Retreat: Exploring Best Practices in Online Education." Paper presented at the Distance Learning Administration Conference (Jekyll Island, GA, June 1–4, 2003). Available in *Distance Learning Administration 2003 Annual*. Carrollton, GA: State University of West Georgia, pp. 101–104.

Montague, Rae-Anne, Linda C. Smith, Bruce R. Kingma, Kathryn A. Allen, Allyson Carlyle, and Grace Beauchane Whiteaker. "Connecting across Campuses: Key Issues in Establishing Collaborative Inter-Institutional Agreements for Online Education." Paper presented at the 9th Annual Sloan-C International Conference on Asynchronous Learning Networks, Orlando, FL, November 14–16, 2003.

Robins, Jenny. "Social Navigation and the Role of Persistent Structures in a Collaborative Virtual Environment." In *Proceedings of the European Perspectives on Computer-Supported Collaborative Learning* (Maastrich, the Netherlands, March 22–24, 2001). Available: http://www.mmi.unimaas.nl/euro-cscl/presentations.htm.

Robins, Jenny. "Affording a Place: The Role of Persistent Structures in Social Navigation." *Information Research* 7, no 3 (2002). Available: http://InformationR.net/ir/7-3/paper131.html.

Ruhleder, Karen. "Network Community: Virtual Space for Physical Bodies." In *Proceedings of the Third Conference on Computer Support for Collaborative Learning*, edited by Christopher Hoadley and Jeremy Rochelle (Palo Alto, California, December 12–15, 1999, pp. 503–509).

Ruhleder, Karen. "The Virtual Ethnographer: Fieldwork in Distributed Electronic Environments." *Field Methods* 12, no. 1 (2000): 3–17.

Ruhleder, Karen, and Michael Twidale. "Reflective Collaborative Learning on the Web: Drawing on the Master Class." *First Monday* 5, no. 5 (May 2000). Available: http://www.firstmonday.org/issues/issue5_5/ruhleder/index.html.

Ruhleder, Karen. "Understanding On-line Community: The Affordances of Virtual Space." *Information Research* 7, no. 3 (2002). Available: http://InformationR.net/ir/7-3/paper132.html.

Smith, Linda C. "Faculty Satisfaction in LEEP: A Web-based Graduate Degree Program in Library and Information Science." In *Online Education Volume 2: Proceedings of the 2000 Sloan Summer Workshop on Asynchronous Learning Networks,* edited by Janet C. Moore. Needham, MA: Sloan Center for OnLine Education, 2001, 87–108.

Smith, Linda C., Sarai Lastra, and Jennifer Robins. "Teaching Online: Changing Models of Teaching and Learning in LEEP." *Journal of Education for Library and Information Science* 42, no. 4 (fall 2001): 348–363.

Twigg, Carol A. "Innovations in Online Learning: Moving beyond No Significant Difference." Pew Learning and Technology Program, 2001. Available: http://www.center.rpi.edu/PewSym/mono4.html.

Tyler, Alyson. "A Survey of Distance Learning Library and Information Science Courses Delivered via the Internet." *Education for Information* 19, no. 1 (March 2001): 47–59.

Contributors

Lanny Arvan is Assistant CIO (Chief Information Officer) for Educational Technologies and an Associate Professor of Economics at the University of Illinois at Urbana-Champaign. Arvan moved quickly from teaching with technology to doing administrative work in the area. As the campus regularized its support of educational technologies, it was Arvan who led the effort. Arvan is the Executive Sponsor of the Illinois Compass project, wherein WebCT Vista will become the enterprise learning management system for the Urbana campus. The project entails migration from prior commercial offerings, both Blackboard and WebCT, as well as some homegrown systems.

Alvan Bregman is Rare Book Collections Librarian and Assistant Professor of Library Administration at the University of Illinois at Urbana-Champaign. He received his Ph.D. in English from the University of Toronto while Northrop Frye was still active there. His research interests include online genre, the history of automation, and early modern medical publications.

Bertram C. Bruce is Professor of Library and Information Science at the University of Illinois at Urbana-Champaign. His central interest is in learning—the constructive process whereby individuals and organizations develop as they adapt to new circumstances. This has led to the development of Community Inquiry Laboratories, simultaneously a suite of Web-based tools, a set of communities, and a research project on inquiry. His recent book, *Literacy in the Information Age: Inquiries into Meaning Making with New Technologies,* examines the relations among new technologies and trends in areas of language, education, work, and democracy.

Amy Bruckman is an Associate Professor in the College of Computing at the Georgia Institute of Technology. She and her students in the Electronic Learning Communities (ELC) research group do research on online communities and education. Amy received her Ph.D. from the MIT (Massachusetts Institute of Technology) Media Lab's Epistemology and Learning group in 1997, and her B.A. in physics from Harvard University in 1987. More information about her work is available at http://www.cc.gatech.edu/~asb/.

Nicholas C. Burbules is Grayce Wicall Gauthier Professor in the Department of Educational Policy Studies at the University of Illinois at Urbana-Champaign. He has published widely in the areas of philosophy of education, technology and education, and critical social and political theory. His most recent books include: Nicholas C. Burbules and Thomas A. Callister, Jr., *Watch IT: The Promises and Risks of New Information Technologies for Education* (Boulder, Colo.: Westview Press, 2000); Nicholas C. Burbules and Carlos Torres, editors, *Globalization and Education: Critical Perspectives* (New York: Routledge, 2000); and D. C. Phillips and Nicholas C. Burbules, *Postpositivism and Educational Research* (Lanham, Mass.: Rowman and Littlefield, 2000). His forthcoming books include Gert Biesta and Nicholas C. Burbules, *Pragmatism and Educational Research,* and Michael Peters and Nicholas C. Burbules, *Poststructuralism and Educational Research,* both to be published by Rowman and Littlefield in 2003.

Leigh S. Estabrook is Professor of Library and Information Science and Professor of Sociology at the University of Illinois at Urbana-Champaign. She currently directs the Library Research Center. From 1986 through 2001 she was Dean of the Graduate School of Library and Information Science where she oversaw the creation and implementation of LEEP (Library Education Experimental Program). Estabrook's current research includes a study of the book as the "gold standard" for promotion and tenure in the humanistic disciplines, funded by the Andrew W. Mellon Foundation.

Jill Gengler is the Manager of Instructional Technology within the Graduate School of Library and Information Science (GSLIS) at the University of Illinois at Urbana-Champaign. Jill has experienced a number of roles during her time with the LEEP program: she began as a LEEP student in 1997, became a graduate assistant with LEEP in 1998, and remained with the program as a full-time staff member in 1999 upon the completion of her master's degree from GSLIS. Before joining GSLIS, Jill taught high school history.

Christine A. Jenkins is Associate Professor at the Graduate School of Library and Information Science, University of Illinois at Urbana-Champaign, where she teaches courses in youth services, young adult literature, and literacy. Her research interests focus on literacy, texts, and young readers, and the various roles that public and school libraries and librarians have played in facilitating young people's literacy. Her work has appeared in *Libraries and Culture; Library Quarterly; Books, Libraries, Reading, and Publishing in the Cold War* (Library of Congress, 2002); *Reclaiming the American Library Past: Writing the Women In* (Ablex, 1996); and the *Encyclopedia of Library History* (Garland, 1994).

Caroline Haythornthwaite is Associate Professor at the Graduate School of Library and Information Science, University of Illinois at Urbana-Champaign. Her research examines how the Internet and computer media support work and social interactions among members of online learning and work communities. Her studies include examination of communication and community among online learners, and of distributed knowledge processes. She recently completed an edited book with Barry Wellman on *The Internet in Everyday Life* (Blackwell, 2002).

Betsy Hearne is a professor at the Graduate School of Library and Information Science, University of Illinois at Urbana-Champaign, where she teaches folklore, storytelling, and children's literature. Her research focuses on story in oral, print, and electronic traditions. Dr. Hearne's articles include "Swapping Tales and Stealing Stories: The Ethics and Aesthetics of Folklore in Children's Literature," *Library Trends*, Winter 1999, and "Ruth Sawyer: A Woman's Journey from Folklore to Children's Literature," *The Lion and the Unicorn*, 2000. She is the author of *Beauty and the Beast: Visions and Revisions of an Old Tale (University of Chicago, 1989)* and *Choosing Books for Children: A Commonsense Guide (University of Illinois, 1999)*, as well as fiction and poetry for young people.

Michelle M. Kazmer is an Assistant Professor at the School of Information Studies, Florida State University. Her research focuses on social processes in online social worlds, especially online worlds that are designed to be temporary. Her current research examines the social world disengagement processes of distance learners and academic researchers. She is also involved with an interdisciplinary research team that uses a hermeneutics approach for studying virtual communities.

Pat Lawton is Visiting Lecturer at the Graduate School of Library and Information Science, University of Illinois at Urbana-Champaign. She has taught in LEEP, GSLIS's nationally recognized Internet-based master's program, since 1997. Her research interests include education for library and information science, online pedagogy, and the impact of new technologies on cataloging and classification theory and practice. She holds the M.L.S. degree from Indiana University, and is a doctoral candidate in the School of Library and Information Science at the University of Wisconsin-Madison.

Rae-Anne Montague is LEEP coordinator and doctoral candidate at the Graduate School of Library and Information Science, University of Illinois at Urbana-Champaign. Her research interests include online education, information literacy, learning technologies, diversity, and lifelong learning. She recently completed several articles emphasizing effective practices in online education. Rae-Anne received a Master of Science in Library and Information Science at the University of Illinois at Urbana-Champaign (2000), taking this degree via the LEEP distance option, and a Master of Education in Curriculum in Instruction at St. Mary's University in Halifax, Canada (1994).

Anna L. Nielsen is a doctoral student at the Graduate School of Library and Information Science, University of Illinois at Urbana-Champaign. Her research interests include formal and informal group communication processes, group identity, and community in online learning groups and distributed work teams. Her work on narratives as information systems extends through children's literature and computer-mediated group communication. She is currently examining the pedagogical and group behavior differences between an on-campus and distance learning children's literature course.

Jennifer Robins is an Assistant Professor in Library Science and Information Services in the Educational Leadership and Human Development Department in the College of Education and Human Services at Central Missouri State University. Her research specialty is information infrastructure in K-12 schools and includes a study of collaboratories and other knowledge-building structures within this environment.

Karen Ruhleder was a member of the GSLIS faculty from 1995 to 2003 with a research concentration in social informatics and computer-supported cooperative work. Past work has included studying the role of the "invisible infrastructure" needed to support distributed computing and the impact of transmission delay on interactions across a video link. She continues to work with Michael Twidale (see the chapter in this volume) on the OTSL (over-the-shoulder learning) project while pursuing a Master of Music in Music Theory at the University of Illinois at Urbana-Champaign. She received her Ph.D. in Information and Computer Science from the University of California, Irvine, and has also been on the faculties of the University of Houston and Worcester Polytechnic Institute in Worcester, Massachusetts.

Susan E. Searing, Associate Professor of Library Administration, is the Library & Information Science Librarian at the University of Illinois at Urbana-Champaign. In this position she provides collections and services to support research and teaching at the Graduate School of Library and Information Science, including its distance education masters degree program. Her research, publications, and professional service revolve around the broad issues of services to library users and library support for interdisciplinary scholarship.

Susan Shoemaker is Assistant Professor at the Graduate School of Library and Information Science at Simmons College, Boston, Massachusetts. Her research interests include social aspects of information technologies, socio-cognitive aspects of library user instruction, and research methodologies. Her previous studies have focused on communication of distance education learners, information needs of older and minority computer users, the role of information in social movement participation, and gender stratification from a comparative/historical perspective.

Linda C. Smith is Professor and Associate Dean at the Graduate School of Library and Information Science, University of Illinois at Urbana-Champaign. Her research interests include information system design, education for library and information science, and the impact of new technologies on reference and information services. She is currently investigating models for online pedagogy and implications for faculty development. She has provided administrative oversight of LEEP since January 1997 and taught LEEP courses on a regular basis since fall 1997.

Michael B. Twidale is Associate Professor at the Graduate School of Library and Information Science, University of Illinois at Urbana-Champaign. His research examines the interaction between human computer interaction, computer-supported cooperative work, and learning issues in computer use. Projects in various different domains use an analysis of how people learn and use software as a way to inform the development of new interfaces and functionalities. Current research projects include the informal learning of computer applications in the workplace, methods for the rapid prototyping and evaluation of novel interfaces and applications, and the usability of open source software.

General Editor: **Steve Jones**

Digital Formations is the best source for critical, well-written books about digital technologies and modern life. Books in the series break new ground by emphasizing multiple methodological and theoretical approaches to deeply probe the formation and reformation of lived experience as it is refracted through digital interaction. Each volume in **Digital Formations** pushes forward our understanding of the intersections, and corresponding implications, between digital technologies and everyday life. The series examines broad issues in realms such as digital culture, electronic commerce, law, politics and governance, gender, the Internet, race, art, health and medicine, and education. The series emphasizes critical studies in the context of emergent and existing digital technologies.

Other recent titles include:

Felicia Wu Song
    Virtual Communities: Bowling Alone, Online Together

Edited by Sharon Kleinman
    The Culture of Efficiency: Technology in Everyday Life

Edward Lee Lamoureux, Steven L. Baron, & Claire Stewart
    Intellectual Property Law and Interactive Media: Free for a Fee

Edited by Adrienne Russell & Nabil Echchaibi
    International Blogging: Identity, Politics and Networked Publics

Edited by Don Heider
    Living Virtually: Researching New Worlds

Edited by Judith Burnett, Peter Senker & Kathy Walker
    The Myths of Technology: Innovation and Inequality

Edited by Knut Lundby
    Digital Storytelling, Mediatized Stories: Self-representations in New Media

Theresa M. Senft
    Camgirls: Celebrity and Community in the Age of Social Networks

Edited by Chris Paterson & David Domingo
    Making Online News: The Ethnography of New Media Production

To order other books in this series please contact our Customer Service Department:
(800) 770-LANG (within the US)
(212) 647-7706 (outside the US)
(212) 647-7707 FAX

To find out more about the series or browse a full list of titles, please visit our website:
WWW.PETERLANG.COM